THE
Penguin History
of
AMERICAN
LIFE

Praise for Patrick Allitt's
A Climate of Crisis

"A wide-ranging history of the American environmental movement . . . A readable account that will provoke and displease many environmentalists . . . An optimistic book." —*Kirkus Reviews*

"This provocative book may become the starting point for future environmental discussions. . . . Deserves a wide audience." —*Choice*

"As . . . Allitt demonstrates in *A Climate of Crisis*, [environmental politics] was a political back-and-forth that became ever less productive. Time and again, Allitt writes, activists and corporate executives railed against each other. Out of this clash emerged regulatory syntheses: rules for air, water, toxins. Often enough, businesspeople then discovered that following the new rules was less expensive than they had claimed it would be; environmentalists meanwhile found out that the problems were less dire than they had claimed." —Charles Mann, *The Atlantic*

"In recounting partisan battles, Mr. Allitt's objectivity is refreshing. . . . Allitt's critique of the relentless crisis mentality will lead many environmentalists to dismiss the book as anti-environmental, while anti-environmentalists will object to his conclusion that much conservation has been achieved at little cost to ordinary Americans."—*The Wall Street Journal*

"Offering historical perspective on the tensions between industrialism, wealth building, and environmentalism, Allitt traces social movements of the 1960s through the creation of Earth Day and the Environmental Protection Agency. Pondering the trade-offs of advancement and economic success vis-á-vis increasing polarization of industrialists and environmentalists, Allitt attempts to balance assumptions about who the good and bad guys are in the drama of the climate crisis." —*Booklist*

"In this sweeping study, Patrick Allitt covers every conceivable major character and event in the modern 'age of environmentalism.' The book is grounded in intellectual history, and seeks to find balance in interpreting the role of environmental advocates and naysayers, in successes and failures of governmental regulation, in objectives and outcomes. The tone is definitely optimistic about the long view of meeting environmental challenges in the United States. At the same time, in linking past to present, Allitt offers caution about what might unfold in the days to come. Above all else, he touts the value of history in assessing America's complex environmental legacy."
—Martin V. Melosi, author of *The Sanitary City* and *Precious Commodity*

"I don't agree with everything in *A Climate of Crisis*, but Patrick Allitt's well-written and provocative book has given me more to think about than any other history of the U. S. environmental movement. *A Climate of Crisis* is both bracing and exciting."
—Adam Rome, author of *The Genius of Earth Day*

PENGUIN BOOKS

A CLIMATE OF CRISIS

Patrick Allitt is the Cahoon Family Professor of American History at Emory University, where he has taught since 1988. He was an undergraduate at Oxford and a graduate student at the University of California, Berkeley, and has held postdoctoral fellowships at Harvard Divinity School and Princeton University. The author of six books, he is also the presenter of eight lecture series with The Great Courses, including *The Art of Teaching*.

A CLIMATE OF CRISIS

AMERICA IN THE AGE OF ENVIRONMENTALISM

PATRICK ALLITT

PENGUIN BOOKS

PENGUIN BOOKS
Published by the Penguin Group
Penguin Group (USA) LLC
375 Hudson Street
New York, New York 10014

USA · Canada · UK · Ireland · Australia
New Zealand · India · South Africa · China
penguin.com
A Penguin Random House Company

First published in the United States of America by
The Penguin Press, a member of Penguin Group (USA) LLC, 2014
Published in Penguin Books 2015

Photograph credits appear on page 372.

ISBN 978-159-420466-1 (hc.)
ISBN 978-0-14-312701-7 (pbk.)

Printed in the United States of America
1   3   5   7   9   10   8   6   4   2

Designed by Marysarah Quinn

FOR
Ernie Freeberg

CONTENTS

PREFACE

Since the early 1990s I have taught undergraduate courses on American environmental history at Emory University. The most dynamic part of this history comes with the decades after World War II. A succession of alarms—about overpopulation, about pollution, about resource depletion, and about climate change—made the environment newsworthy, and these were the years in which an environmental movement developed in the United States. They were also the years in which Congress mandated environmental reforms.

There are many fine books on aspects of this history, by participants and by historians, but until now there has been no general intellectual history of American environmentalism. When the Penguin Press invited me to write such a book I was glad to accept the offer. My editors, Mally Anderson and Scott Moyers, for whose help I am grateful, wanted me not just to describe and explain the environmental debates of this era but to stake out a clear position.

Let me summarize the book's argument. Industrialization caused most of America's environmental problems, but they were the side effects of a phenomenal achievement. Industrialization brought widespread prosperity to millions, along with improved health, greater mobility, and greater life expectancy. Americans became concerned about environmental problems in the 1960s not because their situation was getting worse but because it was getting better. Now that they had a generally high standard of living they were no longer content to live with poor air quality, polluted rivers and lakes, and the indiscriminate use of powerful chemicals around their children, food, pets, and vacation haunts.

In a bipartisan burst of political activity, late in the 1960s and early in the 1970s, their political representatives across the spectrum legislated for improvements in air and water quality, nurture of endangered species, cleanup of contaminated toxic sites, protection for wilderness areas, and the removal of lead from gasoline. The policy objectives embodied in these acts have been largely achieved, with the result that Americans now breathe much cleaner air than their parents and grandparents, can expect longer and healthier lives, have access to more national parks and an improved chance of seeing charismatic animals that have been brought back from the brink of extinction.

No problem was so menacing during these decades as the possibility of nuclear war. The mood of crisis created by the first atom bombs and the Cold War arms race spread to influence popular ideas on many other issues, including population, resources, and climate change. Two contradictory points of view developed among American thinkers interested in these issues. The pessimistic view, often expressed in crisis rhetoric, was that we were running out of basic necessities and faced a future of constraints, restrictions, and even famines. Its corollary was that a new approach to life was essential, one that was more Spartan and more conservation-minded. The optimistic view, by contrast, was that human ingenuity could deal with the problems thrown up by economic growth and technical innovation. As a result, said the optimists, we can anticipate continued environmental improvement along with benign economic growth, here and through much of the developing world. The future would present us with genuine problems, but we were becoming ever more capable of solving these problems.

Each view had, and continues to have, energetic advocates. The arguments on both sides are powerful, often emotional, and freighted with serious policy implications. My own view is that the optimists have been right on most of these questions. Nevertheless, I hope I have given a fair presentation of each side's views, enabling even readers who disagree with me to learn from the chapters that follow.

In addition to explaining the major policy issues, I have followed several interesting byways, such as the work of ecological scientists and philosophers, environmental historians, "deep ecologists" and ecofeminists. Their impact on the political debate was not great but their ways of thinking about the issues have an intrinsic interest and sometimes shed a new and unexpected light on the major controversies.

I am grateful for the help and advice of several outstanding colleagues here at Emory, especially Joseph Crespino, Frank Lechner, Jeffrey Lesser, and Tom Rogers. They do not share my views on all of the issues discussed here, but they are friendly and helpful even when, as often happens, they disagree with me. Thanks also to my research assistant Emily Moore, who, as a new college freshman in the fall of 2012, at once took on the arduous task of checking facts and footnotes. Her steadiness and self-discipline match or exceed those of most people twice her age. Any remaining errors are mine, not hers. It is a pleasure to dedicate the book to my friend and former student Ernie Freeberg. Trumping all other debts of gratitude is the one, unpayable even in a lifetime, that I owe to Mrs. Allitt.

INTRODUCTION

IN THE SUMMER OF 1945 atom bombs were the ultimate secret weapon. Developed and tested in conditions of maximum security in a New Mexico desert camp, they destroyed Hiroshima and Nagasaki that August and ended World War II. In the summer of 1946 a new set of atom bomb tests was designed to make them the ultimate *public* weapon. Three bombs would be detonated in front of movie cameras, journalists, members of Congress, and selected international VIPs at Bikini Atoll in the Pacific Ocean's Marshall Islands. Code-named Operation Crossroads, the display would show the world just how much destructive power America now possessed. The spectacle would intimidate and deter potential aggressors, especially the Soviet Union. The islands' 167 inhabitants were evacuated and given a promise that they could return home later.[1]

But Operation Crossroads did not go according to plan. The two blasts, "Able" (aboveground) and "Baker" (underwater), were less destructive than some scientists and generals had hoped, damaging but not sinking many of the captured German and Japanese warships anchored nearby. On the other hand, the irreversible radioactive contamination of these ships, and the deaths of the trial animals caged on board, demonstrated the bombs' sinister aftereffects. Right after Baker, sailors were sent aboard the damaged ships to clean up, wearing no protective gear. "Out of the four hours we spent on her [the USS *Hughes*], two were spent vomiting and retching as we all became violently ill," wrote one. A medical official on the scene, aware of the danger and dismayed by military negligence, reported that senior navy officers took "a blind, hairy-chested approach to matters of radiological safety." The third bomb test was postponed.[2]

Hydrogen bombs tested at the same site in the early 1950s were literally hundreds of times more powerful than the Crossroads blasts, and these tests too bore witness to the danger of fallout. Mistakes in weather forecasting and an unexpectedly powerful explosion led radioactive ash and debris from the Castle Bravo test in 1954 to rain down on 28 Americans, 236 natives of the Marshall Islands, and the crew of a Japanese fishing boat, the *Fukuryu Maru* ("Lucky Dragon"), which had not been alerted to the danger. Even though the boat was one hundred miles from the detonation site, its crew suffered horribly: "skin discolored and blistered, hands swelled and ached, hair loosened and fell out, eyes and ears oozed a thick yellow secretion." One of them died. The Japanese tuna catch was dangerously radioactive for several weeks, but much of the fish had been sold before American officials notified Japanese authorities of the danger.[3]

After the Lucky Dragon fiasco, controversy broke out among American scientists as to just how dangerous nuclear fallout was. Nuclear physicists and the Atomic Energy Commission (AEC), whose main concern was to build and test the bombs in the context of the Cold War rivalry against the Soviet Union, downplayed its seriousness. The AEC routinely issued statements, in the Pacific and during comparable tests in Nevada, that radioactivity posed no significant health hazard. Biologists, by contrast, emphasized not only that it was serious, but that it could cause genetic mutations that would be felt for generations to come.[4]

The ecological effect of these tests on the Bikini Islands themselves, meanwhile, was catastrophic. The second 1946 blast, Baker, detonated beneath the surface, killed all the fish in the atoll's lagoon, and destroyed its coral reefs. Most of the vegetation died and the topsoil was showered with radioactive debris. The islands remained so contaminated after a decade of tests that even twenty-five years later an attempt at resettlement failed. It caused a high incidence of cancer, birth defects, and accumulations of radiation in the Bikinians' bodies, prompting most to abandon the hope of ever returning. Nuclear fallout, despite being tasteless, colorless, odorless, and invisible, was a fearsome killer. Subsequent studies confirmed that men and women too close to atom bomb detonations, caught there by accident or placed there by design, suffered high rates of radiation sickness and lethal cancers.[5]

Nuclear weapons were paradoxical in many ways. Their explosive power was blatant while their contamination effects were insidious. They were brilliant as technical achievements but horrifying in their indiscriminate destructiveness. The history of the ensuing decades would show that, unlike all previous weapons, they really were too powerful to use, but the threat of using them could paralyze potential enemies. Deterrence policy itself depended on further paradoxes. First, the Soviet Union had to know what weapons the United States possessed—secrecy here would be counterproductive. Second, the Soviets had to believe that the United States would in fact use the bombs when the time came. Their deterrent effect, in other words, depended on showing a willingness to use them as the best way of making sure *not* to.

This paradoxical quality in nuclear weapons applied to plenty of other issues in the years after World War II. Science and technology, after all, had made great strides in the foregoing century, improving standards of living for nearly everyone, creating devices that made life longer, safer, and more enjoyable than ever before. But they had also caused pollution, stress, urban blight, suburban sprawl, car accidents, plane crashes, feelings of anomie and alienation, and all the characteristic miseries of modernity.

Citizens dismayed by nuclear weapons—and aware that other aspects of industrial civilization were a mixed blessing—also knew that the genie could not be put back in the bottle. It was no more possible to destroy the knowledge on which nuclear weapons were based than it was possible to uninvent the blast furnace, the textile factory, or the internal combustion engine. However, it *was* possible to regulate this scientific and technological world. Managing the industrial economy, and striving to mitigate its adverse side effects, was essential.

This was the setting in which the American environmental movement developed. Growing numbers of citizens came to see that economic growth, while usually desirable, could never be a modern society's sole objective. Sometimes it must be forgone for the sake of other aims. Beautiful but vulnerable landscapes needed to be protected from agricultural and industrial degradation. National and state parks, national forests, wildlife preserves, and industrial regulation to prevent the contamination of air, water, and land were essential. Peaceful uses of nuclear power, if there were any, would have to be nurtured in conditions of safety and public accountability.

Debates, disputes, and controversies on a wide range of environmental issues characterized the decades after World War II. In the wake of nuclear fears came new anxieties. In the baby boom years of the 1950s and 1960s, academics, politicians, and the press worried that overpopulation might create famines and mass starvation, not just in the developing world but in Western Europe and the United States. In the early sixties Rachel Carson's *Silent Spring* catalyzed a growing awareness that chemical pollution was threatening the natural world, killing wildlife, and entering the human food chain, contaminating even the milk of nursing mothers. In the seventies, antinuclear activists asserted that nuclear power stations, far from benevolently turning nuclear swords into plowshares, were also a menace, that a meltdown could kill thousands of innocent people, and that spent nuclear fuel rods could not be disposed of safely. Our profligate nation, said environmental economists in those years, was running out of oil and other natural resources, such that we faced a poorer, bleaker, and more constrained economic future. Anxieties about human-induced climate change began in the 1970s and intensified in the ensuing decades.

Every one of these problems was, of course, real. But it is clear, with the advantage of hindsight, that few were catastrophic. None could match nuclear weapons as potential bringers of apocalypse. Population *was* rising, but by the time it prompted headlines, the rate of growth was already slowing. Meanwhile, the global food supply was rising even faster than the population, steadily improving the world's food-to-population ratio. Factories *were* producing high levels of pollution in the form of smoke and chemical waste, but a series of clean air and water acts in the 1970s from a responsive Congress inaugurated a sustained and largely successful cleanup. Poorly monitored nuclear power stations *were* potentially dangerous, but even the worst civilian nuclear power station accident of the era in the United States, at Three Mile Island in 1979, killed no one. The world's climate *was* changing—cooling slightly in the 1960s and early 1970s and warming slightly after that—but these were incremental changes on a planet whose climate had been shifting for millennia.

This book is a history of these environmental concerns and the controversies and debates that swirled around them. I argue that the mood of crisis that surrounded a succession of environmental fears was usually disproportionate to the actual danger involved. Industrial America faced myriad environmental problems, but most of them were manageable problems. What's more, they were the kind of problems that grow out of success, not failure. They became news in an era of rapidly growing national and individual wealth, rising family incomes, improved health, and increased longevity. In no other era in world history had newborns faced such favorable prospects for long and healthy lives. Never before had the United States been such a prosperous place to live. Some environmental problems were noticed only because of an extraordinarily high degree of technological sophistication, which included the development of instruments that could detect trace contaminants in the atmosphere down to a few parts per billion. A society capable of noticing such problems was also capable of remedying them.

Why, then, were there so many alarms? If nuclear dread is part of the background answer, media sensationalism stands squarely in the foreground. To sell newspapers, to attract viewers, and to sell advertising, commercial media companies had an incentive to exaggerate. The science that spurred these alarms was usually extremely complicated. Only when it was simplified could nonspecialist readers grasp its meaning. Only when scientists' cautious conclusions were turned into thrilling headlines predicting disaster would citizens take notice.

Contributing to the mood of crisis was the fact that environmental scientists wanted their work to be noticed. They understood the benefits of publicity. Convinced that their research was significant and their findings potentially ominous, they had an incentive not simply to report their conclusions but to cultivate relationships with journalists and politicians. Many did so. From the 1950s onward, scientists debated among themselves the pros and cons of becoming directly engaged in environmental policy making. Many of them concluded that they *should* play a direct role, but then struggled to prevent it from impairing their scientific objectivity.

Furthermore, a sense of environmental crisis served the interests of a growing number of people whose livelihoods depended on it. The rapid growth of the Environmental Protection Agency after its creation in 1970 turned several thousand federal employees into stakeholders in the idea of an environmental crisis. They were joined by thousands more in the Department of the Interior, the Department of Energy, the Fish and Wildlife Service, the Forest Service, the National Park Service, and by thousands of university and nonprofit workers dedicated to environmental concerns. While of course their efforts stemmed from good intentions, they were nevertheless responsible for spreading and sustaining the idea of an environmental crisis, which helped secure, fund, and justify their work.

The leaders of the Sierra Club, Wilderness Society, Audubon Society, Izaak Walton League, Friends of the Earth, Greenpeace, and other environmental organizations likewise understood that their memberships would swell in the face of dramatic bad news. To broadcast reassuring, upbeat stories of environmental progress—of which there could have been plenty after 1970—would have been to diminish the sense of crisis on which they thrived. They had an incentive to encourage the idea that they stood as guardians of a natural world under threat from the forces of rapacity and greed. In their search for new recruits and political influence, they had an equally obvious incentive to exaggerate the danger posed by each new problem.

Also contributing to the growing mood of environmental alarm was the spread of counterculture values in the 1960s and 1970s. American mainstream culture valued material comfort and was phenomenally successful in achieving it. The counterculture, by contrast, stressed simplicity, warned against hubris, and relished the humbling of the mighty.

It also channeled elements of America's old agrarian tradition, including a veneration of life lived close to the land and in harmony with nature. It channeled elements of America's old religious and political traditions too, condemning greed, vice, and luxury. Environmental and counterculture rhetoric sometimes echoed Puritan jeremiads, sermons rebuking a society that had turned away from virtue in a sinful quest for wealth. Where once vengeance would have come from an angry God, now it would come from an overstressed natural world.

But not everyone was convinced by stories of a world in crisis. In the face of this escalating series of environmental alarms, an opposition began to crystallize. It was made up of business interests that feared that restrictive legislation would reduce profitable enterprises or give an edge to foreign competitors. It also included scientists who doubted their colleagues' conclusions and questioned the accuracy of their grim future projections. Some politicians shrank from passing legislation that would impede economic growth; they opposed excessive federal regulation. Conservative economists shared these fears. Their understanding of recent history led them to believe that as societies grow wealthier, they become more resilient and more capable of solving their problems, including those relating to the environment. Accordingly, they believed that future prospects were bright and would be all the brighter so long as economic growth continued apace.

This opposition did not deny the existence of environmental problems, but rather the idea of an environmental crisis. In the 1980s it found a political place for itself in the Republican Party. Its first famous (or notorious) spokespersons were James Watt, President Reagan's secretary of the interior, and his EPA administrator Anne Gorsuch. Already jaded by a succession of false alarms, some antienvironmentalists began to doubt even the evidence of genuine problems, or to minimize them when evidence was ambiguous. Believers in a severe environmental crisis, conversely, gathered around the Democratic Party, taking Tennessee senator (and later vice president) Al Gore as their principal spokesperson.

Political polarization around environmental questions after 1980 had important consequences that we can still feel today. In the 1960s and 1970s Democrats and Republicans had collaborated to pass clean air and clean water acts, to create the Environmental Protection Agency, and to set aside more land as national parks and national wilderness areas. Since then the general polarization of American politics has mirrored the polarization of environmental politics. By 2014 bipartisan cooperation on the environment had become almost impossible. It was, for example, a standard part of a politician's identity as a Democrat to affirm the gravity of global warming, and a standard part of a Republican's identity to deny that the phenomenon even existed.

My purpose in writing this book is to explain how the environmental debates and controversies developed, why exaggeration and distortion were so widespread, why apparent environmental crises sometimes disappeared or diminished, why the two sides became so rancorous toward each other, and how this rancor and polarization made sensible policy approaches difficult. The continuing polarization is unfortunate. Advocates of environmental concern and their critics for decades have attributed to one another the worst possible motives. Environmentalists see their critics as greedy special interest groups that show no signs of conscience as they plunder the earth. Counterenvironmentalists, by contrast, see their adversaries as the enemies of economic growth whose plans will stop social progress and stifle initiative under an avalanche of bureaucratic regulation. There may be a germ of truth in both views, but more than a germ of falsehood too. It would be more accurate to say that both groups have an idea of how the world should develop in the future to increase human happiness and welfare. Each group regards the other group's plans as certain to prevent the realization of that future.

The best way to understand America's current environmental situation is to study its history. Our history shows, for example, that industries did pollute until they were legally prohibited from doing so, and that many of them set about cleaning up only when forced to do so. The history of this process also shows that once the laws were in place, pollution decreased steadily and was not accompanied by a wave of industrial bankruptcies. On the contrary, compliance with environmental legislation created countless new entrepreneurial opportunities. Rivers and lakes that had turned into sewers regained their vitality. Cities that had been plagued by smog became steadily cleaner even though their populations and the number of vehicles on their streets continued to increase. Toxic lead levels in the atmosphere diminished sharply once leaded gasoline was phased out by 1976 legislation. Americans' life expectancy continued to increase as general levels of health, nutrition, safety, and welfare improved. One lesson to learn from this experience, surely, is that regulation can be effective and should continue. Another is that regulation and environmental improvement are compatible with economic growth.

The historical record also shows that Americans are not so mercenary as some environmentalists seem to think. Support for protecting endangered species and their habitats, for example, has remained popular from the 1970s right up to the present, even though it is costly and difficult. Many species once on the brink of extinction, including wolves, alligators, mountain lions, and bald eagles, have revived and now flourish. A hitherto unknown fish, the snail darter, won tens of thousands of friends when its habitat was threatened by the building of a Tennessee dam in the 1970s. An even bigger constituency favored protecting spotted owls in the Pacific Northwest when their welfare threatened forestry workers' livelihood in the 1980s and 1990s. When a mountain lion killed a jogger in Boulder, Colorado, in 1991, most of the city's citizens nevertheless continued to support plans to protect the lions' habitat and to begin a population recovery project. In all these cases the political resolution of the issue could not and did not please all parties, but it also demonstrated that the forces of economic growth would not always prevail.

Considering environmental issues in light of their history enables us to take the long view. Ever since the Neolithic revolution, the invention of agriculture, human groups have been transforming the environment. Agriculture is itself a highly "unnatural" activity, in that it entails replacing the variety of plants that would grow in a given area with just one, and then protecting it against all rivals. It also entails the selective breeding of domesticated animals to enhance particular characteristics such as their yield of milk, wool, leather, and meat. The industrial revolution intensified the human manipulation and transformation of the environment. Industrialization made the world immeasurably richer and brought an array of technologies that were sometimes harmful but much more often benign. Humans and the natural world both proved adaptable to these changes. Industrialization made possible immense improvements in human health and longevity, while providing ordinary people with greater material welfare than their ancestors could even have dreamed of. If it sometimes created potential threats to the natural world, it also provided more and better remedies.

History also demonstrates that there is a vital link between industrialization, wealth, and environmentalism. Only wealthy societies practice environmental protection on a significant scale. Societies in which most people are poor cannot devote many of their resources to environmental protection—the search for food, clothing, shelter, and work inevitably takes precedence. Wealthy societies like the United States and the nations of Western Europe, by contrast, have secured for most of their people the basic necessities of life. This achievement enables them to devote surplus wealth to fulfillment of other needs, including environmental protection. It is no accident that environmentalism thrived in the United States and Western Europe in the late twentieth century while making little headway in the developing world. It is also no accident that within these wealthy societies affluent people were more interested in environmental protection than poor people. They could afford to devote time and money to the less tangible benefits of environmental protection than their poor fellow citizens, who had more pressing material concerns.

The close connection between wealth and environmental concern also helps explain different nations' reactions to the Kyoto Protocol of 1997. This international treaty was designed to reduce the amount of carbon dioxide being pumped into the atmosphere worldwide by industrial nations, and it won the support of many of the wealthiest. India and China, two nations then in the midst of rapid industrialization, insisted on being exempted from the protocol, however, because conforming to its requirements would restrict their ability to grow. Only with economic growth, they argued, could they reach the baseline of decent subsistence for all their people, after which activities like environmental protection could become worthwhile. The paradox was acute; economic growth causes environmental harm, but the only societies that can remedy environmental harm are those that have experienced rapid economic growth. In the early stages, however, it is much better to have "dirty" industrialization than none at all. Industrialization is the only way for societies to overcome mass poverty.

The United States refused to endorse the Kyoto Protocol if India and China were exempt. By 1997 American environmental skepticism was sufficiently widespread that senators from both major parties could vote against the protocol without feeling that their votes compromised the nation's future. Perhaps they were right. It if were true that the world's temperature had been more or less steady for thousands of years, only to be suddenly wrenched upward by human actions in the second half of the twentieth century, that would indeed be cause for very serious alarm. But the reality was otherwise. Historians, archaeologists, biologists, and paleoclimatologists had accumulated overwhelming evidence by the year 2000 to show that the earth's climate has always been in flux. Even in comparatively recent historic time, distinctly warm periods (such as the one around a thousand years ago in which Greenland really was green, and hosted a colony of Viking dairy farmers) have given way to distinctly cold periods (such as the one around four hundred years ago, when Shakespeare's generation held an annual winter fair on the hard-frozen River Thames in London, which never freezes now). Human activity could not have caused these fluctuations, so it is reasonable to believe that human activity is not the sole cause of the current temperature rise. Neither does history offer us evidence that these cold and warm periods led to catastrophic disruptions of the kind sometimes predicted for the immediate future.

These reflections are not meant to imply that there is no need to worry about responding to global warming or increasing levels of atmospheric carbon dioxide. Of course we should be seeking ways to create a world in which economic growth can be achieved with less pollution and fewer greenhouse gases. The history of industrial and technological progress makes it reasonable to think that we can. The first steam engines, after all, were much more efficient, more powerful, and cleaner than horses. They were displaced by steadily more efficient and economical engines with each passing decade. Internal combustion engines went through the same process, becoming more efficient and getting more work out of the fuel consumed as the technology improved. It is true that the number of engines, vehicles, and factories in the world keeps increasing and that the search for new sources of fuel and new kinds of fuel remains vitally important. As heirs of two centuries of phenomenal technological creativity, however, we can be at least guardedly confident that we will develop new technologies in the face of this challenge, along with better fuels to power them.

Studying the history of environmental debates will, I hope, give readers of this book a better context for understanding each new environmental issue as it emerges. My judgment of these issues and their relative seriousness is based on my experience with the history of ideas and their manipulation. If a scientist hears the claim that global warming is about to transform the world as we know it, he or she is likely to turn to the study of climate. If, on the other hand, an historian hears that global warming is about to transform the world as we know it, he or she is more likely to study the history of claims about the imminent transformation of the world. The historian will discover that claims of imminent disaster have been far more common throughout history than actual shattering transformations—that they are in fact an entirely familiar characteristic of the history of Western civilization.

For the last four decades professional historians have been writing environmental history, often from the starting point of their own environmentalist sympathies. As a result they have tended to give more credence to environmentalists than to their critics. By being receptive to some counterenvironmentalists' ideas, I hope I can redress an imbalance and show that their skepticism was sometimes more than a cold and cynical attempt to protect corporate profits.

In the chapters that follow I will explain the principal environmental controversies of the post–World War II era, beginning with fears of nuclear catastrophe and ending with global warming. I believe this history will demonstrate that America's environmental problems, though very real, were manageable, that the political system was responsive to them, and that it was able—especially before 1990—to differentiate between the genuine problems and the false alarms. Historians, however much they strive for objectivity, are citizens too, with beliefs and convictions about the world that are likely to shine through their presentation and explanation of the past. I make no secret of the fact that I consider industrial civilization a superb accomplishment, very much worth protecting and improving. Industrialization has harmed the environment while improving life for almost everyone. We have the resources to remedy this harm.

CHAPTER 1

THE SCHIZOPHRENIC FIFTIES

IN THE LATE 1940S AND 1950S, there was no environmental *movement* in the United States. A series of controversies from those years, however, foreshadowed the environmental debates of the 1960s and 1970s. The first was the threat posed by nuclear weapons. The American atom bomb attacks on Hiroshima and Nagasaki had demonstrated the technology's apocalyptic power. Now both sides, the United States and the Soviet Union, built them as quickly as possible as the Cold War intensified. One group of scientists argued for a ban on nuclear weapons tests. They believed that increasing levels of nuclear debris in the atmosphere would precipitate increasing levels of genetic damage and a severe health crisis, even if actual nuclear war could be averted. Advocates of an aggressive development and testing program argued, to the contrary, that the nation's defense needs outweighed these health concerns and that the public health evidence was inconclusive. But most important, scientists on both sides of the issue involved themselves directly in this political dispute. Anxious citizens contemplated building fallout shelters in their backyards. Popular culture exploited the possibilities of nuclear fallout too; these were the years when Hollywood featured giant mutant ants and beetles stalking the landscape, and comic book artists created nuclear-genetic freaks like the Hulk and Spider-Man.

A second dispute developed over the idea that the world faced an overpopulation crisis. Despite the fact that more than fifty million people had died in World War II, the rapidly rising population threatened to outstrip the food supply, resulting in famine and political chaos. Demographers disagreed about the gravity of the situation. Some feared the worst, while others argued that new technologies and improved crop strains could meet the challenge of rising numbers. The "green revolution" of the 1950s and 1960s, which yielded much larger harvests than ever before, vindicated the optimists' belief that the food-to-population ratio would actually improve. Among the most impressive achievements of the postwar era was that famine became increasingly rare despite the astonishing rise in the world's population. When famine *did* occur, it was usually in the context of civil wars, in which one side tried to starve the other into submission, or else in the context of ideological fanaticism, such as Mao's politically induced famine in China during the "Great Leap Forward" (1958–1961).

In retrospect, there is something schizophrenic about American life in the 1950s. The potential horrors of nuclear war and overpopulation came along with a much higher standard of living than ever before. Suburbs and superhighways made urban areas bigger, but greatly improved the quality of residential life for most citizens. To most Americans, these new suburbs and highways, and the way of life they represented, were triumphant achievements. An intellectual minority, however, decried them. Sociologist David Reisman's *The Lonely Crowd* (1950) and novelist John Keats's *The Crack in the Picture Window* (1956) were indictments of what their authors saw as a degraded mental and physical landscape, in which conformity and sterility had displaced vitality and individualism.

Disagreement about whether the urban landscape was improving or worsening was mirrored by disagreement over land use in rural and wilderness areas. Conservation leaders like David Brower of the Sierra Club and Howard Zahniser of the Wilderness Society campaigned for enhanced national protection for areas of spectacular natural beauty. Americans for whom economic development remained more important than conservation made the opposite argument, for continuing to exploit the forests, minerals, landscape, and waterways of the United States, fulfilling the promise of material progress for all. Conservationists, in their view, were obstacles on the road to prosperity.

NUCLEAR ANXIETIES

The central argument in favor of the nuclear attacks on Hiroshima and Nagasaki was that ending thousands of Japanese lives saved millions more, Japanese and American. Public reactions in the United States, after initial euphoria, soon began to show signs of ambivalence. American church groups condemned the attacks, while popular books showed American readers just what the weapons entailed. John Hersey's *Hiroshima* (1946) followed six inhabitants of the city, including a minister, a seamstress, and two doctors. Its understated prose depicted a shattered landscape, ruined lives, horrible suffering, and the slow and painful deaths of people the bomb had not killed instantly. After its publication in the *New Yorker* it became a Book-of-the Month Club bestseller, read by tens of thousands. David Bradley's *No Place to Hide* (1948), on nuclear weapon development after the war, sold equally well and was serialized in the mass-circulation *Reader's Digest*. Bradley argued that "there is no real defense against atomic weapons" and that everyone would suffer from "the invisible poison of radioactivity."[1]

In 1951 nuclear weapons tests began in the Nevada desert. In several instances, citizens living downwind of the test sites were not alerted and were exposed to dangerously high doses of radiation. Rumors of a high incidence of cancer in the little towns of Utah and Nevada in the ensuing years were justified, and would eventually become the basis of a class-action lawsuit against the government. Even in areas of the United States remote from the tests, citizens were urged to prepare for nuclear war, to build fallout shelters, and to have their children practice civil defense drills in school. Three popular films from the era, *On the Beach* (1959), *Dr. Strangelove* (1964), and *Fail Safe* (1964) all ended with nuclear war and the annihilation of millions of people. These nuclear-related fears contributed to a building sense of anxiety, making citizens receptive to the idea that the world around them was full of barely perceptible threats that could suddenly become devastating.[2]

Right from the time of the first atom bomb test in New Mexico in 1945, some scientists had opposed their use. The *Bulletin of the Atomic Scientists*, founded by the biophysicist Eugene Rabinowitch (1901–1973) in 1945, struggled to explain the technical and political aspects of nuclear weapons to the general public and to campaign against their proliferation. The cover of the bulletin's early issues showed a clock whose hands had reached seven minutes to midnight in the countdown to catastrophe. In the 1950s the *Bulletin* also carried a succession of stories about growing levels of radiation in the atmosphere and their potential link to rising cancer rates. Rabinowitch himself wrote in 1955 that "the long-range genetic danger of exposure of mankind as a whole to low-level, but widespread and persistent radioactivity—the most ominous but least well understood of all dangers of the new age—is only beginning to be dimly perceived." Peaceful as well as warlike uses of nuclear power, including nuclear power stations and medical X-rays, could contribute to such threats, he noted.[3]

A related concern, much discussed in the *Bulletin*, was the question of scientists' responsibility to society as a whole. A 1955 London conference, attended by Rabinowitch, Albert Einstein, and philosopher Bertrand Russell, issued the "Russell-Einstein Manifesto," which called on humanity to recognize that a nuclear war would be a defeat for all parties and would make life on earth all but impossible. It urged scientists to move beyond their parochial loyalties so that they could spread the understanding of this horrible truth as widely as possible. That meeting was followed by a conference in Pugwash, Nova Scotia, in July 1957, which brought together scientists from both sides of the Cold War and issued a statement on the "Social Responsibility of Scientists." Among its assertions was that scientists should "contribute to the full extent of their opportunities in the formation of national policies." In many subsequent environmental controversies, culminating in the great global warming debate forty years later, scientists would struggle over the extent to which they should involve themselves in politics and advocate specific policy positions.[4]

One prestigious scientist committed to policy involvement was Linus Pauling (1901–1994), a Caltech chemistry professor. A signatory of the Russell-Einstein Manifesto in 1955, Pauling was convinced that atmospheric radiation, even at low levels, caused cancer. In 1957 he and Barry Commoner (1917–2012), a biology professor at Washington University in St. Louis, drafted a petition urging an international ban on nuclear weapons tests. Commoner had come to the issue after discovering rising levels of radioactive materials in children's teeth, which he took as a sign that everyone was being exposed to growing levels of radioactivity. Pauling and Commoner gathered more than ten thousand signatures for their petition, including those of thirty-five Nobel laureates. Pauling presented the petition to the secretary-general of the United Nations early the next year.[5]

Edward Teller (1908–2003), a Hungarian Jewish refugee who had played a leading role in the wartime Manhattan Project, came down on the opposite side of the issue. A passionate anticommunist, Teller argued that natural "background" radiation levels in the atmosphere were already far higher than those caused by atom bomb tests and that national security needs trumped public health concerns on this issue. He and Pauling held a debate on the television station KQED in 1957. Both were talented speakers. One of the issues they debated, the so-called "threshold question," would remain controversial in subsequent battles over environmental carcinogens. Teller took the view that human beings have evolved to tolerate exposure to radioactive compounds up to a certain threshold level. Pauling argued that there is no threshold, such that every increase of radiation increases the number of cancer victims, the number of genetic mutations, and the number of premature deaths. At the time of their debate, in the late 1950s, the evidence in support of either view was ambiguous.[6]

Yet thousands of Americans were convinced that nuclear weapons, ostensibly designed to protect them, were actually threats to their lives and well-being. In a 1957 poll, 52 percent of citizens polled said they believed nuclear fallout to be a danger to their health. That year Norman Cousins and Clarence Pickett founded SANE, the Committee for a Sane Nuclear Policy. It ran newspaper advertisements emphasizing the dangers of fallout, criticized government secrecy ("No contamination without representation"), organized demonstrations, and persuaded prominent figures like pediatrician Benjamin Spock to act as spokespersons. Dagmar Wilson, a children's book illustrator and SANE member, organized the Women Strike for Peace on November 1, 1961, claiming that no American woman could afford to neglect the nuclear issue. Since radioactive strontium was showing up in children's milk, it became a preeminent concern for mothers. Wilson delivered a letter for Mrs. Kennedy at the White House and another for Mrs. Khrushchev at the Russian embassy, urging them to use their influence for peace and against nuclear weapons. Fifty thousand women in cities across the country turned out that day to protest against atmospheric testing. They carried signs that read, "End the Arms Race, Not the Human Race."[7]

President Kennedy witnessed the demonstration and recognized

Dagmar Wilson and Coretta Scott King lead a Women Strike for Peace antinuclear demonstration in November 1963.

the need to respond politically to rising popular anxiety about nuclear fallout. These events led to the signing of a U.S.-Soviet agreement, the Atmospheric Test Ban Treaty, in 1963. From then on nuclear tests would take place only underground in order to prevent the further dispersal of radioactive debris in the atmosphere. But the far worse threat of all-out nuclear war persisted. Barry Commoner went on to found the Scientists' Institute for Public Information, trying to ensure that the public was fully informed about health hazards of this kind and that government would not hide dangerous practices behind the plea of national security. He would later become an important shaper of the environmental debates of the 1960s and 1970s.[8]

POPULATION AND FOOD

No war in the history of the world killed more people than World War II. An estimated fifty million or more people died, yet the world's population was greater when the fighting finished in 1945 than it had been at the outset in 1939. Throughout most of human history, the world's population had been small, reaching one billion for the first time only after the year 1800. It grew immensely in the nineteenth and twentieth centuries because of improvements in sanitation, nutrition, health, and longevity. Some mid-twentieth-century commentators believed that this massive new population, as it kept increasing, would eat up all available food supplies, then fall victim to famine. They were wrong. One of the most astonishing achievements in human history is that food production since World War II has not only kept up with population increases, but has gained on them. This in an era when world population increased from about two and a half billion in 1950 to about seven billion today.[9]

In preindustrial societies, which is to say throughout most of the history of the world, birth rates were very high. Death rates, however, were also high, such that life expectancy was low: many children died before their first birthday, women often died in childbirth, malnutrition was widespread, and epidemic diseases claimed victims of all ages.

These patterns changed with the industrial revolution. Birth rates remained high at first, but death rates began to fall, because of improved nutrition, housing, and health care. As a result, the population rose quickly. Eventually birth rates also began to fall, causing the population curve to begin leveling out, but at a much higher level than before. In 1929 American demographer Warren Thompson named this process "demographic transition." He and other demographers showed that it had happened in Britain, America, and the other industrial societies of Western Europe, and anticipated that it would be repeated in other countries as they went through their own industrial revolutions.[10]

But explaining exactly *why* demographic transition happened was controversial. Reasons included the improvement of contraceptive techniques, women's tendency to marry later and to have fewer years of fertility, new attitudes toward sex, and the changing idea of children as economic liabilities to industrial families rather than labor assets to farming families. Over the course of the mid- and late twentieth century there was plenty of opportunity to watch demographic transition in action around the world, and despite profound cultural variations in different places, it recurred time and again. The experience of particular countries varied widely, however. In the 1920s and 1930s, for example, France believed its population was too low after the carnage of World War I and tried to stimulate a rise in the birth rate. After World War II, conversely, the American birth rate, which might be expected to be low in a mature industrial society, shot up for a decade and a half in the baby boom.[11]

Twentieth-century societies, moreover, were not hermetically sealed off from one another. The actions of developed countries had a profound effect on still developing countries. Humanitarian concern and the search for Cold War allies after World War II led America to begin widespread medical interventions in the developing world. This work could be regarded as a triumph, but writers who were already worried about overpopulation watched in alarm as the population totals of poor countries with high birth rates began to soar. The introduction of life-saving inoculations and vaccines, and the newly found ability to cure malaria, syphilis, yaws, and other chronic killers, were enabling far more children to survive. How could these new millions be fed? American books like *Road to Survival* (1948) by William Vogt and *Our Plundered Planet* (1948) by Fairfield Osborn, both of which became bestsellers, lamented the situation and appeared even to regret that so many lives had been saved. Vogt wrote, "In many areas malaria has actually been a blessing in disguise, since a large proportion of the malaria belt is not suited to agriculture and the disease has helped to keep man from destroying it."[12] These writers followed the lead of the English clergyman and economist Thomas Malthus (1766–1834). Malthus had argued in an influential 1798 essay that population is liable always to outstrip food supply because people can reproduce more quickly than the food supply can increase. He concluded that hunger and epidemics were always going to afflict the surplus population, that wages would always be forced down to near starvation levels by surplus labor, and that it was unrealistic to expect a world of universal plenty.[13]

The development of effective birth control techniques in the twentieth century, however, held out the possibility that population growth might be brought under control by human ingenuity rather than by "Malthusian" diseases and famines. Early birth control advocates actually called themselves "neo-Malthusians." By the 1950s, writers and politicians fearful of overpopulation believed that the drastic application of birth control policies worldwide was the alternative to disaster. In *Standing Room Only* (1955) Karl Sax, a plant biologist and director of the Arnold Arboretum at Harvard, saw it as the only way to avoid mass starvation. Similarly, the novelist Aldous Huxley wrote in *Brave New World Revisited* (1958) that controlling population was the biggest challenge humanity would face in the coming century.[14]

The most forceful advocates of this neo-Malthusian approach in the 1950s were the Planned Parenthood Federation (PPF) and the Rockefeller Foundation, both of which wanted American foreign aid to include the export of contraceptives—and contraceptive education—to poor countries. In 1959, a committee established by President Eisenhower even recommended to Congress that American foreign aid should be given only to nations that also accepted birth control and a pledge to reduce their populations.[15]

But Malthus, after all, had been wrong. No sooner had he made his grim prophecy of inevitable famine and pestilence than a century of unprecedented economic growth began. Population and living standards increased steadily side by side. No industrialized country faced the threat of inadequate food supplies (except briefly, due to enemy action, during the world wars). In fact, the chronic problem of American agriculture by 1900, and ever since, has been *over*production, even though an ever smaller percentage of the American population has made its living through farming.[16]

Danish economist Ester Boserup (1910–1999) offered an alternative analysis of food and population. Rather than assume that population rise followed increases in food supply, she argued that the population rise came first, creating the incentive for farmers to seek new and more effective methods. The implication of her work was that the kind of iron limits Malthus had anticipated did not exist, and that human ingenuity was the most important factor in the equation. Economists by the 1950s also generally ignored Malthus and supported population growth, because of its compatibility with sustained economic growth. As more people are born, and as more of them live longer, said the economists, demand for goods grows steadily, as do employment, investment, work opportunities, and wages. Industrialization thrives on population growth. It encourages constant innovation, increases in efficiency, and a more rational approach to each new problem as it emerges.[17]

Theories like these led to a wave of optimistic literature about the future in the late 1940s and 1950s, agreeing that population growth was dramatic but offering the reassurance that it would not lead to catastrophe. Geography professor Earl Parker Hanson, for example, argued in *New Worlds Emerging* (1949) that overpopulation was a relative rather than an absolute concept, depending on a society's technological achievements. Europe had been *relatively* overpopulated in 1500, but had responded with a policy of expansion into other parts of the world. Hanson explained how technology was now enabling mankind to farm more areas of the earth than ever before, opening up tropical and arctic lands to productive uses and safeguarding the future of ever larger populations.[18]

Similarly, Buckminster Fuller, best known as designer of the geodesic dome, wrote optimistic predictions based on his idea of synergy—that bringing together two complementary products or processes created something better than either could provide alone. In Fuller's view, the industrial revolution had made the ancient fear of scarcity irrelevant "for the simple reason that, if properly managed and utilized, present industrial and agricultural techniques could easily provide not only enough of everything for every living inhabitant of the earth but ample means for a much larger population." He also coined the term "ephemeralization," by which he meant the human capacity to make constant improvements in efficiency and economy, creating superior products while using fewer raw materials than ever.[19]

Agronomists after World War II were working in ways that justified Hanson's and Fuller's optimism and that conformed to Boserup's ideas. The twentieth century had already witnessed phenomenal improvements in agricultural technology, enabling fewer people to grow, harvest, transport, and process more food than ever before. The invention of chemical pesticides in the 1930s and 1940s, of which DDT was, ironically, the most effective and most heralded, sharply diminished farmers' losses to crop pests, greatly increasing harvests and yields per acre.[20]

In the 1940s and 1950s Norman Borlaug and other pioneers of what came to be called the "green revolution" developed a series of hybridized crops: first wheat, and later corn and rice. They discovered ways to help plants ripen more quickly, increase their hardiness and resistance to rust in various climate conditions, and increase their yield per acre. These "dwarf" varieties had shorter

Norman Borlaug, the plant physiologist whose work contributed to increasing food yields worldwide, displaying his Nobel Prize in 1970.

stems, which made the plants less likely to "lodge" (fall over before harvest), while a greater percentage of the volume and weight of each plant was concentrated in the grains themselves. The export of these new varieties to Mexico, India, the Philippines, and other parts of Asia favorably transformed food-to-population ratios there in the 1960s and 1970s, heralding an unprecedented increase in food production. India was finally able to feed itself and even to begin exporting food.[21]

The phrase "population explosion" was used occasionally in American media during the 1950s. Just as for some Americans the campaign against nuclear fallout represented their first step toward environmentalism, so others became active in the Planned Parenthood Federation, thinking not just of their own families but of the welfare of a world threatened by overpopulation. The notion caught on more widely after CBS screened a television documentary, *The Population Explosion*, in 1959. The *New York Times* praised the film for explaining the exponential rise in world population and for reviewing some of the possible remedies. But its critics, most notably Catholics (who comprised about a third of the American population), condemned the show, and the whole notion of a population explosion, as alarmist propaganda for birth control programs. They noted that continuing rises in food productivity per acre were leading to the *withdrawal* of farmland from production in the Midwest, and ended by declaring that increases in the food supply were "almost unlimited in potential." The U.S. State Department, quoting a United Nations report, confirmed that the rate of increase of food production was outstripping the rate of population growth, creating the prospect of large food surpluses in the coming decades.[22]

THE NATURAL WORLD

A group of influential American nature writers rose to prominence in the 1940s and 1950s. Echoing the arguments of Barry Commoner and Linus Pauling, they warned that human blunders could easily upset a delicate natural equilibrium, with very severe consequences. In their view, humanity had become a destructive force by transforming the natural environment and setting off chains of unanticipated consequences. The natural world would support only a population that treated it with respect, they argued, and would avenge itself against a species that abused it.

Among these nature writers, none would have a more lasting impact on later generations of environmentalists than Aldo Leopold, a game management professor at the University of Wisconsin and onetime Forest Service worker. His *Sand County Almanac* (1949) was one of the first popular books to link the love and appreciation of nature to the need for ecological awareness. "Ecology," in Leopold's era, was the scientific study of the interplay between living things and their environment, a science that was rapidly gaining in sophistication and complexity. His work contributed to giving the word "ecology" its later meaning, with its connotations of environmental sensitivity. The first half of the *Almanac*, describing the natural world on Leopold's Wisconsin farmstead over the course of one year, evokes the pleasure he takes from witnessing the reawakening of dormant creatures in spring or splitting firewood on a cold February morning. Leopold experiences an almost mystical sense of connection to the landscape, in passages that link him to the long tradition of American nature writing stretching back to William Bartram, Henry David Thoreau, John Muir, and many others.[23]

But Leopold also takes on more theoretical matters. He warns against thinking of the natural world as something that can be manipulated at will for human convenience. In a passage on predator-prey relationships he recounts an experiment, in which he had participated, of killing all the predators on the Kaibab Plateau of Arizona (wolves, coyotes, mountain lions) in order to safeguard domesticated livestock. This culling had the unforeseen effect of letting the area's deer population swell to unmanageable proportions. They bred freely, stripped the area of vegetation, and then died off in large numbers from starvation. The episode had taught him, he wrote, not only that there is an intrinsic dignity in the life of all creatures, "pests" included, but also that human meddling can destroy an ecological balance built up over the centuries.

Elsewhere he deplores the persistence of ecological ignorance in hunters and fishermen. "Recreational development," wrote Leopold, "is a
job not of building roads into lovely country but of building receptivity
into the still unlovely human mind."

In the book's final essay, "The Land Ethic," Leopold urges his readers to expand their understanding of community. There was a time, he
wrote, when slaves were excluded and could be treated merely as property. The abolition of slavery marked a great advance for humanity in
widening the ethical circle. Now it must be widened again to include
the nonhuman living things, and even the nonliving surroundings of
our world. The human approach to the land must no longer be governed solely by economic considerations. He offered a maxim: "A thing
is right when it tends to preserve the integrity, stability, and beauty of
the biotic community. It is wrong when it tends otherwise." This maxim
became a benchmark principle for generations of environmentalists
while the essay itself became a foundational text for the discipline of
environmental ethics.[24]

Marjory Stoneman Douglas, a Florida newspaper editor, also writing in the late 1940s, eulogized her state's immense wetlands in *Everglades: River of Grass* (1947). Eager like Leopold to reeducate her fellow
citizens, she urged them to look at the area not as a great malarial
swamp, to be drained and transformed into farms and suburbs, but as
a pricelessly beautiful place, "one of the unique regions of the earth,
remote, never wholly known." She lamented the way in which, since
the 1920s, thoughtless development projects, sugarcane plantations,
drainage canals, golf course construction, and uncontrolled burns had
destabilized the environment, menacing fish and animal populations.
That in turn had led to the intrusion of salt water into previously freshwater and brackish zones, killing orchards and sending a warning that
to tamper with a delicate environment is to invite retaliation. Resorting
to the same metaphor as the nuclear scientists, she titled her last chapter "The Eleventh Hour," insisting that only a drastic combination of
political intervention and human self-restraint could save the area from
annihilation. Her narrative, of an Eden-like place gradually degraded

by greedy mankind, yet even now susceptible to rescue, would be repeated in hundreds of subsequent narratives about threatened wild
places.[25]

Another popular nature writer of the era was Rachel Carson (1907–
1964). She had a particular gift for presenting complicated biological
issues in a straightforward way to general audiences. Carson won a wide
following for her trilogy of books about coastal ecosystems, which
blended zoology with a poetic evocation of seaside birds, animals, and
plants. *Under the Sea Wind* (1941), *The Sea Around Us* (1951), and *The Edge
of the Sea* (1955) were so successful that during the 1950s she was able to
give up an administrative job at the U.S. Fish and Wildlife Service and
become a full-time writer. *The Sea Around Us* won the National Book
Award in 1952, and a film documentary based on it won an Oscar the
following year.[26]

Carson shared Leopold's and Douglas's sense of wonder at the variety of nature and the intricate evolutionary adaptations different creatures had made to their environments. She too warned against human
folly and hubris in transforming the natural world. "In all the world of
living things," she wrote in *The Sea Around Us*, "it is doubtful whether
there is a more delicately balanced relationship than that of island life
to its environment." She also knew how easily these precarious arrangements could be broken. The arrival of men on previously undisturbed
islands usually spelled catastrophe. "Man has written one of his black-
est records as a destroyer on the oceanic islands. He has seldom set foot
on an island that he has not brought about disastrous change . . . Upon
species after species of island life, the black night of extinction has
fallen." Her combination of informative exposition with this type of
emotionally charged language elevated Carson, by the early 1960s, to
the status of an environmental prophet. When her *Silent Spring* appeared in 1962 she already had a primed and receptive audience.[27]

A fourth influential nature writer of the 1950s was Sigurd Olson
(1899–1982), a professor of biology and ecology at Ely Junior College,
Minnesota, and a summer canoe guide in the maze of lakes that mark
the U.S.-Canadian boundary. His first two books, *The Singing Wilderness*

(1956) and *Listening Point* (1958), became bestsellers, suggesting a developing constituency of readers eager for nature writing. Olson's writing, even more than Leopold's, blended ecological insight with a sense of mystical awe. To read Olson is to believe that the everyday world disappears completely when you commune with special remote places. Of moments spent on the high ground named Listening Point, he wrote: "[W]hat I have known there is one of the oldest satisfactions of man, that when he gazed upon the earth and sky with wonder, when he sensed the first vague glimmerings of meaning in the universe, the world of knowledge and spirit was opened to him." Children have this sense innately, he believed, but the humdrum reality of life knocks it out of them. In untouched places of great natural beauty we can perhaps recover them. "From this one place I would explore the entire North and all life, including my own . . . For me it would be a listening-post from which I might even hear the music of the spheres."[28]

Sigurd Olson, Minnesota canoe guide, author, and president of the Wilderness Society, 1963–1971.

To have such monstrosities as motorized boats or aircraft in this primitive wilderness was not just an annoyance to Olson but a desecration, and he devoted much of his later life to securing inclusion of the Boundary Waters Canoe Area under the provisions of the 1964 Wilderness Act. In another essay from *Listening Point*, "The Whistle," however, he admitted that he was capable of appreciating the wilderness only because he was part of civilization, many of whose principles and conveniences he valued highly. Olson understood that wilderness and civilization were two aspects of the same reality. "Only through my own personal contact with civilization had I learned to value the advantages of solitude." Like many wilderness advocates, indeed, he valued nature in part as a therapeutic or psychological resource for overstimulated urban Americans.[29]

Olson later became president of the Wilderness Society. He, like all of these nature writers, helped create a constituency for the environmental organizations that were to play a vital role in the politics of the late twentieth century. In the 1950s the most important of these organizations was the Sierra Club. Founded at the end of the nineteenth century by John Muir, it had campaigned for the protection of Yosemite National Park and for the creation of new national parks at Mount Rainier and Glacier. After the San Francisco earthquake of 1906, the club had led a protest movement against the building of a reservoir, Hetch Hetchy, inside Yosemite National Park. Although it lost that campaign, under Muir's guidance it generated immense popular sympathy for the principles of preserving wild areas of special natural beauty and for keeping national parks off-limits for development-oriented projects.

After Hetch Hetchy, the Sierra Club had become, essentially, a mountaineers' club for the next forty years. When David Brower became its executive director in 1952, however, it resumed and intensified its earlier role as a lobbying organization. Brower, like Muir, believed in the quasi-religious sanctity of wilderness, and was a tireless campaigner. Starting in 1954, he created a coalition of wilderness organizations to prevent the Bureau of Reclamation from building the proposed Echo Canyon Dam in Dinosaur National Monument, on the Colorado-Utah boundary. The reservoir behind it would have obliterated canyons of spectacular natural beauty on the Green and Yampa Rivers. The club's leaders addressed congressional committees to prove the economic folly of the project. They also undertook an ambitious publication program, using some of the nation's greatest photographers, including Ansel Adams, and some of its greatest writers, including Wallace Stegner, to show Americans the beauty of a place that was now threatened with flooding. The coalition led by Brower and the Sierra Club finally succeeded in persuading Congress to specify, in the Colorado River Storage Project Act of 1956, that "no dam or reservoir constructed under the authorization of the act shall be within any National Park or Monument."[30]

The Sierra Club's approach to preservation did not go uncontested. It seemed nonsensical to the officers of the Bureau of Reclamation and its energetic commissioner Floyd Dominy. It was obvious to Dominy that dams and reservoirs brought benefits that far outweighed the drawbacks. They offered flood control, hydroelectric power, and steady water supplies in Western areas that suffered seasonal droughts. Without them, he believed, such cities as Tucson, Phoenix, and Las Vegas could scarcely ever have been more than dusty desert villages. Dominy was born on a Nebraska farm in the High Plains, homesteaded by his grandfather in the 1870s. In childhood he had been thrilled by the building of dams and irrigation works that helped farmers in that region of marginal rainfall. Witnessing the Dust Bowl and drought of the 1930s had intensified his conviction that life in the American West demanded the careful control and use of every drop of water. As a county agent in Wyoming he had helped farmers dam local streams and assure their cattle a year-round water supply. Now he was head of a large federal bureau that felt a constant need to justify its existence and increase its budget. No wonder its leaders rarely caught sight of a wild river they did not want to dam. When wilderness advocates argued against dams on the Colorado River, Reclamation bureaucrats regarded them simply as selfish and impractical. The extraordinarily unpredictable flow of the Colorado, they reasoned, was such that the only way to ensure a constant water supply throughout the year, every year, was with a succession of dams and reservoirs in which the flow of many years could be husbanded. In the event, Dinosaur was spared, but many Sierra Club activists later came to regard this as no more than a pyrrhic victory. As a quid pro quo the Glen Canyon Dam, built farther downstream on the Colorado, created a reservoir 186 miles long, flooding a different series of equally beautiful canyons.[31]

Many other activists agreed with Dominy that the natural world was an immense pool of resources and that they were there to be *used*. Charles Park, a professor of mining geology at Stanford, for example, believed that society's need for minerals overrode preservationists' aesthetic concern with wilderness. Park told the Sierra Club's David Brower, "It's criminal to waste minerals when the standard of living of your people depends upon them." His book *Affluence in Jeopardy* argued that natural resources should be used wisely but exhaustively, that affluence was morally defensible, and that its benefits should be extended to everyone. Like Dominy, his outlook was entirely human oriented. Park was not blind to aesthetic concerns, but subordinated them to practical matters. Robert Wernick went further, arguing that wilderness was "precisely what man has been fighting *against* since he began his painful awkward climb to civilization. It is the dark, the formless, the terrible, the old chaos, which our fathers pushed back, which surrounds us yet, which will engulf us all in the end." Wernick added that there was something inhuman about wilderness advocates, and that beneath their hearty and superficially likable exterior they were "decadents, aristocrats, [and] snobs."[32]

Nevertheless, the Wilderness Society and allied environmental organizations were able to secure passage of the Wilderness Act in 1964. It set nine million acres off-limits to economic development and preserved them in a state as nearly pristine as possible. Widespread citizen support demonstrated a growing interest in wilderness as a link to the past and to the heroic earlier stages of American settlement. Popular sociology books of the 1950s like *The Organization Man* and novels like *The Man in the Gray Flannel Suit* described American men as conformist, timid, and "other-directed," in direct contrast to their assertive, "inner-directed" grandfathers. Perhaps the increasing popularity of wilderness among the white, urban middle classes, even those who never visited it, was their way of paying tribute to their forefathers' achievements. If so, it was an ironic tribute, since the pioneering homesteaders and Western settlers had not regarded wilderness as something to cherish but as something to overcome and subdue. The prodevelopment advocates were the pioneers' real descendents.[33]

CITIES AND SUBURBS

The fifteen years after World War II witnessed an immense building boom, not just in Western areas served by massive new dams but throughout the entire country. Depression in the 1930s, followed by a scarcity of building materials in the war years of the early 1940s, had led to an accumulation of demand that could now finally be satisfied. The building boom was pushed along by the baby boom and by the fact that millions of demobilized military personnel had access to low-interest loans through the GI Bill of Rights. These loans enabled a larger percentage of the population to buy single-family houses than ever before. Suburbs grew rapidly after 1945 because the new generation of home-buyers also owned motor vehicles and could afford to commute to their jobs. Mass-produced suburbs, like the Levittowns built on Long Island and in Pennsylvania, became famous for the speed at which they turned acres of farmland into new communities.[34]

The rights and wrongs of suburbanization became a point of controversy in the 1950s and 1960s. Those who approved the process pointed proudly to the fact that far more Americans than ever before could live in low-density neighborhoods, away from city smoke, and in houses that permitted them to express their individuality. They enjoyed access to cheap electricity and the new miracle of efficient air-conditioning, attaining greater levels of comfort than any earlier American generation. Remembering their Depression-era childhoods, these members of what would later be called the "Greatest Generation" were acutely aware of how much richer they were than their parents. Suburban houses with large verdant yards also gave their owners at least a hint of rural life. Critics who disliked suburbanization, by contrast, called it "urban sprawl." Sociological arguments against suburbs included the idea that, far from being zones of individualism, they encouraged bland conformity.[35]

The building of suburban houses also provoked some of the earliest of what would later be called environmental concerns. Houses were often sited on sloping ground, floodplains, or wetlands, making them prone to erosion and flooding. They often lacked adequate sanitation, particularly early on, when builders relied not on mains drainage but on septic tanks, which could contaminate groundwater and lead to epidemics. Poorly insulated postwar suburban houses were also energy inefficient. Finally, profit-oriented developers had an incentive to use every available lot for housing, and neglected to diversify the new communities by building parks, unless compelled by the government to do so.[36]

Early generations of suburbanites enjoyed access to neighboring tracts of untouched woodlands and fields, but not for long. All too soon, another tract-housing estate would obliterate them, simultaneously destroying wildlife habitats and creating wider zones of suburban uniformity. The historian Adam Rome, speculating on why so many members of the baby boom generation that grew up in these houses became environmentalists as adults, remarks that "again and again the destruction of nearby open spaces robbed children of beloved places to play—and the losses hit home . . . The desire to preserve wilderness was the tip of an iceberg, the most visible part of a much larger concern about the destructive sprawl of urban civilization."[37]

The growth of suburbs also changed the cities they ringed. The population of inner cities declined as aspiring suburbanites moved out, usually leaving poorer people and minorities behind. Urban planners believed that neighborhoods should be organized by function in the name of efficiency, rather than having housing, shops, warehouses, factories, and railroads all jumbled together. Early postwar city planners, of whom New York's Robert Moses was the most famous, favored the building of freeways to facilitate rapid movement into and out of the cities for the new suburban commuters, even though the building of freeways sliced old neighborhoods in half and worsened the quality of life for the people who had been left behind.[38]

Jane Jacobs's now classic book *The Death and Life of Great American Cities* (1961) protested against such changes. Jacobs (1916–2006) lived and worked in Greenwich Village and was an editor at *Architectural Forum*. She hated the dehumanizing scale, noise, and speed of the freeways and helped defeat Moses's planned Lower Manhattan Expressway.

The packed, jostling variety of cities was just what had always made them so interesting, she added, citing mixed-use neighborhoods like her own Greenwich Village, Boston's North End, and Back of the Yards in Chicago. Fascinating neighborhoods with their distinctive communities and traditions were now, alas, being replaced by zones of specialization, which were alienating, crime ridden, and depressing. Worst of all were the massive high-rise public housing projects, which segregated "problem" populations from everyone else. When new buildings are built, she argued, let them rise amid older buildings in mixed-use settings, preserving the mood, distinctiveness, and organic community of their locale.[39] Embodying a kind of informal folk anthropology, her book warned against the idea that experts can fully grasp the intricacies of a system as complex as a city. Jacobs is not usually considered an environmental writer, but several themes in her great book can be seen, in retrospect, as auguries of later environmental attitudes. One was her criticism of intolerant experts' high-handedness and their false prioritizing of efficiency. Another was her recognition that cities were where most Americans actually lived, and that making a humane and livable world ought to begin at home.[40]

A wide variety of American writers in the 1950s also began to address what we now call urban environmental issues. The economist John Kenneth Galbraith, for example, argued in his popular and influential book *The Affluent Society* (1958) that the nation devoted far too many of its resources to the pursuit of private wealth and far too few to public welfare. One result was environmental neglect and squalor. Now that we had cured the age-old problem of feeding, housing, and clothing our population, he said, we needed to achieve a new social balance and a new wisdom in spending our money. In one of the book's most famous passages Galbraith wrote:

> The family which takes its mauve and cerise, air-conditioned, power-steered, and power-braked automobile out for a tour passes through cities that are badly paved, made hideous by litter, blighted buildings, billboards, and posts

for wires that should long since have been put underground . . . They picnic on exquisitely packaged food from
a portable ice box by a polluted stream and go on to spend
the night at a park which is a menace to public health and
morals. Just before dozing off on an air mattress, beneath
a nylon tent, amid the stench of decaying refuse, they may
reflect vaguely on the curious unevenness of their blessings.

Galbraith believed that only government action could improve water
quality, order utilities to bury the wires, mitigate urban blight, and improve the landscape. His work offered a theoretical justification for
government action on behalf of the environment, and would influence
the activist mood of the Kennedy and Johnson administrations in the
following decade.[41]

A range of scholars was also beginning in the 1950s to think holistically about humans' impact on the natural world. A conference at
Princeton in June 1955 on "Man's Role in Changing the Face of the
Earth," convened by geographer Carl Sauer, zoologist Marston Bates,
and urban planner Lewis Mumford, was a pioneering attempt at
interdisciplinary scholarship. What, the participants asked, could the
nation's leading biologists, economists, ecologists, and geographers
teach one another about threats to the future welfare of the earth?
Foreshadowing countless subsequent debates, the conference's participants were split in their judgments. The ecologists generally argued
that humans should restrain themselves to achieve "a condition of equilibrium with the environment, so that the use of earth's resources will
not represent a net deterioration of the capital base." The economists,
by contrast, spoke of transforming natural systems on behalf of increasing human health, wealth, and welfare. They scoffed at conservationists
"who are willing to freeze to death sitting on top of a coal mine." Pessimistic contributors foresaw the coming exhaustion of natural resources
like oil, copper, and iron, whereas optimists anticipated an inexhaust-
ible supply of new resources into the indefinite future, thanks to human
inventiveness and versatility.[42]

. . . .

THE GREAT POSTWAR debate over nuclear weapons persisted into
the subsequent decades. How does it stand now, in 2014? The consensus
view on the danger of nuclear fallout, established by 1960, has stood the
test of time. The importance of adhering to the principles of the Atmospheric Test Ban Treaty of 1963 was widely accepted, with the result that
atmospheric radiation levels have declined steadily since 1964. Between
1950 and 2014, Britain, France, China, Israel, India, Pakistan, North
Korea, and South Africa all developed their own nuclear weapons, but
none used them in war. When the Soviet Union broke up into its con-
stituent republics after 1990, Belarus, Kazakhstan, and Ukraine all in-
herited stockpiles of warheads. These they subsequently turned over
to Russia for decommissioning, in accordance with the Nuclear Non-
Proliferation Treaty, which has been in force since 1970. As a result of
these treaties and historic changes, there are many fewer nuclear warheads in the world today than in the peak year of 1985, an estimated
decline from seventy thousand to twenty-three thousand, many of
which, moreover, are warehoused, eventually to be dismantled.

These developments have almost certainly made the threat of nuclear war more remote than it was in the 1950s, and at such Cold War
flashpoints as the Cuban Missile Crisis of 1962. Anxieties and uncertainties remain, of course, including the threat that militant or unstable
regimes might acquire nuclear weapons, and the threat of nuclear-
armed terrorist groups. The overall picture concerning this worst of all
environmental threats, nevertheless, is one that gives ground for cautious optimism.

The great postwar debate over population also persisted down the
ensuing decades, as we shall see in the following chapters. Here too the
news turned out to be surprisingly positive. World population continued to grow, passing the seven-billion mark in 2011. By then, however,
birth rates in most of the developed industrial nations were at or below
replacement level, obliging ever smaller cohorts of working-age people
to shoulder the burden of caring for larger, older generations. Future
projections vary, but many demographers now suggest that world pop-

ulation might peak in the mid-twenty-first century and then begin a gradual decline as the processes of worldwide industrialization and demographic transition continue. Increases in food production, meanwhile, have continued, such that famine and malnutrition, though still dismayingly widespread, are more often the result of war, political instability, or tyranny than simply of inadequate supplies. The plant physiologist Lloyd Evans, at the end of a survey of agricultural innovations over the last half century, concludes that "we can be reasonably sure of producing enough food for ten billion by 2050." Just as political changes were decisive in reducing the threat of nuclear war, however, so benign political changes are essential if the poverty, inequality, and mass unemployment that contribute to world hunger are to be reduced in the coming decades.[43]

CHAPTER 2

POLLUTION AND PESSIMISM

POLLUTION WAS THE ISSUE that crystallized the mass environmental movement of the 1960s. Visible pollution was widespread, ugly, and threatening to human health. It came from factory chimneys belching smoke, smog over industrial cities, and immense open dumps at the edge of every city, often smoldering and sending ash into the sky. Streets and parks were marred by litter, while dead fish floated belly-up in rivers near factory outlets. The destruction of a once thriving vacation industry on the shores of Lake Erie, whose beaches were coated with algal slime, and the destruction of California beaches by a massive oil spill in 1969 were only the worst among the decade's many pollution scandals. A patchwork of state and local ordinances against pollution, underfunded and inadequately enforced, was rarely effective against large-scale dumping into waterways, on wasteland, and into the atmosphere. Often the city governments that made the rules were also among the leading polluters.

The timely convergence of new facts about pollution, books about invisible hazards, and a new activism among scientists helped to develop environmentalism as a popular social movement. Its development in the mid- and late 1960s coincided with mass protests against the Vietnam War, a succession of bloody urban riots, and large-scale student demonstrations on college campuses. The mood of the 1960s was mistrustful of government and skeptical about tradition. It embodied an amorphous but powerful youth revolt. All these movements favored street demonstrations, polar antagonisms, demonization of adversaries, and a white-hot rhetoric of righteous indignation. Environmental protection and improvement, which in other times might have remained a marginal matter of ordinary politics, became briefly one of the flashpoints of a society in crisis, drawing in millions of concerned citizens.

The new environmentalism was not, on the whole, a radical movement, but it inevitably resonated and drew energy from the new counterculture. Counterculture gurus like Timothy Leary and Abbie Hoffman believed that sex, drugs, and rock 'n' roll were superior to monogamy, suburban tract homes, and nine-to-five sobriety. The counterculture also included a protest against conspicuous waste and the "plastic" falsehoods of consumer society. It favored a return to sincerity, simplicity, selflessness, and "Mother Earth." It claimed the moral high ground and sought to embody a superior way of life in self-sufficient communes. Environmentalism taught similar lessons: respect for the earth, mistrust of synthetic things, mental liberation from traditional but destructive approaches to life, and the idea of finding harmony with nature.

The sixties generation of writers and activists left a strong and permanent mark on American environmentalism. They were largely responsible for its transformation from a set of special interests into a mass movement, without which much of the political progress of the seventies would never have been achieved. But their influence also left behind a heritage of exaggeration and pessimism, damaging the movement's long-term plausibility and setting the stage for an antienvironmental backlash. The environmental debates of our own day still carry the marks of conflicts begun in the 1960s.

POLLUTION IN THE NEWS

"Pollution" was a religious idea before it became an environmental one. It meant that something holy—a person, place, or food—had been ritually defiled and was no longer acceptable to God. Using "pollution" metaphorically, to describe the side effects of industrialization, carried with it the idea that rivers, lakes, and the atmosphere were themselves holy, deserving of a quasi-religious veneration and protection. In the early days of the industrial revolution, smoke and factory effluent had seemed no more than minor inconveniences. Indeed, they could be welcome signs of productivity and increasing wealth. By the mid-twentieth century, however, they were a menace.

The Pittsburgh area, with its concentration of iron and steel plants fueled by soft coal, had long been one of the dirtiest places in the United States. In late October 1948 twenty residents of Donora, a low-lying town on the Monongahela River, died in a dense cloud of contaminated smog containing oxides of nitrogen and sulfur. Six thousand more residents suffered paralyzing headaches, severe coughing fits, shortness of breath, and nausea; some never fully recovered. Hospitals were crowded as doctors administered oxygen to men and women, es-

Severe pollution in Donora, Pennsylvania, where an
atmospheric inversion incident killed twenty people
and injured hundreds more in 1948.

pecially the elderly, as they struggled for breath. A hotel basement had to be turned into an annex to the city morgue. A suffocating smell of sulfur, originating at the American Steel and Wire plant and the Donora Zinc Works, intensified in the windless air; residents had long known that no vegetation could live within a mile of the zinc smelter. Government agencies, responding to the disaster, realized that they must start to take pollution more seriously. "We have to get over the idea that smog is just a nuisance," said one of the leaders of the U.S. Public Health Service after the disaster. "There is no condition confronting us that is more terrifying." A detailed report on the tragedy, published the following year, established "for the first time that air contamination in an industrial community can actually cause acute disabling diseases."[1]

After Donora, media attention to the problem of air pollution increased gradually—but so did the pollution itself, as a consequence of the postwar era's immense economic boom. Coal use was declining in favor of oil and natural gas, but the national surge in motor vehicles was a growing source of new pollution. No American city suffered as badly as London, England, where an estimated four thousand people died in a killer smog in 1952, but New York health authorities reported elevated death rates from atmospheric inversion episodes in 1953 and 1963. New York produced 730 pounds of atmospheric pollutants per inhabitant per year, according to one account from 1965; the city government's garbage incinerators and local power stations were the leading sources of smoke. The whole metropolitan Northeast was forced to breathe air high in sulfur dioxide, carbon monoxide, and lead compounds from fuel additives. Los Angeles, similarly, suffered from "a mist of hydrocarbons, soot, lead, acidic gases, and particles that made entire mountain ranges disappear." Residents became familiar with the eye-stinging, lung-burning air, reduced visibility, and chronic breathing complaints that these pollutants brought.[2]

Water pollution was equally serious, and no body of water suffered worse than Lake Erie. Ringed by industrial cities and fed by heavily polluted rivers, it was subjected to large volumes of raw sewage, outflow from factories and oil refineries, and agricultural chemical runoff. These contaminants, above all phosphorus from detergents, upset the lake's biological equilibrium in a process known as eutrophication. High nutrient levels fed the immoderate growth of algae and other marine plants, which used up all the available oxygen in the lake and killed off the fish. Massive volumes of algae washed ashore and rotted on the beaches, becoming infested with flies and other insects, forcing all but three of sixty-two swimming beaches to close. *Time* magazine wrote in 1965 that "beaches once gleaming white with sand are covered with smelly greenish slime" and that "most of [the lake's] tributaries have turned into little more than open sewers." The Lake Erie vacation industry was ruined and its local fishermen nearly lost their livelihood.[3] Raritan Bay, New Jersey, part of New York Harbor, was also a health hazard to recreational swimmers because of untreated raw sewage and effluent from adjacent factories and refineries. Shellfish from the bay

Dead fish, oil, boards, and debris in the Rouge River, Michigan, 1969.

were known to carry hepatitis. James Ridgeway, a young journalist at the *New Republic*, campaigned for years to clean up what he called America's own River Styx.[4]

News stories also criticized other forms of local pollution, particularly noise from airports and sickening smells from pulp mills in the Pacific Northwest and chicken rendering plants in the Northeast.[5] Laws against pollution already on the books, however, proved hard to enforce. States were reluctant to shoulder the financial burden of cleaning up rivers and lakes. Politicians knew that the industries responsible for pollution also brought jobs and prosperity. If they imposed stringent pollution controls, industries might move to more lenient states and cities. Local governments were slow to improve sewage treatment because paying for it meant raising taxes. Environmental violations involving more than one state often went unresolved as various government agencies disclaimed responsibility or agreed merely to undertake further studies—a classic stalling tactic—rather than assign blame and act decisively.

Detergent pollution in Sudbury, Massachusetts, 1963.

Media from across the political spectrum began to argue that these issues could be addressed only by a federal agency, enforcing a uniform set of standards nationwide. Appealing for such standards from the left, the *Nation* noted that "it is obviously inequitable for a low-standards upstream state to impose filth on a more conscientious state downstream." From the political center the *New York Times* opined that the cry of "invasion of states' rights" was really "the rallying cry of the chemical, leather, paper, steel, power, and other industrial firms that oppose Federal action because they find it much easier to put pressure on state and local governments." Even the right-wing *National Review*, while continuing to favor the principle of states' rights, admitted that "Washington could help in constructing uniform state laws governing pollution control." Congress, in response to this widely shared view, passed comparatively modest clean air acts in 1963 and 1967 and clean water acts in 1960 and 1965. It supplemented them with more decisive legislation in the early 1970s (by which time the Environmental Protection Agency had come into existence as an umbrella organization to supervise most forms of environmental regulation).[6]

As the sixties neared their end and the volume of pollution-related stories in the news increased, a catastrophic 1969 oil spill from a drilling platform off the California coast seemed to epitomize America's pollution woes. Forty miles of pristine beaches were coated in oily slime as the Union Oil Company tried for eleven days to seal the leak, which eventually spread over four hundred square miles. Dispersants meant to mitigate the oil's effects often proved even deadlier than the oil itself to birds, fish, and seals. Thousands of animals died. Local residents and conservationists tried to use the disaster as a pretext to shut down all the offshore drilling platforms, but Union Oil officials retorted that the locals were hysterical, that the damage was temporary, and that the oil was an indispensable national resource. Fred Hartley, the head of Union Oil, made a bad situation worse by remarking, "I'm amazed at all this publicity for the loss of a few birds."[7] Previous oil spills had been equally severe, but the timing of this one, along with the wealth of the community affected, prompted a national outcry. The Nixon administration, then just eight days old, recognized that the passions aroused crossed party lines and that it might profit from taking bold steps on environmental issues. It delighted environmental groups by ordering a temporary halt to all drilling in the region.[8]

Also in 1969, the heavily polluted Cuyahoga River—so choked by chemical waste, oil, and fermented gases that its water was brown— caught fire and burned fiercely for twenty minutes, badly damaging two railroad bridges before being extinguished. This was just the latest of nine fires to afflict the river in recent decades (a 1952 blaze had been far more serious), but the timing of the 1969 fire coincided with the peak of popular outrage against pollution. As historians David and Richard Stradling note, "[T]he Cuyahoga fire evolved into one of the great symbolic environmental catastrophes of the industrial era" and was cited in dozens of subsequent analyses and exposés of American pollution. The next year, *National Geographic* featured a foldout double-page photograph of the dirty, factory-lined river, depicting it as emblematic of everything that was wrong with polluted industrial America.[9]

By the end of the sixties, journalists and politicians alike were recognizing the connection between the many forms of pollution and the need for an effective response. "This man-made pollution is bad enough in itself," wrote *Time*, "but it reflects something even worse: a dangerous illusion that technological man can build bigger and bigger industrial societies with little regard for the iron laws of nature." Americans would have to rid themselves of "the false assumption that nature exists only to serve man." Instead they would have to learn a new form of restraint and a new way of living in harmony with nature.[10]

A different kind of atmospheric health hazard—not usually described as pollution at the time—became the subject of political action for the first time in the mid-1960s. This was tobacco smoke, which Surgeon General Luther Terry identified in January 1964 as one of the causes of lung cancer, emphysema, and heart disease. The invention of cigarette-making machines in 1882 had stimulated an aggressive marketing campaign to increase cigarette sales. By the mid-twentieth century, with help from Hollywood and Madison Avenue, smoking was linked to ideals of sexual attractiveness, independence, health, and heroism. Scattered evidence about its health *hazards* was already accumulating, however, and in the 1930s insurance companies had begun to link smoking to reduced life expectancy and elevated cancer rates.[11]

In 1950 two British scientists, Richard Doll and Austin Hill, published an article in the *British Medical Journal* linking smoking directly to the incidence of lung cancer. Their American counterparts, E. L. Wynder and E. A. Graham, came to the same conclusion soon afterward. *Reader's Digest*, the single most widely read magazine in America during the 1950s, ran a series of articles about these findings entitled "Cancer by the Carton." The tobacco industry fought a tenacious rearguard action against the accumulating medical evidence. The leading cigarette manufacturers created the Tobacco Industry Research Committee, which hired its own scientists, conducted its own studies, and emphasized ambiguities in the evidence for as long as possible. It was true that not all smokers contracted lung cancer and that nonsmokers sometimes *did* contract it. Nevertheless, the industry acknowledged in private that the science was conclusive—an acknowledgement that would later lead to prosecutions for fraud and conspiracy. The surgeon general was convinced by 1964 that government was justified in warning citizens of the risks of smoking. For the first time, in 1965, health warnings were printed on cigarette packets.[12]

Cigarette sales fell sharply in the months after the surgeon general's warning but rebounded the next year, demonstrating the addictive character of tobacco and the determination of the tobacco industry to compensate for the report by stepping up its advertising campaigns. In fact, the average American smoked 4,318 cigarettes in 1965, the highest number ever. Tobacco use remained high, demonstrating some of the paradoxical aspects of this new cluster of health issues. Citizens could, at the same time, express anxiety about relatively low levels of exposure to pollutants in the environment while voluntarily drawing into their lungs large quantities of smoke, which ever accumulating evidence showed to be carcinogenic.[13]

FIVE PESSIMISTIC INTELLECTUALS

Rising national awareness of pollution led to a series of influential books and articles about the use and misuse of science and technology. Rachel Carson's *Silent Spring* was the first of these studies to win national acclaim. Based on a series of articles in the *New Yorker*, it was published in book form in 1962 and rose rapidly to the top of national bestseller lists. Her central image was of a new year in which the traditional signs of spring never arrive, because all the songbirds have been killed by pesticides. Carson argued that government agencies and the nation's farmers were using herbicides and pesticides indiscriminately, poisoning other species, damaging habitats, and possibly threatening human lives.[14] Carson believed that toxins were being concentrated in the bodies of the birds and fish that ate poisoned insects. People in turn would eat the contaminated fish, such that mothers could be unwittingly harming babies in the womb and through contaminated breast milk.[15]

Rachel Carson, whose surprise bestseller *Silent Spring* (1962) helped catalyze the environmental movement.

Carson cited cases where city governments undertook aerial spraying that killed domestic pets. Detroit had been sprayed with aldrin in 1959, ostensibly targeting Japanese beetles but collaterally killing thousands of birds, squirrels, rabbits, muskrats, possums, cats, and dogs. Moreover, repeated spraying of the same area, while it killed most of the targeted insects, was never 100 percent effective. The small number that survived due to some level of natural immunity would pass this immunity to their offspring, making the chemical progressively less effective with the passage of each generation. Meanwhile the preference of American commercial farmers for monoculture, or the planting of a single crop over wide areas, created perfect conditions for the most troublesome insects to thrive. Diversified crop planting, by contrast, would diminish the problem by creating opportunities for a wide diversity of insects and birds to compete, preventing the local dominance of any single species.[16]

Readers drawn into *Silent Spring* by its dismaying opening might have recalled the DuPont Corporation's longtime slogan: "Better Things for Better Living . . . Through Chemistry." Carson raised the possibility that it was a glaring falsehood. "The central problem of our age has . . . become the contamination of man's total environment with such substances of incredible potential for harm—substances that accumulate in the tissues of plants and animals and even penetrate the germ cells to shatter or alter the very material of heredity upon which the shape of our future depends." Carson pointed out that although the human body can adapt to new substances over long periods of time, it could not possibly adapt to the dozens of ever more powerful compounds that were appearing on the market every year.[17]

Carson did not argue that the use of chemical pesticides was wrong in all times and places. She hoped that the currently primitive uses of science would be displaced by *better* science. She appealed for restraint and prudence and argued the virtues of biological rather than synthetic chemical alternatives. Even so, the book ended with an anguished condemnation of human folly. "As crude a weapon as the cave man's club, the chemical barrage has been hurled against the fabric of life . . . The 'control of nature' is a phrase conceived in arrogance, born of the Neanderthal age of biology and philosophy, when it was supposed that nature exists for the convenience of man . . . It is our alarming misfortune that so primitive a science has armed itself with the most modern and terrible weapons, and that in turning them against the insects it has also turned them against the earth."[18]

Silent Spring sold forty thousand copies just after its publication and dominated the *New York Times* bestseller list for most of the next year. But by that time, Carson herself was already severely ill with breast cancer and undergoing radiation therapy. She promoted her book in a variety of television broadcasts and in 1963 addressed a congressional committee on pesticide control, but she died in the spring of 1964, at the age of only fifty-six.[19]

By the time of her death, she had witnessed the full range of responses to her book, from enthusiastic support on one hand—from such luminaries as Supreme Court justice William O. Douglas—to bitter opposition on the other. It was possible to overlook the mean-spirited personal attacks by some chemical corporations that had an obvious material interest in the case. More damaging were the adverse scholarly responses. Reviewing *Silent Spring* for *Science*, University of Wisconsin biologist I. L. Baldwin wrote that although the book was well written and raised important safety questions, it was deplorably one-sided. Carson had almost certainly exaggerated the degree to which the new chemicals were carcinogenic and mutagenic, he believed. She had also neglected to mention any of the benefits that various chemicals and modern inventions conferred. Since World War II, after all, "the development of new fibers, new plastics, new medicinals, and new agricultural chemicals has produced profound changes in our lives. Public health has been improved; the span of life has been greatly extended . . . and our rate of productivity in agriculture has been greatly expanded." Worst of all, in Baldwin's view, Carson's argument about the "balance of nature" was obviously false, implying that until very recently humans had lived in harmony with the natural world. In fact, he wrote, "modern agriculture and modern public health, indeed modern civilization, could not exist without an unrelenting war against a return of a true balance of nature." Lamont Cole, a Cornell University biologist, wrote in *Scientific American* that Carson had underestimated the importance of insects and overestimated the importance of birds, perhaps for emotional reasons. He also recalled witnessing the extraordinary effectiveness of DDT (one of her principal targets) in halting a typhus epidemic in Italy in 1944. Like Baldwin, he chided her for failing to place the issue in an ecological context, remarking that the idea of a "balance of nature" was "an obsolete concept among ecologists."[20] Brickbats notwithstanding, Carson became and has remained an honored figure in the environmental pantheon; the book itself, though outdated as science, remains in print.

Many writers in the 1960s drew inspiration from Carson's work. Some were scientists who had learned from the controversies of the 1950s that laboratory work was sometimes best combined with political action. Barry Commoner, for example, first aroused to the political implications of his work in the nuclear fallout controversy of the 1950s, published *Science and Survival* in 1966. Like *Silent Spring,* Commoner's book envisioned a world bound for destruction because of the perversion of science by greedy, shortsighted, and unimaginative people. We build complex systems, but then they turn on us, he wrote, citing the self-reinforcing power failures of November 9, 1965, which had blacked out the whole Northeastern United States for twelve hours. He also agreed with Carson's condemnation of DDT, adding that the pollution caused by nuclear fallout, detergents, phosphates, and an ever growing array of industrial chemicals constituted a vast experiment that humanity was conducting on itself without adequate safeguards. It was bad enough that we should use ourselves as guinea pigs, he wrote, but worse that we might be endangering the health and genetic well-being of future generations.[21] The cover of *Sci-*

Paul Ehrlich, the Stanford biologist who predicted famines for the United States and Europe in his bestseller *The Population Bomb* (1968).

ence and Survival pictured a mother pushing her baby in a carriage, both wearing gas masks.

Commoner was also alarmed that an increasing amount of basic scientific research was being conducted in secret, either because of national security or because of its lucrative commercial implications. Both scenarios violated the long-standing tradition of sharing scientific knowledge, enabling scientists impartially to monitor one another's work. "Mistakes made in secret will persist," he wrote, and could have appalling consequences for the lives of millions. The scale of government and corporate funding was so immense, moreover, that it attracted the most ambitious scientists and distorted the process of deciding which scientific questions were most important and pressing.[22]

A third scientist to step outside the laboratory and enter the world of environmental politics was Paul Ehrlich (born 1932), an entomologist and butterfly specialist at Stanford University. His 1968 book *The Population Bomb* created nationwide alarm about overpopulation. Even more sensational than *Silent Spring*, it sold two million copies in its first two years and sustained strong sales through the 1970s.[23] Ehrlich's book was a synthesis of the arguments about population formulated over the previous twenty years. *Time* magazine had run a cover story about overpopulation in 1960, and—as we saw above—the issue of obligatory contraception had become entwined with debates over foreign aid and agricultural policy in the Eisenhower years. In 1967, Paul and William Paddock had published *Famine 1975!*, a book of pseudo-prophecy arguing the inevitability of mass starvation and recommending the discontinuation of most foreign aid. None of these works, however, could match Ehrlich's when it came to clever marketing or artful overstatement.[24] Paperback editions of *The Population Bomb* bore a picture of an old-fashioned black anarchist bomb with its fuse fizzing and the slogan "The population bomb is ticking." Above it was the title *The Population Bomb* in lurid red letters, and the query: "Population Control or Race to Oblivion?" Below the title came the declaration: "While you are reading these words four people will have died from starvation. Most of them children."[25]

The Population Bomb begins by describing a horrible, burning-hot evening in Delhi when Ehrlich and his family had been surrounded by tens of thousands of swarming poor people. "People thrusting their hands through the taxi window, begging. People defecating and urinating. People clinging to buses. People herding animals . . . As we moved slowly through the mob, hand horn squawking, the dust, noise, heat, and cooking fires gave the scene a hellish aspect." He went on to summarize the acceleration of population growth since World War II, the way in which medical advances had (regrettably, in his view) increased human longevity, and what he claimed was the inability of rises in food productivity to keep pace. He then declared: "The battle to feed humanity is already lost, in the sense that we will not be able to prevent large-scale famines in the next decade or so. It is difficult to guess what the exact scale and consequences of the famines will be. But there *will be* famines." He predicted that Western Europe and the United States would be unable to feed themselves by 1980 and that citizens would be dying of starvation even in the most advanced societies.[26]

Drastic population control policies were therefore necessary. Widespread use of contraceptives and abortion were desirable, voluntarily if possible but compulsorily if necessary. "Abortion is a highly effective weapon in the armory of population control." Unfortunately, he added, "it is condemned by many family planning groups—which are notorious for pussyfooting about methodology." Sterilization, he said, should be guaranteed as a right to all who sought it. Ehrlich treated the Catholic Church, whose recent encyclical letter *Humanae Vitae* (1968) had upheld the traditional ban on artificial contraception, as almost criminally negligent. "It takes a great deal of patience for a biologist familiar with the miseries of overpopulation to read through documents that represent the views of even 'enlightened' Catholics."[27] Ehrlich mentioned the possibility of introducing contraceptives into the water supply or imposing punitive taxes on childbearing women. He proposed the creation of a "Department of Population and Environment" that would be empowered "to take whatever steps are necessary to establish a reasonable population size."

In an enthusiastic foreword to *The Population Bomb*, the Sierra Club's David Brower argued that population, pollution, and environmental

protection were directly connected issues. The preservation of wilderness areas and the limitation of pollution presupposed a restricted
population. Ehrlich agreed. In a chapter entitled "A Dying Planet," he
strove to link overpopulation to the era's other environmental concerns:
industrial pollution, urban smog, soil erosion, water contamination,
and the development of pesticide resistance in insects. A larger population, he argued, would make every one of these problems worse. He
ended the book by urging readers to proselytize their neighbors, teach-
ers, ministers, and local college professors on the issue of stopping
population growth, and to join his new organization, Zero Population
Growth (ZPG).[28]

Critical responses to the book were not lacking. There were already
plenty of reasons in 1968 to doubt that Ehrlich's "inevitable" mass famines would materialize. In a sharp retort entitled "The Nonsense Explosion," the journalist Ben Wattenberg pointed out that the United States
was one of the *least* densely populated nations in the world, that the
birth rate in 1968 was the lowest on record (seven hundred thousand
fewer births than in 1958), and that one in three counties in the United
States was actually *losing* population. He also denied that population growth worsened pollution. It might even help. After all, national defense would cost about the same whether the population was
two hundred million or three hundred million, but the additional tax
contributions of all those extra people could be devoted to the costs
of environmental research and pollution cleanup. It was a question of
political will, said Wattenberg, not gross numbers.[29]

Wattenberg's essay appeared in an anthology, *The American Population Debate*. Many of the contributors were professional demographers,
and the majority also expressed skepticism about the alleged inevitability
of famine. They pointed to the concept of demographic transition,
which correlates a decline in birth rates with the advance of industrialization. Therefore we could expect that as the world grew richer and
more industrialized, the danger of overpopulation would continue to
diminish. They also noted that population growth was attributable
above all to the twentieth century's impressive and laudable achievements in public health and medicine. These achievements included the

near elimination of smallpox and a huge reduction in the incidence of polio, tuberculosis, cholera, typhus, yellow fever, and other scourges.[30]

While *The Population Bomb* seized headlines and turned Ehrlich into one of the most popular lecturers in America, other writers investigated the connections between population, pollution, and the depletion of the world's limited resources. Garrett Hardin (1915–2003), a professor of human ecology at the University of California, Santa Barbara, offered support to Ehrlich's claim that coercion would be necessary in an effective population policy. In an article for *Science*, also published in 1968, Hardin introduced the idea of "the tragedy of the commons," a theory that would play a role in many subsequent environmental controversies.[31]

For the last two centuries, wrote Hardin, humans had been impressed by the power of Adam Smith's idea in *The Wealth of Nations* (1776) that the way to create prosperity is to let as many self-interested citizens as possible pursue their own wealth without government obstruction. The "invisible hand" of the market was better able to regulate supply and demand than any political authority, wrote Smith, and there was no surer incentive, for market participants, than self-interest. Hardin wrote that it was now time to discard Smith's approach because self-interested economic actors never consider the incidental harm their actions cause. He proposed to replace it with "mutual coercion, mutually agreed on." The idea of coercion may sound offensive, he wrote, especially to liberals, but liberals needed to consider that there are many areas of life in which they actually favor it. For example, everyone agrees that bank robbery must be prevented and that taxes are sometimes necessary. In other words, we have learned to live with a coercive policy against bank robbers and a coercive policy in favor of taxes, and we have been right to do so. These policies do not restrict our freedom—instead they make us *freer* than we would be without them.[32]

The reason that coercion sometimes promotes freedom, Hardin argued, will be clear when we consider the alternative. He gave the example of a group of herdsmen letting their cows graze on common land. At first there will be grass enough for all. Eventually the herdsmen begin to realize that the land's carrying capacity has been reached.

Each new cow brought onto the land therefore contributes to overgrazing it. Nevertheless, each herdsman also sees that the benefit of each new cow *he* brings onto the land accrues to himself alone, whereas the drawback of overgrazing is shared among all. It is therefore economically *rational* to overuse the common land. The catch is, of course, that every other herdsman makes the same calculation, with the result that they collectively destroy the common. This example appeared to be the perfect disproof of Adam Smith's idea that economically rational actors were sure to help one another spontaneously by acting each in his own self-interest.[33]

The practical consequences of men acting in this way were all around us, wrote Hardin. Overfishing of the oceans was already a notorious example of the tragedy of the commons, with the result that rational fishermen from each of the many maritime nations were collectively destroying the resource on which they all depended. Only the enforcement of an international treaty, imposing coercive limits on everyone, could save the fisheries. In the same way, the right to reproduce should no longer be considered a "commons." Instead it must be regulated, and it must be regulated coercively. As pollution regulation increased in the following years, analysts and legislators pointed out that the atmosphere and the nation's waterways could no longer be thought of as "commons." As economists would say, they were no longer "externalities" but had to be considered as costs of production and regulated accordingly. There was no technological fix to the population problem, Hardin insisted, because it was a political and moral problem.[34] Unlike Commoner and Ehrlich, Hardin never became a celebrity intellectual, but his phrase "the tragedy of the commons" showed up repeatedly over the following decades whenever environmental intellectuals and policy makers discussed the question of restraint in the use of scarce resources.

Another writer of the 1960s, UCLA medieval history professor Lynn White (1907–1987), regarded the achievements of science and technology as menacing rather than triumphant. His article "The Historical Roots of Our Ecological Crisis," published in 1967, became an environmental classic. White argued that the alarming combination of pollution, overpopulation, and resource depletion could be traced back to the era when science and technology first began to collaborate in the mid-nineteenth century. Until then, science had been "aristocratic, speculative, intellectual," whereas technology had been "lower-class, empirical, action-oriented." But as the high and low classes began to mix during the democratic revolutions of the late eighteenth and early nineteenth centuries, social barriers broke down and "tended to assert a functional unity of brain and hand." Science and technology came together as never before, as European inventors realized that systematic scientific research would have a huge payoff in the development of practical new devices. The ecological crisis, accordingly, was "the product of an emerging, entirely novel, democratic culture."[35] White went on to argue that Judeo-Christian religion had created a disposition in Western civilization to exploit the natural world. In Genesis, after all, God makes the world entirely for man's benefit; "no item in the physical creation had any purpose save to serve man's purposes." Christians had few scruples about modifying the natural world because they had rejected the pagan idea that trees, rocks, rivers, and air were sacred: "By destroying pagan animism, Christianity made it possible to exploit nature in a mood of indifference to the feelings of natural objects." By now, the exploitation had been going on for centuries and was becoming calamitous.[36]

Science and technology, therefore, had now produced a severe ecological crisis. For that, wrote White, "Christianity bears a huge burden of guilt." The only hopeful figure White could find in Christian history was Saint Francis of Assisi, who understood the need for humility in the face of nature, "not merely for the individual but for man as a species." He ought to be the patron saint of ecologists. Meanwhile, he wrote, "we shall continue to have a worsening ecological crisis until we reject the Christian axiom that nature has no reason for existence save to serve man." In other words, White looked on the achievements of the industrial era, even though they had lifted society out of perpetual poverty, as a curse.[37]

While their works were very different, Carson, Commoner, Ehrlich, Hardin, and White together drew up the indictment on which the environmental movement acted. Even before the first Earth Day in

1970, thousands of citizens joined organizations to combat pollution and improve their neighborhood environments. That same year, when *Time* magazine sought a figure to embody the environmental awareness sweeping the nation, it chose Barry Commoner.

The magazine's cover, on February 2, 1970, was a painted portrait of Commoner, showing half of his face as a color print, backed by a sunny, idyllic landscape of hills and rivers, and the other half in black and white, backed by smoking factories, polluted canals, and a shoal

ECOLOGIST BARRY COMMONER
The Emerging Science of Survival

Time magazine's ecology cover, February 2, 1970.

of dead fish. One feature story in that issue, "Fighting to Save the Earth from Man," described the efforts of a handful of scientist-activists to increase environmental awareness. Another, "The Paul Revere of Ecology," sketched Commoner as "an uncommon spokesman for the common man." As a prolific writer and as a public speaker, it declared, "he personifies the New Scientist—concerned, authoritative and worldly, an iconoclast who refuses to remain sheltered in the ivory laboratory."[38]

Commoner, by then a popular figure on the college speaking circuit, wrote a sequel to *Science and Survival* entitled *The Closing Circle* (1971). Commoner elaborated on the themes of the earlier book, but in the context of American politics and economics and his own socialist beliefs. *The Closing Circle* indicted not just reckless pollution, but American industrial capitalism itself. Free-market capitalism, he wrote, encourages production and consumption on a lavish and unsustainable scale. New technologies since World War II had achieved great profitability, but only through greater pollution—and now the survival of humanity was at stake.[39]

The Closing Circle linked America's worst environmental problems to the perverse incentives of contemporary capitalism. The environmental crisis, as Commoner saw it, was more than a limited but manageable side effect of recent progress: "In our unwitting march toward ecological suicide we have run out of options. Now that the bill for the environmental debt has been presented, our options have become reduced to two: either the rational social organization of the use and distribution of the earth's resources, or a new barbarism." The barbarism he feared was represented not only by capitalism, however, but also by some other environmental writers, notably Ehrlich and Hardin. They thought of the environmental crisis as a *biological* question of too many people, rather than a political and economic question of a dysfunctional system.[40]

The Closing Circle also featured Commoner's "four laws of ecology," in effect a set of principles to be applied in thinking about pollution and the natural world. Commoner was not an ecologist, but the term "ecology" by then had become almost interchangeable with the neologism "environmentalism" (which was first used by the *Washington Post* in 1966). These laws were:

1. "Everything is connected with everything else."
2. "Everything must go somewhere." What we think of as "waste," and what we throw away, does not disappear. It remains in the natural world—in the ground, water, or atmosphere, sometimes changing its chemical form as it interacts with other substances—and often affects other plants, animals, and natural processes.
3. "Nature knows best." For humanity to make and distribute new organic compounds in huge quantities was recklessly to ignore this immense fund of "experience" accumulated in the natural world itself, argued Commoner, "yet this is precisely what we have done with detergents, insecticides, and herbicides."

4. "There's no such thing as a free lunch." Sooner or later, our misuse of the environment and our resources will come back to haunt us.[41]

The Closing Circle met with mixed reviews. It made the most readable and comprehensive case yet published for the idea that America faced a general environmental crisis. But several reviewers chided Commoner for overdramatizing the issues and for implying that the ecological crisis had created a simple binary opposition between "bad guys," like the Atomic Energy Commission, industry, government, and the older generations of scientists, and "good guys," like Commoner himself, as they tried to enlighten mankind and save the world. One reviewer noted that "between these two Cassandras of ecodoom Commoner is generally regarded as the more sensible, while Ehrlich has been charged with hysteria" but that in *The Closing Circle* Commoner himself "becomes quite hysterical." For example, Commoner offered no explanation or evidence for his assertion that society now had only a twenty-five year window of opportunity to transform itself in an environmentally responsible way before it was too late.[42]

Commoner and Ehrlich had already disagreed publicly on whether overpopulation was the worst environmental problem. Their dispute was exacerbated by the publication of *The Closing Circle*, which Ehrlich perceived as a personal attack. He described it as a "dreadful book" full of "self-righteous philosophical ramblings." The journal *Environment* printed Ehrlich's review and Commoner's rebuttal, even though both articles had originally been scheduled for publication in the *Bulletin of the Atomic Scientists*. Ehrlich was furious and believed that Commoner, a founder of *Environment*, had breached professional ethics in "scooping" the *Bulletin*. He then called for the scientific community to develop a court to judge controversial theories such as "Commoner's one-sided treatment of the complexities of the environmental crisis." *The Closing Circle*, he said, was "typical of a dangerous trend of politically active scientists who appeal to the public for support when they receive little or none within their professions." Commoner responded by sabotaging Ehrlich's address at a major environmental conference in Stockholm.

The acrimony between these two leading lights of the new movement became so toxic that other environmental writers urged them both to make a truce, lest their squabble "threaten the cause of a better environment that they and most other responsible persons espouse."[43]

THE COUNTERCULTURE

By the late 1960s a range of environmental issues had become newsworthy. Population pressure, pollution, and wilderness preservation were making the jump from special issues to the subject of mass politics. At the same time the 1960s counterculture was arguing for a new approach to life. Hippies in the San Francisco "summer of love" (1967) acted on Timothy Leary's advice to "turn on, tune in, drop out." Reject the rat race, they said, and refuse to let yourself be defined by how much you earn, how much you consume, and the size of your house, car, and luxurious possessions. Attend instead to humane values, love one another, go back to the land, and learn to settle for less. So long as this message came—or appeared to come—from dirty, long-haired, barefoot dropouts, it was never going to be widely persuasive. In milder form, however, their message was similar to the one being preached by the new environmentalists. They too wanted Americans to settle for less, accept limits, and humble themselves before the majesty of nature rather than try to conquer it.[44]

The hippie generation found a nature writer of its own. Just as Sigurd Olson had offered wilderness canoe trips to the man in the gray flannel suit during the mid-1950s, so now Edward Abbey burst on the scene with an irreverent, countercultural take on living close to nature. Abbey (1927–1989) was born in Pennsylvania and raised in New Jersey, but travels in the American West during his teens had sparked a lifelong love affair with the desert. He was already a published novelist by the mid-sixties, but his essay collection *Desert Solitaire* (1968) turned him into a celebrity. It became one of the late twentieth century's most influential books about the human encounter with the natural world.[45] *Desert Solitaire* is based on the journals Abbey kept while working as a park ranger at Arches National Monument in Utah. He was familiar with the American tradition of nature writing, but wanted to rethink its conventions and tropes:

> The personification of the natural is exactly the tendency I wish to suppress in myself, to eliminate for good. I am here not only to evade for a while the clamor and filth and confusion of the cultural apparatus but also to confront, immediately and directly, if it's possible, the bare bones of existence, the elemental and fundamental, the bedrock which sustains us. I want to be able to look at, and into, a juniper tree, a piece of quartz, a vulture, a spider, and see it as it is in itself, devoid of all humanly ascribed qualities . . . I dream of a hard and brutal mysticism in which the naked self merges with a nonhuman world yet somehow survives still intact, individual, separate.

A few days into his lonely stay at Arches, he describes catching sight of a jackrabbit nearby, flinging a stone at it and—to his astonishment— killing it instantly. Expecting to feel guilty, he actually feels elated. "What the rabbit has lost in energy and spirit seems added, by processes too subtle to fathom, to my own soul . . . No longer do I feel so isolated from the sparse and furtive life around me, a stranger from another world. I have entered into this one. We are kindred, all of us, killer and victim, predator and prey."[46]

Several months later, Abbey joins a search party that finds the body of a man who'd gotten lost and died from heat exhaustion. He reflects that it was not such a bad way to die, out in the dazzling wilderness. He even offers advice to travelers who realize they are about to die of thirst in the Utah backcountry: "Crawl into the shade and contemplate the lonely sky. See those big black scrawny wings far above, waiting? Comfort yourself with the reflection that within a few hours, if all goes as planned, your human flesh will be working its way through the gizzard of a buzzard, your essence transfigured into the fierce greedy eyes and unimaginable consciousness of a turkey vulture."[47]

Abbey, a good-natured anarchist, also cracked jokes about his employers, drank beers in his pickup truck and threw the cans out the window, chatted with old cowboys and uranium prospectors, and railed against what he called "industrial tourism." In playful, argumentative, and provocative prose he argued that wilderness should be left alone as much as possible, and that anyone who wanted to see it should have to *work* for it. (In this respect, at least, his sensibility was similar to that of Aldo Leopold.) Motor vehicles should be banned from all the national parks and people should be forced to get out and walk, or ride bicycles and horses. As Abbey pointed out, the parks would in effect instantly become much bigger because it would take pedestrians and riders a very long time to cross them. As for the rangers themselves: "Lazy scheming loafers, they've wasted too many years selling tickets at toll booths and sitting behind desks filling out charts and tables in the vain effort to appease the mania for statistics which torments the Washington office. They're supposed to be rangers—make the bums *range!*" Abbey had a profound influence on the rising generation of young environmental activists—he would become the inspirational guru of the direct action group Earth First! in the 1980s.[48]

Environmentalism became a popular mass movement in 1969 and 1970. The sudden surge of interest stemmed from a rising sense of anxiety about pollution, population, pesticides, and nuclear fallout, and from a dismaying sense that Americans were, through greed and negligence, destroying their natural environment. Achievements that had seemed unquestionably positive in the immediate postwar years, such as the spread of high-quality housing, good roads, automobiles for nearly everyone, and thousands of consumer conveniences, could now be reinterpreted not as signs of success, but as a fall from grace. Even the free market and the Judeo-Christian tradition, long regarded as sources of American strength and moral integrity, fell under suspicion. It was also clear to a growing number of Americans that blame rested not merely with sinister external forces and people, but with themselves. *They* threw out the trash, flew in the aircraft, bought the consumer goods, and drove the automobiles that were polluting their world. In another example of the time-honored tradition of American self-renewal, they would have to reform themselves.

At its best this new mood encouraged Americans to demand a more careful approach to the environment. To a great extent, they accomplished it in the 1970s and subsequently. The air pollution that had caused so much anxiety in the 1950s and 1960s was drastically reduced in the next four decades, restoring the atmosphere even in cities whose population and traffic volume continued to increase. At its worst, the new environmentalism stimulated a mood of apocalyptic thinking, demonizing business and government, denigrating the human capacity to reform, and creating successive scares about imminent disasters that never materialized. The idea of coercive family limitation never caught on in America, luckily, though it did catch on later in China, where the compulsory one-child-per-family policy would provoke two generations of odious human rights violations.

What happened to the most polluted places in America, whose plight had helped set in motion the movement for improvements to air and water quality? Donora, Pennsylvania, site of the 1948 smog disaster that killed twenty residents, celebrated the event's sixtieth anniversary by opening a Smog Museum in 2008. A sign at its front door now reads "Clean Air Started Here" and the exhibits inside explain and illustrate the appalling conditions residents once endured. In 1966 U.S. Steel closed down the plants that generated the deadly fumes, though without ever accepting responsibility for the deaths. One of the museum's curators reminisced with journalists, in 2010, that toxic smoke in Donora had for decades made it impossible for grass and trees to grow. Now, by contrast, "the hills on both sides of the river are green today and the air is much cleaner."[49]

The situation with waterways was more equivocal. The Cuyahoga River and Lake Erie recovered from their nadir sufficiently to become once more attractive for fishing and boating. After the 1972 Clean Water Act the recovery of Lake Erie was particularly impressive; one biologist described it as "the best example of ecosystem recovery in the world." Beaches reopened and tourist fishing boats plied the lake every summer. By 2012, however, the lake was once more troubled by algal blooms like those that had blighted it in the 1950s and 1960s. The source was no longer factory emissions and sewers but, chiefly, agricultural runoff. The tendency of farmers to use ever larger quantities of fertilizers, including many that were yet to be developed in the 1970s, combined with the reduction of wetlands on the lake's edge, made Lake Erie vulnerable again and demonstrated the need for continued vigilance and tougher regulation. An obvious weakness of the 1972 act, identified at the time and apparent in retrospect, was the need to exempt farmers in order to win farm-state senators' support. The EPA nevertheless estimated that whereas in 1972 two-thirds of the nation's lakes and rivers had been unfit for fishing and swimming, that fraction had now fallen to one-third. The agency marked the fortieth anniversary of the act by signing a new Great Lakes Water Quality Agreement with the government of Canada to address the continuing problem.[50]

CHAPTER 3

POLITICS AND THE ENVIRONMENT

AMERICAN DEMOCRATIC POLITICIANS want to be reelected or move up the ladder to positions of greater power. To be reelected, they have to say what the voters want to hear and do what the voters consider right. They monitor their constituents' interests and concerns; if a new issue becomes popular, the politicians become interested in it. There is no surer evidence that the environment was becoming a major worry by the end of the 1960s than the fact that politicians of all stripes suddenly became environmental enthusiasts. For a brief time, it was the leading issue of American politics, bringing together Republicans and Democrats, national, state, and local politicians, legislatures and executives. Between 1969 and 1973, in a sustained burst of bipartisan cooperation, they transformed the politics of the environment more drastically than at any time before or since.

This four-year period saw the passage of the National Environmental Policy Act and the Endangered Species Act, the creation of the Environmental Protection Agency and the National Oceanic and Atmospheric Administration, greatly strengthened clean air and clean water legislation, and new efforts to protect coastal regions and to restrict pesticides. These actions decisively shifted the balance of power in environmental disputes, giving new opportunities to antipollution activists. For the first time, polluters faced uniform federal rules

Earth Day organizer
Denis Hayes, 1970.

and severe penalties for noncompliance. Bowing to necessity, corporations started to change their ways, beginning a long period in which the pollution of America's air, land, and waters diminished.

The shift in public opinion was never more visible than on the first Earth Day, Wednesday, April 22, 1970. Proposed by Democratic senator Gaylord Nelson of Wisconsin and Denis Hayes, a Harvard Law School student, it was modeled on the era's anti-Vietnam "teach-ins." It surpassed their wildest hopes by mobilizing thousands of schools, colleges, businesses, and governments across the nation. Politicians and business leaders as well as environmental activists gave conservation-themed speeches while local communities assembled to pick up trash and celebrate "Mother Earth." Among the issues debated, that day as throughout the era, were pollution and population. Another idea that had begun to generate interest and publicity was the alleged exhaustion of the earth's resources. According to various writers, more people on the planet and more economic development were using up the oil, coal, metals, water, and soil on which modern civilization was based. Studies such as the 1972 Massachusetts Institute of Technology (MIT) report *Limits to Growth* urged a switch to the "steady-state" economy in place of sustained economic growth. Economist E. F. Schumacher's *Small Is Beautiful*, which argued for a localized, human-scale economy in place of corporate or state gigantism, became an environmentalist classic.

Despite the superficial plausibility of these claims, however, resources were *not* running out, opportunities for growth were *not* seriously limited, and small usually was *not* beautiful. On the contrary, improvements in recovery technique, recycling, and substitution were making most natural resources more plentiful and cheaper than ever before. An array of economists mounted a powerful counterattack against the claim of resource exhaustion and looked with dismay on the idea of halting economic growth. To do so, they believed, would push the world into depression, unnecessarily prolonging the misery and suffering of millions of people. In their view, it was possible to sustain economic growth *and* improve the environment, while feeling confident that the raw materials of industrialization would not run out. They emphasized, moreover, that the surest way to improve the environment was to generate more wealth, because rich societies are much more capable of cleaning themselves up than poor ones.

ENVIRONMENTAL LEGISLATION

There were auguries of change before 1969. President Lyndon Johnson, a Democrat, began to mobilize federal power on behalf of environmental reforms in the mid-1960s. He signed the Wilderness Act in 1964, protecting nine million acres of wild lands from development. In his "Great Society" speech that year, he declared that "America the beautiful" was in danger: "The water we drink, the food we eat, the very air we breathe, are threatened by pollution. Our parks are overcrowded, our seashores overburdened. Green fields and dense forests are disappearing." His wife, Lady Bird Johnson, worked for passage of the Highway Beautification Act of 1965 while the president urged Congress to establish two new agencies, the Federal Water Pollution Control Administration and the National Air Pollution Control Administration. In his five years as president, Johnson signed nearly three hundred conservation measures.[1]

President Richard Nixon, a Republican, who entered the White House in 1969, followed suit. Almost immediately his cabinet had to confront the Union Oil spill crisis off Santa Barbara. Having shown no previous interest in environmental matters, Nixon now put them at the top of the national agenda; his advisers and pollsters confirmed that it was politically shrewd to do so. He supported the National Environmental Policy Act passed by Congress later that year, and created a presidential Council on Environmental Quality. In his State of the Union address the following spring, Nixon declared:

> The great question of the seventies is: shall we surrender to our surroundings, or shall we make our peace with nature and begin to make reparations for the damage we have done to our air, to our land, and to our water? Restoring nature to its natural state is a cause beyond party and beyond factions. It has become a common cause of all the people of this country. It is a cause of particular concern to young Americans, because they more than we will reap the grim consequences of our failure to act on programs which are needed now if we are to prevent disaster later. Clean air, clean water, open spaces—these should once again be the birthright of every American. If we act now, they can be.

Nixon went on to declare that he would ask Congress to legislate for improved municipal waste treatment, protection and preservation of endangered green spaces, more fuel-efficient vehicles, and regulations to ensure the maintenance of clean air and water. Artfully mixing Cold War rhetoric with a sense of environmental commitment, Nixon ended with the remark, "We need a fresh climate in America, one in which a person can breathe freely and breathe in freedom."[2]

On Wednesday, April 22, 1970, the nation celebrated its first Earth Day and was rewarded, in most places, by beautiful spring weather. Events were held in every large American city and among high schools, colleges, churches, citizens' groups, businesses, trade unions, and members of Congress (Congress recessed for the day). It generated a great deal of press attention, mostly favorable, and drew in far more participants than any antiwar, civil rights, or feminist demonstration of

The planet itself wears a gas mask
on Earth Day, April 22, 1970.

Fifth Avenue in New York City closed
to traffic for Earth Day.

the 1960s. In New York, Fifth Avenue was closed for two hours, enabling people to stroll along the suddenly quiet avenue and enjoy speeches and "ecological" street theater. Mayor John Lindsay, a Republican, declared that all the complicated environmental issues of the day boiled down to a simple question: "Do we want to live or die?" Elsewhere communities arranged trash pickups or symbolically buried gas-guzzling cars in the ground—a group of one hundred Tacoma, Washington, teenagers rode horses to school along the freeway. Senator Gaylord Nelson, who had dreamed up the whole thing, remarked later, "Earth Day worked because of the spontaneous response at the grassroots level. We had neither the time nor the resources to organize twenty million demonstrators and the thousands of schools and local communities that participated."[3]

Some corporations were eager to support Earth Day, especially automobile and oil companies that had been criticized for their dirty and damaging conduct over the last few years. Like politicians, they were susceptible to changing popular moods and eager to embrace them, for the sake of good public relations. Before long Ford, Mobil, and Atlantic Richfield would launch "green" advertising campaigns, claiming that no one was more alert to the needs of the suffering earth than they. A later generation would denounce such campaigns as cynical "greenwashing." The organizers of Earth Day itself, however, refused to accept corporate contributions.[4]

The event also met with criticism from both left and right. Some radicals regarded environmentalism as a right-wing hoax, designed to distract citizens' attention from the unfinished civil rights movement, the unfinished war on poverty, and the interminable war in Vietnam. The radical journalist I. F. Stone, speaking at the Washington Monument, for example, described Earth Day as a "snow job." Militant black students and SDS radicals protested against the environmental teach-in at the University of Michigan, with one student declaring that the environment was merely a "new toy" for the white middle class. Another added that it was designed "to divert our energy . . . to forget there is a criminal war going on in Vietnam . . . to forget that 50 million people in a country that put a man on the moon don't have enough to eat."[5]

If some young activists scoffed at environmentalism as a distraction, however, others argued that it was closely linked to these other pressing issues. The military's use of defoliants like Agent Orange in Vietnam, for example, prompted some antiwar critics to accuse the American military of conducting a "war against nature," a form of "ecocide." Similarly, the battle over People's Park, a square block in Berkeley near the University of California campus, symbolized for some radicals the confrontation between nature and the soulless state. The university planned to turn the area, currently occupied by homeless hippies, into a parking lot. Demonstrators fought to preserve the block and turn it into a green space. In the tense confrontations that followed, the National Guard killed James Rector, one demonstrator, blinded another, and wounded more than one hundred on "Bloody Thursday," May 15, 1969. Rector became a martyr to the idea of preserving nature.

One radical wrote that the killing had "given the dispossessed children of the tract homes and the cities a feeling of involvement with the planet, an involvement proved through our sweat and our blood."[6]

Conservatives, like radicals, had mixed reactions. Some saw the new environmental politics as an example of federal power grabbing at its most blatant. They feared that a short-term fad for "ecology" would have long-term consequences in shifting the balance of power from individual states to Washington, D.C., and that the price of reducing pollution would be astronomical. On the other hand, there was much about the conservation movement to attract conservatives, as the similarity of the two words suggests. America's leading conservative journal, *National Review*, editorialized that "the violation of the land, the violation of the natural environment generally, is felt without even the possibility of argument to be the quintessence of evil," and that conservation was "likely to be a powerful, indeed an overriding *spiritual* issue, which it would be political suicide to concede to the Left." At the same time it emphasized the complexity of the issue and the need for a levelheaded approach, with a careful calculation of the relevant costs and benefits.[7]

In 1970 the pace of federal environmental legislation accelerated. Congress created the Environmental Protection Agency, which brought together a variety of different agencies and placed them under the aegis of the Department of the Interior. The EPA grew rapidly in the 1970s and became a major player in subsequent environmental controversies. Its first administrator was William Ruckelshaus (born 1932), an Indiana lawyer, former prosecutor, and Republican politician. From the start of his tenure he worked energetically against polluters. "The core of his strategy," writes the historian Richard Andrews, "was to use high-visibility enforcement lawsuits to establish the agency's power and credibility, and thus to generate mass public support, as a counterweight to the entrenched power of industrial and municipal polluters." In the second year of his tenure at EPA, Ruckelshaus responded to a series of lawsuits by banning DDT, bringing an end to American use of one of the chemicals Rachel Carson had condemned in *Silent Spring*. As the 1970s progressed, the EPA dedicated its efforts above all to countering perceived environmental threats to human health.[8]

President Nixon looks on as William Ruckelshaus is sworn in as the first EPA administrator, 1971.

Between the first Earth Day and 1980, Congress passed twenty-eight major environmental laws, a testament to the breadth and depth of public interest in the issue. The laws stipulated improvements to air and water quality, acted to rescue endangered species and their habitat, abolished the use of lead in gasoline, restricted pesticides, created the Superfund to clean up severely polluted chemical waste dumps, and set aside more land for national parks, forests, wilderness areas, and wildlife refuges. An unusually high degree of bipartisanship in Congress testified to Democrats' and Republicans' shared perception that such legislation would be popular with their constituents.[9]

At the same time as the EPA became a major presence in Washington so did the major environmental organizations, most of which created or enlarged their offices in the nation's capital. For example, the Sierra Club opened an office in Washington and hired a staff of full-time lobbyists in the hope of influencing environmental legislation and its enforcement. Brock Evans, who ran the club's D.C. office from 1972, described how he made the switch from an emotional regional volunteer to a sober national professional, trying to create the right image for the organization inside the Beltway. "I always thought it was very important for me to go to lots of meetings and wave the banner of the Sierra Club and show the flag . . . because it sort of adds credibility and respect." He said he worked to "soften the image of the Sierra Club" among politicians in order to make it "part of the power structure . . . of this whole town." The historian Susan Schrepfer agrees with Evans that the Sierra Club was changing its image in order to become a serious player in national politics: "Was the cry of outraged conscience and principle to prevail, or was that impulse to be restrained by the need for credibility, cohesiveness and respect for authority?" Restraint won out in the end. The club suffered the usual organizational growing pains as it became larger, more bureaucratic, less charismatic, and more willing to compromise, which sometimes offended its more zealous members.[10]

The growth of environmental legislation and regulation gave prominence to a generation of administrators who could bridge the gap between a genuine concern for the environment and knowledge of how to operate in the labyrinth of Washington politics. William Ruckelshaus at EPA was one; another was Russell Train. He too was a moderate Republican, but with an established reputation as a conservationist. He had resigned a federal judgeship in 1965 to become president of the Conservation Foundation. Train was appointed deputy secretary of the interior in the first Nixon administration, then the first head of the Council on Environmental Quality, and later the second administrator of the EPA.[11]

A third of these conservationist-administrators was John Quarles, who worked first in the Department of the Interior, then for Ruckelshaus, then became Train's second-in-command at EPA. His book *Cleaning Up America* (1976) draws a vivid picture of the difficulties involved first in drafting the new laws, then in getting them through Congress, and finally putting them into practice on the ground. Congress members, manufacturers, unions, consumer groups, and citizens' alliances all lobbied to influence the legislation. Prosecuting polluters also raised nettlesome questions. Quarles wrote of his days in the fledgling EPA:

Ahead lay hard realities that would force EPA to make choices, to take positions that would draw attack. The most basic of these would be the conflict between the environment and the economy, and here the heat was first felt. Controversy broke out over EPA's handling of one of its first major enforcement actions [the Armco Steel prosecution], in a case that not only posed the fundamental question of which comes first, pollution control or jobs, but that illustrated the complexities of the interplay between politics and the formation of national policy.

Quarles quickly recognized that whatever measures the agency took would be regarded as too mild by environmental lobbyists and too punitive by polluters, who could always pose as the champions of job creation for working people.[12]

The novelty of environmental politics and the clash of wide-ranging interests sometimes resulted in confusing situations. Historian Adam Rome shows in his history of suburban housing and the environment that "the government's conservation and land-management agencies often pursued policies that were anathema to environmentalists." At the same time, however, he notes that "officials in the government's scientific agencies were often the first to sound alarms about the environmental problems caused by suburban development." Depending on their particular missions, in other words, federal agencies could be either the best friends or the worst enemies of the environment, and often worked at cross-purposes. By the 1970s an earlier generation's faith that government agencies worked simply for the public good had given way to the realization that they were deeply self-interested organizations with interests and commitments of their own.[13]

Corporations responded to this new era of environmental legislation in various ways. In the 1960s, their first instinct had been to lobby against clean air and clean water laws that imposed stricter emissions standards on their factories. They pleaded the high cost of developing cleaner technology and pointed out ambiguities in the research that suggested their products were causing such problems as the eutrophication of the Great Lakes. By the time of Earth Day in 1970, however, corporations were becoming wary of offending against a new ortho-doxy in public opinion. Some actually switched their position and began to *seek* uniform federal regulation rather than trying to navigate through a maze of different state and local laws. The auto industry wanted to be sure that mass-produced vehicles made in Detroit could be sold in all fifty states without the need for irksome modifications in each place. Soap and detergent manufacturers similarly recognized that a single set of standards was preferable to a patchwork of conflict-ing rules and regulations at the local level.[14]

Manufacturing corporations also had to face the rise of consumer advocacy, pioneered by a young attorney named Ralph Nader (born 1934). Learning that General Motors was neglecting safety issues in its cars, notably the Chevrolet Corvair, Nader gathered information about its development and in 1965 published a scathing attack on the corpo-ration, *Unsafe at Any Speed*.[15] General Motors retaliated by setting pri-vate detectives on Nader's trail, tapping his phone, even hiring prostitutes in an attempt to compromise him. They hoped to uncover embarrassing or criminal secrets, but their plan backfired when Nader discovered their scheme. He sued GM, won, and used the $284,000 settlement they were obliged to pay to establish a consumer-oriented advocacy group, the Center for the Study of Responsive Law. Soon nicknamed "Nader's Raiders," the group investigated environmental issues, corporate scandals, and political corruption, while Nader him-self became a major figure in the anti–nuclear power movement of the 1970s. He was sharply critical of lawyers' and scientists' tendency to be passive in the face of what seemed to him an overwhelming crisis of environmental destruction. He urged both groups toward a new activ-ism and militancy and encouraged citizens to be skeptical of corporate and government rhetoric, and to stand up for their rights.[16]

Another young attorney, Victor Yannacone, shared Nader's con-cerns. He helped create a new organization, the Environmental De-fense Fund (EDF), in 1967. The EDF was "a scientific organization dedicated to use of the courts for environmental protection." Begin-ning in Suffolk County on Long Island, New York, the group sued governments and corporations to prevent the use of pesticides. Where Nader worked behind the scenes and was media shy, Yannacone was brash, confrontational, and adversarial—his hallmark phrase was "Sue the bastards!" He was one of the founders of what we now call environmental law, litigating on behalf of threatened places of natural beauty or against the use of hazardous chemicals. This new cause was aided in part by judges' willingness to grant standing (the right to litigate) to citizens even if they did not have a direct *economic* stake in environmental controversies.[17]

In a Wisconsin DDT case in 1968–1969, EDF raised twenty-five thousand dollars from local conservationists for its costs and recruited faculty and graduate students from the University of Wisconsin by soliciting their testimony on the scientific issues. The case drew significant public attention: so many people came to watch and listen that the case had to be moved to the chamber of the Wisconsin state assembly. Academic scientists who felt professionally uneasy about participating directly in public campaigns against DDT *were* willing to testify against it in court. As a reporter for *Science* commented at the time, this willingness had profound implications for environmental cases that followed. In his argument to the court, Yannacone asserted the novel doctrine that citizens have a constitutional right to an environment unspoiled by pollutants such as DDT. By its pioneering effort EDF hoped to establish important legal precedents and to carve out a role for itself analogous to the roles the American Civil Liberties Union and the Legal Defense Fund of the NAACP had played so successfully in civil rights law. Representatives of the industry, by contrast, had been caught off guard and made an inadequate defense of DDT. This was a mistake they would not repeat as environmental litigation mushroomed in the 1970s.[18]

The arguments to be made in favor of DDT were not trivial. Invented in the 1930s by a Swiss chemist, Paul Müller, it had proved to be a phenomenally powerful and effective insecticide. When the Allied armies liberated Naples in 1943, their medical staffs suppressed a typhus epidemic by using DDT against the lice and fleas that transmitted it, saving thousands of lives. In postwar spraying campaigns public health workers virtually eliminated malaria from Sardinia and Taiwan, places where it had been endemic for centuries. Even in India DDT dramatically reduced the number of cases for three decades. Resistant strains of lice and mosquitoes eventually developed, and DDT was never going to be able to annihilate mosquitoes once and for all. Even so, the mosquito historians Andrew Spielman and Michael D'Antonio argue that, when used carefully, DDT remains even today the best remedy against malaria. In their view, "a worldwide ban on DDT would be a severe loss for public health workers."[19]

The cumulative effect of citizens' environmental awareness, stronger environmental laws, and activist groups was to make American business more environment conscious in the early 1970s. Corporations lobbied hard in Washington to establish rules, or interpretation of rules, favorable to their interests, but they also worked to cultivate a "greener" image consonant with new popular attitudes. Entrepreneurial initiatives sprang up to remedy pollution and to help industries meet new requirements of clean air and water. Recycling and recovery of minerals and metals from effluent often proved cost-effective.

POPULATION, RESOURCE EXHAUSTION, AND ECONOMICS

The United States was the world's richest nation in the 1960s after two centuries of almost uninterrupted economic growth. A handful of economists began to ask whether this high rate of economic growth could continue—and whether it *should* continue. The 1960s was also the first decade of space travel, in which it became possible to see photographs of the earth taken from lunar orbit. How beautiful it looked, but how vulnerable, and how alone! Kenneth Boulding, an economist at the University of Michigan, published "The Economics of the Coming Spaceship Earth" in 1966, comparing the earth to a spaceship in which every resource is limited and nothing can be wasted. He argued that we must abandon the old "cowboy" form of economy, in which there was no need to worry about where resources came from or where waste went, and switch instead to a "spaceman" economy, in which every process was sustainable and in which producers had to recognize that the water and air they used were scarce and valuable. Turning the conventions of economics on their head, he argued: "The less consumption we can maintain a given state with, the better off we are. If we had clothes that did not wear out, houses that did not depreciate, and even if we could maintain our bodily condition without eating, we would clearly be much better off." What matters, he added, is the *use*, not the *using up*, of resources, a point he believed most economists had not yet grasped.[20]

In 1972, a group of computer modelers at MIT led by Donella and Dennis Meadows published *The Limits to Growth,* to great media fanfare. Twelve thousand copies, in six different languages, were mailed free of charge to world leaders. The report caused an instant sensation. "The premise of this cliff-hanger is even more spine-chilling than the swapping of human hearts," wrote one commentator. "Can civilization save itself from smothering in its own malignant growth?" The group's computer projections indicated, they wrote, that if present economic trends continued, "the limits to growth on this planet will be reached some time within the next one hundred years. The most probable result will be a rather sudden and uncontrollable decline in both population and industrial capacity." They anticipated that unmanageable levels of pollution would make the continuation of life impossible. On the other hand, changing our ways and learning how to create a condition of "ecological and economic stability that is sustainable far into the future" was still possible, so long as the entire world committed itself right away to this strenuous alternative.[21]

The Limits to Growth emphasized that it would be easy for the world to be taken unawares by sudden crises of food production, population, pollution, and industrialization, all of which were undergoing exponential growth. Why? They offered a thought experiment. If a pond lily is growing exponentially, doubling in size each day, its size seems unremarkable for a long time because it started out so small. It would be easy to let many days pass without considering the implications of its exponential growth. Suppose that on day twenty-nine everyone began to take notice because it now covered half of the pond's surface. They would have waited too long, because just one more day's growth would cause it to cover the whole pond, crowding out everything else. The same kind of alarming growth was happening in reality throughout the world, as the book's abundance of graphs bearing exponential curves purported to show. Current trends showed that "one can move within a very few years from a situation of great abundance to one of great scarcity. There has been an overwhelming excess of potentially arable land for all of history but now . . . there may be a sudden and serious shortage."[22]

The authors predicted that as the limit conditions approached for food, nonrenewable natural resources, population, and pollution, the world would enter an era of turbulence and crisis. To prevent it, the leading nations of the world needed to abandon economic growth as an objective for themselves, even while encouraging developing nations to achieve food security and basic amenities. The members of the governing board of the Club of Rome, which had commissioned the project, most of them politicians, scientists, and executives, wrote in an afterword, "We have no doubt that if mankind is to embark on a new course, concerted international measures and joint long-term planning will be necessary on a scale and scope without precedent." Their rhetoric, with its authoritarian overtones, echoed Paul Ehrlich's sinister comment at the end of *The Population Bomb* that a new department of population must take "whatever steps are necessary" to end population growth.[23]

The idea of sustainable development, or the steady-state economy, caught on in the 1970s, and has often reappeared in recent decades. Among its advocates was Herman Daly, who argued that conventional economists had failed to acknowledge certain hard truths. Beyond a certain point of economic development, wrote Daly, marginal costs rise and marginal benefits decline, to the point that economic growth becomes dysfunctional, causing more harm than good. We make a fetish of increasing our gross national product, he wrote, often forgetting that these increases are using up nonrenewable resources and creating pollution that worsens the quality of life. A steady-state economy, as he envisioned it, was not frozen at a given level of technology: "As values and technology evolve we may find that a different level is both possible and desirable. But the growth . . . required to get to the new level is a temporary adjustment process, not a norm." He pointed out that the economists' term "growth" was a metaphor taken from human development. But human growth ends in maturity unless the individual becomes morbidly obese. Surely we don't want that! What was needed, he believed, was a paradigm shift in economists' thinking, in which the ideal to strive for was long-term stability, a high degree of equity in wealth distribution, and a stable population (whose members would be allowed to trade reproduction licenses depending on the number of children they wanted, but only up to replacement level).[24]

In 1973 English economist E. F. Schumacher (1911–1977) published *Small Is Beautiful,* which rapidly became a cult classic in America and around the world. Schumacher, like Boulding, had been impressed by the photographs of earth taken from the moon by astronauts. He too liked the "Spaceship Earth" metaphor. If man wins "the war against nature," wrote Schumacher, he'll find himself on the losing side. That was the paradox of the human situation; the way out was not merely a new approach to conservation but a changed understanding of what it means to be human. Society must become decentralized, must give up an economy based on greed and envy, and must restore the dignity of work and the human scale.[25]

Schumacher advocated what he described as "Buddhist economics." Unlike the Western economic tradition, he wrote, "the Buddhist point of view takes the function of work to be at least threefold: to give man a chance to utilize and develop his faculties; to enable him to overcome his ego-centeredness by joining with other people in a common task; and to bring forth the goods and services needed for a becoming existence." Labor-saving devices were not necessarily improvements under these circumstances, and the achievement of leisure was not necessarily a desirable goal. Mechanization that robbed the traditional craftsman of his skill, far from being a manifestation of progress, was a crime. Not surprisingly, Schumacher was sympathetic to Gandhi's idea of manual craftsmanship for all instead of mass industrialization for postimperial India. He emphasized that he was not opposed to technology as such, but rather that he favored the simpler "intermediate" technologies.[26]

What would a society look like if it actually acted on the proposals of *The Limits to Growth* and *Small Is Beautiful?* Ernest Callenbach's futuristic novel *Ecotopia* (1975) drew heavily on these sources. In the story, Ecotopia is the name of a separate country, made up of Northern California, Oregon, and Washington, which has seceded from the rest of the United States. It has closed its borders and become completely estranged from the materialistic and growth-obsessed United States. An American journalist, William Weston, gets permission to visit Ecotopia, and the book consists of his journal entries and the news stories he files for publication back in the States. Weston finds that Ecotopia consists of many small, self-contained local communities using simple technologies. There are electric monorail trains but no cars, and the streets are quiet. It's possible to hunt deer close to downtown San Francisco. Clothes are simple, all fibers are organic, food is wholesome and locally grown, schoolchildren do farm work as well as study, and everyone is committed to a sustainable no-growth economy. Emotional spontaneity, expressive sex, and close community bonds all puzzle Weston at first, but with the passage of time he comes to love the whole thing so much (along with loving one of its comely inhabitants) that he decides never to leave.[27]

Callenbach (1929–2012) lived in Berkeley and worked for the University of California Press. He was impressed by the counterculture that flourished there in the late 1960s and early 1970s, and by the era's sudden acute interest in the environment. *Ecotopia* was rejected by twenty New York publishers before struggling into publication through a local cooperative. After that, however, it became a cult classic, picked up a trade publisher, was widely translated, and eventually sold an estimated one million copies worldwide. Callenbach wrote later that he had tried "to make sure that readers could learn what Ecotopians ate, what their living quarters were like, how they traveled . . . and so on. The book thus had the unexpected effect of inspiring people who had been groping for better ways to live." Along with Stewart Brand's *Whole Earth Catalog* (another Bay Area product), *Ecotopia* became a practical handbook for individuals and groups committed to the idea of living in a sustainable way.[28]

"Spaceship Earth," *The Limits to Growth*, the steady-state idea, and *Small Is Beautiful* all sought to revolutionize economics. A wide variety of writers and politicians despised this literature, arguing that on all the important questions the old economists, not the new ones, had got it right. Growth, although it should be undertaken intelligently and with more environmental care than in the past, was still necessary and still benign. Critics of *The Limits to Growth* noted a succession of scientific and logical fallacies committed by its authors, and that their computers had been programmed in such a way as to encounter a "doomsday" scenario no matter what data were used. Either famine, population crisis, pollution, or resource exhaustion was certain to bring an end to "life as we know it," according to the programmers' assumptions. "What the doomsday machine proves, in effect," wrote one critic, physicist Petr Beckmann, "is that if you have no other means of subsistence than a box of poisoned candy, then you are doomed . . . Who needs a computer to derive such trivialities? . . . They run a computer to prove a point that every sane man must concede." But the programmers had hopelessly underestimated human inventiveness and technological creativity. The great danger we faced now, Beckmann believed, was "technophobia," the possibility that humanity would turn against science and technology. John Maddox, editor of Britain's (and indeed the world's) leading science journal, *Nature*, agreed. His faith in the resourcefulness of science and technology made him, like Beckmann, dismiss the population and resource alarms ("the doomsday syndrome") as needlessly pessimistic.[29]

Other critics noted that throughout history population and economic growth had advanced together in a close causal relationship, a point emphasized by Nobel laureate Simon Kuznets. If population is stable or declining, economic growth is almost impossible; the result is not a steady state but the misery of mass unemployment. When population is rising, by contrast, people have much greater incentives to develop new resources, improve efficiency, save and invest more constructively, take entrepreneurial chances, raise labor productivity and standards of living, enjoy economies of scale, and take an interest in environmental protection.[30]

Wilfred Beckerman, a British economist, made a particularly impassioned case for economic growth in *Two Cheers for the Affluent Society* (1974). Dismayed by the growing chorus of voices denouncing growth, he wrote, he had decided to make the case for the defense, by a careful presentation of all the relevant evidence. Economic growth was now in the position of an innocent man, wrongly accused of a crime: "A mistake in a criminal trial may mean imprisonment for one innocent man. A failure to maintain economic growth means continued poverty, deprivation, disease, squalor, degradation and . . . soul-destroying toil for countless millions of the world's population." He argued that environmental decline and a decline in the quality of life did *not* necessarily accompany growth in population and the economy. Overwhelmingly, growth promoted both human and environmental well-being.[31]

Beckerman described *The Limits to Growth* as "a brazen, impudent piece of nonsense," which would never have been taken seriously by anyone had it not been for the false prestige attached to big computerized projects. He agreed with other critics that the report suffered from the "garbage in, garbage out" fallacy, giving the operators what they wanted to hear from the outset on the basis of their tendentious assumptions, rather than actually forecasting the world's future. Pollution was certainly a real problem, he wrote, but the way to correct it was by ensuring that the polluters paid a price for their degradation of the air and water. Until recently, pollution had been an "externality" of production, something not reckoned into the price because no one owned the air or the water. That problem could be set right either by government regulation of maximum pollution levels or by a pollution-permit-trading scheme to give manufacturers an incentive to reduce their costs as they reduced pollution, making purchase of the permits steadily less necessary.[32]

Beckerman understood that the public was unlikely to have access to reliable information on these highly divisive subjects, partly because the press preferred to render them in sensationalistic terms and partly because they were often counterintuitive. He also noted that the reputation of science, which had perhaps been unrealistically high in the years immediately after World War II, had now swung sharply, so that "the fickle public went too far and began to blame science and technology for all the ills of present day society." He even speculated that the middle classes and the privileged youth of developed nations felt guilty about the much higher standards of living they enjoyed than the world's less fortunate peoples. "One way of expiating this guilt is to attack the very prosperity of which they are the 'victims'" in the name of the environment. It might be high-minded and well meant, but it was nevertheless, he believed, fatally misleading.[33]

Ben Wattenberg, a former adviser and speechwriter to Lyndon Johnson, also dismissed such gloomy literature as *The Limits to Growth*. His upbeat 1974 account of current trends, *The Real America*, was crammed full of polling data and economic statistics of a highly reassuring kind. The trends of the postwar years, he wrote, had been extremely encouraging in almost every way. A "Failure and Guilt" complex had nevertheless grown up in those years of success, and had come "quite close to dominating the intellectual discourse of our time, spewing forth reams of rhetoric organized around these closely related ideas: crisis, failure, guilt." Populationist "doomsayers" and environmental alarmists were two of the groups that contributed to this pessimistic complex, but on nearly all the important issues, he argued, they were mistaken.[34]

Wattenberg had written, as we have seen, one of the sharpest rebuttals to Paul Ehrlich's *Population Bomb*. He now pointed out that the United States, far from facing a population explosion, was undergoing a "birth dearth." In 1972, for the first time on record, the American birth rate had fallen below the replacement level of 2.1 and was continuing to decline. With the exception of the post–World War II baby boom, moreover, the American birth rate had been trending down for 150 years. The spread of widespread and effective contraception since 1960 and the rise of middle-class values among the great majority of the American people made it probable that the low birth rate would continue. The typical small American family had far more disposable income than ever before, and lived in uncrowded suburban conditions. Suburbanization could be criticized as "urban sprawl," but this was a problem of success, not of failure: "Suburban Sprawl is a pejorative phrase that describes perhaps the most comfortable mass residential living conditions in history."[35]

Wattenberg also denied that there was a connection between over-population, pollution, and the threat to endangered species. On the contrary, he wrote, the passenger pigeon had been driven to extinction, and the buffalo nearly so, by far smaller American populations because they lacked the interest and the political will to prevent it. "If the bald eagle becomes extinct it will become extinct not because of too many humans but because of lax and lenient laws . . . The same holds with regard to protecting the wilderness. It can be destroyed by 100 million or preserved by 300 million. If you want it preserved, preserve it; but don't look for phony crutches to support a feeling of inevitable despair."[36]

Finally, Wattenberg argued that pollution was entirely manageable and could be remedied in the ways Beckerman had outlined. It was certainly not a crisis in the sense of threatening human life; otherwise life expectancy would be diminishing whereas, in fact, it was continuing to increase. And "as pollution abatement laws take hold, such harm as now exists will probably diminish." His study of survey data also showed him that the vast majority of Americans, while hoping to see pollution controlled, had no interest in accepting lower standards of living. The antimaterialist animus, he concluded, was the concern of a small intellectual elite, most of whose members were already wealthy.[37]

The leaders of America's major environmental organizations—Sierra Club, Audubon Society, National Wildlife Federation, and Izaak Walton League—were uncomfortably aware that this was true; their members were generally well heeled and they found it extremely difficult to attract poor, working-class, or minority recruits. MIT economist Lester Thurow explained why. Members of the upper middle class already have good homes and cars, good educations for their children, and the chance to travel abroad. They ask themselves: what could make our lives better? They answer: a cleaner environment. Just as they consume a wide variety of other goods, so now they want to "consume" the environment, and they understand that if they want it, they are going to have to pay for it, by joining organizations that lobby for changes in the law. Poorer people, by contrast, are still preoccupied with more immediate forms of consumerism as they try to acquire the goods that their wealthier contemporaries already possess. Environmental objectives seem insignificant to people who still lack decent, well-paying jobs, houses, and cars of their own. They are also afraid that environmental legislation might even restrict their employment opportunities.[38]

Thurow encouraged his readers to think of the environment in economic terms. If we want a cleaner environment, we must pay for it. The people who want it cleaner will benefit, whereas others will suffer by being made to pay more than they think it is worth, either through taxes or through the increased price of goods that have to be made by cleaner technologies. He cautioned: "'Small is beautiful' sounds beautiful, but it does not exist because it does not jibe with human nature. Man is an acquisitive animal whose wants cannot be satiated . . . To try to straightjacket human beings into 'small is beautiful' is to impose enormous costs; yet these would yield only modest benefits in terms of less pollution and slower exhaustion of resources."[39]

After the mid-1970s, population gradually diminished in importance as a headline environmental theme. The nonappearance of the famines Ehrlich and others had predicted for the late 1970s and early 1980s, and the unchanged reality that American and European farmers' worst problem was *over*production, meant that the issue had lost most of its power to alarm.[40] Even so, the anxious mood of the late sixties and early seventies did not disappear. In 1977, for example, President Carter asked his Council on Environmental Quality to collaborate with the State Department in drawing up a study of the major trends in world resource use, population, food supplies, and pollution, and to project their probable development up to the year 2000. The resulting eight-hundred-page report, written by Gerald Barney, made for gloomy reading. "Barring revolutionary advances in technology," it concluded, "life for most people on earth will be more precarious in the year 2000 than it is now." It projected continued population growth, increased disparities between rich and poor countries, and catastrophic environmental deterioration. Problems of soil erosion, deforestation, desertification, urbanization, intensified pesticide use, pollution, and scarce water supplies would all worsen. Forty percent of the world's remaining forest cover would be cut down. It anticipated mass extinctions, perhaps of as many as 20 percent of all species by the year 2000.[41]

CLEANING UP

One of the biggest success stories of the years 1970–2010 has been the cleaning up of American air, land, and water. Once effective laws were in place, corporate compliance, lawsuits, and improvements in technology combined to achieve astonishing reductions in emissions from factories, cars, and incinerators. It was certainly not clear in 1970 that such achievements were going to be possible. Writers and politicians noted anxiously at the time that increases in population and production were going to put immense pressure on the environment in the coming decades. They feared that pollution abatement projects were likely to find themselves running at full speed just to prevent the situation from getting even worse. In the event, these fears proved groundless; air and water quality *improved* substantially even while the total number of people, vehicles, power stations, and factories increased.

How did it happen? This "great cleaning" has been studied by businesses, economists, and scientists, but has rarely made headlines, because it has no villains and lacks the alluring flavor of tragedy and danger that colors so many environmental news stories. Some studies emphasize that success stemmed from the strict new rules introduced by the legislation of the early 1970s, and from the EPA's vigor in prosecuting offenders. Other studies argue that polluters had incentives to improve their methods and would have cleaned up even *without* closer supervision. After all, smoke and polluted water usually meant imperfect combustion, wasted fuel, and wasted raw materials. As production technology improved in efficiency, fewer waste products were left over—hence, less pollution. Others again suggest that the energy crises of 1973 and 1979 made America far more energy conscious than it would have been otherwise and prompted serious conservation efforts.

A few observers, taking a libertarian approach, have even suggested that the new laws *delayed* air and water quality improvements. By exempting old factories and old cars from new standards, according to this argument, they gave producers a perverse incentive to stick with the old plants for longer rather than pay the high price for a new generation of environmentally sound ones. Whatever the merits of this argument in the abstract, the historical record shows clearly enough that many manufacturers polluted the air and water until they were forbidden to do so, at which time they stopped. The history of the great cleaning clearly favors centralized government regulation and national standards.[42]

Before 1970, a clutter of different agencies—local, state, and national—was responsible for monitoring pollution and trying to remedy it. Once the stronger laws had passed, by contrast, uniform standards began to prevail. Corporations could no longer credibly threaten to move to different states in response to tough state laws. The EPA under Ruckelshaus also showed that it was less interested in coming to an understanding with polluters than in forcing them to comply. What's more, citizen groups like Nader's Raiders and the Environmental Defense Fund were now able to step in if the EPA faltered. As the historian Richard Andrews notes, "Citizen environmental advocacy organizations were armed with expanded rights to disclosure of government documents, with access to administrative proceedings, and with new rights to challenge government agencies in the courts. These changes had far-reaching implications both for the environment and for American governance."[43]

Among the challenges facing the EPA in its early years was to decide what standards to apply in legislation. Should it specify particular methods of cleaning up smokestack emissions, for example, or simply establish a standard and require all polluters to meet it by a given deadline? In general, they opted for this second approach, known in the business as "command and control," rather than letting themselves become mired in the minutiae of particular systems. After surveying the industry in question, the EPA would require firms to match the pollution reduction then being achieved by the best available abatement systems, or else to invent others that were equally effective. Its primary intention was to mitigate six common pollutants that were well known as threats to human health: sulfur and nitrogen oxides, carbon monoxide, particulates, lead, and ozone. The National Ambient Air Quality Standards (NAAQS) used public health criteria to set enforceable limits, but also added a set of secondary standards to improve visibility and prevent damage to plants, animals, and buildings. Not surprisingly, polluters, public health advocates, and environmentalists all had different ideas about exactly where the line should be drawn.[44]

EPA administrators eventually realized that it would be better to allow manufacturers to trade in the right to pollute. They applied the idea in the 1990 amendments to the Clean Air Act. The scheme worked like this: every polluter was issued with annual certificates granting the right to emit a certain amount of pollution. If he already polluted less than the permitted amount, he could sell his permits to other manufacturers, whose factories were, for the moment, "dirtier." In this way, the buyer could stay in business while working to clean up his factories, and the seller would profit from his socially desirable decision to run a clean factory. With each passing year, however, the overall amount of pollution permitted by the certificates would diminish, obliging dirtier manufacturers to improve their technology and preventing cleaner ones from resting on their laurels. The system, with its ever diminishing total of allowable pollution, forced manufacturers to acknowledge that water and air were not "externalities," but scarce resources that had to be paid for.[45]

Like all big bureaucracies, EPA could be inefficient, not least because it brought together a motley array of scientists, lawyers, and administrators who had previously worked for other agencies with traditions and cultures of their own. Some pollutants, such as nitrogen oxides from cars, proved harder to suppress than others, and compliance schedules were not always met. Nevertheless, the nation's overall accomplishments in pollution reduction were impressive almost from the start. As one historian notes, "Between 1970 and 1990 smoke pollution (particulates) decreased by nearly 80 percent, lead emissions by 98 percent and most other air pollutants by at least one fifth to one third, even as economic production and growth continued to increase." As a result, "it was unlikely that the U.S. would ever again experience the severe air pollution emergencies that had occurred in earlier decades."[46]

America did not give up manufacturing, nor did it give up suburban living, automobiles, or high levels of consumption. It simply behaved more efficiently and cleanly. "Scrubbers" on factory chimneys to remove sulfur dioxide and devices to remove lead compounds and waste gases from car engines improved steadily from the 1970s to the 1990s, becoming a major area of entrepreneurial initiative. Small cars with efficient engines caught on widely in the 1970s and 1980s. Companies like Envirotech sprang up to serve the rising demand for cleaner technology, and before long a trade group, the Manufacturers of Emission Controls Association, could be found lobbying *in favor* of strict regulation. For them it meant more business. Power stations switched to burning low-sulfur coal. Corporations found, despite their earlier claims, that compliance with the new standards would not bankrupt them, and that it was possible to save money on fuel and raw materials through

Los Angeles dispatch riders wear antismog gas masks, 1955.

greater efficiency. Citizen groups and environmental organizations continued to lobby for tighter controls, and cities worked to improve their "green" image.[47]

To explain these improvements, some academic observers developed a concept called the environmental Kuznets curve (EKC), named for Nobel economics laureate Simon Kuznets. The curve, an inverted U, suggested that in the early stages of industrialization pollution would rise rapidly, then begin to decline as per capita GNP increased. Wealthier populations had incentives to improve their quality of life, and so long as they lived in democratic societies that were responsive to citizens' opinions, they would be able to achieve a decline in pollution, even as production and GNP continued to rise.[48]

Perhaps this sounds very abstract, but the 2008 book *Smogtown*, by Chip Jacobs and William Kelly, draws a vivid picture of what this abatement actually meant to people living through these decades. A pollution history of Los Angeles, *Smogtown* begins with vivid descriptions of appalling smog incidents in Los Angeles in the 1940s, 1950s, and 1960s, and the city's long struggle to recover the air quality that had attracted residents in the first place. It shows that by 2005 automobile exhausts were 90 percent cleaner than in 1990 and 99 percent cleaner than in 1960. The number of smog days had fallen from 152 in 1983 to 68 in 2003, even though the definition of smog days had been tightened, making it harder than ever to meet

Southern Californians at an antismog rally in Pasadena, 1954.

the requirements. As a result, "Southern Californians can breathe easier than at any time since the beastly murk [first] engulfed the West
Coast's glamour city . . . Sixty-five years of revolutionary gadgetry, civic
feistiness, hard-won regulation, and population survival constitute an
enormous success." Plenty of other environmental problems remain for
Los Angeles, not least the fact that its immense, sprawling population
drives millions of vehicle-miles per year and still pours greenhouse
gases like carbon dioxide into the atmosphere. The cleanup of smog,
however, has been so successful that it has ceased to be an urgent issue
for the area's environmentalists.[49]

A MOOD OF COLLECTIVE CONCERN about the environment ener-
gized politicians on both sides of the party divide in the early 1970s.
It prompted a wave of significant legislation, resulting in a steady reduction of pollution. The political situation in the second decade of
the twenty-first century is very different. Politicians, as sensitive as ever
to their constituents' concerns, are now more worried about unemployment and taxes, more skeptical about assertions of environmental crisis, and far more polarized. Tea Party pressure inside the Republican
Party has pushed GOP members of Congress to oppose environmental
initiatives and to criticize every Democratic appointee to environ-
ment-related jobs. Republican politicians such as David Vitter of Louisiana, John Hoeven of North Dakota, Rand Paul of Kentucky, and
Marco Rubio of Florida treat every environmental initiative by the
Obama administration as another excuse to "feed the beast" (i.e., further increase the size of the federal government), destroy jobs, and
erode individual citizens' freedom. Conservatives regard the EPA as
too cozy with environmental groups and too reluctant to consult businesses and landowners that will be adversely affected by its rules.[50]

There are exceptions even now, however. If environmental legislation has a clearly beneficial effect for American businesses in addition
to increasing public health and safety, it can still gain political traction.
In 2013, for example, Republican senator David Vitter and Democratic
senator Frank Lautenberg (New Jersey) cosponsored the Chemical

Safety Improvement Act, designed to make the cumbersome Toxic Substances Control Act of 1976 more effective. Of the eighty-four thousand chemicals registered for use in the United States, most have never been subjected to systematic safety tests and only five have ever been banned through operation of the law. Although its implementation would mean more federal oversight, Vitter and other Republicans were aware of business groups' enthusiasm, such as that offered by the Biotechnology Industry Organization, whose statement in support of the law read, in part: "Growing worldwide demand for cleaner, safer chemical alternatives is creating a market opportunity for renewable chemicals. Providing clarity in the law will help US-based chemical companies capture a share of the growing market." The Environmental Defense Fund and the American Academy of Pediatrics also supported the proposed law, which would increase the EPA's ability to test the safety of chemicals in everyday use, indicating that creating a widely shared political consensus on an environmental issue—though extremely rare—was still at least conceivable.[51]

---||||||||||||||||||||||---

CHAPTER 4

ENERGY POLITICS

THE UNITED STATES WAS WELL EQUIPPED to begin solving its pollution problem in part because its political system was responsive to citizens' concerns. When enough citizens protested against filthy rivers, dying lakes, and smoggy air, their representatives took notice and legislated remedies. There was a great deal of bureaucratic friction and public disagreement along the way, but the eventual outcome was cleaner land, air, and water. Political tyrannies such as the Soviet Union and China were insensitive to public concerns, so their environmental situations worsened. Industrial areas behind the Iron Curtain in the Cold War era (1946–1989) were incomparably dirtier and more dangerous than their American counterparts. Moreover, as we shall see, poorly planned projects could have catastrophic environmental effects, such as the explosion at the Chernobyl nuclear power station and the destruction of the Aral Sea.

The history of America's environmental debates is, in this sense, a vindication of democratic institutions, the rule of law, freedom of the press, and citizens' rights. The fact that citizens could band together to sue not only polluters but also the EPA, if they thought it was failing to fulfill its mandate, kept all relevant parties alert and made environmental abuses much less likely. So did investigative journalism. After

1970, monitoring of the environment and lobbying on its behalf were fully institutionalized in Washington, D.C., and in the state capitals.

But American democracy has weaknesses as well as strengths. It is susceptible to short-term enthusiasms, such as the widespread vogue for "ecology" in the late 1960s and early 1970s. This trend lasted long enough to provoke a profound political reorientation in environmental affairs, but suddenly lost momentum in 1973 when oil supplies dried up, threatening jobs and the American standard of living. Furthermore, most environmental issues were extremely complicated, difficult even for highly trained specialists to understand, and not easily reduced to simple either-or alternatives for voters. Majorities of voters sometimes get their way even when they are wrong on the facts.

If population and pollution were the great environmental issues of the 1960s, energy was the great issue of the 1970s. Concern about short energy supplies transformed the environmental and political landscape. The decade began with a heated controversy over whether to build a trans-Alaska pipeline that would bring oil from the state's arctic north to ports in the south. Mistrust of oil companies by then was so widespread that the pipeline project was almost defeated, but the first oil crisis of 1973 saved it. The decade continued with an even sharper controversy over nuclear power generation, for which strong arguments were deployed on both sides. When they worked well, nuclear power plants generated immense quantities of nearly pollution-free electricity, and might be regarded as the environmentalist's best friend. When they went wrong, however, they could contaminate wide areas beyond recovery, making them the environmentalist's worst nightmare. No wonder the debate they generated was so intense, a debate that remains unresolved in 2014.

THE FIRST OIL CRISIS AND THE ALASKA PIPELINE

After years of warnings that resources were being used up at an unprecedented rate, the United States faced its first actual resource shortage in the fall of 1973, when the price of gasoline rose steeply. For a few weeks gasoline supplies dwindled and almost gave out completely, not because supplies were exhausted but for political reasons. When Israel and its Arab neighbors went to war (the Yom Kippur War), the United States resupplied Israel, its ally, with weapons, ammunition, and communications equipment. The Arab nations in the Organization of the Petroleum Exporting Countries (OPEC) retaliated by cutting off or restricting supplies to the United States. By the time regular supplies were restored in 1974, the price to American consumers had tripled.[1]

The response to this first "oil crisis" took two forms. One group of pundits took it as confirmation of their predictions that "business as usual" could not continue and that the United States must get serious about radical conservation measures, reduced economic growth, and a far greater commitment to energy efficiency. Schumacher's *Small Is Beautiful* was ready at hand, explaining how to do it. Another group argued that the United States must wean itself from dependency on foreign oil suppliers, especially those in the Middle East, by more aggressively developing domestic sources.

The Santa Barbara oil spill of 1969 had made offshore drilling unpopular and even helped create an environmental mass movement. Oil discoveries made by geologists on the North Slope of Alaska, by contrast, had opened up the possibility of American self-sufficiency. In the early 1970s, Alaska therefore became the focal point of a dispute over whether oil should be drilled at all and, if so, how it might best be transported to the lower forty-eight states. Supertankers could not sail safely in these arctic waters—they were not sufficiently maneuverable and could not evade icebergs, even during the three or four months in summer when the sea was not frozen solid. The alternative was a pipeline running from the oil fields across Alaska to a terminal on the southern coast—nearly always ice-free—where tankers could take on the oil.[2]

Alaska itself was, by the 1970s, freighted with symbolism. It represented "the last frontier" to many Americans concerned about the environment. They took the view that Alaska ought to be exempted from the commercialization that had overtaken the lower forty-eight states. A state in the Union only since 1959, Alaska had already been the scene of fierce debates relating to its environment. Two development projects had been prevented by the power of public opinion: Project Chariot, which would have excavated a deepwater harbor by the controlled use of nuclear explosions, and the proposed Rampart Dam on the Yukon River.[3]

Building a pipeline appeared to be the logical approach, but the project presented formidable technical and political difficulties. Land would have to be acquired from the native peoples living along its path, and compensation offered. Eight hundred miles in length, the line would have to cross the Brooks Range and the Alaska Range, numerous small rivers and a few big ones, including the Yukon, and several earthquake faults. It would have to accommodate a temperature range of more than two hundred degrees, reflecting the difference between winter and summer temperatures and the difference between its condition when empty and when full of hot, fast-flowing crude oil. Critics also pointed out that the pipeline would cross caribou migration routes and could have damaging effects on Alaskan wildlife, especially if it leaked. Burying the line also presented difficulties because it would melt the permafrost.[4]

The events of the late 1960s and early 1970s, in particular the Vietnam War and the Watergate scandal, had undermined public confidence in politicians; it was painfully obvious that they did not always tell the truth. Big business had also suffered a sharp decline in popularity and credibility. The fact that it was the *oil* industry that planned to exploit the North Slope and build this pipeline while its hands were still dirty from the Santa Barbara disaster added to the intensity of the Alaska debate. The historian Peter Coates explains:

> The tone of the [congressional] hearings [of the early 1970s] reflected the influence of the new ecological perspective, which, in its extreme form, resembled abolitionism and prohibitionism in the strength of its moral ardor. Some critics viewed the proposal as a symptom of a sick, "gluttonous," and sordidly materialistic society that was over-dependent on technology and built precariously on a

profligate and highly polluting economy as much as they saw it as an insult to the last great American wilderness . . . The project became a prime target for the assault on so-called technocratic chauvinism and runaway science, which, many believed, bore a heavy responsibility for the ecological crisis.

Most Alaskans, by contrast, supported the project because it would bring jobs and revenue into their state. One local journalist, criticizing delays to the pipeline and the road that would run adjacent to it, wrote that "for conservationists to attempt to block a single road being built to open up an area of Alaska roughly the size of Texas makes as much sense to us as an attempt to block a Daniel Boone from cutting a trail through the Cumberland Gap."[5]

Environmentalism had become such a powerfully emotional issue that the pipeline might well have been voted down in Congress had it not been for the Yom Kippur War and anxieties about the Middle East. Vice President Spiro Agnew ultimately broke a 49-49 deadlock in the Senate, voting in favor of the pipeline in 1973 (shortly before revelations of a financial scandal forced him to resign). In order to get work going as quickly as possible, Congress permitted a cursory environmental impact statement rather than subjecting the project to the full rigors of the new National Environmental Policy Act. Construction began in 1974 and the state-of-the-art pipeline was completed in 1977, much of

The 800-mile-long Alaska pipeline under construction, 1975.

it aboveground. Sections traversing the caribou migration route were buried, which necessitated insulating the pipe so that it would not thaw the permafrost.

The pipeline operated relatively smoothly into the twenty-first century, delivering tens of millions of barrels of oil to Port Valdez and thence to the lower forty-eight states, reducing America's dependency on imports from the politically volatile Middle East. It was also, at least in this author's opinion, an example of a win-win situation. The pipeline is unobtrusive, silent, and efficient, far better and cleaner than convoys of trucks on a superhighway would have been. It runs mainly through areas whose population is less than one per square mile, required no evictions, terminated no one's traditional way of life, and had no long-term effect on regional wildlife. Alaska is so immense (more than twice the land area of Texas, the next largest state) and so empty that the pipeline appears as a minuscule feature on the landscape.

Alaskan natives, meanwhile, gained official recognition of their land tenure by the terms of the Alaska Native Claims Settlement Act of 1971, offered as a quid pro quo for their cooperation in the project. No other group of native peoples had been so well treated by the federal government in negotiations over land and resources. At the same time, environmentalists annoyed by the pipeline, which some saw as a symbolic desecration of America's largest remaining wilderness, were mollified by the vast extension of national parks and wildlife refuges in the state. The Alaska National Interest Lands Conservation Act of 1980 created or extended nineteen national parks, wildlife refuges, wilderness areas, and national preserves, totaling more than one hundred million acres of land (which is to say, greater than the total land area of most individual states in the lower forty-eight).

Of course, the project was not cost-free in environmental terms. It showed a preference for confronting the era's energy dilemma not with radical conservation measures (as the mood of the early 1970s might have suggested) but with a decision to retrieve oil from ever more inaccessible places, which might be regarded as postponing the ultimate day of reckoning. Worse, the pipeline created the conditions for the *Exxon Valdez* disaster of Easter 1989, in which a tanker laden with crude oil from the pipeline went aground in Prince William Sound, ripped open its hull, and poured eleven million gallons of crude oil into the coastal sea.[6]

NUCLEAR POWER

The crisis of 1973 showed that America could be severely embarrassed if the oil-rich nations of the Middle East imposed an embargo. This fact was underlined by a second crisis in 1979. Was there an alternative to oil? Could nuclear power be the answer? Ever since the American attacks on Hiroshima and Nagasaki, the peaceful possibilities of nuclear fission had been widely debated. In December 1953 President Eisenhower gave what came to be known as the "Atoms for Peace" speech at the United Nations in New York, using powerful "swords into plowshares" rhetoric. The science that had made the terrible destruction of the bombs possible, he declared, must now be turned to peaceful uses.[7]

Sure enough, the 1950s and 1960s witnessed the building of America's first nuclear power stations, with the active encouragement of the Atomic Energy Commission (AEC) and the bipartisan Joint Committee on Atomic Energy (JCAE) in Congress. The Price-Anderson Act, passed by Congress in 1957, limited utility companies' liability in the event of an accident at a nuclear power station. The new technology sparked a uranium rush in Utah and, at first, a utopian literature about its possibilities. Early advocates claimed that nuclear power stations were incomparably cleaner than traditional coal-fired stations. They would brighten the atmosphere in previously smoggy cities and enhance the quality of life, meanwhile bringing down the cost of electricity for all consumers. They would produce electricity almost too cheap to meter.[8]

Some environmental groups shared this vision and saw nuclear-generated electrical power as a benign alternative to the ash, soot, carbon dioxide, and sulfur by-products of coal-powered plants. In the mid-1960s, for example, the Sierra Club split on the question of supporting nuclear power. Moderate members, including photographer Ansel

Adams, in consultation with the Pacific Gas and Electric Company (PG&E) suggested Diablo Canyon on the California coast as a suitable site for a nuclear power station, proposing it as an alternative to the utility's original suggestion, the scenic Nipomo Dunes. Later, the discovery of a geological fault beneath Diablo Canyon would make the site a flashpoint of environmental activism, but in the early 1960s Adams saw this cooperative approach as evidence of a sensible maturity among conservationists. David Brower and other more radical spirits, by contrast, refused to negotiate with PG&E. This was one of the issues that led to Brower's eventual ouster from Sierra Club leadership.[9]

In the first half of the 1970s, the number of civilian nuclear power stations in operation jumped from thirteen to fifty-five. A frail pronuclear consensus in public opinion, however, was starting to break down. Nuclear power stations proved more expensive to build than early optimistic estimates had suggested. Moreover, they had profound environmental effects of their own. The first of these to draw widespread attention was thermal pollution. Sited beside rivers or the sea, stations drew in water for their cooling systems and expelled it at the end of the generating process twenty or more degrees hotter. This hot water transformed river habitats and damaged or destroyed the local ecology.[10]

The subject of nuclear waste disposal caused increasing concern as the 1970s progressed. Used uranium fuel rods were no longer potent enough to work in the reactor core, but they were still highly radioactive and would remain so for thousands of years. What to do with them? Pronuclear writers argued that they could be stored in geologically inert areas, either salt beds or granite bedrock. Encased in glass cylinders, then locked inside stainless steel containers and buried two thousand feet deep, the waste would be unable to escape and leach back to the surface. After all, uranium came from the earth in the first place and a lot of it was still there: "Mother Nature," wrote the pronuclear advocate Petr Beckmann, "keeps 30 trillion cancer doses of radioactivity in random places under the US."[11] Opponents, meanwhile, remained skeptical on this and other points. Ralph Nader, whose Center for the Study of Responsive Law was now a significant contributor to environmental debates, began to challenge nuclear power advocates. He believed that the electric utility companies had rushed to embrace the technology with politicians' encouragement before reaching answers to a long series of difficult questions.

The major hazards already clearly identified by the 1970s were the radioactive waste disposal problem; the possibility of a meltdown (whether by accident, sabotage, or earthquake); the problem of uranium theft, in transit or on site; the problem of nuclear proliferation through the export of technology abroad; and the potential for accidents abroad. All these concerns, combined with the fact that the power stations turned out to be far more expensive to build and maintain than had originally been expected, convinced Nader that the industry was more menace than panacea. That it was shrouded in secrecy (the "ion curtain") made everything worse; it threatened citizens' constitutional rights and made every power station a potential national security target. Resources poured into nuclear power development also drained them away from sustainable alternatives like wind and solar.[12]

Supporters of nuclear power believed that Nader, and like-minded critics, were exaggerating the risks of nuclear waste, and more generally that radioactive materials were not nearly as toxic as environmentalists alleged. It became a cardinal element of their defense that the risks of nuclear power were smaller than those attending other electricity-generating technologies. In 1976 Petr Beckmann wrote a booklength analysis, *The Health Hazards of NOT Going Nuclear*, in which he admitted that nuclear power was dangerous, but that its dangers were smaller than those presented by any other form of power generation. Activists who campaigned against nuclear power stations, in his view, were arguing, "consciously or not, for more deaths by mining accidents, Black Lung, air pollution and chemical explosions: to crusade, consciously or not, for increased American dependence on medieval sheikdoms and other unstable dictatorships." He added that the nuclear waste disposal problem was also minuscule by comparison with coal-fired power, which was then producing 320 pounds of toxic ash per person per year.[13]

Whatever the scientific evidence, however, pronuclear intellectuals found themselves unable to garner media and public support in the early 1970s. "What we were to discover," wrote AEC chief Glenn Sea-borg, "was that the public was not disposed or equipped to deal with probabilities. What many people seemed to demand of nuclear power was zero-risk, never mind the comparison with other risks. This was frustrating to technical people trained in numerical analysis, but there it was."[14]

Some defenders of nuclear power even offered their own bodies in support of their convictions. Bernard Cohen, a professor of physics at the University of Pittsburgh and one of the most energetic defenders of nuclear power, wrote a reassuring paper on plutonium toxicity in 1976. When Ralph Nader accused him of "trying to detoxify plutonium with a pen," Cohen countered by offering "personally to inhale 1000 particles of plutonium of any size that could be suspended in air, or 10 micrograms of plutonium in any form (ten times the dose that Nader claimed would be lethal)." He sent this offer to the television networks, including the popular shows *60 Minutes* and *The Tonight Show*, "asking that I be given a few minutes to explain why I was doing this: my risk, according to my calculation, was equivalent to the risk faced by a soldier in wartime, and I felt that my demonstration would be an important service to the country." No one took him up on the offer, but Cohen remained confident in his calculations.[15]

As the debate over nuclear power intensified, reactor safety itself came under scrutiny. The AEC, which was responsible both for promoting civilian nuclear power and for regulating it (which critics understandably saw as a conflict of interest), held hearings on emergency core cooling systems in 1972. It encountered the organized opposition of the Union of Concerned Scientists (UCS), which had been founded by a group of MIT faculty in 1969. Two of the union's members, Henry Kendall and Dan Ford, were anxious about the risk of nuclear power station accidents or failures, but, realizing the complexity (and potentially the obscurity) of the issue, looked for a way to make headlines. "We wanted Ralph [Nader] to take the issue of nuclear power and to colloquialize it," said their attorney. "He could merely raise an issue and it would be instant news. For us to make instant news, we needed a seminal event. He could say nuclear power was bad and people believed it."[16]

Nader's "Critical Mass '74," held at the Statler Hotel in New York City, was the first nationwide antinuclear conference. Its theme was that the technology's hazards outweighed the benefits. Hollywood celebrities like Paul Newman and important academics such as Margaret Mead were in attendance. Scattered groups of activists from areas where nuclear power stations were being built began to assemble a coordinated national opposition to the technology. In 1975 the UCS sent to President Ford and Congress an antinuclear petition signed by twenty-three hundred eminent scientists, urging that the whole technology be abandoned.[17]

In 1976 the defection and whistle-blowing of three high-level nuclear engineers against their former employers, and a *60 Minutes* story about one of them, Robert Pollard, bolstered antinuclear advocates' claims. They said that standard safety procedures were not being followed in the construction or operation of power stations, and that the industry and the Nuclear Regulatory Commission (the successor to the AEC) were colluding to cover up evidence of dangers. Questions also surrounded the mysterious death in 1974 of Karen Silkwood, a union activist and nuclear power worker from Oklahoma. She died in a car accident en route to a meeting with a *New York Times* reporter to hand over evidence of mismanagement at the plant where she worked. The industry said she crashed because she was a recreational drug user under the influence of Quaaludes; the antinuclear movement believed she had died due to corporate foul play. The second Critical Mass conference met on the anniversary of Silkwood's death and held a candlelight vigil in her honor.[18]

Critics like the Union of Concerned Scientists and the Critical Mass group argued, among other things, that nuclear power stations violated the American democratic tradition. Although most stations were privately owned by utility companies, they had been developed in intimate collaboration with a secretive federal agency, the AEC. Their sheer scale and cost made them remote from local control and led their neighbors to feel helpless and vulnerable. The fact that nuclear fuel could also be used for weapons created more layers of government secrecy while increasing the hazard of nuclear terrorism. Citizens living near the power stations learned that a catastrophic accident could create a "China Syndrome" meltdown that might kill thousands outright, contaminate others with radiation sickness, and force them to abandon their homes permanently. The AEC's own Rasmussen Report of 1974, designed to be reassuring to the industry, admitted as much.[19]

Vietnam and Watergate had cast dark shadows over the idea of benign technology and trustworthy government. "A public which had only recently regarded scientists and technologists with awe and admiration," wrote the former head of the AEC, "was becoming increasingly critical and mistrustful of them." In the late 1970s, citizen groups like Mobilization for Survival undertook orderly direct-action protests against all forms of nuclear energy, sometimes on environmental grounds, sometimes as part of the pacifist movement. The Clamshell Alliance assembled groups of several thousand demonstrators to stage a sit-in outside the half-built Seabrook, New Hampshire, nuclear facility in April 1977. By insisting on nonviolence and getting fourteen hundred well-trained participants arrested, the demonstrators revived the tactics of the civil rights movement, "packed the jails," and won the moral high ground over a tactless and confrontational state governor. The fact that many of those arrested were respectable middle-class citizens brought a new wave of media attention to the issue and proved highly favorable to the antinuclear cause.[20]

To add to the utility companies' woes, they recognized in the late 1970s that demand for new sources of electricity was not rising as rapidly as they had expected. Throughout most of the twentieth century electricity had been a superb investment opportunity because demand consistently rose between 7 and 10 percent per year. The provision of new power stations had always been met with increasing demand and stimulated further building. Anticipating a continuation of this cycle in the 1960s, nuclear power station planners appeared to be acting rationally. The first energy crisis of 1973, however, prompted a new interest in insulation and energy conservation, such that the demand curve for electricity began to level off, with rate of increase in demand falling to about 3 percent per year. By the late 1970s and early 1980s a combination of high interest rates, cost overruns on nuclear power stations, inflation, and reduced electricity demand had brought to an end the golden era of electric utilities. Some companies, notably the Washington Public Power Supply System (WPPSS) were on the brink of bankruptcy. Nuclear electricity, touted in the 1950s as almost "too cheap to meter," was actually becoming too costly to be viable.[21]

THE CHINA SYNDROME AND THREE MILE ISLAND

These fears and doubts gained ground and were sufficiently familiar parts of American popular culture by 1979 to form the basis of a Hollywood film, *The China Syndrome*, starring Jane Fonda, which portrayed the technical side of the nuclear industry as incompetent and the financial side as callous and greedy. Hardly had this disaster movie begun its profitable theater run than a real-life accident at a nuclear power station, Three Mile Island, near Harrisburg, Pennsylvania, on March 28, 1979, seemed to bring the movie script to life. Faulty designs, faulty equipment, poor maintenance, and incompetent management left the owners of the plant, Metropolitan Edison, unsure of what was happening when the meltdown began. They were not sure how much danger they were in, nor whether to order an evacuation of the area.[22]

No one died and dangerous amounts of nuclear materials were not released into the atmosphere or water. Even so, the accident gravely weakened the prospects of American commercial nuclear power. The sharply critical Kemeny Commission report, released that October, along with lengthening delays, staggering cost escalations for all new plants, and organized political opposition, discouraged utility companies from ordering any new nuclear plants and prompted them to cancel dozens that were on order or already begun. The Long Island Lighting Company (LILCO) carried on building its Shoreham nuclear power station, but the public resistance movement became so intense that the utility was never able to bring it online. Eventually it sold the plant, which had cost tens of millions of dollars, for just one dollar, in order to have it dismantled.[23]

Public opinion shifted away sharply from nuclear power after Three Mile Island. A New York City demonstration shortly after the accident attracted an estimated two hundred thousand people. Speakers reiterated the case against nuclear power in terms of health, government and official deceit, democracy, and future uncertainties. *The Anti-Nuclear Handbook*, a popular cartoon-format polemic from the era, asked readers to imagine how airline passengers would react if their captain announced: "We only have fuel for the early stages of this flight but we think we can solve that en route . . . As for sabotage, well, it's always a possibility . . . after all, we live in dangerous times. But you'll have noticed that you're all handcuffed to your seats and gagged. Finally I'm sure you'd like to know your destination . . . so would we." Such, said the cartoonist, was the situation of a nation that committed itself to nuclear power![24]

Defenders of nuclear power knew that they were losing ground in the battle for the moral high ground, and that critics were challenging their arguments with increasing success. Three Mile Island forced them onto the defensive, but they did not abandon their faith. They continued to make the case for nuclear power as technologically realistic, and environmentally, economically, politically, and strategically desirable. Many of them, such as nuclear physicist Edward Teller, former AEC commissioner Glenn Seaborg, and Oak Ridge National Laboratory chief Alvin Weinberg, had come of age with the Manhattan Project, had spent much of their adult lives at work on nuclear projects, and continued to believe that the benefits outweighed the dangers. David Lilienthal, former head of the Tennessee Valley Authority and the AEC, and Weinberg, both included the phrase "a new start" in the titles of their books on the topic, recognizing that something had gone badly amiss the first time around.[25]

These pronuclear advocates' outlook was primarily technocratic. They believed that the issues could not really be understood except by experts and that the answer to technological difficulties was simply to improve the technology. They believed that centralized management and control were appropriate, and that the economic, waste, and safety issues were all manageable. To turn against the technology itself, in their view, was to deny the possibility of a better future. The journalist Mark Hertsgaard, who wrote a study of nuclear power executives after Three Mile Island, explained the moral fervor they felt. Both sides in the nuclear power dispute, he wrote, "are absolutely certain that they are right, that theirs is the moral and just cause, and that therefore they are destined to triumph while their opponents are destined to fail. The executives regard nuclear power as humankind's salvation and feel honored to help bring it into being. They shield themselves against castigation and ridicule by reassuring one another that societies have always reacted hostilely to those who, like themselves, were ahead of their times." The executives and their intellectual supporters mounted their counterattack on a broad front. They tried to concentrate on matters of cost-benefit analysis and comparative risk assessment. They also tried to seem practical and levelheaded but, as Hertsgaard's remark suggests, they periodically gave way to emotional outbursts and a moralistic rhetoric that mirrored that of their antinuclear opponents.[26] They pointed out that no one had died at Three Mile Island and that, alarming as the incident had been, it could not fairly be described as a public health catastrophe. Bernard Cohen argued that average radiation exposure of Three Mile Island area residents was only 1.2 millirems. "Such exposure," he wrote, "has one chance in eight million of causing a fatal cancer, which corresponds to reducing life expectancy by 1.1 minutes." It was, he added, comparable to the amount of life expectancy "we would lose from taking three puffs on a cigarette." Edward Teller appeared in a *Wall Street Journal* advertisement in July 1979 under the caption "I was the only person injured at Three Mile Island." In the text Teller described how stress in days following the accident had led him to suffer a heart attack, not because of events in the power station itself, however, but from countering the inaccurate allegations of Ralph Nader, Jane Fonda, and other antinuclear celebrities.[27]

A key element of the public health controversy was the issue of "linearity." If exposing laboratory animals to high levels of radiation caused numerous cancers, could scientists make a linear extrapolation and expect a proportionally lower number of cancers from lower doses? Scientists who became spokespersons for the antinuclear movement, like John Gofman and Thomas Mancuso, said yes, and even argued for "supralinearity"—the tendency of low doses to cause proportionally *more* cancers than a linear curve would suggest. Pronuclear power scientists, by contrast, interpreted the growing volume of studies the opposite way, arguing that the linear hypothesis overstated the risks because "nature provides mechanisms for repair of radiation damage at low doses." Many substances, they noted, are harmless at low doses— common salt, for example—but become toxic in high concentrations. They added that everyone is subject to low-level or "background" radi- ation all the time, from the bricks in their houses and (at quite high levels) from the components of jet aircraft when they travel by air.[28]

Pronuclear advocates attributed America's growing energy vulnera- bility to disruptions in the oil supply. Three Mile Island in 1979 coin- cided with the overthrow of the shah of Iran and the seizure of the American embassy in Tehran, whose personnel were taken hostage by the Ayatollah Khomeini's revolutionary guards. Iran, formerly a de- pendable ally and source of oil, was now a rabidly hostile power, soon to become embroiled in war against Iraq. These events contributed to the "second oil crisis" of 1979 and made self-sufficiency in energy a politically attractive option. Nuclear power, said its advocates, could assure that self-sufficiency.[29] They also interpreted the nationwide wave of antinuclear demonstrations after Three Mile Island as a display of scientific ignorance and political scaremongering. Environmentalists, in their view, simply were not facing up to certain hard realities about contemporary energy needs. The Canadian nuclear scientist Gordon Sims wrote a book-length rebuke to antinuclear activists, claiming that they were deliberately arousing unnecessary fears and manipulat- ing a credulous media. All forms of energy production, wrote Sims, carry adverse environmental consequences and risks to human health and safety, but no form of production involves lower risks than nuclear power.[30]

Supporters of nuclear power also learned how to make use of some standard environmentalist arguments. They pointed out, for example, that if America were to abandon nuclear power, it would remain more dependent on coal-fired and hydroelectric power stations. That meant more deaths for coal miners—directly in cave-ins and flash fires, indirectly in lung diseases—and it meant atmospheric damage and more lung diseases from carbon and sulfur compounds produced by the power stations themselves. "Every time a coal-burning power plant is built," wrote Bernard Cohen, "about 1000 people are condemned to an early death from air pollution."[31] The advocates of nuclear power pinned their hopes on the fast breeder reactor, which, when perfected, would generate an immense additional quantity of fuel. In the 1960s, plans for a fast breeder began in part to counteract the popular perception that available supplies of uranium were limited. By the 1980s the experimental Clinch River fast breeder had consumed more than a billion dollars of federal money, along with $250 million in contributions from utilities (which expected to benefit from the technology in the long run), and was an attractive target for political budget cutters. "Those of us who had enthusiastically pushed the program," wrote Glenn Seaborg, "—and I was certainly one of those—had underestimated the difficulties involved, for example, the need to have materials and components that could withstand extremely high temperatures and neutron flux levels with minimum absorption of neutrons." By then future uranium supplies did not seem so limited, but it was still possible to make a case for the breeder on environmental grounds and on the grounds of (very) long-term economy.[32]

The international situation added insult to injury, from pronuclear advocates' point of view. While the growth of American nuclear power had become politically unlikely, it was thriving in other parts of the world. The two nations most dedicated to self-sufficiency through nuclear power were France and Japan, which had shown that strong national leadership and rational planning made it possible to conceive, plan, build, and operate nuclear power plants in the same years that they were faltering in America. By the early 1990s over 70 percent of French electricity was nuclear generated. Communities were given financial incentives by the central government to accept the plants, so they were often regarded as welcome additions to the local economy

rather than sinister intruders. The licensing obstacles were less daunting, the public less adversarial, and plants were moving from the drawing board to completion in less than half the time of American plants
even in their heyday.[33]

Pronuclear intellectuals held out little hope for solar or wind power,
the alternatives most often proposed by environmentalists. In the fore-
seeable future, they said, these technologies would generate far too
little electricity to be cost-effective. Besides, if attempted on a commercial scale, solar and wind power stations consumed immense areas of
real estate for miserly returns, and solar power for domestic use, while
effective in the Sunbelt, was a forlorn prospect in areas of America with
four-month winters.[34]

At the same time, pronuclear intellectuals after Three Mile Island
admitted that their industry was far from blameless. After the accident,
Alvin Weinberg argued the need for greater professionalism among
reactor personnel, more rigorous self-criticism, further refinement
of nuclear technology and safety, and public education on nuclear-
generated electricity. He also advocated the concentration of nuclear
reactors at a few large sites, so that their staffs could be mutually sup-
portive and build up a "priesthood" of expertise in the design, building, management, and safe operation of the facilities. These reactor
parks, moreover, should be remote from population centers and should
be subjected to strong centralized controls. In Weinberg's view, the dispersal of reactors in America, their location in populated areas, and
poor management by utility companies had all contributed to the industry's many failures. He held up France as an ideal example of the
right ways to handle nuclear power.[35]

A further source of anxiety to supporters and detractors of nuclear
power alike was the continuing accumulation of used nuclear fuel rods.
Military nuclear facilities were also accumulating used rods, pending a
decision about where to build a permanent disposal facility. A succession of congressional acts between the 1970s and early 2000s was unable to resolve the question of where this site would be. Literally billions
of dollars were spent on assessments of potential sites, with Yucca Mountain, Nevada, one hundred miles northwest of Las Vegas, eventually

becoming the consensus choice. More than eight hundred nuclear explosions had taken place close to this remote desert setting during the Cold War and it was among the least populated areas of the lower forty-eight states. But Nevada politicians, along with objections by Shoshone Indians, uncertainties about the site's geological inertness, and fears about the vulnerability of the fuel in transit all delayed the opening of the facility. Its eventual cancellation by the Obama administration in 2011 in the face of this intense political opposition further embarrassed the nuclear industry. The ultimate destination of the used fuel rods as of 2014 remains uncertain.[36]

AMORY LOVINS

The intensity of the energy debate in the 1970s stimulated the interest of numerous inventive writers. One of the most original was Amory Lovins, a brilliant and hardheaded polymath who began life as a mathematical and musical child prodigy in Washington, D.C. After two years

Amory Lovins, energy guru, advocate of efficiency and of alternatives to an oil-based economy.

as an undergraduate at Harvard in the mid-1960s, he moved to Oxford, in England, where a dazzling academic career in physics led to his election as a fellow of Merton College. He began studying the economic, technical, and ethical aspects of international energy policy in ways that drew widespread and generally favorable attention from environmentalists and governments. (He also became the UK representative of David Brower's organization Friends of the Earth, and ran a campaign to prevent new mining and smelter projects in Snowdonia, a national park in North Wales.)[37]

Lovins's 1973 book *World Energy Strategies*, published when he was only twenty-six, surveyed the energy dilemma just as the first oil crisis was taking hold. Industrialized nations, he wrote, have enjoyed a prolonged era in which oil has been cheap and plentiful. The rate of increase of oil use, however, and the fact that more nations are competing for it, would drive up costs, even leaving aside the political volatility of the Middle East. We also know enough about world inventories to be sure that supplies will eventually be exhausted. Some new energy supplies, such as natural gas, can come online quickly, but there is no evidence that more quick fixes are going to be available. Nuclear power stations take a very long time to build, are unpopular, and present unprecedented dangers. We have already reached the situation in some specialized areas, such as high-tech agriculture, where we use far more energy to grow the food than the food itself provides to its consumers. Learning to live with less energy, he argued, is therefore essential: "Most technical fixes that increase energy supply are slow, costly, risky, and of temporary benefit; most social or technical fixes that reduce energy demand are fairly quick, free or cheap, safe and of permanent benefit." Governments therefore needed to begin planning on reduced use, low-tech alternatives, and much increased efficiency.[38]

In a subsequent book, *Soft Energy Paths* (1977), Lovins expanded this argument. It costs far less to economize on energy use, to make more fuel-efficient cars, and to develop alternative energy resources, he wrote, than it does to build more power stations and import more oil. It also generates more employment and reduces pollution. In addition to increasing efficiency with traditional energy sources, however, it was time to move to what he called "soft energy" alternatives. "Soft" meant "flexible, resilient, sustainable, and benign." These sources depended mainly on energy flows that were "always there whether we use them or not, such as sun and wind and vegetation," and were designed to be user-friendly, appropriate in scale to their users, and keeping production physically close to ultimate use. Lovins was an implacable foe of nuclear power. He linked technology to the global search for peace, arguing that the current world energy situation was a powder keg, likely to become even more dangerous if the world shifted further to nuclear power, and that, accordingly, soft energy was the road to peace.[39]

By the time Lovins published *Energy/War: Breaking the Nuclear Link* (1980), the lessons of Three Mile Island were beginning to sink in. The years 1979 and 1980 also bore witness to an intensification of the Cold War as the Soviet Union invaded Afghanistan, and Ronald Reagan, the victorious candidate in the 1980 presidential campaign, launched a tougher anticommunist policy than the détente favored by his three predecessors. It was now clear, wrote Lovins, that most of the world was abandoning nuclear power generation and that it was right to do so. Nuclear power had shown itself to be too big, too dangerous, and too uneconomical to survive in the free market—it proved successful only in strongly centralized regimes like France and the Soviet Union. This move toward abandonment was good news, since nuclear energy and nuclear weapons proliferation were closely linked. Soft energy paths would not merely bring affordable, renewable power to more people; they might even prevent a nuclear Armageddon.[40]

In the ensuing decades Lovins remained a prominent figure in the national and international debates over energy. In 1982 he and his wife Hunter founded the Rocky Mountain Institute, a nonprofit organization in Snowmass, Colorado, dedicated to fostering "the efficient and sustainable use of resources as a path to global security." They were convinced that progress was possible simply by making the technology we already possessed more efficient. Lovins was careful never to let his image become that of a countercultural figure. He described himself as an economist rather than an environmentalist, stating that "we don't have to become vegetarians and ride bicycles to save the

Earth." He financed the institute partly by working as a policy adviser to corporations and government agencies in the United States and abroad, arguing that more efficient vehicles, better building techniques, better insulation methods, and better lightbulbs make immense energy savings possible. Lovins was one of relatively few prominent figures in the environmental debates whose work seemed to gratify more people than it antagonized.[41]

There is something likable about Amory Lovins's approach to energy questions. He was fully aware, as we all should be, that successful handling of energy and the environment depends more on weighing many issues together than by clinging to single causes and solutions. Among these issues are cost, cleanliness, conservation, public trust, and democratic responsiveness.

Nuclear power was probably the best and cleanest way of making electricity in the United States during the 1970s, but it could not ultimately work because it aroused too many fears. Despite its advocates' many strong arguments—that it promised cleaner skies, fewer mining-related deaths, and cheaper electricity—it lacked public support, which, in a democracy, is decisive. Antinuclear protestors who saw nuclear power as intrinsically undemocratic were right. The danger of nuclear fuel rods being stolen or hijacked, along with the danger of a serious accident, meant that power stations had to be surrounded by barriers of security and secrecy. If a serious accident did take place, it might irrevocably destroy entire communities. Better, on balance, to stick with coal- and natural gas–fired power stations and with hydroelectric power—imperfect as they were—while pressing on with research into "greener" alternative forms of energy.

In the 1970s and the ensuing decades, America demonstrated a continuing thirst for oil and only the most limited willingness to sacrifice. Congress could have mandated far stricter gas mileage on the Detroit automakers, but never did so—its imposition of a speed limit of fifty-five miles per hour in 1974 never proved effective as a fuel conservation measure. It could also have taken Europe's example and imposed high taxes on gasoline as a revenue-raising device, to penalize gas-guzzlers, and to discourage driving altogether. Citizens could have returned en masse to public transport, but declined to do so—they lived in suburbs and loved the convenience of driving their own cars. Millions could have elected to live without electricity, but, so far as I can tell, only an infinitesimal number of alternative-lifestyle radicals ever tried it, and usually not for long! Oil and power companies, widely mistrusted by the general public, always claimed that they were simply providing what the people actually wanted.

TWO OF THE GREAT ENERGY issues of the 1970s are once again at the center of public discussion in the second decade of the twenty-first century. If the Alaska pipeline pitted environmentalists against development enthusiasts in the 1970s, the Keystone XL pipeline has created a comparable face-off since 2010. Some of the arguments for it, and some of those against, have been heard before, while others are new. The seventeen-hundred-mile pipeline, if completed (at an estimated cost of around $7 billion), will bring one million barrels of crude oil per day from Alberta, Canada, through Montana, Wyoming, Nebraska, Kansas, and Oklahoma to refineries around Houston, Texas. Its advocates argue that this oil will reduce America's dependence on imports from abroad, create greater energy security, and reduce the price of gasoline in the United States. The pipeline, buried throughout its length, will rely on a well-tested and safe technology, they say, and will remove the need for hundreds of tanker trucks, barges, or tanker trains (all polluters and all vulnerable to accidents). It will also stimulate employment and contribute to recovery from the post-2008 recession. Marty Durbin, then of the American Petroleum Institute, claimed in 2011 that the pipeline makers were deeply preoccupied by environmental and safety concerns and that "the pipeline will not only meet industry standards but exceed them."[42]

Keystone's opponents counter that the oil in question comes from tar sands and consists of a thick bitumen that burns dirty. It is so viscous that it has to be mined rather than pumped from the ground and will damage irrevocably the mined area in Canada. It then has to be diluted with toxic additives (into a substance known in the business as "dilbit") before being able to flow through the pipeline. Its refinement and use as fuel will worsen the greenhouse effect and accelerate global warming. The building of the pipeline, moreover, means forcible intrusion into many landowners' properties with writs of eminent domain. It is a threat to the environmentally sensitive Sand Hills region of Nebraska and will cut across the High Plains' great Ogallala Aquifer. Leaks there would be catastrophic to the region's farmers. Denying that the technology is safe, they cite recent pipeline ruptures in Mayflower, Arkansas, Marshall, Michigan, and the catastrophic BP oil well spill in the Gulf of Mexico of 2010. Nor are they convinced that the oil, once refined, will be used in the United States or bring down prices—from Houston it could easily be shipped abroad, making it advantageous and profitable only to a handful of oil companies, not to the nation in general.[43]

The environmental writer Bill McKibben and the NASA scientist James Hansen (already a prominent figure in the global warming debate) organized demonstrations outside the White House early in 2013 with support from the Sierra Club. For the first time in the club's history it authorized its members to participate in acts of civil disobedience and expose themselves to the possibility of arrest. They challenged President Obama to make good on his 2008 election promise to end America's dependence on fossil fuels by vetoing the project, knowing that he was under intense congressional pressure to approve the pipeline. Seventy protestors locked themselves to the fences, including McKibben, Hansen, the actress Daryl Hannah, Michael Brune (executive director of the Sierra Club), Robert Kennedy, Jr., and even an old veteran of the civil rights movement, Julian Bond. They were arrested for trespass and failure to disperse. Meanwhile, protestors in Nebraska and Oklahoma obstructed bulldozers or chained themselves to heavy equipment to block progress on the pipeline itself. Two visions of the nation's future were in stark opposition over the Keystone pipeline, one treating it as an obvious economic and political asset, the other seeing it as a vicious assault on the environment by greedy climate change deniers.[44]

With President Obama still undecided about Keystone as these words are written, another reviving controversy with roots in the 1970s is the question of nuclear power. Here, too, strong voices are speaking out on both sides, but the new issue of global warming is changing the configuration of forces. Long-term advocates of nuclear power remain enthusiastic that their technology is the best way to produce clean electricity in sufficient volume. Their PR experts have created the "Clean and Safe Energy Coalition" and hired a former EPA administrator, Christine Todd Whitman, to act as its mouthpiece. They have now been joined by at least some environmentalists who see it as the best way of generating electricity, superior to coal, natural gas, and hydro. James Hansen, prominent in the anti-Keystone movement, regards nuclear power as the best available option because it alone among bulk production methods creates no greenhouse gases. James Lovelock, originator of the Gaia hypothesis, agrees. So does Stewart Brand, lifelong environmental campaigner and father of the *Whole Earth Catalog*. He was antinuclear in the seventies but now believes that "environmentalists have much less to fear from the current nuclear power industry than they think, and much more to gain from new and planned reactor designs than they realize. Hansen is right. Nukes are green." After studying the field, he is convinced that new, safer reactor designs, an improved method of waste storage known as "dry cask," and an unparalleled ability to produce a lot of power for a tiny amount of waste combine to make it the best available solution. As more of the world's people struggle out of poverty, he writes, and as more of them migrate to cities, they too will demand electrical power. Attempting to provide it from coal-powered stations would entail dumping tens of millions of tons of greenhouse gases into the atmosphere.[45]

Passionate in their continued opposition to nuclear power, by contrast, are many of the groups and figures who opposed it in the 1970s, including most of the mainstream environmental organizations. The Natural Resources Defense Council still thinks it's a bad idea. So do the Sierra Club, the National Wildlife Federation, and the Union of Concerned Scientists. They argue that, without political subsidies, nuclear power stations are still so expensive to build and run that they cannot compete on the open market. Designs may be safer, waste disposal may be a little more sophisticated, but the big questions have not been answered. Nagging fears about terrorists acquiring spent nuclear fuel to make "dirty bombs" persist in the long aftermath of the 9/11 attacks.[46]

History often plays tricks on human hopes. No sooner did nuclear power seem set for a comeback than an earthquake-induced tidal wave severely damaged a Japanese nuclear power station on the Pacific coast at Fukushima Daiichi in 2011. Nearby towns had to be evacuated; workers fled from the radioactive damage, while helicopters dumped seawater onto the reactor to prevent a meltdown. Releases of radiation, failure of safety equipment, bewilderment on the part of officials, and continuing leaks of radioactive water into the ground from temporary holding ponds have emphasized all over again the fallibility of projects designed and built by humans, and their inability to anticipate every contingency. Japan closed all fifty of its reactors for safety review. The chancellor of Germany, Angela Merkel, responded to news of the disaster by closing down all seventeen of her own country's nuclear power stations and insisting the technology is just too dangerous. Nuclear safety officials elsewhere, including those at the U.S.'s remaining plants, hurried to review their own safety procedures.[47]

About a hundred reactors are currently producing electricity at sixty-five different sites around the United States, generating around 20 percent of American electricity. All were already built, or were under construction, in 1974 and some are now old enough that their close-down dates are approaching. Two new reactors at an active power plant in Georgia and two in South Carolina have been commissioned in recent years but no new nuclear plant has been built from scratch. Several utilities planned new ones over the last five years, but the low price of natural gas has discouraged them from going ahead, from fear that they could not make electricity cheap enough to compete on the market. As a result, the future of the whole technology, at least in the United States, still hangs in the balance.[48]

CHAPTER 5

CRISES AND CRITICS

By 1977, as Gerald Ford left the White House, the bipartisan tide that had transformed environmental politics was ebbing. The energy crisis of 1973 made clear that the nation faced hard choices and that environmental protection would always have to be measured alongside other—usually economic—issues. The new president, Jimmy Carter, discovered early and often that the nation had little appetite for self-sacrifice.

The events of the foregoing years, however, had demonstrated a widespread sympathy among voters for environmental improvements on grounds of public health, economic welfare, and even aesthetics. Strong support for the Endangered Species Act of 1973, passed almost unanimously in both houses of Congress by Republicans and Democrats alike, also showed that citizens had more than a utilitarian concern for other species. If building a dam in Tennessee would annihilate the snail darter, a small fish of no apparent practical benefit, many took the view that the dam must not be built. There was, in their view, an intrinsic value to the existence of the species itself. Others, including most Tennessee politicians, however, spoke up in favor of the dam and against the fish, because the project would bring federal money, jobs, and economic growth to the area.

Most environmental controversies in the late 1970s and 1980s involved scientific disagreements. Toxic waste dumping at Love Canal, New York, and Times Beach, Missouri, for example, represented to some observers a gruesome object lesson in industrial greed and negligence at their worst. But how acute was the danger, who was really to blame, and how well did the political response rest on sound epidemiology as opposed to the clamor of panicked residents? The construction of waste facilities in minority districts represented "environmental racism" to some observers. To others environmental racism was an imaginary problem, since dumps and incinerators were often built in nonminority districts. Some observers looked on acid rain—first identified in the 1970s—as a scourge of major proportions, while others saw it as no more than an annoying but remediable problem affecting a particular type of spruce tree in mountain districts.

A combination of anxious citizens, activist scientists, antagonistic politicians, and headline-seeking journalists made each of these issues complicated and difficult to assess. That is what we should expect in a free society. Genuine scientific uncertainties, combined with disagreements about national priorities, are the perfect recipe for contentious politics. These were issues on which reasonable people could and did disagree. A highly educated population was eager to join the discussion. All had access to the press and television, all were able to speak freely, and all found sympathetic academics and journalists to amplify their concerns.

In retrospect, agencies and citizens who regarded these concerns as real but manageable appear to have been justified. The number of deaths from exposure to toxic wastes, acid rain, and ozone depletion was very small—hundreds of times smaller than the annual number of smoking-related deaths, for example. Meanwhile, positive trends in pollution abatement continued, demonstrating the success of federal policies and the likelihood that environmental fatalities would continue to diminish. The nonlethal character of America's environmental problems in the 1970s and 1980s is significant. The 1980s was also, after all, the decade in which environmental accidents abroad—above all the toxic gas leak at Bhopal, India, in 1984 and the horrifying nuclear power station explosion at Chernobyl, Ukraine, in 1986—killed thousands. Sometimes in history what *doesn't* happen is as important as what does—a point Sherlock Holmes once made about a dog that did *not* bark in the night.

ENDANGERED SPECIES

By the late 1970s environmental issues were integral to American political life. The increasingly professional environmental organizations lobbied members of Congress fiercely, while business lobbyists worked equally hard to minimize their influence. Once laws were passed, both sets of lobbyists migrated to the Environmental Protection Agency, hoping to influence the way in which the agency carried out its congressional mandate. All knew that small variations in the way rules were applied could have large economic and environmental consequences into the future.

New legislation sometimes had unexpected side effects. Environmentalists discovered, for example, that the Endangered Species Act (ESA) of 1973 could be useful in holding up proposed engineering projects that they opposed for other reasons. If the environmental impact report (itself a new phenomenon) indicated that a project threatened the habitat of an endangered species, the project itself might have to be abandoned. Such was the situation with the Tellico Dam, a proposed addition to the network of dams built over the last half century by the Tennessee Valley Authority (TVA), a creation of the New Deal. By the mid-1970s many environmentalists regarded the TVA as a menace whose self-justifying bureaucratic momentum was backed by the enforcement power of the federal government. It had flooded many of the area's fertile valleys, destroyed towns, and displaced populations. Then it had turned to building coal-fired power stations and strip-mining, creating some of the ugliest examples of pollution and blight in the entire nation.[1]

Opponents of the Tellico Dam, which was already near completion, were pleased to learn from University of Tennessee biologist David Etnier's environmental impact report that the Little Tennessee River, site of the dam, was home to a small fish, the snail darter, that could be found nowhere else and whose habitat would be destroyed by the dam and reservoir. These opponents brought a lawsuit, *Hill v. Tennessee Valley Authority*, which ultimately went all the way to the Supreme Court. In a 1978 decision, the court upheld the objectors by a vote of six to three, citing the exact language of the Endangered Species Act. For a time it seemed the dam would never be finished.[2]

The case was rife with ironies. On the one hand most environmentalists had never heard of the snail darter until it became a pretext for stopping the dam. It was not at all the kind of animal Congress had had in mind when writing endangered species legislation—Congress members had been thinking about dramatic and symbolically powerful creatures, predators like the bald eagle, the wolf, or the California condor. On the other hand the dam was itself of dubious benefit. Even prodevelopment economists doubted whether it was economically justifiable. The chairman of President Carter's Council of Economic Advisers, Charles Schultze, wrote scornfully: "Here is a project that is 95% complete, and if one sets the cost of finishing it against the total project benefits, and does it properly, it doesn't pay, which says something about the original design." It seemed to him a case of pork barrel politics, pure and simple, designed to help construction companies and a self-justifying bureaucracy far more than the area's residents.[3]

Twentieth-century members of Congress were almost unanimous in their love for federal dam projects, however, because they brought so much work and federal money into their districts. Howard Baker, a Tennessee senator who had voted for the ESA in 1973, now introduced an amendment to the act into Congress, proposing that when a major project bumped up against an endangered species, a special committee—which was soon nicknamed the "God Committee"—should resolve the issue. He feared that without such a mechanism all future projects might be prevented by the timely discovery of ever more obscure creatures in danger of annihilation. In an artful speech, Baker strove to make the snail darter and its defenders sound ridiculous:

Mr. President, the awful beast is back. The Tennessee snail darter, the bane of my existence, the nemesis of my golden years, the bold perverter of the Endangered Species Act, is back . . . In the midst of a national energy crisis the snail darter demands that we scuttle a project that would produce 200 million kilowatt hours of hydroelectric power and save an estimated 15 million gallons of oil . . . I have nothing personal against the snail darter. He seems to be quite a nice little fish, as fish go, [but] the snail darter has become an unfortunate example of environmental extremism, and this kind of extremism, if rewarded and allowed to persist, will spell doom to the environmental protection movement in this country.

Nevertheless, the God Committee voted *not* to exempt the Tellico project from the ESA.[4]

Baker followed up by attaching a clause to another piece of legislation, exempting the Tellico Dam from the act and sneaking it through the House of Representatives without discussion on a quiet day in 1979 when most members were absent. He then called in as many favors as possible to persuade the Senate to go along with his maneuver. Even Al Gore voted for the dam. President Carter, fearing ridicule if he vetoed it in the midst of the second energy crisis of the decade and needing political help on other issues, signed it into law, which permitted the dam to be finished and the valley to be flooded. For the TVA, it was a pyrrhic victory. As two of its historians note, "By the time the Tellico project was completed, the chasm between TVA and its critics was unbridgeable. Most Tellico opponents had come to believe that the TVA had conspired to foist a bad project on the public for the purpose, they argued, of providing continued employment for the personnel of a bureaucratic agency that had outlived its usefulness." In one final irony, however, very soon afterward snail darters were found elsewhere in the Tennessee Valley river system, and have continued to thrive into the new millennium.[5]

The possibility that Tellico Dam would drive the snail darter to extinction was simply a convenient argument for some participants in the controversy, but the possibility of *any* creatures becoming extinct was truly dismaying to many others. Paul and Anne Ehrlich's book *Extinction* (1981) argued that letting species go extinct was as reckless as removing the rivets from the wings of an aircraft immediately before it took off. Permitting extinctions was a way of gambling recklessly on the world's future viability. There were, wrote the Ehrlichs, obvious direct incentives for humanity to preserve biodiversity. Food and medicines came from a wide variety of plants and animals; new sources of nutrition and medicine were being discovered every year from species that might once have appeared useless. In addition, the variety of species on earth was intrinsically fascinating. Human compassion alone ought to ensure the preservation of every species, along with a more humble attitude toward the natural world. In line with their work on human overpopulation, the Ehrlichs added that curtailing the number of humans was one of the surest ways of granting to other species the space they needed to survive.[6]

The Ehrlichs recognized, and indeed celebrated, the importance of the Endangered Species Act. By the early 1980s the act was helping numerous American species to recover. It also had a strong educative function, teaching people that they should want to help species avoid extinction. The passage of time sustained these trends, especially once the act had been strengthened by congressional amendment in 1988. The longer a species was on the list, the greater the probability of its recovery, not least because it then enjoyed "recovery plans, protection from unauthorized take, protection of critical habitat, scientific research, captive breeding, public education, and habitat restoration and acquisition." The courts regularly upheld stringent enforcement of the act, and an array of federal agencies contributed to making it work. The brown pelican had recovered sufficiently well to be removed from the endangered list in 1985, and the alligator followed in 1987. Others were delisted when further research revealed greater numbers of survivors than had earlier been identified.[7] This was, surely, a superb achievement for an advanced industrial society, most of whose people lived in urban areas and had no personal familiarity with the animals and plants in question.

By contrast with the United States, most other nations had no endangered species legislation. An influential book from 1979, Norman Myers's *The Sinking Ark*, argued that the twentieth century had witnessed a steady acceleration in the rate of extinctions worldwide. Myers, an English environmental activist, had worked in Africa and was particularly concerned about the destruction of tropical rainforests. By the late twentieth century, he claimed, the rate of extinction exceeded one species per day, and the planet was going to lose hundreds of thousands more species by the end of the century, perhaps even a million. The reason was a combination of industrial pollution, habitat destruction for agriculture, and the rising human population. Like the Ehrlichs, he believed that creatures and plants should be saved both for their own sakes and also because they represented a great trove of genetic wealth, with implications for nutrition, pharmacology, and medicine. It was not enough to single out particular sympathetic species like eagles and whales—entire biomes must be set aside in which large numbers of species, many of them obscure, could continue to coexist. He noted that pollution problems could be often mitigated in a matter of years but that species loss was irrevocable.[8]

Myers also emphasized that to address this problem nation by nation was hopelessly inefficient. The first United Nations environmental conference (in Stockholm, 1972) had emphasized the worldwide significance of issues like nuclear proliferation but had not taken a holistic approach to most other questions. It was hamstrung by the fact that newly independent nations, such as Europe's ex-colonies in Africa and Asia, refused to submit to international bodies regulating issues that affected their sovereignty or their pursuit of economic growth. They were struggling to start industrial revolutions of their own and had little energy or resources to spare for conservation. Still, said Myers, "the earth's stocks of genetic variability surely belong, in some sense at least, to all inhabitants of the earth . . . They cannot, in equity, be deemed to be the sole concern of nations within whose territorial boundaries they happen to exist." The great challenge for the rest of the century, accordingly, would be to work *above* the national level to forestall further extinctions.[9]

Myers, like many other advocates of species preservation, was aware of philosophical conundrums in working to save biodiversity. Was his motive a purely human one: that *people* would benefit from the existence of these many different species? Or did the animals themselves have *rights* that should be honored and protected? If they did have rights, did they belong to the species as a whole or to individual members of the species? What about microorganisms, especially those that posed a direct threat to humans' well-being? Did they have rights too?

Peter Singer, an Australian philosopher, had definite answers to these puzzling questions. He published the landmark text *Animal Liberation* in 1975, extending the utilitarian principle of the greatest good for the greatest number from people to individual animals. Singer borrowed from consciousness-raising techniques used by the women's movement. He used the word "speciesism" in the way feminists used "sexism" and civil rights workers used "racism." There was the obvious difference that women and members of racial minorities can make moral judgments about their situation, whereas animals, as far as we know, cannot. Nevertheless, he urged readers to recognize that they must act toward animals in the knowledge that they can experience pain. Rethink familiar ideas about the treatment of animals for food, he wrote, and recognize that animal experiments, even those undertaken in search of cures for cancer, are forms of torture. He wrote lurid descriptions of factory farming, with its characteristic overcrowding, immobilizing, and psychological stressing of animals, especially geese force-fed for pâté de foie gras and calves for veal. He also made a pitch for a mass conversion to vegetarianism.[10]

Singer's central criterion was sentience, the ability to feel, so he did not propose to grant rights to bacteria. He said he drew the line "somewhere between a shrimp and an oyster." He could not deny, however, that many animals are themselves carnivorous and predatory, and that they are biologically incapable of making the switch to vegetarianism. There was, in other words, a profound asymmetry to his ideas about rights and responsibilities, which offered a critical vantage point to skeptical reviewers. His approach was the opposite of an ecologist's, for whom predation is an integral element of the energy exchanges in an ecosystem, and to whom the idea of individual rights for members of all the animals in the system is meaningless. Even so, Singer enjoyed many respectful reviews and posed an interesting set of new ethical challenges.[11]

LOVE CANAL

Meanwhile, as the Tellico Dam controversy came to a head, so did the drama of Love Canal. It was the most galvanizing pollution crisis since the publication of *Silent Spring*. Many places had suffered from smoke, smog, river pollution, oil slicks, lead paint, pesticides, and various other forms of low-level contamination over the years, but Love Canal was a suburban community built literally on top of a toxic waste dump. The Hooker Chemical Company had used the area, part of Niagara Falls, New York, as a dump in the 1940s and early 1950s, placing oil drums full of chemical residues in the bed of a disused canal, in accordance with laws of the time. Later the company sold the land to the school board for one dollar, mentioning its former use and the presence of 21,800 tons of buried waste. The board had nevertheless gone ahead with its plan to build a school on the site and had sold the balance of the land to a developer, who built several hundred single-family houses. By the 1970s, the oil drums, now more than thirty years old and rusting, were releasing their contents into the ground, including the backyards, pools, and basements of the unfortunate residents.[12]

Citizens dismayed by bubbling chemicals and evil-smelling gases began to compare notes about high rates of miscarriage, birth defects, cancers, seizures, and other health problems in the neighborhood. They appealed to the city for help but received contradictory advice or mere bland reassurances. Conflicting jurisdictions hamstrung the political and epidemiological response, with the chemical company, the city, the state, and the federal government at first shirking responsibility, then all undertaking separate—and sometimes conflicting—studies of their own. Large public health experiments take a long time. The experimental group has to be paired with a comparable control group if the study is to yield meaningful results. Then the scientific peer review process is slow and painstaking. Love Canal residents were understandably reluctant to wait for months or years before learning how much danger they faced. The early results of one experiment, alleging chromosome damage among Love Canal citizens, was leaked to the press, intensifying the residents' anxiety.[13]

The scene became a media circus, with regular TV and newspaper stories about children in danger. Lois Gibbs, a local mother of school-age children whose son had developed epilepsy, emerged as a talented organizer for the residents' association and something of a folk hero.

Lois Gibbs organized the residents of Love Canal, New York, who discovered in 1978 that their homes were built on a toxic waste dump.

New York governor Hugh Carey ordered the compensated evacuation of 239 families closest to the canal at the end of 1978. Two years of bickering over the danger to the rest of the neighborhood ended when furious residents, including Gibbs, briefly kidnapped two EPA officials. At that point President Carter declared the area a national emergency zone and authorized the compensated evacuation of another seven hundred families.[14]

The extent of the actual health danger remained unclear, and the response was guided more by political than scientific considerations. Politicians were acutely aware that there were thousands of similar dumps throughout the nation. A welter of lawsuits raised the question of whether the chemical company should be held liable, even though it had not acted illegally at the time of either the dumping or the sale of the land. Should conclusive scientific evidence of harm be necessary before government intervention, or did a lower level of evidence suffice in such cases? And how could the necessary impartial studies take place when the residents were maddened by contradictory reports and inflammatory headlines?[15]

Among the consequences of the episode was Congress's passage of the Comprehensive Emergency Response, Compensation, and Liability Act (CERCLA), better known as the Superfund Act, to clean up such sites. It recognized that in many cases only the federal government would be able to mobilize resources sufficient to undertake the necessary massive and complex cleanup operations. The most dramatic of the EPA's Superfund jobs in the ensuing years took place in the small Missouri town of Times Beach, beginning in 1983. A local contractor named Russell Bliss had regularly sprayed waste oil on the town's dirt roads to suppress dust during the 1970s. He mixed it with chemical waste that contained dioxin and other toxic compounds, which he possessed because he ran a waste disposal service and was paid to take it from the manufacturers. The fact that Bliss sprayed the oil mixture around his own home suggests that he was unaware of the danger it constituted, though he eventually became the target of several lawsuits. EPA tests in late 1982 found dioxin levels one hundred times higher than the one part per billion then regarded as a safe level for human exposure. The EPA responded by evacuating and demolishing the entire town in February 1983, with compensation to its residents. It undertook an immense cleanup over the next fourteen years, eventually restoring the area and turning the former town site into a state park.[16]

Superfund was politically controversial from the beginning. It imposed part of the cleanup costs on the original polluters, even if they had acted within the law at the time they originally dumped the chemicals. They understandably felt that they were being victimized by ex post facto legislation. Worse, if only one of many original polluters could be identified, that one might still be liable for the whole cost of the cleanup; if it failed to act, EPA would do the work but then sue to recover *three times* the amount expended. The law imposed an excise tax on companies most likely to create such hazards (oil and chemical companies), and it required that Superfund sites be cleaned to a very high standard, which escalated the cost of remedial work. A decade after the program began, one analyst estimated that the cost per life saved at the worst sites was around $340,000, but that at the less severely contaminated sites the cost was around $77 *billion* per life saved. Clearly, more cost-effective ways of increasing human safety could be found.[17] A large percentage of the fund—one study showed it to be 55 percent— had to be devoted to litigation arising out of early cases rather than to actual cleanups. The opening paragraph of a *New York Times* story from 1991, on the cleanup of the Helen Kramer landfill in Mantua, New Jersey, may explain why:

> Now that work is under way the litigation over who will pay is rapidly escalating. The Federal Government is suing 25 companies and New Jersey is suing the same companies and 25 others. A handful of these defendants have sued 239 other parties they say are responsible for most of the waste, including Philadelphia and other municipalities . . .
> Long delays, regiments of lawyers, blizzards of documents, a widespread sense of being unfairly singled out to shoul-

der others' responsibilities—this is life in the clutches of
the . . . Superfund.

The story's author pointed out various other paradoxes. If, for example,
a company that owned a cleanup site went bankrupt and the bank fore-
closed, the bank itself could become liable for the cost of the cleanup.[18]

Most states, in addition to the federal government, passed laws similar to CERCLA, imposing cleanup costs on current landowners rather
than original polluters. They too created plenty of scope for personal-
interest journalism, in which the environmental agency appeared as
villain rather than hero. For example, the owner of Pappy's Diner in
Totowa, New Jersey, who had built up his business over thirty years of
hard work, bought a piece of land adjoining his property in 1981 to
create a parking lot. New Jersey officials told him, after the purchase,
that the previous owner, Sunoco, which had run a gas station there,
had suffered leakage from underground storage tanks and that *he* was
now responsible for cleaning the ground and must comply in 120 days
or face civil and criminal charges. The state told him he could seek
redress from the previous owner, but the small-business owner was
understandably pessimistic about his chances against a corporate giant.
He told the local newspaper that failure to meet the state environmental protection department's deadlines would also provoke fines of fifty
thousand dollars per day.[19]

Love Canal put the issue of toxic waste dumps firmly on the national
environmental agenda for the 1980s. Lois Gibbs, the local activist, was
the central figure in a made-for-TV movie about the controversy and
became a minor national celebrity. She went on to found the Citizens'
Clearinghouse for Hazardous Waste (later the Center for Health, Environment, and Justice), locating communities around the country that
were in danger from exposure to poisonous chemicals, informing citizens of the risks, training local activists, and helping them to mobilize
government aid and to sue recalcitrant authorities. Superfund remained
controversial but steadily, one by one, cleaned the most hazardous
sites, and thus reduced the hazard faced by local residents.[20]

Equally significant, the Resource Conservation and Recovery Act

(RCRA) of 1976 outlawed the dumping of toxic wastes in the oceans and laid down rules for the monitoring of poisons from their moment of manufacture until the ultimate disposal of residues. Thousands of substandard dumps were closed while new ones, built to much higher standards, were monitored closely. As the historian Richard Andrews observes, "The increased cost of safe landfilling and incineration . . . fueled dramatic growth in recycling and waste reduction, adding new incentives for more efficient use of materials and stabilizing markets for capital investment in recycling facilities." These improvements in waste management were, he writes, "one of the most impressive yet least noted successes of American environmental policy." Companies eager to avoid liability and high waste-disposal costs now had a great incentive to recycle and optimize use of raw materials from the outset.[21]

ENVIRONMENTAL RACISM

During the 1980s the issue of toxic wastes prompted activist movements among racial minorities for the first time. The "Big Ten" environmental lobbies, concerned mainly with wilderness, national parks, wildlife habitat protection, birds, and fishing, had been unable to recruit poor and minority members up to that point. But minorities had sometimes responded to health threats in their own neighborhoods. In Warren County, North Carolina, in 1982, for example, residents protested against the proposed construction of a hazardous waste dump where soil contaminated with PCBs (polychlorinated biphenyls), which had previously been illegally sprayed along roadsides, was scheduled to be buried. Of one hundred counties in the state Warren ranked ninety-seventh in wealth and had the highest percentage of African-American residents. Blacks and whites joined hands in protest and civil rights celebrities like Joseph Lowery visited the area. More than five hundred people were arrested for sitting in front of dump trucks as they arrived with their loads of contaminated earth. The protestors were unsuccessful in preventing the creation of the dump, but they brought media attention to the question.[22]

A subsequent study by the United Church of Christ, released in 1987, claimed that dumps of this kind were systematically sited in places whose populations were poor and black and where organized protest and resistance were least likely. The result, said the report, was high levels of chemical-related cancers and associated illnesses in those areas. The church's spokesman coined the term "environmental racism." He admitted that this was not the kind of racism in which a racial majority singled out a minority population for systematic discrimination, but he said the result was often the same. Richer white populations were able to assert the NIMBY principle ("Not in my backyard!"), which left the poorer black population, less vocal and less well organized, to defend itself as default recipient of the toxic waste.[23] Robert Bullard, an urban sociologist, also studied the issue at the prompting of his wife, an attorney acting on behalf of a middle-class black community in Houston that was trying to prevent the development of a municipal landfill in its neighborhood. Bullard discovered that race was an even stronger marker than class and economic status in the location of dumps, which prompted him to write the first book-length study of environmental racism, *Dumping in Dixie*.[24]

Battles over proposed construction often led to divisions in minority communities because hazardous sites were also sources of work in places that sometimes offered little alternative employment. Some communities welcomed the arrival of a dump or factory, especially when its potential health hazards were not fully disclosed. Conversely, to close down a hazardous waste site deprived local residents of work; some of them regarded the risks as worth taking. As the authors of one study admitted, it was difficult to start a movement against a massive Alabama landfill that received hazardous waste from forty-eight states and three foreign countries "because the landfill offered higher paying jobs compared to other places within the county, donated money to civic and church organizations, and paid about half the county's tax revenues. Those 'hooked on toxics' fought any effort to destroy their jobs at the landfill; these were the best paying jobs they ever had, giving them a chance to improve their living conditions."[25]

Probably the single most heavily contaminated place in the entire nation was "Cancer Alley," the stretch of the Mississippi River between Baton Rouge and New Orleans. Heavily industrialized, dense with oil refineries and factories that used toxic chemicals, it bore witness to an intensive citizen protest movement beginning in 1988, even though it was now far cleaner than it had been before passage of the Clean Water Act of 1972. The Louisiana Toxics Project, an alliance of environmental, health, and trade union groups, staged an eight-mile march, reminiscent of the civil rights-era Selma to Montgomery march, to publicize and protest against the region's contamination. Spokespeople for the area's chemical industry denied accusations of racism, pointing out that the first generation of workers in these plants had been overwhelmingly white, and that black workers had migrated to the area later in search of jobs. "The idea that we intentionally put plants in predominantly black neighborhoods really isn't true," said a spokesperson for the Louisiana Chemical Association in 1993.[26]

William Reilly, President George H. W. Bush's EPA administrator, affirmed the reality of environmental inequities related to race and established a task force to study it in 1990. In light of the task force's proposals, and in response to an influential study in the *National Law Journal*, the president established an Office of Environmental Equity inside the EPA in 1992, whose report "Environmental Equity: Reducing Risks for All Communities" established principles for preventing and redressing environmental racism. President Clinton later issued an executive order directing federal agencies to be aware of the problem and to avoid it, while ensuring better access to information where communities were likely to be affected.[27]

Critics argued that the actual effect of this policy would *worsen* minorities' job opportunities by scaring away potential employers. A *New York Post* editorial noted that "any corporation in its right mind would avoid areas with large concentrations of minorities—like New York City—like the plague," lest it face accusations of environmental racism. The *Post* also denied that dumping correlated with minority populations. New York's Fresh Kills landfill on Staten Island, whose population was 85 percent white, was "the destination for virtually all the trash from heavily minority neighborhoods in Brooklyn, Queens and the Bronx."[28]

Other commentators denied that environmental racism even existed, and therefore deplored the attempt to remedy it. "The government's hasty response to a potentially bogus issue," wrote one, "costs money and jobs, thickens already dense layers of government bureaucracy, substitutes paternalism for community self-direction, and polarizes the citizenry." An economist at the University of Chicago who led a study of thirty hazardous waste sites in the area, expecting to uncover further evidence of environmental racism, found to his surprise that at least in his city there was no correlation between sites and minority population concentrations.[29]

A test case for the new policy arose in the mid-1990s when the Shintech Corporation planned a polyvinyl chloride (PVC) plant in Convent, Louisiana, most of whose population was black. The plant lay in an area that the state had designated for improving minority employment opportunities, and the company guaranteed that it would provide permanent and well-paying jobs to 165 local residents in manufacturing plastic PVC pipes. Its plans met all EPA emissions requirements. Greenpeace, which was opposed to PVC manufacturing on other grounds, took advantage of the new regulations to sue. The EPA then suspended its approval on the grounds that the opening of the plant might violate the rule signaling a "disparate impact" on minorities. The community divided sharply over whether the plant would represent a gain or a loss for the town. Lois Gibbs, now nationally famous, came to speak out against the plant. By then, however, the EPA had itself conducted a study showing that the neighbors of Superfund sites were *not* disproportionately members of minority groups, which supported skeptics' doubts about environmental racism as a genuine problem (Love Canal and Times Beach were both primarily white communities). Even so, Shintech abandoned its plans for Convent and built upriver at Plaquemines instead, where it would not face the accusation.[30]

It remained true in the 1990s and early 2000s that minorities would become active in response to local health-related movements but would not get involved in the wilderness and wildlife issues prioritized by the major environmental organizations. No wonder; as one academic observer wrote, "[I]t is unrealistic to expect someone subsisting at the margins of the urban or rural economy, or who is unemployed, to support wildlife and wilderness preservation if she or he has no access to or cannot utilize these resources." She added, "[T]he same groups and organizations which preach biological diversity in nature, and which spend small fortunes to achieve this end, practice their craft in very homogeneous racial, cultural, and social settings." Was not diversity in human groups, she asked, as important as it was in nature?[31]

OZONE AND ACID RAIN

The late 1970s and early 1980s bore witness to two new, more intangible environmental threats: the depletion of atmospheric ozone and the increase of acid rain, both of which had international implications and both of which became politically controversial.

Ozone is a form of oxygen that can be hazardous to humans at ground level but has a benign function in the upper atmosphere, where it screens out ultraviolet-B radiation. Two atmospheric scientists from the University of California, Irvine, Frank "Sherry" Rowland and Mario Molina, concluded from experiments and observations in the 1970s that the ozone layer was thinning due to the breakdown in the upper atmosphere of chlorofluorocarbons (CFCs). CFCs, best known under the trade name Freon, were a class of industrial chemicals perfected in the late 1920s by the American inventor and engineer Thomas Midgley, Jr., and widely used in air conditioners, refrigerators, and as propellants in aerosol cans. Seemingly inert and much safer than the products they had displaced, CFCs were believed, at midcentury, to enter the atmosphere and stay there, harmlessly. Rowland and Molina realized, to the contrary, that CFCs eventually broke down, interacted with stratospheric ozone, and impaired its protective function. The implications included a rise in skin cancer and blindness rates. Their studies, verified in subsequent experiments, led eventually to a Nobel Prize.[32]

In 1978 Congress responded to this discovery with legislation that phased out the use of CFCs in favor of safer substitutes. A second stage in the ozone story came with the discovery of a seasonal ozone "hole" over Antarctica in 1985. That in turn led to the signing of an international treaty, the Montreal Protocol, in 1987, by which all the major industrial nations bound themselves to phase out CFCs in the coming decades. As the scale of the danger was more thoroughly recognized, the terms of the treaty were then tightened by amendment four times during the 1990s, and CFC production shrank dramatically between the original treaty and the year 2000. Although CFC manufacturers offered scattered opposition to these restrictions, the strong scientific consensus was converted relatively easily into political action. The Montreal Protocol became the model for all subsequent international environmental agreements, though its success was rarely matched.[33]

Acid rain as a political problem followed a similar timetable to ozone. First identified in the 1960s and made newsworthy in a 1974 article in *Science* by Gene Likens, an ecologist at Cornell University, acid rain could be traced to the emission of sulfur dioxide and nitrogen oxides from factories and power stations. These chemicals had the effect of acidifying rain and snow downwind. The acid was, ironically, becoming more noticeable than in the past because the clean air legislation of the early 1970s had removed the particles from factory emissions that had previously helped neutralize the acid. New England, New York, Pennsylvania, New Jersey, and the Appalachian Mountain states were affected by acid rain originating in emissions from factories in the Midwest and Great Lakes region. Some reports suggested that it was contributing to the deaths of trees, springtime fish kills when acidified snow melted, decline of lakes' water quality, reduced atmospheric visibility, and damage to the facades of buildings. European studies even suggested that acid rain was causing catastrophic "waldsterben" (forest death), and for a while acid rain provoked frantic headlines like *Reader's Digest*'s "Scourge from the Skies" and *Field and Stream*'s "Rain of Terror." A National Academy of Sciences report from 1980 also called it "a new silent spring."[34]

Acid rain from American sources also appeared to be damaging

Canadian forests, and so became a diplomatic issue between the two nations. The Carter administration established a national monitoring system in 1979, the National Acid Precipitation Assessment Program (NAPAP), which undertook extensive studies. The scale of the problem and the large distances involved made it difficult for smaller jurisdictions to act effectively. The state of Wisconsin, for example, undertook an ambitious acid rain study program in the 1980s, but soon concluded that on its own it could achieve little. Its authors remarked: "Since much of the acid deposition in Wisconsin originates outside the state, even a 90 percent reduction of Wisconsin sulfur emissions would only slightly decrease acid deposition in Wisconsin." It added that the scientific evidence of harm remained, at that stage, in 1984, highly ambiguous.[35]

Lobbyists for the coal and power station industries, anticipating federal legislation that would be expensive to them, tried to downplay the gravity of the situation and found receptive ears in the Reagan administration, which urged further studies rather than prompt action. This approach was to be repeated by industry on many subsequent environmental issues—to delay action by emphasizing ambiguities in the science and then to call for further studies. As the historians Naomi Oreskes and Erik Conway point out, science is a probabilistic enterprise that always includes doubts and uncertainties. The policy question then becomes: what degree of scientific certainty should be sufficient to provoke political action?[36]

On the other hand, acid rain was indeed an area in which many issues were not fully understood, including the extent of a direct linear correlation between the amount of emissions at source and the amount (and strength) of acid rain downwind. A variety of scientific studies in the 1980s had already cast doubt on whether damage to forests was attributable to acid rain. Two government-sponsored panels submitted contradictory reports. The first, the 1984 Nierenberg Committee report, expressed serious concern about acid rain's effects and encouraged remedial action. The second, a massive NAPAP study costing $540 million, concluded in 1990 that acid rain was *not* threatening to destroy America's forests and played only a minor role in the acidification of lakes in the Adirondacks. Acid rain from industrial sources was real, it said, but on the scale of a nuisance rather than a catastrophe. Its most significant impact was on red spruce trees on Appalachian mountain-tops that received heavy rainfall and were frequently enveloped in clouds. At lower elevations damage was much less significant.[37]

The Reagan administration failed to act on the first report, perhaps emboldened by the fact that one of its nine authors, Fred Singer, dissented from the majority view. The George H. W. Bush administration, by contrast, under diplomatic pressure from Canada and eager to live up to Bush's declaration that his would be "the environmental presidency," decided it would act on the issue, cutting sulfur dioxide and nitrogen oxide emission levels in the 1990 revision of the Clean Air Act. Meanwhile, the tardy NAPAP report affirmed that sulfur and nitrogen compounds from industry had caused acid precipitation but that the problem was entirely manageable in scale. It "contradict[ed] the doomsayers of a decade ago who predicted widespread collapse of aquatic and terrestrial ecosystems under assault from acid rain."[38]

Using an approach suggested by Dan Dudek from the Environmental Defense Fund and Robert Hahn of the American Enterprise Institute, the amended Clean Air Act instituted an emissions trading arrangement (often referred to as "cap and trade"), according to which a total annual ceiling on the pollution was specified by government, which then distributed pollution permits to power stations and manufacturers. Companies that already emitted low levels of sulfur dioxide were allowed to sell the right to emit to companies that had not yet reduced their emissions. In other words, being a heavy polluter became more expensive and created an incentive to clean up. The most efficient companies profited from their cleanliness, whereas the laggards were allowed to keep operating at a cost, while preparing to reduce their own emissions.[39]

EPA chief William K. Reilly wrote the legislation and was able to see it through Congress despite intense lobbying from business and labor groups that anticipated severe economic losses. As the journalist Gregg Easterbrook wrote, "All the entrenched lobbying interests lost their fights regarding acid rain controls," whereas spruce trees at high altitude came out as winners. "In a profound display of the power of environmentalism . . . mere trees defeated an armada of traditionally indomitable interests: the coal lobby, the labor lobby, the business lobby, the utility lobby, the old-line Senate lobby, the conservative anti-government lobby."[40]

American industry groups had opposed the law but admitted that cap and trade was preferable to mandatory reductions at source or punitive taxation. American sulfur dioxide emissions declined 66 percent between passage of the act in 1990 and 2006, without provoking a sharp rise in the price of electricity. This was an impressive achievement, especially considering that coal burning for power generation was increasing steadily over those years. On the other hand, as the historian Ted Steinberg notes, "Germany confronted a similar acid rain problem, but managed to use stringent industry regulation, as opposed to market incentives, to reduce sulfur dioxide emissions by roughly 90 percent in just six years." The historian of technology David Hounshell also concludes that mandatory reductions across the board ("command and control") were a more effective way of lowering pollution rates quickly, because they created an immediate rather than deferred incentive to innovate.[41]

The acid rain controversy did not end with the legislation, however. Scientific studies by Edward Krug, Charles Frink, and others had already shown that the acidity of rivers and lakes was more closely connected to the surrounding soil and vegetation than to the acidity of local rainfall. Often, neighboring lakes had sharply different pH levels (sometimes by two orders of magnitude), suggesting that other factors, such as disturbance of the watershed by fire or the blowdown of trees, rather than acid rain, was the cause. Krug's study of ancient lake bed samples further suggested that in many cases the acidity had been there for millennia. Other scholars noted that some of the most acidic lakes in the United States were in Florida, which was not downwind of any major industrial area.[42]

After the NAPAP study, even *60 Minutes*, a show normally sympathetic to environmental concerns, scoffed at earlier press stories claiming that acid rain was annihilating forests and aquatic life over wide areas of the Northeast. James Mahoney, the new head of NAPAP, lamented on the show that his agency's reassuring report had been largely ignored by the mainstream media. Krug also appeared and remarked that in Northeastern lakes the acid rain problem was "so small that it's hard to see." The deputy administrator of the EPA, which took a graver view of acid rain than NAPAP, responded by attacking Krug's credibility, even though Krug had been one of the acknowledged experts on the issue over the foregoing decade, publishing extensively in peer-reviewed journals. When Krug threatened to sue for slander, the EPA official (himself not a scientist) was forced to back down and issue an apology.[43]

Aaron Wildavsky (1930–1993), a political scientist at Berkeley, argued that the original alarm was based on the assumption that "pristine" rainfall had a pH of about 5.6. He discovered that studies of rainfall in pristine settings around the world, however, showed a wide variation in acidity. Ice core samples also showed that prehistoric rain had a lower pH than 5.6 (i.e., was more acidic) in many areas. Proof of industrially induced acid rain, he argued, would be established only if long-term data from the same place showed a steady rise in rain acidity. But, he wrote, "it turns out that data from sites that have been continuously monitored since at least the early 1960s indicate that the pH of precipitation either remained the same or increased slightly [i.e., became *less* acidic]. None of the studies found rain getting more acidic."[44]

The threat of acid rain turned out, like environmental racism, to be evanescent. After seeming for a time like a grave hazard, it gradually diminished in significance and even, in the opinion of a few scholars, disappeared altogether. By the early 1990s most regarded it as a manageable but diminishing problem. On the other hand, reducing the sulfur dioxide and nitrogen oxides in the atmosphere remained desirable as a simple matter of pollution abatement. The rate of improvement of antipollution technology enabled power plants and factories to reduce emissions in line with the 1990 act, at a rate of ten million tons of sulfur dioxide per year. National action had again proved effective, making the issue of acid rain progressively less newsworthy.[45]

CANCER CONTROVERSIES

Another environmental health controversy of the 1970s and 1980s was the rising incidence of cancer among Americans. Some cancer researchers believed that a principal cause was carcinogenic compounds in the atmosphere, ground, and water supply proliferating as the chemicals industry flourished. Headlines from Love Canal and Times Beach encouraged this view, especially since the evidence of a close link between smoking and lung cancer was, by the late 1970s, overwhelmingly strong. Samuel Epstein, a British-born doctor and professor of environmental medicine at the University of Illinois, believed that environmental factors in the etiology of cancer were as high as 70 to 90 percent. He made his case with particular force in *The Politics of Cancer* (1978):

> If one thousand people died every day of cholera, swine flu, or food poisoning, an epidemic of major proportions would be at hand and the entire country would mobilize against it. Yet cancer claims that many lives daily . . . and most people believe they can do nothing about it . . . But cancer has distinct, identifiable causes . . . It can largely be prevented, but this requires more than just scientific effort or individual action. The control and prevention of cancer will require a concerted national effort.

Epstein believed that epidemiological studies and studies with laboratory animals had identified numerous industrial chemicals as carcinogens, but that industry groups, public relations campaigns, and political pressures then prevented the truth from being told clearly and unambiguously. He included chapters on vinyl chloride, asbestos, benzene, estrogen, and saccharin and defended the use of experiments in which animals were administered very high doses of these chemicals. In his view, since nearly all cancer was caused by environmental carcinogens, the best way to combat cancer was by cleaning up the environment and by pressuring government agencies to monitor industry much more strictly. Rather than focus so intensely on curing cancer, he urged, let us prevent it. It infuriated him that tobacco farmers were still receiving over $50 million per year in government subsidies. He also argued that the growing number of government agencies and organizations relating to health and environment, each with bureaucratic interests of its own (USDA, EPA, OSHA, FDA, and many others), should be rationalized and coordinated to improve the coherence of research and to prevent unnecessary duplication.[46]

But cancer research at that point was dogged by uncertainty. Even sympathetic colleagues questioned Epstein's assertion that *most* cancer was caused by environmental factors. His theory might prove to be true eventually, wrote one, but "it is unfortunate that his line of argument seems to require trying to prove the almost exclusive etiological importance of these agents." Might not genetic and "lifestyle" factors (smoking, drinking, overeating of junk food and fats, lack of exercise) also play a role, and might not money spent on identifying and remedying potential environmental carcinogens be better spent elsewhere? Reviewers also deplored Epstein's conspiratorial tone and his tendency to regard "industry" as a singular and malignant force.[47]

Richard Peto, an epidemiologist at Oxford University, was among Epstein's strongest critics. His review in *Nature* suggested that Epstein had faked some of the evidence, had omitted data that weakened his claims about the carcinogenicity of saccharin, and had understated the central role of smoking in the etiology of cancer. Peto added that while some cancers had indeed increased in recent decades, others had *decreased* (including cancer of the stomach and cervix), yet Epstein had failed to mention them. In Peto's view, it was too soon to concentrate solely on environmental factors, and much too soon to follow Epstein's proposed bans on numerous alleged carcinogens.[48]

The most concerted response to Epstein came in journalist Edith Efron's *The Apocalyptics* (1984). Paradoxically, she wrote, the rising incidence of cancer was a sign not of a worsening environment but an *improving* one. It was, when properly understood, one of the problems of success. In other ages, she argued, large numbers of people had died prematurely from diseases and accidents that they were now able to survive because of immense improvements in public health, medicine, and surgery. It was true that they became vulnerable to cancer as they aged, but this was simply because more of them lived longer than the members of any previous generation. Most cancers attacked people in the later decades of their lives.[49]

Efron, after a long digression to denounce the ideological blinders of radical environmentalists—they were the "apocalyptics" of her title—attacked Epstein's view that most cancers were caused by carcinogens in the environment. Like Peto and other critics, she did not think he had established a cause-and-effect relationship. She also took him to task on the question of "linearity." If many laboratory animals die from exposure to large doses of a potential carcinogen, does that mean that reduced doses will cause correspondingly fewer deaths, so that the death-to-dose curve on a graph will be a straight line? She doubted it, for evolutionary reasons. Humans have evolved in a world that constantly exposes them to low doses of many chemicals and to a low level of background radiation. They have therefore evolved a tolerance toward these low doses. It is reasonable to infer, therefore, that experiments in which laboratory animals were exposed to very high levels of these chemicals and developed cancers did *not* imply that humans exposed to far lower doses would share the same fate in proportional numbers.[50]

Efron believed that scientists working in government-funded cancer research institutes had a vested interest in exaggerating the degree of carcinogenicity in everyday chemicals. Their jobs depended on maintaining a high level of public alarm and anxiety. Her book was immensely successful in the United States and abroad. One historian notes that its appeal was "similar in certain ways to the sweeping simplicity of Epstein's *Politics of Cancer*; both assume that powerful, ill-willed men in high places are making us sick (with cancer, according to Epstein; with fear of cancer, according to Efron). Both recognize that politics saturate research in these areas."[51]

Cancer and carcinogens were, of course, highly emotional issues and tended to draw a great deal of media and political attention. Environmental organizations became steadily more effective at cultivating the national media with cancer-related stories. As they did so, they developed the power to shape public opinion in a way that itself became controversial. For example, the Natural Resources Defense Council (NRDC) won unprecedented coverage in February 1989 for its report "Intolerable Risk: Pesticides in Our Children's Food." With the help of a professional public relations company, it offered an exclusive to *60 Minutes*. The show's host, Ed Bradley, told an audience of about forty million one Sunday evening that apples and apple juice were contaminated with a carcinogenic growth and ripening agent called Alar, and that it was going to cause premature cancer deaths in thousands of children. Supermarkets reacted by taking apples and apple juice out of their stores, while schools urged children and their parents to stop consuming them. A week later Meryl Streep and other celebrities gave a press conference on behalf of an NRDC action group, Mothers and Others for Pesticide Limits, timed to revive the controversy just as the first wave of headlines subsided.[52]

After a surge of claims and angry counterclaims, *60 Minutes* aired a second segment on Alar in May 1989 that featured the apple industry's rebuttal, casting serious doubt over the NRDC's claims. Numerous apple growers were nevertheless bankrupted that year and the industry took two years to recover, by which time Alar's manufacturer, Uniroyal, had taken the product off the American market. As its title suggests, the NRDC report was not a peer-reviewed scientific study but a call to action. EPA had tested the chemical daminozide (Alar was its trade name) in the early 1980s and tests with laboratory mice had shown a perceptible carcinogenic effect from very high dosages over an animal's lifetime. Different branches of the agency had disagreed over whether it would cause as many as five premature cancer deaths per one hundred thousand people or as few as one per million. Still, it was the public relations campaign, as one observer wrote, that "elevated the Alar controversy from the level of regulatory dispute to that of national pandemonium." A 1991 United Nations study eventually showed that the amounts of Alar actually in use had virtually no health consequences for human consumers of any age.[53]

The Alar case caused much soul-searching among journalists, some of whom admitted that they had let themselves be manipulated by an artful public relations campaign. An editorial in *Science* pointed out that to start rumors of this kind—disproportionate to the actual danger—was to imitate the boy who cried wolf. When a real danger came along, a jaded public would be far less likely to believe it. But public interest groups have conflicts of interest, just as do business groups. Businesses prefer to be out of the limelight; public interest groups prefer to be in it. "Because they are selling products in the marketplace, businesses downplay discussions of hazard. Because public interest groups acquire members by publicity, they emphasize hazards. Each group convinces itself that its worthy goals justify oversimplification to an 'ignorant' public. Businesses today have product liability and can incur legal damages if they place a dangerous product on the market." But, said *Science*, "public interest groups have no such constraints," even today, and victims of irresponsible scares have no redress.[54]

Most other academic scientists who commented on the case believed that it said more about sensationalistic journalism and a gullible public than about real health risks. NRDC, on the other hand, continued to assert that its conduct was justified and that the danger had been real. It took the view that the EPA's supervision of pesticides was slack and that it was too willing to permit the industry to use dangerous chemicals simply for cosmetic and commercial reasons.[55]

MAJOR ENVIRONMENTAL DISASTERS

If Alar turned out not to pose an "intolerable risk" after all, the 1980s certainly bore witness to the fact that some environmental risks really were intolerable. Two disasters abroad, in particular, demonstrated the gulf between conditions in the United States, where regulation and oversight were becoming more rigorous, and those in countries where regulation was weak or where private ownership, freedom of the press, and citizen participation in politics were prohibited.

In 1984 a leak of methyl isocyanate from a Union Carbide pesticide factory in Bhopal, India, exposed hundreds of thousands of people to a highly poisonous toxin, killing about twenty-five hundred people outright and several thousand more in the ensuing weeks. This was almost certainly the worst industrial disaster in the entire history of the world, more than one hundred times more lethal than the Donora, Pennsylvania, disaster of 1948, the worst in U.S. history. Safety precautions at the factory were far inferior to those at a comparable Union Carbide plant in the United States, local managers were poorly trained, and the company had severely cut the workforce after putting the plant up for sale. India, then in the midst of its own industrial revolution, bore witness to Dickensian scenes of suffering and inequality, as well as horrifying levels of managerial negligence. To add insult to injury, the Indian government reacted to survivors' demonstrations for compensation with repression. The accident raised not only a worldwide humanitarian response but also a series of challenging questions about the morality of America-based multinational corporations maintaining lower standards abroad than at home.[56]

In 1986 an explosion at Chernobyl, a nuclear power station in the Ukraine, showered radioactive debris over parts of Ukraine, Russia, Belarus, Georgia, Poland, Sweden, Germany, and Turkey, and elevated levels of atmospheric radiation as far away as Japan and the United States. It killed thirty-one people immediately, caused widespread exposure to high levels of radiation to thousands more, and forced a mass evacuation of the area, eventually leading to the relocation of 350,000 people. Estimates of the eventual death toll from cancers that developed gradually after exposure to radiation ranged as high as 200,000 (Greenpeace), though the World Health Organization suggested 4,000.[57]

The Chernobyl disaster, like that at Bhopal, was attributable largely to faulty design, bad maintenance, and negligent management. The response to the accident was delayed by the Soviet government's obsessive secrecy, but detection of elevated radiation throughout Europe soon thwarted its plan to avoid an announcement. Astonishingly, the three surviving reactors at the power station were kept in operation (though another one was severely damaged by fire in 1992). Nothing in the United States was remotely comparable, though that may be partly because the Americans were luckier at Three Mile Island than the Soviets at Chernobyl. One report comparing the two noted that in both cases "mechanical systems were defeated by operators who did not understand what they were doing and took actions that deliberately overrode safely systems." Grave design weaknesses in the Soviet reactor, however, gave its operators a far shorter time in which to respond.[58]

There was certainly nothing about the United States to suggest that it was exempt from the possibility of human-error-related accidents. A severe maritime accident in March 1989 added another chapter to the intense environmental disputes that had surrounded the building of the Alaska pipeline in the 1970s. Minor by comparison with Bhopal and Chernobyl, it was nevertheless a turning point in the history of American environmental regulation. The supertanker *Exxon Valdez*, laden with thirty-eight thousand tons of crude oil, foundered on the Bligh Reef in Prince William Sound soon after leaving the southern terminal of the pipeline at Port Valdez. The accident happened at midnight in bad weather, due chiefly to the negligence of the ship's captain, John Hazelwood, who was alleged to have been drunk at the time and who had left the bridge in the hands of an unqualified junior officer. Oil began to pour from the torn hull of the tanker, creating an immense slick that flowed south and west for the next several weeks. Stretching five hundred miles and affecting thirteen hundred miles of beaches, it massacred local wildlife. Vivid and dismaying photographs in the press and on television brought the reality home to watchers throughout the world. Seabirds blackened, choking, and filthy and sea otters dying in the oily water created a public relations nightmare for Exxon.[59]

The various authorities involved had underestimated the potential dangers they faced and had neglected to prepare for the worst. Contingency plans were soon overwhelmed by the scale of the spill, and almost at once the organizations that should have hastened to react began worrying about legal liability. "Lawyers representing Exxon, Alyeska (the pipeline consortium), the state of Alaska, and the Coast Guard . . . all urged their clients not to risk taking the initiative in cleanup efforts because of potential for later liability claims." The company eventually flew in cleanup crews to rescue what animals it could and to clean the soiled beaches. Many of these workers labored long hours in oil-soaked clothes with no respirators. This situation led to charges of a hazardous work environment and endangerment of workers' health and safety.[60]

Exxon eventually spent four years on the project, at a cost of about $2.5 billion. It also paid $125 million in fines to the government for violation of the Clean Water Act and other laws. Civil lawsuits persisted for the next nineteen years. Journalists who wrote the first books about the disaster noted that Exxon itself wielded great power over the communities affected by the spill by offering them employment and tempting them to cooperate with the company's public relations and damage control operations. One of these authors, John Keeble, argued that Exxon seemed to be at least as interested in cleaning up its image as in cleaning up the oil itself.[61]

Some subsequent studies discovered that the long-term toxicological impact of the spill was profound, depressing wildlife population rates and increasing mortality long beyond the initial phase of critical destruction. Other studies emphasized the relatively rapid rate of recovery, as the oil dispersed or broke down naturally, enabling fish, bird, and otter populations to rebound. Ironically, several observers concluded that the areas that *were* cleaned exhibited durable problems of their own. The combined presence of large numbers of people, the detergents and high-temperature water they used as they tried to clean the beaches, and the trash and sewage they left behind had adverse consequences sometimes as bad as those caused by the spill itself. Ironically, the best response might even have been no response, though for political reasons that would also have been intolerable.[62]

THE ENVIRONMENTAL CRISIS of the late 1960s and early 1970s had centered on the visible menace of pollution. Polluted skies, rivers, lakes, and landfills looked horrible and smelled worse. By the 1980s environmental crises were becoming increasingly massive—sometimes global—

but also increasingly invisible. No one could see the hole in the ozone layer, acid rain, environmental carcinogenicity, or environmental racism, and plenty of voices questioned whether they even existed. To be understood they required a level of abstract and conceptual thinking, which in turn made reaching agreement about how to react to them all the more elusive. These were also the years in which difficult questions about remediation arose, even when there was widespread agreement about a problem. Everyone agreed that toxic waste dumps should be cleaned up, for example, but the degree of cleaning and its cost-effectiveness were difficult to decide—on both technical and economic grounds.

While a wide array of such environmental controversies persists up to the present, occasional dramatic events continue to show that environmental change is not always invisible or abstract. The most appalling accident of recent years is the Deepwater Horizon disaster of April 2010. An explosion on an oil rig in the Gulf of Mexico, about forty miles off the coast of Louisiana, killed eleven men outright, injured dozens more, forced an evacuation of the blazing rig, and set off a crude oil leak from the seabed that gushed for nearly three months before it could be capped. An immense oil slick, formed from the two hundred million gallons lost, spread across the northern Gulf, killing birds, fish, and marine animals, contaminating beaches with tar balls, blackening marsh grasses, and once again exceeding the scope of contingency plans to contain the damage. Vast quantities of oil seem to have remained far beneath the surface, difficult to study and with environmental consequences not fully understood. Nearly two million gallons of toxic oil dispersants used to combat the gusher contributed to the environmental damage. Entire communities whose livelihoods revolved around fishing and tourism were paralyzed in what was referred to by President Obama as the biggest environmental disaster in American history. Some of them had only recently recovered from the impact of Hurricane Katrina in 2005.[63]

BP, owners of the sunken rig, pleaded guilty to charges of criminal negligence in a 2012 trial and paid a fine of $4.5 billion. They also faced literally thousands of civil suits from people whose livelihoods and communities had been affected, most of which, as these words are written, have still not been resolved. Four states, Florida, Alabama, Louisiana, and Mississippi, alone have sued to recover lost revenues that they estimate at $34 billion.[64]

The Deepwater Horizon disaster was, not surprisingly, compared with the *Exxon Valdez* disaster from twenty-two years before. The good news of the intervening years was that the number of tanker incidents had declined steadily. Tanker ships were now built with double hulls and with multiple sealed compartments so that collisions or ground-ings were much less likely to cause large-scale spillage. The develop-ment of global positioning technology had also improved navigation safety, while the creation of one-way sea-lanes in narrow waters such as the English Channel had cut down on the number of collisions. The bad news was that oil rig blowouts had become *more* common as exploration teams worked in ever deeper waters and drilled to record depths, where pressures were extremely high. When something did go wrong, moreover, it was incomparably more difficult to remedy because it required coordinated work on the seabed. BP's first efforts to stop the oil flow failed—it was working in an unfamiliar and difficult set-ting, at the limits of current technical knowledge.[65]

The assignment of blame for the Deepwater Horizon disaster is complicated, but certain points seem fairly clear. Most studies agree that BP and Transocean, the rig's owners, had cut corners on safety procedures for the sake of making quicker and cheaper progress on the project in the months leading up to the disaster. This was in part a reaction to the slack regulatory environment of the business-friendly George W. Bush administration between 2001 and 2009. The Interior Department's Minerals Management Service expedited BP's permits and exempted the company from submitting detailed environmental impact statements. Once the accident happened, the Obama adminis-tration was determined to make BP pay the lion's share of cleanup costs and to tighten regulation to prevent another accident. At the same time, it wanted to be sure the company did not go bankrupt, lest tax-payers be left to foot the bill. The Gulf itself, as a primary source of American domestic oil production, could not be closed down, though the president did place a six-month moratorium on new exploration. The relevant federal agency issued new regulations to ensure that subsequent wells would be drilled according to stricter safety standards and with closer supervision. Environmental scientists noted that the unprecedented depths at which the drilling now took place required an overhaul of the regulators' assumptions about how oil entered the environment.[66]

Everyone involved in responding to the disaster agreed that it ought never to have happened, that nothing comparable must happen in the future, and that greater care was essential in managing deepwater drilling projects. Beyond that, the usual divergence of opinions took place. To environmental groups the accident was symptomatic of a sick society that had made itself slavishly dependent on cheap oil, no matter how dangerous its pursuit had become. To business groups it was a deplorable but unrepresentative event, in which the culprit was not improper societal values but poor management and negligence in one particular corporation.[67]

CHAPTER 6

ANTI- AND COUNTER-
ENVIRONMENTALISTS

THE ELECTION OF RONALD REAGAN in 1980 transformed the
character of environmental politics and intensified the national environmental debate. Reagan's White House predecessors, Johnson,
Nixon, Ford, and Carter, had shared the broad public concern about
the environment and supported an active national policy to improve it.
Reagan was far less sympathetic. In his view environmental protection
had already gone too far, with regulation that was too intrusive and
costly. He believed that regulation slowed economic growth, making
America vulnerable in its Cold War competition against the Soviet
Union. He appointed to key federal positions at the Environmental
Protection Agency and the Department of the Interior men and women
who were bluntly and openly critical of the recent legislation and opposed to the entire concept of environmentalism.

For the first two years of the administration, Reagan's appointees
tried to dismantle or weaken the regulations they were supposed to be
enforcing and to shrink the agencies over which they presided. An outcry not only from angry Democrats but also from within Reagan's own
Republican Party, however, made this approach politically untenable.
He was forced to dismiss his antienvironmental appointees in 1983 and

replace them with less confrontational figures. These events marked a watershed in American environmental politics. On the one hand they established the principle that from now on every candidate, every office holder, and every federal appointee must at least pay lip service to the ideal of a clean, safe, and beautiful environment. On the other hand they bore witness to a growing disenchantment with environmental regulation among conservative Americans.

From the 1980s and through the millennium, an influential *counter*environmentalism developed in the United States, bringing together politicians, foundations, journalists, scientists, and intellectuals who questioned national environmental policies. They were part of the rising conservative movement, the "New Right," which had swept Reagan to power. The New Right favored militant anticommunism and economic growth; it hated big government, federal regulation, and high taxes. New Right activists also developed an intellectual critique of mainstream environmentalism, challenging what they saw as its excessive pessimism and asserting that economic growth and environmental improvement could advance together. Paradoxically, they believed that environmentalists could not be trusted to safeguard the environment.[1]

Counterenvironmentalists noted that the ghastly famines predicted by Paul Ehrlich and others for the late 1970s and early 1980s, though now due, were *not* happening in America and Europe, that the country was *not* running out of raw materials, that air and water quality were improving, not worsening, and that life expectancy was continuing to increase—all of which suggested high and rising levels of health and well-being. As we saw in earlier chapters, scattered objections had already greeted the glum prophecies made by Vogt, Osborn, Carson, Commoner, Ehrlich, and the Club of Rome. The passage of time appeared to give cogency to these objections and to offer support to a more optimistic vision of the future.[2]

In addition to criticizing the costly and highly bureaucratized programs established by the federal government during the 1970s, the counterenvironmentalists scorned environmentalists as a group. Their five major accusations were

1. That environmentalists were really socialists in disguise, threatening American freedom in the name of a centralized, planned economy

2. That environmentalists were really devotees of a sectarian religion, pagans and Earth-worshippers

3. That environmentalists were a selfish, privileged elite who wanted to protect their advantages from everyone else

4. That environmentalists were well-meaning but ignorant souls who failed to understand that economic growth was the necessary prelude to environmental protection

5. That environmentalists were hippies who rejected American values but now aimed to foist their alternative values on everybody else

There was much caricature in these views, but also a few grains of truth. Several environmental writers emerging from the New Left of the 1960s *were* sympathetic to socialism, many of them had been involved in the counterculture and back-to-the-land movement, and a few radical environmentalists *were* developing a religious ecospirituality.

Counterenvironmentalists liked to depict themselves as embattled outsiders to the establishment, but their access to corporate funding, to the major media, to influential conservative think tanks, and increasingly to congressional staffs made such claims disingenuous. They laid the foundations of the environmental skepticism that would be embodied in America's 1997 rejection of the Kyoto Protocol.

This chapter, on the history of political and intellectual critics of environmentalism, distinguishes between *anti*environmentalists on the one hand and *counter*environmentalists on the other. It is an important distinction. President Reagan and James Watt, for example, were antienvironmentalists in the sense that they saw no benefit to the environmental achievements of the foregoing decade. By contrast, many other figures considered here, including Ben Wattenberg, Julian Simon, Gregg Easterbrook, and Wallace Kaufman, are better understood as counterenvironmentalists,. They were seriously interested in environmental problems but deplored the attitudes, methods, and rhetoric of mainstream environmentalists. These two categories, "anti-" and "counter-," are heuristic, offering what seems to me a necessary opportunity to distinguish between very different objections to American environmentalism. "Counterenvironmentalism" was not part of the era's vocabulary, so far as I can discover, not least because these figures did not use the word themselves and because their critics labeled all of them as "antienvironmentalists" without making the distinction.

THE REAGAN ERA

Complaints about the environmental bureaucracy were sometimes justified. The bureaucracy usually did move slowly and was often more responsive to political imperatives in Washington than to real environmental problems on the ground. The new requirement for environmental impact statements before any major new project could get started, and the opportunities the statement process offered for delaying construction, infuriated conservatives. "Regulations of the EPA," wrote Arizona senator Barry Goldwater in 1979, "have added hundreds of billions of dollars to the cost of our mineral products, electric power, highway construction, food, automobiles, and housing. It almost seems as though the government regulators were determined we should all freeze to death in the dark." He believed that it also diminished America's position in the Cold War, since the Soviet Union continued to develop at full speed without concern for environmental niceties.[3]

One part of counterenvironmentalism, the "Sagebrush Rebellion," was particularly strong in Goldwater country, the Western states, where the federal government remained a major landholder (of about 760 million acres). The federal Bureau of Land Management (BLM) administered much of this land and had for decades sold grazing rights to local farmers and ranchers. The ranchers nearly always pressed for permission to graze more cattle on the land. The BLM countered that overgrazing would lead to erosion, and therefore it restricted the number of cattle. Since the ranchers rarely owned enough land of their own to run big herds, the BLM was in effect deciding how many cattle each farmer could own, and was coming up with numbers the ranchers thought too low. This was a form of federal paternalism they strongly resented. On the other hand, local traditions, and the fact that the ranchers and local BLM managers lived side by side and knew each other, could lead to compromises that mitigated the rigors of official policy.[4]

The Sagebrush rebels were an alliance of Western ranchers, developers, outdoor groups, and politicians who wanted the federal government to hand over its landholdings to the several states, leaving them to decide how it should be used. Congress passed the Federal Land Policy and Management Act (FLPMA) in 1976, which declared the *permanent* character of the BLM lands as a national asset, proposed a survey to establish some of them as wilderness areas, and ordered a new policy of grazing-related environmental impact statements. From the ranchers' point of view, a bad but familiar situation was about to get worse. Western user groups "saw it as the end of an era of western control . . . a violation of an implied trust that public lands would eventually be turned over to the states for disposal. They perceived a transfer of power and decision-making authority from BLM field managers to Washington bureaucrats amassing power on the Potomac."[5]

The Nevada legislature declared in 1979 that it intended to take over all the federal lands in the state. It hosted a conference that year, attended by senior representatives of the other Western states. Several more legislatures followed Nevada's lead by passing symbolic legislation, though none actually made good on its threat to seize the federal lands within its borders. The victory of Ronald Reagan in the presidential election of 1980 appeared to give the rebels the kind of sympathetic support at the top they had hoped for.

Reagan declared himself a friend of the Sagebrush Rebellion. He proposed selling off much of the land or ceding it to the states. Ironically, this offer at once knocked the stuffing out of the "rebellion," partly because closer studies had shown that many of the lands would be a financial liability rather than an asset, the burden of which financially hard-pressed state governments could not afford. Outdoor and off-road groups, which had wanted easier access, lost interest if the land was going to be privatized and fenced. Ranchers also recognized that privatization might *worsen* their situation if they had to buy and then pay taxes on the land instead of just paying a grazing fee. On reflection they were content to resume the relatively easy conditions that had governed their use of the public domain before 1976. Western urban interests also opposed the rebellion because they foresaw that if states acquired the lands and put them on sale, a

James Watt, President Reagan's Secretary of the Interior, 1981.

sudden glut of available land would knock the bottom out of the real estate market. Few rebellions have ended so quickly, with scarcely a whimper.[6]

Reagan himself had no interest in environmental issues. As a candidate for governor of California in 1966 he had remarked, "If you've looked at a hundred thousand acres or so of trees—you know, a tree is a tree, how many more do you need to look at?" The remark was often paraphrased as, "If you see one redwood, you've seen them all." In one of the state's old-growth redwood groves in 1967 he had denied that the trees were beautiful and remarked simply that they were "just a little higher than the others." He, like Goldwater, was a hard anticommunist who wanted to maximize economic growth, making the United States as strong as possible in the Cold War.[7]

Reagan's key appointments reflected his prodevelopment views.

James Watt, his secretary of the interior, came from Colorado, where he had been closely identified with antienvironmental and prodevelopment corporations and foundations. Outspoken, tactless, and confrontational, Watt came to D.C. from the presidency of the Mountain States Legal Foundation, a Denver organization founded by the Coors brewing family. At the foundation he had led litigation on behalf of oil, chemical, power, and agribusiness companies, often *against* the Department of the Interior, trying to create a more favorable (and more laissez-faire) regulatory situation for Western development interests. Watt opened previously sequestered lands to logging, mining, and oil drilling, and declared: "We will mine more, drill more, cut more timber."[8]

Watt imposed a moratorium on creating new national parks, even though the number of visitors to the existing parks had risen during the 1970s from 172 million to 300 million. He closed down the Office of Surface Mining, which was supposed to regulate the conduct of strip-mining operations, and he leased far more federal land for new strip mines than any predecessor. He wanted to see more exploratory drilling for oil offshore and proposed to ease the licensing process. "I don't believe government should stand in the way of the free market," he declared in a characteristic speech, "and I'm here to do what I can to make sure it doesn't."[9]

Watt did not merely oppose environmentalists on the issues; he disliked them personally and showed that he intended to take their philosophical disagreements to heart. He affronted the "green" lobbyists in Washington from the outset by refusing to maintain his predecessor Cecil Andrus's policy of regular meetings to discuss issues of mutual concern. It was, ironically, one of the best things that could have happened for environmental groups. They ran successful membership drives, depicting Watt as a menace to the future of the country. Membership of the Sierra Club jumped from 181,000 to 346,000 between 1981 and 1983. The Environmental Defense Fund sued him for postponing the addition of forty-four new species to the endangered species list.[10]

Conservative columnist George Will was among the first Republicans to realize that Watt was more of a liability than an asset to the administration:

> He has no patience for the to-ing and fro-ing practiced by persons who understand that in politics the straightest line between two points is rarely the easiest route. He speaks almost too clearly, indifferent to the bureaucratic art of constructing whole paragraphs perfectly devoid of substance. His cocksureness, his thirst for conflict, his tone-deafness regarding his own shrillness, have invigorated environmental groups . . . He sometimes seems un-reconciled to government's stewardship concerning community assets. Some assets, such as wilderness areas, cannot survive if unprotected from the morals of the marketplace.[11]

Businesspeople also recognized that, whatever his intentions, Watt was making their public relations problem worse rather than better. George Keller, the chairman of Standard Oil of California, told a journalist, "Jim Watt has done more to harm our industry than any other government official in recent history. You couldn't carry on a conversation with him without getting aggravated." Even the White House staff presented Watt with a plaster model of a human foot with a hole in it, symbolizing his tendency to shoot himself in the foot with provocative remarks.[12]

Anne Gorsuch at EPA was no better. She was unusual in the history of Washington bureaucracy in that she took pride in trying to make her agency smaller—the opposite of a normal administrator's approach. In her two years at EPA she laid off employees, failed to replace those who retired or resigned, and applied for smaller budget allocations. Inheriting a workforce of 14,075, she had trimmed it to 10,396 by early 1983. She was also far less aggressive in suing polluters—prosecutions fell from 230 in 1980 to just 42 in 1981—and she declined to follow her predecessors' interpretation of the pollution legislation. A former Carter employee at EPA, William Drayton, wrote: "Knowing that the public will never stand for the repeal of these environmental laws, Reagan is gutting them through the personnel and budgetary back doors. With only the shattered shell of an EPA left, our environmental statutes will be virtually meaningless." Employees who had been proud of the agency's mission became progressively more disillusioned and leaked news of every controversial initiative to the media.[13]

Rita Lavelle at Superfund, like Gorsuch at EPA, dragged her feet with cleaning up the most dangerous waste dumps. She had previously worked for Aerojet, which the EPA had identified as having illegally dumped toxic chemicals. When an EPA engineer, Hugh Kaufman, blew the whistle on Lavelle for making sweetheart deals with the companies she was supposed to be regulating, she retaliated by having him followed and harassed.[14]

Republicans as well as Democrats appealed in public for the removal of Watt, Gorsuch, and Lavelle. A racist joke Watt told at a public hearing in 1983 gave the president the pretext he needed to get rid of him. By then Gorsuch had also been forced out under a cloud of suspicion. She and Lavelle were both prosecuted for misconduct in office—the so-called "Sewergate" scandals, in which they had allowed favored companies to avoid compliance with environmental laws and regulations. Lavelle was sentenced to six months' imprisonment for perjury and misuse of CERCLA funds while Gorsuch was condemned for contempt of Congress.[15]

Reagan then ostentatiously invited William Ruckelshaus, the original EPA administrator and one of the Republican heroes of the Watergate era, to return and to restore order and morale at the agency. Ruckelshaus improved enforcement of the pollution laws, increased the number of Superfund investigations, and won the applause of most mainstream environmental organizations. William Clark moved from the position of national security adviser to secretary of the interior. He believed in the general Reagan approach to the environment but was far more circumspect and less confrontational than Watt. As *Time* put it, his appointment "would assure western right wingers, an important part of the president's political power base, that [Reagan's] policies would continue without being enmeshed in the controversies set off by Watt's loose-lipped remarks." Reagan himself had learned a lesson about the emotional power of the environment as a political issue. From then on, he was careful to speak respectfully on all environmental questions and to avoid giving the impression of negligence or indifference. The year 1983 marked the moment at which public denigration of environmentalism became politically impossible. His Republican successor, George H. W. Bush, campaigned in 1988 on the promise that he would be "the environmental president."[16]

COUNTERENVIRONMENTALIST IDEAS

Environmentalists and counterenvironmentalists each tried to depict the other as selfish and greedy. While environmentalists saw themselves as high-minded advocates for an abused environment, their opponents answered that they were in fact selfish elitists trying to consolidate their advantages. For example, wrote these opponents, federal restrictions on land use were threatening ordinary folks' livelihoods by preventing them from living where they wanted and from pursuing their favorite outdoor recreations. According to this view, a wealthy and privileged minority had secured favorable political treatment by clothing its ambitions in the rhetoric of environmental protection. Local people, by contrast, were being excluded from the best places to live, work, and play. The environmental movement posed as people-friendly but was really an upper-middle-class assault against blue-collar workers aspiring to middle-class dignity, against small-business owners and against the poor. "What is nowadays called protecting the environment," wrote one journalist sympathetic to these claims, "is in fact the protection of economic and social privilege." Titles from the late 1970s and early 1980s embodying the idea included Bernard Friedan's *The Environmental Protection Hustle* (1979) and William Tucker's *Progress and Privilege* (1982). Both authors showed that the wealthy owners of prime locations knew how to use environmental rules to prevent any further building in their neighborhoods.[17]

A journalist from the Pacific Northwest, Allen May, echoed this view while neatly inverting the familiar rhetoric of wilderness advocates. While they spoke about the overbearing power of lumber and mining corporations, he described the *environmentalists* as the holders of "crushing power." Communities whose members worked in the forests of Oregon and Washington, he wrote, suffered "the frustrations of years of looking on, helpless and voiceless, while the hated wilderness conservationists remorselessly destroyed the things loggers value most."[18]

Even citizens who had managed to acquire land in the most desirable areas found, sometimes, that they were prevented from using it. For example, if an area was wetland on which migratory birds rested or if it was the habitat of endangered species, building was forbidden. Owners who had bought land on which to build only to find that subsequent legislation now prohibited them from doing so were especially embittered, arguing that such rules infringed their property rights and that they should be compensated. A clause of the Fifth Amendment specifies compensation when private land is seized under eminent domain to realize a compelling public good. But here was a situation in which the owners did not have to surrender the land itself but rather to submit to restrictions on how it might be used. Were they entitled to compensation for "regulatory takings"?[19]

University of Chicago law professor Richard Epstein said yes. His book *Takings* (1985) offered an interpretation of the Fifth Amendment that justified compensation for anyone restrained by environmental regulations, health and safety rules, or even zoning regulations. Judges appointed by Presidents Reagan and Bush in the 1980s and early 1990s sympathized with this approach, notably Judge Loren Smith of the U.S. Court of Federal Claims, who gave "takings" awards to a series of litigants when they were prohibited, by environmental rules, from quarrying, mining, and building on their own land. In 1992 the Supreme Court heard a "takings" case. Developer David Lucas had bought land on the South Carolina barrier islands in 1986 with the intention of building vacation homes. In 1988 the state government restricted building in ecologically fragile areas such as those he owned, prompting Lucas to sue for compensation, since the effective value of the land had

Julian Simon, the economist who denied overpopulation
and the exhaustibility of natural resources.

fallen to zero. The Supreme Court agreed with his claim in a six-to-three decision, *Lucas v. South Carolina Coastal Council*. The effect of the case was, potentially, to strengthen landowners' rights and limit those of regulators.[20]

Another strand of counterenvironmentalism could be found in the work of economists and social scientists who questioned the prevailing environmental orthodoxy. Among the best known and most provocative was Julian Simon (1932–1998), a professor of business first at the University of Illinois and later at the University of Maryland. Simon had at first shared the prevailing view that overpopulation was a serious problem and had published *The Economics of Population Growth* (1977) as a contribution to alleviating it. Further scrutiny of the economic and demographic situation in the late 1970s, however, gave him second thoughts. He then received an emotional push that prompted a complete change of heart. In Washington one day, at the Iwo Jima memorial, he recalled the funeral eulogy delivered by an army rabbi after the battle on Iwo Jima in World War II. The rabbi had asked: "How many who would have been a Mozart or a Michelangelo or an Einstein have we buried here?" That question prompted Simon to reflect: "Have

I gone crazy? What business do I have trying to help arrange it that fewer human beings will be born, each of whom might be a Mozart or a Michelangelo or an Einstein—or simply a joy to his or her family?" In subsequent works, he argued that rising population was making the world better, not worse, that more industrialization was desirable, and that we had every reason to be optimistic about the future. His first general statement of these themes came in *The Ultimate Resource* (1981), whose title referred to humans. A growing population, he now believed, was "a moral and material triumph."[21]

In Simon's view, it was misleading to regard a growing population solely as "more mouths to feed." Every mouth, after all, was attached to two hands and a brain, whose creativity and capacity for work far outweighed the demands they made on resources. It might be true in the short run that a family with four children is able to give each one a little less than a family with two, but once those four have grown up, their contributions to society will more than outweigh the cost of their upbringing. Prosperity and rising population go hand in hand.[22]

Meanwhile, said Simon, the food supply was rising more quickly than the population, disproving neo-Malthusian fears. Even more impressive, "the quantity of land under cultivation has been decreasing because it is more economical to raise larger yields on less land than to increase the total amount of farmland." Immense yield increases from year to year were being achieved thanks to improved crop strains and the green revolution, even though the percentage of the American population employed in agriculture continued to decline. As a result, "land for recreation and for wildlife has been increasing rapidly in the U.S."[23]

Simon regarded Paul Ehrlich and other environmental pessimists as wrong not only on population but also on the question of resource depletion. As an economist, he believed that the way to test whether a commodity was plentiful or scarce was to look not at remaining reserves throughout the world (itself a technically difficult and unreliable method) but to look at *prices*. If a commodity was scarce or in high demand, its price would rise. If it was plentiful, its price would fall. He included in *The Ultimate Resource* a series of graphs showing the trend in prices for numerous commodities over the last two centuries. The graphs showed that nearly all of them had been getting steadily cheaper, in real terms, decade after decade and century after century, even though the world's finite supplies had presumably been diminished.[24]

Why was that? It was because "resources" themselves were not mere minerals in the ground, but a combination of minerals and human ingenuity. Throughout human history, he noted, the volume of oil in the world had been immense. That didn't make it a resource. It only became a resource when someone worked out how to extract it and refine it into usable kerosene and, later, usable gasoline. The history of the last two centuries showed countless new materials becoming "resources" for the first time. It was reasonable to believe, Simon added, that other materials not currently being used would *become* resources. Each generation built on the achievements of its predecessors, developed new and improved technologies, and became more adept in recycling, such that later generations enjoyed ever increasing abundance.[25]

From time to time, he agreed, short-term crises of supply did push up the cost of a commodity or resource. When that happened, however, there was a renewed incentive to seek an alternative. It was true, said Simon, that we cannot *guarantee* that crises will always bring forth remedies, but the fact that they have so often done so in the past makes it reasonable for us to believe that the process will continue. The longer a trend has continued, the more likely it is to persist into the future. He also noted that improvements in efficiency, in recycling, in resource extraction, and in manufacturing using fewer raw materials all had reassuring long-term implications. Buckminster Fuller had made a similar argument with the idea of "ephemeralization."[26]

Simon was so confident of the rightness of his view about resources that he offered a challenge to anyone who doubted him. He offered "to stake $10,000 in separate transactions of $1000 or $100 each, on my belief that mineral resources (or food or other commodities) will not rise in price. If you are prepared to pay me now the current market price for $1000 or $100 worth of any mineral you name (or other raw material including grain and fossil fuels) that is not government controlled, I will agree to pay you the market price of the same amount of that raw material on any future date you now specify." Paul Ehrlich rose to the challenge. In collaboration with two colleagues, John Harte and John P. Holdren, Ehrlich chose copper, chromium, nickel, tungsten, and tin and "bought" two hundred dollars worth of each one, on paper, to make one thousand dollars worth in all. The two men then agreed to watch price fluctuations over the next decade until the end of the stipulated period of the bet. If the real price had risen by September 1990, Simon would have to pay the balance above $1,000 to Ehrlich. If the real price had fallen, Ehrlich would pay Simon the shortfall.[27]

Simon was vindicated in the case of all five metals, some of which had gone down significantly in price. He would have won even without adjustments for inflation. Ehrlich ruefully mailed him a check for $576, noting that he was particularly surprised by the sharp fall in the price of copper since 1980, whose price had been climbing steeply in the late 1970s. Simon replied that the rise, though real, had been a short-term effect and had created the highest possible incentive to seek a substitute. Sure enough, this was the era of the invention of fiber-optic cables, which could now be substituted for copper in many electrical systems, while improved plastics in place of copper pipes could be used for plumbing. Satellites had also taken over some of the work previously done by copper telephone wires. As Simon observed, no one is interested in copper for itself, but only in the service it can provide. Inventors and technologists are constantly looking for cheaper and better ways of providing that service.[28]

Coming to Ehrlich's aid, sympathetic commentators speculated that on the really important issues he might be right despite having lost. One reason for the fall in the price of metals could be the tendency of employers to reduce wages (especially if a rapidly rising population created a glut of labor). Another reason could be that employers had shifted their production to overseas sites where environmental regulation was lax or nonexistent and where production costs would be correspondingly lower. Ehrlich, despite losing the bet, retained a wide following for his more pessimistic ideas and even won a MacArthur "genius" grant. A journalist sympathetic to Simon noted that "a bizarre reverse-Cassandra effect" seemed to be at work: "[W]hereas the mythical Cassandra spoke the awful truth and was not believed, these days 'experts' spoke awful falsehoods, and they *were* believed. Repeatedly, being wrong actually seemed to be an advantage, conferring some sort of puzzling magic glow upon the speaker."[29]

Julian Simon was an unconventional figure, as his anguished autobiography bears witness. Victim of recurrent acute bouts of depression, he found intense hard work to be the best antidote. Despite claims that he was a solitary figure, his ideas began to catch on. The World Bank's 1984 *World Development Report* on the relationship between population and economics adopted his view that moderate population growth was compatible with economic growth, that it stimulated demand, and that it was not likely to provoke subsistence crises. The National Research Council in 1986 drew similar conclusions, making Simon "more a part of mainstream thinking than is commonly realized." The passage of time also confirmed his view that as developing societies went through the industrialization process, they would also experience the demographic transition that prevents exponential population increases. In other words, the logical response to overpopulation fears was to industrialize.[30]

Simon was not without company in American academia. Another figure who came to similar conclusions was Herman Kahn (1922–1983). Kahn, a mathematics prodigy and a pioneer in the development of game theory, had played a prominent role in nuclear war planning after World War II at the RAND Corporation. His book *On Thermonuclear War* (1960) had made him one of the most influential figures in the defense policy community with its argument that nuclear war *was* "thinkable"—and winnable. The American nuclear posture of "massive retaliation" in the 1960s was based partly on his ideas, designed to convince the Soviet Union that no matter how powerful its first strike against American forces might be, the American nuclear "second strike" retaliation would still be decisive.[31]

In 1961 Kahn founded the Hudson Institute, which developed into a "futurology" think tank. He too became convinced in the late 1960s and early 1970s of the essential wrongness of Ehrlich and other resource and population pessimists. In 1984 Kahn and Simon collaborated as editors on *The Resourceful Earth*, which was designed as a systematic refutation of President Carter's *Global 2000* report. Its language was, in places, a near parody of *Global 2000*:

> If present trends continue, the world in 2000 will be less crowded (though more populated), less polluted, more stable ecologically, and less vulnerable to resource-supply disruption than the world we live in now. Stresses involving population, resources, and environment will be less in the future than now . . . The world's people will be richer in most ways than they are today . . . life for most people on earth will be less precarious economically than it is now.

The detailed chapters that followed were studies of pollution, population, nuclear power, endangered species, cancer, farmland, and water resources. In one representative chapter, D. Gale Johnson, writing on agriculture, confirmed Simon's earlier claim that world food supplies were increasing more rapidly than world population. It was true, he added, that people still go hungry, especially in the developing world, but this is nearly always due to political factors rather than a simple inability to grow enough food. The resilience of the world as a producer and distributor of food had never been greater. As better infrastructure (more roads) was built in the developing world, remote areas would continue to become more accessible, further reducing the hazard of famine.[32]

The plausibility of the Simon-Kahn view was sustained in the 1990s by other economists, notably the Indian Nobel laureate Amartya Sen. Malthus and his heirs, Sen wrote, had been proven wrong by two centuries of experience. Population had risen dramatically, but productivity in food and all other goods had risen even faster, making the food-to-population ratio more favorable than ever before. Surveying experiments in the developing countries, Sen argued that the worst approach to restraining population was the coercive one, then being undertaken in China with its draconian one-child-per-family policy. It violated basic human freedoms and led to neglect of female children and possibly even to female infanticide. Much better were voluntary schemes that coupled access to contraception with access to health care and education, especially women's education. "Central to reducing birth rates . . . is a close connection between women's well-being and their power to make their own decisions and bring about changes in the fertility pattern . . . It is thus not surprising that reductions in birth rate have

Ben Wattenberg, a journalistic critic of environmental pessimism.

typically been associated with improvement of women's status and their ability to make their voices heard—often the result of expanded opportunities for schooling and political activity."[33]

The challenge for Sen, as for Simon and Kahn, was to respond to environmental problems in a way that protected personal choice and preserved human dignity. Ben Wattenberg agreed. His book *The Good News Is the Bad News Is Wrong* (1984) drew readers' attention to the continuing successes of the American economy, even as the nation alleviated its worst environmental problems. Short-term difficulties, he wrote, could not alter the fact that the majority of Americans were living longer and qualitatively better lives than any previous generation. One of the most serious continuing problems they faced, ironically, was the unrelenting negativity of the media. A free press was certainly greatly to be desired, as was journalists' willingness to look below the surface and find out what was really going on. Unfortunately, this tendency had developed in only one direction, seemingly paralyzing journalists' willingness to tell good news. "They are missing some of the biggest stories of the era—about progress—and missing them regularly, consistently, structurally, and probably unwittingly."[34]

Life expectancy in America was still increasing, more people were surviving diseases that had once been fatal, standards of living had increased, and higher levels of education were within reach of more people than ever before. Environmental progress was, Wattenberg added, undeniable. The number of accidental deaths had declined radically since World War II, the number of acres in national parks had doubled over the same period of time, and vast improvements in air and water quality had been achieved since 1970. Cars were twice as fuel efficient as they had been twenty years earlier, and lead compounds had been removed from gasoline, making it far safer than before. Never a doctrinaire libertarian, Wattenberg admitted that many of these improvements *had* come about through government-mandated changes, which themselves were the result of environmentalists' lobbying. Why, then, would the people who had helped bring about these benign changes, and those who reported on them, decline to celebrate?[35]

Wattenberg, despite his generally upbeat demeanor, was afraid of one future problem: *under*population. One chapter of *The Good News* explored the implications of the fact that the American fertility rate was now a mere 1.8 children per woman, a figure below the replacement rate of 2.1. "From the environmentalist view, it should be deliriously good news. In fact, we all should share a portion of their unstated, unpublicized joy. It is important to know that population rates can go down as well as up." On the other hand, a declining population might present worse problems than one that was rising. Among these problems were a decline in economic incentives and an aging population, such that a smaller and smaller number of working people would have to look after an ever greater cohort of the elderly. The high cost of raising children, the high percentage of women in the workplace, and the proliferation of contraception and abortion all made it reasonable to suppose that low rates of childbearing would persist in the developed world. He added that the exponential growth of population that had agitated the neo-Malthusians in the 1960s was a two-way street, and that population could also *shrink* exponentially. In a subsequent book, *The Birth Dearth* (1987), he elaborated on the problems that lay ahead for societies that were *too* successful in curbing their birth rate.[36]

Berkeley political scientist Aaron Wildavsky was as optimistic about most environmental questions as Simon and Wattenberg. He too was baffled at environmentalists' apparent resistance to reassuring news. Why were they so downbeat about prospects for the future? He and British anthropologist Mary Douglas (1921–2007) coauthored *Risk and Culture* (1982), a study of how different cultures think about the risks they must confront, and the degree to which the *perceived* risks differ from the dangers they actually face. Douglas and Wildavsky showed that perceived risk is directly related to a culture's overall values and its vision of the good life. "Questions about acceptable levels of risk can never be answered just by explaining how nature and technology interact. What needs to be explained is how people agree to ignore most of the potential dangers that surround them and interact so as to concentrate only on selected aspects." Many more Americans are going to die from car accidents than from nuclear waste exposure every year, for example, yet the first is not regarded as a severe environmental risk and the second *is*.[37]

They theorized that since the 1960s the counterculture's "sectarian" vision of the good life had profoundly influenced the educated public.

In the amazingly short space of fifteen to twenty years, confidence about the physical world has turned into doubt. Once the source of safety, science and technology have become the source of risk . . . How can we explain the sudden, widespread, across-the-board concern about environmental pollution and personal contamination that has arisen in the Western World in general and with particular force in the United States? Our argument is that a complex historical pattern of social changes has led to values that we identify as sectarian being more widely espoused.

The sectarian view idealized nature "uncorrupted by social artifice." The rapid spread of this sectarian view was, in their view, regrettable, especially in an economically advanced industrial democracy, which needed its citizens to be well informed and rational. Public policy ought to concern itself with *actual* degrees of risk. At the moment the two were completely out of sync.[38]

Wildavsky went on to survey the alleged environmental emergencies of his era. His book, *But Is It True?* was subtitled *A Citizen's Guide to Environmental Health and Safety Issues.* Its goal, he wrote, was to help readers gauge the relative danger of the risks they confronted. He began by noting the extraordinary difficulty faced by an ordinary citizen trying to grasp the scientific issues at stake in many of these controversies. It was, however, essential that citizens in a democracy make the effort, rather than permitting themselves to be flung from one anxiety to the next by feverish headlines. He recruited graduate students at Berkeley to read the conflicting scientific reports on a wide variety of environmental and health issues, then collaborated with them in writing up each of the book's principal chapters.[39]

Repeatedly, Wildavsky and his students, some of whom were environmental activists, concluded that the perception of risk was utterly disproportionate to the real danger, especially in the midst of media scares, and that several substances had been banned by government regulators even though their benefits outweighed the hazards. After a survey of the history of DDT research, for example, he wrote: "The most important understanding to be gained from the history of DDT is that there are few unalloyed good things in the world. Rarely does one find a substance that has benefits but no costs. Why, then, do we expect technologies, including their chemical components, to be entirely benign, unlike anything else in our lives—our friendships, marriages, children, parents, colleagues?" The decision to stop using DDT, taken by the EPA in 1972, had almost certainly consigned thousands of people around the world to chronic sickness and premature death from malaria. Similarly, a chapter on the dioxin scare that had led to the evacuation and destruction of Times Beach, Missouri, concluded that the government had overreacted. "Studies of potentially exposed people from Times Beach and other Missouri dioxin sites have discovered no serious adverse health consequences that can be linked to dioxin." Nevertheless, the town had been destroyed.[40]

Wildavsky concluded with a plea to abandon the current policy of regulating substances that showed even a possibility of harm, however low. Each intervention incurred costs, disrupted lives, and diverted manpower, which precluded wiser actions elsewhere and did not fulfill the criterion of "erring on the safe side." Again and again, in his view, the real harm had been tiny by comparison with the lurid alarms sounded by the press and taken up by the regulatory agencies. "With the exception of CFCs thinning the ozone layer, the charges are mostly false, unproven, or negligible."[41]

Americans' illogical approach to risk also baffled Stephen Breyer, a legal scholar and future Supreme Court justice, when he published *Breaking the Vicious Circle* in 1993. Breyer, approaching the question from the point of view of public policy, argued that we should devote the greatest energy to combating those hazards that are in fact the most lethal. Take the process out of the hands of the politicians and media, he suggested, and put it in the hands of a committee of scientists instead, insulating them from political pressure. Otherwise our response to risks will be driven by a succession of media scares and health crazes rather than a systematic study of what is most likely to harm us. He pointed out that more people were killed each year by *toothpicks* than by asbestos (which was then a source of acute concern; millions of dollars were being spent on removing it from buildings). It might be true that citizens felt differently about these two hazards, said Breyer. But "if you think it is reasonable to spend more money to save a life when asbestos is at issue, you should at least ask yourself how much more, and you should try to explain to yourself why." He added that political responses to risks were haphazard and inconsistent; established programs also dedicated far too many scarce resources to cleaning up "the last ten percent" in cases of hazardous waste sites, when the money could be put to much better uses elsewhere.[42]

Counterenvironmentalists like Simon, Wildavsky, Douglas, Kahn, and Breyer were academics and social scientists, drawing on the traditions and insights of their disciplines to explain the inconsistencies and weaknesses of current environmental policy. They were joined in the 1980s and early 1990s by a group of popular nonfiction writers and journalists who were interested in the same questions but generally lacked specialized training. These writers also doubted the conventional wisdom. Among them were Ronald Bailey, Gregg Easterbrook, Dixy Lee Ray, Lou Guzzo, and Wallace Kaufman. Reporting on environmental affairs had convinced them that, on balance, the world was becoming healthier rather than sicker, richer rather than poorer, better fed rather than hungrier, cleaner rather than dirtier, and steadily more sensitive to environmental concerns. The future seemed to them bright so long as environmental pessimism did not lead to the creation of misguided policies.

They feared that too much government intervention might make matters worse rather than better, partly because uniform regulations are a blunt instrument when applied to the diverse landscapes of the United States and partly because bureaucracies are always self-interested, motivated by political as well as environmental issues. Bailey was especially emphatic on this point. A libertarian conservative, he despised "timid, ass-covering regulators" and argued that they had imposed an enormous deadweight of unnecessary costs and regulations on American industry, which would be more creative and better able to improve the environment if left unmolested. An influential neoconservative author, Charles Murray, had suggested in *Losing Ground* (1984) that America's antipoverty programs of the last two decades, though well intentioned, had been worse than useless; he believed poverty would have diminished faster if the government had done nothing. Bailey now made the same claim for environmental policy.[43]

Not all counterenvironmentalists were libertarians, however. Gregg Easterbrook, whose 1995 book *A Moment on the Earth* was an encyclopedic survey of the principal environmental issues, praised federal anti-pollution programs and Congress's willingness to protect the habitat of endangered species. Easterbrook, making a pitch for the sober middle ground, which he termed "eco-realism," emphasized that markets cannot solve every problem and that a judicious blend of federal oversight and entrepreneurial initiative generally worked best, in such programs as the emissions trading arrangements of the 1990 amendments to the Clean Air Act.[44]

These writers, in addition to their shared faith in the improvement of environmental conditions, also shared the belief that environmentalists had to be understood as a special psychological or religious type. They were analogous to the many Americans who, in earlier eras, had prophesied the imminent end of the world, only to be proven wrong by the *absence* of catastrophe on the predicted day. Wallace Kaufman, for example, used a language similar to that of Douglas and Wildavsky to convey his belief that environmental leaders were intolerant sectarians who had developed an orthodoxy, one that required an extremely high degree of conformity from its members, who were expected to be more committed to a set of favored outcomes than to scientific truth. "After thirty years in the environmental movement," he wrote, "I am worried that as it gains power, it cares less and less about reason and science. Its influence on movies, academia, and literature has already turned history into fiction and propaganda . . . it has almost lost touch with reality." He added that it also had an unpleasant vengeful streak, eager to harm American businesses and citizens whose values and interests did not jibe with its own.[45]

Kaufman felt that contemporary environmentalists fell far short of their predecessors in the nineteenth and early twentieth centuries. The best of the old conservationists, including George Perkins Marsh, John James Audubon, Frederick Law Olmsted, Theodore Roosevelt, and Gifford Pinchot, he wrote, were enthusiastic about the possibility of managing nature through the careful application of science and technology, and were openly anthropocentric. The new environmentalists, by contrast—people like Paul Ehrlich and Barry Commoner— were intellectual descendants of the Romantics, who had protested against the new power of science and technology. In one startling passage Kaufman even argued that no one had done more harm to the cause of sensible conservation than Henry David Thoreau, "the mes-

siah of the environmental movement." Thoreau's sentimental veneration for solitude and poverty, the themes of *Walden*, was the worst
possible model for actual developing societies. His ideas about science,
technology, and nature were superficially attractive but utterly wrong-
headed. Kaufman noted, pointedly, that Thoreau, after extolling the
superiority of natural over medical remedies, died of tuberculosis at
the age of forty-four, "nature's victim."[46]

Several of these writers, including Kaufman, were themselves former environmental activists. Another was Dixy Lee Ray (1914–1994). A
near contemporary of Rachel Carson and, like her, a marine biologist,
Ray had moved out of academia and into politics, becoming the first
female head of the Atomic Energy Commission, during the Nixon administration, and then the first female governor of her home state,
Washington, between 1977 and 1981.[47] In retirement she and an old
journalist friend, Lou Guzzo, cowrote a pair of books casting doubt on
the environmental orthodoxy of the times, *Trashing the Planet* (1990)
and *Environmental Overkill* (1993). In their view, the evidence just did
not support claims about impending disaster. The threats posed by
acid rain, ozone depletion, pesticides, and nuclear waste were real but
entirely manageable, they wrote. Citizens and governments must not
overreact. Instead they should depend on science and have faith in the
"resilience and recovery power of nature."[48]

Authors skeptical of environmental gloom became more confident
and more articulate in the late 1980s and early 1990s. Editorials in the
Wall Street Journal, National Review, Fortune, and the business press often
echoed these themes. None implied that environmental matters were
insignificant—the comic opera blunders of Watt and Gorsuch had put
an end to public expression of such views. But steady denigration of
bureaucracy, overregulation, and gloom and doom continued, putting
environmentalists on the defensive. *Fortune* itself argued in 1992 that
"laws have made the environment cleaner, the workplace safer, and the
consumer healthier than the unguided invisible hand could have," but
that they worked best with the "light touch." By now, unfortunately,
overregulation was crushing American business and absorbing a disproportionate part of the nation's gross domestic product.[49]

FREE-MARKET ENVIRONMENTALISM AND "WISE USE"

Conservatives interested in environmental protection had an alternative to offer: free-market environmentalism. Two think tank intellectuals, Terry Anderson and Donald Leal, for example, argued that the best way to ensure responsible stewardship of land and resources was through private ownership. Owners are much more likely than employees of a remote Washington bureaucracy to know in detail what they own, what it needs, and how to look after it. Just as the Soviet Union was breaking down, demonstrating vividly the weakness of a command economy, Anderson and Leal stressed the superiority of self-interest as motivation. Owners know the exact character of their property and do not have to apply to it general rules that were written to cover many different locations and contingencies. Above all, private owners face the full consequences of the decisions they make rather than being insulated by bureaucratic process. They are therefore likelier to act wisely.[50]

Anderson and Leal recognized that political intervention had arisen to combat pollution and protect endangered places and resources. Unfortunately, they said, government management of lumber, water, recreation, and federal land had become dysfunctional because the appropriate incentives were missing. Political rather than environmental motives activated the government managers, which meant that the assets in their care were not their first concern. It was true that private owners had often earned bad reputations for pollution and for nonsustainable practices. What government should do, accordingly, was to create strict and impartial rules of conduct and uphold them through the court system, leaving the market and individual entrepreneurs to take care of the environment itself. Owners would be liable for environmental damage and would have strong incentives to prevent it. "Imagination is crucial to free-market environmentalism, because it is in the areas where property rights are evolving that resource allocation problems occur. Where environmental entrepreneurs can devise ways of marketing environmental values, market incentives can have dramatic results." The trading of pollution permits, already a familiar idea, seemed to them greatly superior to the attempt by government to micromanage factory emissions.[51]

The "Wise Use" movement of the late 1980s and early 1990s attempted to put free-market environmental ideas into practice in the American West. It aimed to relax the tight regulations that governed land use in much of the West and to restore local property owners' rights to act as they wished on their own land. Founded at a Reno, Nevada, conference in 1988, the movement was a coalition of loggers, miners, gun owners, property owners resentful about "takings," along with off-road vehicle users who wanted more access to trails on public land. Backed by lumber and motorcycle corporations, it also enjoyed the legal support of groups like the Mountain States Legal Federation (former interior secretary James Watt's old employer). Unlike the Sagebrush Rebellion, the Wise Use movement used populist rhetoric and depicted itself in press releases as a coalition of ordinary folks being victimized by a remote and overmighty government.[52]

Wise Use's founder was Ron Arnold, a Seattle writer and ex–Sierra Club member who ran the Center for the Defense of Free Enterprise. Arnold did everything he could to emphasize the "just folks" character of the movement because he realized that "citizens' groups have credibility and industries don't." He was aided by a direct-mail fund-raiser, Alan Gottlieb of Bellevue, Washington, and together they wrote and self-published *The Wise-Use Agenda*. The agenda asserted that Wise Use too was environmentally concerned, but with different priorities from the mainstream. Their book *Trashing the Economy* (1993) was a sustained attack on the Endangered Species Act. The Sierra Club, horrified, described the Wise Use movement as "a super-financed environmental juggernaut that is craftily masquerading behind a totally deceitful public relations 'wise use' blitz to conceal their profit-driven designs."[53]

Environmental journalist William Poole covered the Wise Use 1992 conference for *Sierra* magazine and was dismayed at the speakers' rhetoric and their plans to open up protected wilderness areas to more economic activities. He admitted, however, that there were some eerie parallels to environmentalists' own meetings. The chunky, outdoorsy

clothes worn by the participants, the men's beards, and the overwhelming whiteness of the faces present were all close matches to meetings of
his own group. Even the titles of the presentations sounded similar,
such as "How to Deal with the Media" and "How to Move Forward with
Our Agenda." Secretary of the Interior Manuel Lujan, meanwhile,
urged President George H. W. Bush to lend a sympathetic ear to the
Wise Use movement in the run-up to the 1992 election. "I have never
seen a positive reaction from environmental groups no matter what we
do," he told a reporter. Here, by contrast, was a group likely to help re-
elect the jeopardized president, especially if a few of the rules restraining logging, grazing, and mining projects in the West were relaxed.[54]

Bush eased the rules but nevertheless lost in 1992 to Bill Clinton.
The Wise Use movement demonized Clinton. Its best-known political
representative was Republican congresswoman Helen Chenoweth, a
freshman legislator from Idaho who came to Washington in the
great GOP sweep of 1994. She described environmentalism as a
government-sponsored cult: "This religion, a cloudy mixture of New
Age mysticism, Native American folklore, and primitive earth worship—
pantheism—is being promoted and enforced by the Clinton administration in violation of our rights and jobs." Widely disliked in
Washington, Chenoweth gained further notoriety in 1999 when she
married Wayne Hage, a property rights activist from Nevada who had
conducted a highly publicized lawsuit against the U.S. Forest Service.[55]

The prominent environmental historian Richard White, struggling
to understand the Wise Use phenomenon, recognized that the federal
government was a huge and visible presence in the West, especially on
Western lands, in a way that it was not in other parts of the United
States. The history of the area had demonstrated in the late nineteenth
century that government aid was essential to the formation of most
communities and enterprises there. Unaided small-scale homesteaders
had failed in large numbers in the arid lands, and only federal aid had
been adequate to get major irrigation schemes started. That reality,
however, was regularly forgotten by Westerners, who liked to think of
themselves as self-reliant and found the federal presence abrasive to
their pride. "The West has long resented federal control," he wrote,

"but it has resented it . . . the way a person might resent a scratchy woolen shirt in winter: it was uncomfortable but it's all that is keeping the wearer warm." Throughout the twentieth century, money, jobs, and opportunities in the West nearly all depended on federal spending, which was both necessary and deeply resented. There was, White noted, no simpler way to confirm this reality than to propose withdrawing all federal subsidies from Western economic interests.[56]

Journalists of the 1980s and 1990s often referred to the disputes of their era as the "culture wars." Conservative and liberal partisans faced off angrily about whether to teach creationism as well as evolution in schools, about race and gender, about the canonical status of certain works of art and literature, about the relativity of intellectual and moral standards, and about the alleged subversion of students by "tenured radicals" in America's universities.[57]

The environment was certainly one of the issues in these culture wars, in which each group tried to depict its opponents as mad, bad, or both. Counterenvironmentalists like Aaron Wildavsky and Wallace Kaufman saw a "sectarian" mentality among their adversaries. Environmentalists, conversely, sometimes described their critics as "deniers." The term was powerful because it made an implicit comparison with Holocaust deniers, people who refused to believe that the Nazis had exterminated six million Jews during World War II. In both cases the implication was that the adversary was not merely misinformed, but mendacious or even mentally ill.[58]

Paul Ehrlich was among those most often named as the archetypal sectarian, doomsaying environmental radical. Undeterred after years of intellectual combat, he condemned what he described as the rising environmental "brownlash" in America, a combination of skepticism and denial on a wide range of environmental issues. In *The Population Explosion* (1990), he and his wife, Anne Ehrlich, reasserted the major themes of *The Population Bomb*, admitting that human ingenuity permitted some flexibility in response to new crises, but repeating that the sheer number of people now in the world, and their collective impact on resources, was catastrophic.[59]

In a follow-up volume, *Betrayal of Science and Reason* (1996), the Ehrlichs argued that scientists should not merely do their work and systematically counter falsehoods with truths, but should also *publicize* what they found, to refute antienvironmentalists' misstatements among a broad public. Doing so, they believed, would promote sounder public policy. This suggestion drew a predictable range of responses, depending on the reviewers' faith in the authors' assertions about which elements of the science were beyond dispute. A reviewer for *Science* noted that the Ehrlichs' professed aim of "reaching out to a broad audience of readers" was "undermined by their elitist tone. They sprinkle 'Harvard' and 'Stanford' attributions throughout the text like holy water. And while they point out many egregious examples of misuse and manipulation of data by brownlashers, they fail to consider similar selectivity in the cause of environmentalism." Besides, no amount of scientific information could, of itself, show what a society *ought* to do— these were questions of value, not simply of knowledge. On many issues, especially the population question that had initially made Ehrlich a celebrity, there was still plenty of uncertainty. Authors dissenting from his neo-Malthusian position were not necessarily being dishonest, because scientific differences of opinion were far more often genuine than tendentious.[60]

To UNDERSTAND THE OPPOSITION from the 1970s to the 1990s, we need to make a clear distinction between *anti*environmentalism and *counter*environmentalism. The first, represented by President Reagan, James Watt, and Anne Gorsuch, lacked all patience with the reforms of the 1970s and sought to turn back the clock to an era of aggressive industrialism. The second, represented by Julian Simon, Aaron Wildavsky, Gregg Easterbrook, and others, was sympathetic to environmental goals but unsympathetic to the developing environmentalist orthodoxy. Counterenvironmentalists thought of nature as resilient and adaptable and remained convinced that human ingenuity and the human capacity for work could more than compensate for the stress that growing populations and rising living standards imposed on the natural world. They doubted that resources were being exhausted once and for all and believed that improvements in efficiency and substitution would more than make up for increases in demand and production. They were also clear-eyed about the fact that different people can disagree about the kind of future environment they want, and that under these conditions it is appropriate to maximize freedom and minimize coercion.

The question of whether the federal government was usually a help or a hindrance divided these critics of environmentalism. Angry Westerners, first in the Sagebrush Rebellion and later in the Wise Use movement, were simply wrong on the facts. Without extensive federal help, as Richard White recognized, the settlement of the West could scarcely have begun or been sustained. To deny that fact, and to deny the continued centrality of government subsidies to Western prosperity, was simply to deny the historical truth. Similarly, libertarian free-market environmentalists, whatever the theoretical beauty of their claim that market mechanisms could solve all problems, had no adequate answer to the fact that they had failed to do so until government intervened. That regulation sometimes moved slowly and clumsily suggests not that there should be no regulation but that it should be reviewed, improved, and streamlined better to fulfill its mission.

Straight antienvironmentalism has largely disappeared by now, but counterenvironmentalism is alive and well. Turn to any recent issue of the *Wall Street Journal, National Review, Weekly Standard,* or *American Spectator* to find articles that simultaneously accept the need for environmental care and deny that contemporary organized environmentalism is capable of providing it, especially in ways consonant with economic reality. More recently, the American edition of the *Economist* has joined them by, for example, casting doubt on climate change alarms.[61]

Among the many issues under debate in 2014 is hydraulic fracturing, or "fracking," a technique for extracting natural gas from subsurface rock strata that requires the injection of high-pressure liquids to create fractures. The advantage of this method is that it vastly increases available reserves of hydrocarbons, creating for the United States the possibility of near self-reliance for decades to come. Many environmental organizations, including the Sierra Club, condemn it because it creates the hazard of groundwater contamination, escape of methane and toxic gases, and the return to the surface of "flowback water" at the end of the process, which has to be processed for safety or recycled in subsequent operations. The filmmaker Josh Fox created the documentary *Gasland* in 2010, depicting communities affected by contaminated water and related health hazards, while Matt Damon starred in an antifracking drama, *Promised Land*, in 2012. The major environmental organizations held a Washington rally, Stop the Frack Attack, in July 2012, at which the president of the Sierra Club said, "The out-of-control rush to drill has put oil and gas industry profits ahead of our health, our families, our property, our communities, and our futures." A comparable demonstration took to the streets of New York the following month.[62]

Counterenvironmentalist writers recognize the potential hazards of fracking but argue that safety techniques are improving rapidly and that the national benefits easily outweigh the drawbacks. In the *Weekly Standard*, for example, Robert Nelson, an environmental policy professor at the University of Maryland, takes seriously the hazards, admits abuses among early users of the technology, and emphasizes the need for close government regulation. At the same time he sees the potential benefits of shale gas in particular as "a windfall with which the United States has been blessed" and speculates that antifracking activists have come to depend on a quasi-religious view of the issue rather than on quantifiable or logical objections. Similarly, Kevin Williamson, writing in *National Review*, emphasizes the environmental superiority of natural gas over oil and coal, notes its role in stimulating economic recovery after 2008, its clean burning qualities, and its national security advantages. He admits that the drilling phase is extremely noisy, intrusive, and potentially dangerous if not done carefully. But in his view also, a comparison with coal and oil recovery techniques makes it highly desirable. Fracking, he writes, provides "cheap, relatively clean, ayatollah-free energy, enormous investments in real capital and infrastructure, thousands of new jobs for blue-collar workers and Ph.D.s alike . . . Who could not love all that?"[63]

The transformation of the American energy situation since President Obama's first election is in fact striking. Oil production has risen steadily despite the Deepwater Horizon disaster. Gas production has risen even faster, while evidence about human-induced global warming has not followed the more pessimistic scenarios laid out at the turn of the century. Alternative energy sources, wind, solar, geothermal, and ethanol, have proven difficult to generate in sufficient quantities, or have other adverse environmental consequences, as we shall see below. The overall effect has been to give a new lease of life to the traditional methods. In the counterenvironmentalists' eyes this situation is neither surprising nor deplorable.[64]

CHAPTER 7

ECOLOGISTS AND HISTORIANS

ENVIRONMENTAL ACTIVISTS from the 1960s to the 1990s feared that a once healthy and stable natural world was being damaged or even destroyed by thoughtless human actions. Environmental skeptics, by contrast, doubted that human action threatened the natural world, partly because they saw it as adaptable and resilient and partly because they believed human ingenuity could compensate for whatever damage might happen along the way. The academic discipline of ecology provided the basic concepts, in particular the concept of the ecosystem, for many intellectuals in these disputes. In the 1970s and 1980s, however, a younger generation of ecologists began to doubt the value of the "ecosystem" concept, pointing out that it was as much a human construct as a reality out there on the ground. The rise of chaos theory and the spread of Heisenberg's uncertainty principle from physics to other sciences eventually affected ecologists, imposing a new modesty on their ability to say what the world *was* like and what it *should* be like.

At the same time, a generation of environmental historians began to demonstrate that the natural world itself had a history, one that was stormy and variable rather than stable and serene. They pointed out that even such an apparently obvious term as "nature" had in fact meant very different things at different times in human history, that it too was a cultural construct rather than a simple external reality. The size and vitality of American universities in the postwar decades ensured that hundreds of skillful and imaginative scholars subjected every ecological and historical orthodoxy to rigorous challenge. The cumulative effect of their work was to create a new awareness of the importance of language in the discussion of environmental issues, a new modesty about the predictive power of the environmental sciences, and a new and deeper level of uncertainty about the future.

ECOLOGY

Ecology as a distinct intellectual discipline began in the nineteenth century. It was so named by the German biologist Ernst Haeckel (1834–1919) after reading Darwin's *On the Origin of Species* (1859). Ecology is the study of living organisms in relation to one another and to their nonliving surroundings. Where biology isolates individuals or species for close scrutiny, ecology studies their interactions.

By 1945 a talented group of European and American ecologists had created a set of general principles based on years of careful observation and deduction. Central to their science was the concept of the "ecosystem." An ecosystem, according to this idea, is a setting in which a variety of plants and animals live cooperatively and in a condition of relative stability. Frederic Clements (1874–1945), a major contributor to this theory, argued that in its early stages an unvegetated place would be "colonized" by pioneer plant species, but that later arrivals would eventually displace them. A wider variety of species would come to coexist in the system, which Clements named a "climax community." If undisturbed, the climax community would reproduce itself over the generations, exhibiting a high degree of stability and equilibrium. Clements thought of the ecosystem as an organism in its own right. Popular phrases such as "the balance of nature" were based on this idea.[1]

Clements's successors, notably Arthur Tansley (1871–1955) and Charles Elton (1900–1991), elaborated the concept of the ecosystem (Tansley actually invented the term in 1935). They studied the operation of food chains and pyramids, in which large quantities of primary food sources (algae and plants) fed a moderate number of small animals, which in turn supplied food to a very small number of top predators. Raymond Lindeman (1915–1942) added a mathematical rigor to these ideas, explaining how energy, derived originally from the sun, circulated through ecosystems' living and nonliving elements. Lindeman tried to move ecology in the direction of becoming a hard and precise science with predictive as well as descriptive powers.[2]

One of the most influential ecologists after World War II was Eugene Odum (1913–2002), a professor of ecology at the University of Georgia who shared his immediate predecessors' faith in the ecosystem concept and regarded it as essentially stable and predictable, unless disturbed by humans. His textbook, *Fundamentals of Ecology* (1953), cowritten with his brother Howard, sold widely and summarized the orthodox view into the 1980s. It encouraged students to think holistically and to imagine that the ecosystem not only witnessed a high level of symbiosis among its parts, but also that it employed "strategies" to preserve and strengthen itself. Odum, like Clements, came close to arguing that the ecosystem, even though much of it was inorganic, was nevertheless somehow a kind of intelligent being in its own right.[3]

The early environmental movement of the 1960s and 1970s drew on this set of ideas, which could also be taken to mean that ecosystems wanted certain things to happen and tried to prevent others. The most radical application of the organism metaphor came from an eccentric English scientist and inventor, James Lovelock, who argued at a Princeton conference in 1969 that the whole earth was one immense, homeostatic organism. He named it "Gaia" after the Greek goddess of the earth and theorized that all the living beings on the planet cooperated to make it habitable and benign. Life itself had *created* the oxygen-rich atmosphere, so different from those of all the other planets, and collaborated in preserving it. Lovelock further believed that Earth-Gaia was self-regulating, essentially with an immune system of its own, which was able to cope with, and correct, such threats as pollution. (Agricultural monoculture and the reduction of species diversity seemed to him worse threats than industrialization.) He codified the Gaia idea in a popular book, which began, "The quest for Gaia is an attempt to find the largest living creature on Earth . . . If Gaia does exist, then we may find ourselves and all other living things to be parts and partners of a vast being who in her entirety has the power to maintain our planet as a fit and comfortable habitat for life." Many young environmentalists latched on to the idea and it quickly gained spiritual overtones.[4]

In the 1970s and 1980s, however, a younger generation of hard-headed scientific ecologists, shrinking with distaste from the idea of quasi-mystical superorganisms, began to challenge aspects of the old orthodoxy. In 1973, for example, William Drury and Ian Nisbet wrote that their study of a New England forest showed few of the characteristics of an Odum-type ecosystem. Change appeared to them random; there was no sign of cooperation among species, and there was no equilibrium state that the system as a whole sought to preserve. A few years later, in 1977, Joseph Connell and Ralph Slayter added that they had not been able to verify the idea, important in ecosystem ecology since Clements, that a given area was populated first by pioneer species and later by a secondary group that established itself as a mature or "climax" community. On the contrary, they wrote, the first arrivals usually held on unless destroyed by some calamity, like fire or destructive windstorms.[5]

Another surprise was the discovery that complex ecosystems were not necessarily more stable and more durable than simple ones. This intuitively plausible idea had been strongly held for decades until the influential Australian scholar Robert May disproved it empirically. His contemporary Paul Colinvaux agreed that "the claim that complex communities are more stable than simple communities is invalid." It was a case of wishful thinking, he believed, and had "done mischief by distracting people from real problems."

> It has, for instance, been invoked in the controversy over
> the Alaska pipeline, in the claim that the arctic ecosystem
> is "fragile" . . . But this is nonsense. The animals and plants
> of the arctic spend their whole lives and evolutionary expe-
> rience struggling against adversities far mightier than any

pipeline or road . . . I happen to think that the Alaskan
pipeline is a disaster . . . but the argument that it is damaging a fragile ecosystem is false.

Colinvaux, an English immigrant working at Ohio State University,
anticipated that the trans-Amazonian highway, built through more
complex ecosystems, was likely to do far more damage than the Alaska
pipeline.[6]

PATCH DYNAMICS

The challenge to the old orthodoxy reached a new intensity with the
publication of *The Ecology of Natural Disturbance and Patch Dynamics*
(1985), a series of essays edited by S. T. A. Pickett of Rutgers University
and P. S. White of the University of Tennessee, which summarized recent developments in many areas of ecological research. "Disturbance,"
which their predecessors had regarded as exceptional and (implicitly)
as regrettable, these authors regarded as normal, pointing out the near
universal effects of fire, winter conditions, sudden surges in ant or bad-
ger populations, human action, and other unpredictable and irregular
effects. All such disturbances changed the structure of an area's vegetation and the availability of resources. The book's contributors were
aware that disturbance could take place at many different scales, sometimes affecting microorganisms over the space of a few square centime-
ters but sometimes transforming thousands of acres. Relevant periods
of time also varied greatly, depending on whether annual plants or
trees with the potential to live for hundreds of years were under consid-
eration. "Failure to recognize the importance of disturbance," they
wrote, "has led to two kinds of frequent misinterpretation in field
ecology: (a) extrapolation of events measured during disturbance-free
years to predict future system states, and (b) use of a plot scale that in-
tegrates different kinds of patches." "We seek," they added, "to present clearly a framework that can stimulate the generation of explicit

hypotheses and theory and thus form an alternative to equilibrium concepts of the evolution of populations, compositions of communities and functioning of ecosystems."[7]

Pickett and White understood the practical consequences of a new paradigm, which depended on temporary and shifting "patches" rather than durable and stable ecosystems. Policy makers could no longer assume that stability was somehow normative and would have to face the paradox that preserving an area in its present form could now be thought of as "unnatural" if the intention was to forestall disturbance.

Also in the 1980s, Daniel Simberloff, a professor at the University of Florida who was a practicing ecologist and a philosopher of science, argued that ecologists should rid their discipline of old philosophical baggage. He argued that Darwin had made the great breakthrough in separating science from philosophical idealism, being more interested in *variants* of species than in ideal forms. Darwin and his successors had emphasized the primary role of *randomness* in mutations. The physical sciences had followed suit in the late nineteenth and early twentieth centuries, ridding themselves of the "demonic reifications of typology, essentialism and idealism." Einstein and Heisenberg cast doubt on the idea of immutable "laws" of science and showed science to be a probabilistic enterprise. After a delay of more than half a century, ecology was now following suit, emphasizing the probabilistic character of community development.[8]

Simberloff knew from practical experience that the plant communities studied by ecologists—himself included—had rarely conformed to the theoretical precision Clements or Odum claimed. Apart from anything else, they rarely had clear boundaries and were likely to be visited by animals, insects, and birds from elsewhere. Local conditions, in every particular study, were all important—no wonder different ecologists had come to such different conclusions. To him the significance of each community study was its distinctiveness rather than its conformity to a standard type. Ecology, he insisted, must get rid of its physics envy: "What physicists view as 'noise' is music to the ecologist; the individuality of populations and communities is their most striking, intrinsic, and inspiring characteristic, and the apparent indeterminacy of ecological systems does not make their study a less valid pursuit." The materials physicists worked on were simple and relatively unchanging. The materials worked on by ecologists, namely living things and systems, were immensely complicated, often with thousands of entities in the same community, all of them subject to evolution. Simberloff suggested that chaos theory was more likely to be useful to ecology than mechanical analogies.[9]

In 1990 Daniel Botkin, professor of environmental studies at the University of California, Santa Barbara, followed this new line of thinking with *Discordant Harmonies*, in which he too used metaphors from music rather than mechanics. He criticized environmental policy makers for acting according to discredited ecological ideas and for remaining captive to Greek metaphysics. Old theories about the natural world as itself a kind of organism had been discredited by rigorous analytical studies, he wrote. So had the mid-twentieth-century idea that ecosystems were analogous to machines, mechanically cycling nutrients and energy through their various components in a highly predictable way. Instead he offered readers what he called the "nature of chance," in which a mixture of regular and wildly irregular events took place side by side. Botkin shared his generation's enthusiasm for sophisticated computer modeling but showed that the models had greater ability to imitate actual natural environments when an element of randomness was introduced, unlike the machinelike regularities assumed by his predecessors.[10]

In one striking passage, Botkin challenged Aldo Leopold's claim that the killing of predators on the Kaibab Plateau had led to a surge in the mule deer population, overbrowsing of local vegetation, and widespread death of the deer themselves. Leopold had written in one of the best-known passages of his *Sand County Almanac* that as he watched a mountain lion that he had shot a few moments before breathe its last, he had seen the "fierce green fire" go out in its eyes and learned that he should protect rather than destroy such magnificent creatures. A generation of environmentalists had treasured this story, Botkin wrote, because it justified the protection, preservation, or even reintroduction of mountain lions, wolves, and other top predators and supported the idea that the predators would maintain a "natural balance." However, as a later biologist of the Kaibab area, G. Caughley, had shown, the removal of the predators was only one of many possible reasons for the violent fluctuation in the deer population. It could also have been affected by changing weather, changing grazing practices among local farmers, and shifts in the frequency of local fires.[11]

Botkin believed that even rigorous ecological scientists were susceptible to wishful thinking and that they had clung to equilibrium ideas for psychological reasons, even as evidence to discard them had gathered force and cogency:

> As long as we could believe that nature undisturbed was constant, we were provided with a simple standard against which to judge our actions, a reflection from a windless pond in which our place was both apparent and fixed, providing us with a sense of continuity and permanence that was comforting. Abandoning these beliefs leaves us in an extreme existential position; we are like small boats without anchors in a sea of time; how we long for safe harbor on a shore.

It was time, nevertheless, to break the old myths and metaphors and face up to a more uncertain future. Botkin was as dedicated as anyone to environmental protection, and despite his critique of Leopold's parable of the mule deer, he honored Leopold's ethical approach to the natural world. He suggested that nature was not always harmonious, and that ecologists must now learn about its discords. That learning could be empowering, because it would teach us that intervention in the natural world to compensate for "dissonances" was often necessary and could be benign.[12]

THE ORIGINS OF ENVIRONMENTAL HISTORY

Historians as well as ecologists reacted to the environmental movement and to new challenges in knowledge theory. The events of the 1960s and 1970s prompted historians to ask some new questions about the past. If soil erosion, resource depletion, pollution, overpopulation, and new risks to human health and welfare were afflicting our own era, had such problems confronted humanity in earlier generations? How had people reacted? More generally, what was the history of the interplay between people, plants, animals, the weather, and microbes? The term "environmental history" appears to have been first used in 1969 and spread quickly in the early 1970s, though scattered works from earlier eras had anticipated several of its themes.

In 1934, for example, Hans Zinsser had tried the thought experiment of studying an epidemic disease not from the point of view of the humans, but from the point of view of the rats and lice that carried and spread it. Zinsser (1878–1940) was a bacteriologist at Harvard Medical School who devoted much of his career to the study of typhus but was also a poet and writer. He wrote *Rats, Lice and History* as a spare-time entertainment, and in a whimsical style, but to make a serious point.[13]

"In the course of many years of preoccupation with infectious diseases," he wrote, he had "become increasingly impressed with the importance—almost entirely neglected by historians and sociologists—of the influence of these calamities upon the fate of nations, indeed upon the rise and fall of civilizations." After years of working with them, said Zinsser, he had started to sympathize with lice as well as men—after all, they too were victimized by the bacillus. "If lice can dread, the nightmare of their lives is the fear of some day inhabiting an infected rat or human being . . . Man is too prone to look upon all nature through egocentric eyes. To the louse, *we* are the dread emissaries of death." He showed the role the disease had played in the collapse of armies and the decline of cities, vitally affecting the fate of great cultures from the past, and he warned that up to the present it had lost none of its "vigor, cruelty, and stealth."[14]

The following year Paul Sears published *Deserts on the March* (1935). Taking the catastrophic Dust Bowl storms of the American plains (which were then taking place) as his starting point, Sears (1891–1990) surveyed earlier civilizations—the Mayans, the ancient Chinese, the civilizations of the Fertile Crescent, and the Romans—that had over-farmed fragile lands, failed to undertake soil conservation practices, and paid a ruinous price as their once fertile environments turned to desert. "Man, who fancies himself the conqueror of it, is at once the maker and the victim of the wilderness." To use the soil faster than it could recover was to be living on borrowed time, and nature would always exact a terrible vengeance. Sears was a professor of ecology at the University of Oklahoma when he published the book. Living in the midst of the Dust Bowl, he could bear witness to the appalling reality of soil erosion simply by stepping outside his office.[15]

Zinsser and Sears were groping toward a holistic, ecological understanding of the relationship between living things and their inanimate surroundings that would be further developed by their environmental history successors. They recognized that natural forces were sometimes decisive in changing the course of history. Many other historians of medicine, travel, science, and exploration in the midcentury decades were also glimpsing connections of these kinds and offering what would later be called ecological or environmental explanations.

Roderick Nash's *Wilderness and the American Mind* (1967), coinciding with the increased environmental awareness that followed *Silent Spring*, was perhaps the first major work of American history to be informed by a mature ecological outlook. Nash wrote the original version of the manuscript as his doctoral dissertation at the University of Wisconsin, completing it in the same year that Congress passed the Wilderness Act, 1964. As a graduate student Nash also persuaded the university's archives to acquire the papers of Aldo Leopold, a former faculty member whose significance he was quick to appreciate, and he devoted one summer to sorting them out. He was also the first historian to write extensively on Leopold's work. Moving to a faculty position at the University of California, Santa Barbara, he founded the university's environmental studies program and worked locally as an environmental activist.[16]

Nash published a revised version of his thesis to enthusiastic reviews in 1967. He argued that ideas about wilderness were one of the defining characteristics of Americans' self-understanding. The first generation of European settlers were terrified by the extent of its "wilderness." From the Bible, they thought of wilderness as the place where the Devil dwelt and where Jesus was tempted by Satan. At the same time, however, a memory of the fact that the Children of Israel had escaped from Egyptian captivity into the wilderness also gave it the image of a *sanctuary*, a place of testing and preparation, before entry into the Promised Land. Generations of Americans had struggled to conquer the immense interior wilderness, so that it would no longer be a place where wild beasts and wild men threatened a fragile civilization.[17]

The great drama of American history, accordingly, was the tension between civilization and wilderness. Puritan divines feared that men who pushed too far into the interior were reverting to barbarism, though the pioneers countered that they were taming the wilderness and creating a new Eden. In the Romantic era writers like Henry David Thoreau had spoken up for the first time on behalf of wilderness as something positive, a place where God, not the Devil, might be found. By the end of the nineteenth century the closing of the frontier and the rapid spread of settlement across the United States had led to a movement for the preservation of at least some bits of distinctively American wilderness. Wilderness advocates like John Muir thought of it as a place for physical and spiritual refreshment and as the antidote to an overbearing commercial civilization.[18]

As Nash pointed out, "wilderness" was as much a beholder's state of mind as an actual condition of particular pieces of land—it was a noun that acted like an adjective. It was nonetheless real for that, however, and had stamped itself indelibly on the minds of generations of Americans—hence the intensity of the political debate in the 1950s and 1960s over how to define wilderness and how to preserve it. He ended by pointing to the irony that the *popularity* of wilderness recreation had itself, by the 1960s, become a threat to its well-being. Supporters and detractors of extending American wilderness areas alike cited Nash's book. In effect, *Wilderness and the American Mind* set the ground rules for discussion of wilderness, and was reprinted and updated repeatedly in the 1970s and 1980s.[19]

In the 1970s, as environmentalism entered the mainstream of American politics, more historians began to work on its origins. Alfred Crosby's *The Columbian Exchange* (1972) became another classic. Its title introduced what is now a thoroughly familiar concept, though at the time Crosby struggled to find anyone willing to publish the book. Crosby (born 1931), a professor at Washington State University, had been active in the civil rights movement and the struggles of migrant farm laborers during the 1960s. This work had led to an interest in "the histories of people who were victimized, economically exploited or enslaved in the advance of European imperialism and capitalism." He wanted to explain their fate without arguing the superiority of their conquerors, which prompted him to explore "the influence . . . of nonpolitical, nonreligious, and largely ignored factors—especially infectious disease."[20]

The Columbian Exchange is a study of how contacts between Europe and America starting in 1492 transformed environmental conditions on both continents. Crosby describes the way in which an array of Old World plants and animals was taken to the New World by the conquistadores and their successors, sometimes for food (pigs and grain crops), sometimes for military reasons (horses, the terror weapon of their day against the Aztecs), and sometimes for religion (grapevines, to facilitate the making of communion wine). He also shows how New World plants transformed life in Europe, especially potatoes and corn, whose high yields facilitated subsequent European population growth, and tobacco, whose addictive character transformed European leisure habits after 1500.[21]

Crosby emphasized the importance of European diseases, to which Native Americans had no immunity and which annihilated them far more effectively than European armies: "When the isolation of the New World was broken, when Columbus brought the two halves of this planet together, the American Indian met for the first time his most hideous enemy: not the white man nor his black servant, but the invisible killers which those men brought in their blood and breath." He stressed throughout that the decisive characteristics of the Columbian exchange took place *below* the level of conscious intention. The conquistadores, and later the Pilgrim Fathers, may have thought they were beneficiaries of God's goodwill—in fact they were beneficiaries of a favorable epidemiological situation. Determined not to glamorize Columbus, he ended: "The Columbian exchange has left us with not a richer but a more impoverished genetic pool. We, all of life on this planet, are the less for Columbus, and the impoverishment will increase." He also lamented that the process had led to as many extinctions in the five hundred years since Columbus as would normally take a million years.[22]

The sometimes melodramatic style and sorrowing tone of Crosby's rhetoric, highly characteristic of their era, could not disguise his intellectual achievement. Although other historians, including Zinsser, had already identified the importance of medical factors in history, Crosby brought together the full range of environmental issues better than any predecessor. William McNeill's *Plagues and Peoples* (1976) built on this achievement. Earlier historians had shied away from disease as an explanatory historical device, he wrote, because of its apparent randomness. "We all want human experience to make sense, and historians cater to this universal demand by emphasizing elements in the past that are calculable, definable, and, often, controllable as well." McNeill believed it was now possible to make the role of disease explicable rather than capricious. He introduced historians to the concept of "disease boundaries," pointing out that epidemics were incomparably more devastating when they reached a new population for the first time ("virgin soil epidemics") than when they afflicted populations that had had previous experience with them. We now knew enough about epidemics, he argued, that these historical moments could be identified and explained with the same kind of logic as other historical phenomena.[23]

McNeill (born 1917) was a professor at the University of Chicago and specialized in writing books on big themes. His *Rise of the West* (1963) emphasized the interplay of civilizations over the course of history and aimed to explain the gradual rise to dominance of Western civilization after about 1500. *Plagues and Peoples* complemented that work. It urged historians to reconceptualize human life, in environmental terms, as "caught in a precarious equilibrium between the microparasitism of disease organisms and the macroparasitism of large-bodied predators, chief among which have been other human beings." After pointing to various episodes in which epidemics appeared to have played a crucial role, he ended with an account of medical progress since 1700, which had transformed this long process of coevolution and mutual parasitism. In the nature of things, he warned in closing, the parasites, big and small, will always be with us, even as their forms and degrees of lethality change.[24]

Environmental history won acceptance as a legitimate field of study in the 1970s. In 1976 the *Environmental Review* (later called *Environmental History Review*) began publication, and a growing number of talented scholars began to investigate the history of environmental problems. One among them, Donald Worster (born 1941), won the Bancroft Prize, the American Historical Association's highest award for an American history book, in 1980. Worster's *Dust Bowl* (1979) explained the catastrophic events on the High Plains during the 1930s as an example of human folly, environmental mismanagement, and economic shortsightedness. Worster, turning his back on the traditional historiography of the Great Plains, which emphasized the triumph of the human spirit in taming a wild and difficult land, concentrated instead on the cumulative missteps settlers and their descendants had taken between the late 1860s and the early 1930s.[25]

For millennia, he wrote, a complex of grasses had adapted to the area's high winds and periods of low rainfall, binding down the earth and making the best use of available water supplies. It had even adapted to the intermittent visits of the vast buffalo herd. Homesteading farmers, however, plowing up the land after the Civil War, and their descendants' intensification of this process during the brief boom of the World War I era, had destroyed the grassland and replaced it with crop monocultures. Tractors and mechanical harvesters had vitiated the area's capacity to defend itself. The next time the rains stopped, the friable soil turned to dust and the high winds blew it away, never to return.[26]

The exploitation of the land up to 1930, moreover, was not an anomaly, but rather the outcome of "a culture that deliberately, self-consciously set itself [the] task of dominating and exploiting the land for all it was worth." This culture was capitalism, which regarded the natural world as something to be *used*, exploited to the maximum in yielding ever greater returns, and to which no reciprocal obligation was owed. Capitalist farming sought the highest possible returns and rewarded short-term risk takers, which put it on a collision course with ecological reality. It substituted a delusional optimism for critical self-appraisal and left its victims unable to appreciate the justice of their fate. In Worster's view it was no coincidence that the Dust Bowl and the Great Depression should have happened at the same time; both were signs of the dysfunctionality of capitalism.[27]

In a long and anguished epilogue, Worster recounts a visit, during the mid-1970s, to some of the worst afflicted counties of the Dust Bowl era. Capital-intensive agribusiness had transformed the scene; deep wells into the aquifer, intensive irrigation, the use of artificial pesticides and fertilizers, and giant harvesters were creating immense crops year after year whether it rained or not. According to the farmers he interviewed, technology had provided the perfect answer to old troubles, such that the bad days would not return. In Worster's view, by contrast, the scene demonstrated that America's capitalist high-tech farmers had learned nothing. They were continuing to work in an unsustainable way, devoting far cheaper subsidized energy to growing food than the energy it could give back to its ultimate consumers. He ended with an appeal to Americans to "discipline our numbers and our wants," recognize the deep flaws in capitalism, and turn our attention to helping less fortunate peoples throughout the world, "making them more self-sufficient in ways that are ecologically sensitive." Worster's next book, *Rivers of Empire* (1985), argued that the same aggressively exploitative culture that had almost destroyed the Great Plains was at work in the damming of all the West's rivers and in the commercial diversion of every drop of water. This project too, he felt certain, was unsustainable.[28]

SECOND-GENERATION ENVIRONMENTAL HISTORY

Worster was, unmistakably, an environmental advocate as well as an environmental historian, and to read *Dust Bowl* or *Rivers of Empire* is to feel the intensity of his indignation. William Cronon, by contrast, lowered the rhetorical temperature while bringing a new level of intellectual subtlety to environmental history. Born in 1954, Cronon had undertaken a meteorically successful education, which culminated in a Rhodes Scholarship to Oxford. He published his first influential book, *Changes in the Land* (1983), before his thirtieth birthday. A study of the way New England changed between the first English settlement in 1619 and the American Revolution, it demonstrated the interplay between human cultures and environment, emphasizing that the *meaning* of land, lakes, trees, rivers, and plants was very different to the settlers than to the Indians. Agreeing with Worster that the Europeans' introduction of capitalist principles had led to exhaustion of the land and to unsustainable practices, he added that they had set to work on a landscape that was already heavily marked by human modifications. He emphatically re-

William Cronon, the leading figure among the second generation of environmental historians.

jected the old fallacy that the settlers had encountered a "virgin land" whose Indian population had lived in harmony and equilibrium with the plants and animals.[29]

In an introductory discussion of method, Cronon pointed out the pitfalls a careful historian must avoid in drawing conclusions about the ecology of a place. If early colonists mentioned white pine trees often, was that because they were so common, or was it simply because they were more *valuable* to onlookers than the other species among which they were found? He also cautioned readers against thinking the worst of the settlers:

> When reading colonial accounts describing floods, insect invasions, coastal alterations, and significant changes in climate, we are perhaps all too tempted to attribute these . . . to the influence of the arriving Europeans. This will not always do. Not all the environmental changes which took place after European settlement were caused by it. Some were part of much longer trends, and some were random: neither type need have had anything to do with the Europeans. Trickier still are instances where Europeans may or may not have altered the *rate* at which a change was already occurring.

Cronon was also well versed in recent developments in ecology. Discarding the old organic metaphor of a "climax community," he was also skeptical of the "ecosystem" idea, because it made stability, rather than change, seem normal. But New England had seen "environmental changes on an enormous scale, many of them wholly apart from human influence," and there had never been a "timeless wilderness in a state of perfect changelessness." Ecologists, he argued, had become increasingly aware that it made no sense to think of human involvement as an aberration because human intervention was all but universal. History itself, in other words, was coaxing ecology toward a more realistic understanding of the role humanity had played in shaping the natural world.[30]

If the first great works in this new field of historical study took on wilderness, desertification, and rural New England, fine studies of urban environmental history were not far behind. Martin Melosi (born 1947) was a graduate student at the University of Texas just as the environmental movement was getting under way in the late sixties. In an early article he recognized that urban pollution itself needed to be understood historically, in ecological context as well as in the history of progressive reform. His own book *Garbage in the Cities* (1981) shared Worster's and Cronon's insight that capitalist societies can be wasteful and destructive as well as productive, that the waste has environmental consequences, and that it has a history of its own. In a bravura passage on urban horses, however, he reminded readers to guard against assuming that the situation only ever got worse. More than three million horses lived and worked in American cities in 1900, generating hundreds of thousands of gallons of urine and tons of manure every day. They presented a horrible dilemma to civic authorities when they died and their heavy, cumbersome corpses began to decay in the gutters before teams of other horses could arrive to drag them away. We think of cars as sources of pollution, said Melosi, and they are, but to the generation that first saw them replacing the horses they could easily be depicted as miracles of cleanliness. Studies of the history of pollution, sewage disposal, smoke, noise, detergent, and phosphates appeared in growing numbers through the 1970s and 1980s, fleshing out the skeleton of urban environmental history.[31]

Environmental themes also influenced new departures in American Western history. Just as a pattern of ideas established at the start of the twentieth century had cast a long shadow over subsequent work in ecology, so a powerful orthodoxy from the same era had dominated the study of the American West. This was Frederick Jackson Turner's "frontier" thesis, first enunciated in 1893 and widely persuasive to subsequent generations of Western historians. Turner and his disciples claimed that the ongoing encounter with the frontier through centuries of American history had stripped away the vestiges of European-ness from generations of American pioneers, leading them to seek democratic, individualistic, and egalitarian solutions to their common problems. The frontier, in other words, not the European heritage, had decisively shaped the distinctive American character.³²

Historians had been chipping away at various aspects of this influential thesis for decades, but Patricia Nelson Limerick's *Legacy of Conquest* (1987) was a frontal attack. Recent developments in the history of race and the environment facilitated her approach. Central to the frontier thesis had been the confrontation of the noble pioneer with the Indian "savage." Limerick, a professor at the University of Colorado, Boulder, reconceptualized the pioneers as invaders and plunderers. Consciously or unconsciously, she did for whites in the American West what Rachel Carson had done for the American chemical industry: she turned a group of self-perceived benefactors of mankind into a group of rapacious environmental destroyers. She noted at the outset that one of her models was the historian C. Vann Woodward, whose *Burden of Southern History* (1955) had summarized the tragic character of the American South and its inability to deal humanely with the race question. Her book was, in effect, a comparable study of the burden of Western history, in which the tragedy consisted of both racial and environmental injustice. Like Crosby's *Columbian Exchange*, Limerick's *Legacy of Conquest* was, and was meant to be, an indictment as well as a history.³³

Also central to the Turner thesis was the idea that the census of 1890, which had announced the disappearance of a perceptible "frontier line" from the American map, marked a divide in American history. To the contrary, said Limerick; the most striking aspect of Western history is its *continuities*. Far from being independent minded and self-reliant, Western settlers from the outset depended on federal aid in all its forms and continued to do so into the present. White Westerners persecuted and marginalized ethnic and racial minorities from the outset and continued to do so through the twentieth century. Far from creating a small property holders' utopia, they created near monopoly conditions in mining, railroads, ranching, and irrigation farming, duplicating the forms of exploitation that had grown up in the East. Their

economic activity was essentially extractive, geared to short-term profitability rather than long-term self-sufficiency. Western farming in
practice had often been almost as much an extractive industry as gold
mining.[34]

Legacy of Conquest drew widespread attention, admiration, and
awards, and historians recognized that it provided a new model for
thinking about regional history in general and the West in particular, along with an imaginative application of environmental insights.
Equally ingenious was Stephen Pyne's creation of another new subfield,
fire history. Just as the ecologists were emphasizing disturbance rather
than stability, Pyne, a professor at Arizona State University, found a way
to give historical shape to an apparently formless and universal phenomenon. Fire, he wrote, "is a cultural phenomenon. It is among man's
oldest tools, the first product of the natural world he learned to domes-
ticate. Unlike floods, hurricanes, or windstorms, fire can be initiated
by man . . . Mankind is the primary source of ignition in the world, the
chief vector for the propagation of fire, and the most significant modi-
fier of the fire environment."[35]

Pyne showed how domesticated fire had been used in land clearance, in hunting, in warfare, and in other culturally recognizable
ways. Selective setting of fires by American Indians had contributed to
improving forage conditions for the animals they hunted. Pyne, like
Cronon, rejected out of hand the romantic notion that the Indians
lived in an unchanged wilderness. To the contrary, he wrote, they
worked actively with fire to modify the landscape in their own interests,
so much so that their decline, in the face of competition from settlers,
led in many places to an *increase* in woodland. In the early twentieth
century, the Forest Service came to regard its mission primarily as the
prevention of forest fires and the protection of wood supplies, which
linked it closely to the forestry industry and created the preconditions
for rarer but much fiercer fires. In subsequent books Pyne elaborated
on these insights, writing in 1990 that "fire and humanity have co-
evolved, much as fire and life have, an endless dialectic for which terrestrial ecosystems are both medium and message." He even offered
readers the intriguing thought that history itself originated among

ing scholars, notably Richard White and Patricia Nelson Limerick, had discarded old myths about Western history (such as Turner's frontier thesis) in favor of a more complex, more nuanced, and less heroic vision. Environmental history had grown up side by side with the environmental movement. Its first stars, Nash, Worster, and Crosby, had openly identified with the environmental movement. As environmentalism itself encountered contradictions and complications in the 1970s and 1980s, so did environmental history, leading to a richer, more complex, and less polemical version.

THE COMBINED EFFECT of these changes in the study of ecology and history was potentially profound. Advocates of environmental reform had often implicitly appealed to the idea of an old baseline era when humanity was in harmony with nature, arguing that conditions since then had deteriorated. They had assumed that a formerly stable world in equilibrium had been upset and that humans had done the damage. It was no longer easy to make such claims, because one could no longer assume that there had been an equilibrium state or that any earlier condition had been "normal." Just as it was impossible to say what nature *wants*, so it became impossible to say what nature was actually *like* before the people came along and began to change it. Human intervention was continuous for as long as people had been walking the earth—and perpetual transformation certainly predated humanity.

Other academic disciplines were delivering versions of the same message. Geologists, paleoclimatologists, astronomers, and evolutionary biologists all had versions of the same story to tell, of a volatile shifting earth. The planet they depicted in publications of the late twentieth century was, and had always been, vulnerable to seismic, volcanic, climatological, and meteorological transformations, sudden reversals of the earth's magnetic field, meteor strikes, mass extinctions, and vast shifts of continents, ice sheets, sea levels, atmospheric composition, and species distribution. As some of the new ecologists had observed, it was certainly possible to find times and places of stability within this universe of disorder, but that depended largely on the relevant timescale.

It was no longer possible to say that stability was normal and distur-bance exceptional.

This new idea did not gain credence everywhere, to be sure, and some elements found a readier audience than others. It certainly was still possible to stand in judgment over human actions in the environ-ment and to condemn them. Radical environmentalists did exactly that. The next chapter, which traces the philosophy, spirituality, and activism of radical environmentalists, can also be seen, in a sense, as a digression. The radicals' impact on national policy was negligible. On the other hand, they had a substantial impact on mainstream environ-mentalists, going back to first principles, testing consciences, and que-rying assumptions about the rights and wrongs of environmental exploitation.

CHAPTER 8

DEEP AND RADICAL ECOLOGY

THE MAJORITY OF AMERICANS with an interest in the environment hoped that necessary reforms and improvements would be accomplished voluntarily, as public standards changed or as government intervened. A small minority came to believe that only direct action would be sufficient, even if it meant breaking the law. They viewed the environmental crisis as so serious, and prevailing attitudes toward the environment as so wrong, that only shocking actions would be enough to compel the nation to take its environmental responsibilities more seriously. Some environmentalists, inspired by the civil rights movement of the 1960s, undertook nonviolent actions such as sitting in trees slated for felling or lying down in front of bulldozers. Others favored minor forms of sabotage such as "spiking" threatened trees or pulling up road surveyors' stakes, while a few committed more violent acts, such as cutting down power lines, destroying road-building equipment, even setting fire to car dealerships, logging company offices, and ski resorts.

Their justification for such acts was usually couched in the language of "deep ecology," an approach that began in the mid-1970s and regarded mainstream environmentalism as compromised and superficial. Not all deep ecologists broke the law, to be sure; for many, deep ecology was a form of philosophical or spiritual exploration. The most militant among them, however, felt that human actions toward the natural world were atrocities and that they were morally obliged to resist.

An intense debate arose inside the radical environmental movement between the "social ecologists," for whom *human* welfare remained paramount, and those who declined to regard humans as privileged over other species in any way. The obvious weakness of this latter group was that they were all people themselves, trying to speak on behalf of a natural world that expressed no preferences of its own. They were really voicing their own ideas about how other people should think and act toward nature.

Some moderate environmentalists felt a grudging respect for the radicals. Here were people willing to act on their beliefs rather than follow the slow, safe path of lobbying congressional representatives or contributing to the funds of the mainstream organizations. By the 1980s, and especially after President Reagan's foolish assault on environmentalism, the mainstream—represented by such groups as the Sierra Club, Natural Resources Defense Council, National Wildlife Federation, Izaak Walton League, Audubon Society, Wilderness Society, Environmental Defense Fund, and the Nature Conservancy—were an important part of the Washington establishment. Their leaders sometimes helped draft legislation and draw up agency rules, commanded a wide following among voters, raised funds nationwide, bought and preserved vulnerable natural areas of special interest, and made sure that the environmental aspect of all government activities was monitored thoroughly. Their credibility was at stake, prompting others among them to deplore the radicals, fearing that the environmental cause as a whole would get a reputation for recklessness and even violence.

DEEP ECOLOGY

Deep ecology asked humans to regard the other parts of nature, the plants and the animals, as their equals. Rejecting the idea that the earth exists primarily for human use, and that people are entitled to manipulate it at will, deep ecology asked for a new humility and, in practice, a form of voluntary poverty. Scattered insights in the work of Saint Francis of Assisi, Henry David Thoreau, John Muir, and Aldo Leopold had prefigured deep ecology, especially Leopold's "land ethic," but none of them had defined it as such.

An influential 1973 article by the Norwegian philosopher Arne Naess, "The Shallow and the Deep," was the urtext of this new approach. Naess pointed out that the purpose of the "shallow ecology" movements then springing up in developed nations was simply to "ensure the health and affluence of people in the developed countries." Deep ecology would go much further, requiring ecocentrism (earth-centeredness) instead of anthropocentrism (human-centeredness), and would ask its practitioners to be *involved*, not merely to comment from a detached academic standpoint. Deep ecology rejected hierarchies of all kinds and was radically egalitarian:

> The ecological field-worker acquires a deep-seated respect, or even veneration, for ways and forms of life. He reaches an understanding from within, a kind of understanding that others reserve for fellow men and for a narrow section of ways and forms of life. To the ecological field-worker the equal right to live and blossom is an intuitively clear and obvious value axiom. Its restriction to humans is an anthropocentrism with detrimental effects upon the life quality of humans themselves . . . The attempt to ignore our dependence and to establish a master-slave role [toward nature] has contributed to the alienation of man from himself.

Deep ecology entailed decentralization and the recovery of local self-sufficiency. It also asserted that humans must never reduce the diversity of nature except to fulfill vital needs, and that only with a sharp reduction of the human population could all the other species thrive. Naess also cautioned that deep ecology was not something that could be explained in an entirely detached way or with calm rationality. It was a praxis, understood only through doing, and was affective, intuitive, and existential.[1]

Bill Devall, a sociology professor at Humboldt State University in California, popularized Naess's ideas in the United States. In deep ecology, he wrote, "the American dream is understood as a nightmare and the assumptions of higher and higher standards of living or the desirability, or even possibility, of continuing rapid economic growth are criticized."[2]

Devall collaborated with philosopher George Sessions on a deep ecology anthology in 1985, urging readers to repudiate the mechanistic mind-set of contemporary American life and to develop a new sense of harmony with all of nature:

> It can potentially satisfy our deepest yearnings; faith and trust in our most basic intuitions; courage to take direct action; joyous confidence to dance with the sensuous harmonies discovered through spontaneous, playful intercourse with the rhythms of our bodies, the rhythms of flowing water, changes in the weather and seasons, and the overall processes of life. We invite you to explore the vision that deep ecology offers.

Devall and Sessions's book was an eclectic jumble of prayers, poems, practical tips on social activism, snippets of news from the new European green parties, and advice for achieving local self-sufficiency. They also included a list of eight deep ecology principles that Sessions and Naess had drawn up the previous year during a camping trip in Death Valley, California. The most important was that "the well-being and flourishing of human and nonhuman Life on Earth have value in themselves," a value that was "independent of the usefulness of the nonhuman world for human purposes."[3]

Central to the deep ecology outlook was the idea that humanity had evolved gradually over millions of years alongside other species and that industrialization was dysfunctional and unnatural. Dolores LaChapelle, another deep ecology advocate, regarded this separation from nature not as progress but as a form of alienation from a bigger reality: "We still have the sophisticated body and highly complex brain of the hunter, yet in the last 400 years we've been trying to force this body/ brain into the tight, dull, limited violent view of modern industrial culture. The breakdown is showing up all over the place—in stress-related diseases, alcoholism, suicide, devastation of land, and so on." The philosopher Holmes Rolston added that deep ecology asked vitally important ethical questions. "There comes a point when we want to know how we belong in this world, not how it belongs to us. We want to get ourselves defined in relation to nature, not just to define nature in relation to us."[4]

Deep ecologists condemned mainstream environmentalism because it was anthropocentric. National parks and wilderness areas ought to exist not for the benefit of human visitors, they said, but for their own sake. Any relationship toward nature that presupposed human dominance, even the model of stewardship, was wrong, because it singled out one species for control over all the others. As the historian Roderick Nash noted, mainstream environmentalists' campaigns for improved stewardship of nature struck deep ecologists as equivalent to slave owners' campaigns for improved treatment of slaves, when they should have been devoting themselves to abolishing slavery.[5]

What should deep ecologists actually do in a world where they were outnumbered hundreds to one, not only by "shallow" ecologists but by people who had no interest in the topic at all? Arne Naess published *Ecology, Community and Lifestyle* (1989) in an attempt to provide some guidance on the question. When it came to politics, he was a nonviolent Gandhian. He shrank from the idea of revolutionary violence but affirmed that instituting a deep ecological approach to life would be revolutionary:

> I envisage a change of revolutionary depth and size by means of many smaller steps in a radically new direction. Does this essentially place me among the political reformists? Scarcely. *The direction is revolutionary, the steps are reformatory.* I can only say that I do not think that some-

thing resembling the revolutions we read about in history textbooks . . . would be of help in the industrial countries.

Deep ecologists should, in practice, welcome and work for steps in the right direction rather than shun practical politics altogether. He believed they should also struggle to remain sympathetic to their antagonists, whose ultimate conversion to a deep ecology outlook was essential.[6]

The philosophy of deep ecology appealed to some radical feminists, who speculated that the earth itself was vulnerable to human predation in the same way that women were vulnerable to predatory men— hence such phrases as "rape of the earth." Ynestra King, one of the most energetic first-generation ecofeminists, wrote that "the hatred of women and the hatred of nature are intimately connected and mutually reinforcing." The abolition of hierarchy and the achievement of full human liberation would involve a radical reconceptualization of the relationship between people and nature as well as the relationship between men and women. King had roots in the American left, but wrote that she had become dissatisfied with the "economism, workerism and authoritarianism of a myopic socialism that has not challenged the domination of nonhuman nature or taken ecology seriously." She added that, unlike liberal feminists, she was not going to struggle just for "a piece of a rotten carcinogenic pie."[7]

Some ecofeminists, borrowing from the work of gender theorist Carol Gilligan, tended to emphasize that men and women were *essentially* different; women were closer to the earth and to nature: more peaceful, more cooperative, less egotistical, and of course more fertile. The archaeologist Marija Gimbutas, for example, theorized that before the Neolithic revolution (the invention of agriculture), matriarchal, goddess-worshipping societies had flourished in Europe, but male-dominated warrior societies with male deities had displaced them with patriarchy and hierarchy. In the same vein, Riane Eisler's *The Chalice and the Blade* (1987) argued that the great struggles of prehistory in the eastern Mediterranean had pitted nurturing, caring, communitarian women against savage, hierarchical, destructive men, whose invasions shattered this achievement and brought patriarchal domination ("androcracy") into the world. Starhawk (née Miriam Simos) and the theologian Carol Christ took these insights in a religious direction.[8]

Not all ecofeminists liked the idea of an essential difference between the genders, however, and warned that this kind of dualism might lead to perpetuating old forms of subjugation. They also criticized the essentialists' tendency to veer away from practical action and into New Age spirituality. In an indignant 1991 polemic, *Rethinking Ecofeminist Politics*, Janet Biehl scoffed at the kind of wishful thinking that offered women the illusion that there had once been a feminist golden age, replete with goddess worship and no hierarchical oppression. She objected to the "magic, goddesses, witchcraft, privileged quasi-biological traits, irrationalities, Neolithic atavisms and mysticism," all of which struck her as counterproductive and backward looking. She even declared that "the very word *ecofeminism* has by now become so tainted by its various irrationalisms that I no longer consider [it] a promising project."[9]

In the same vein, Susan Griffin (born 1943), a Bay Area writer, argued that overemphasizing the link between women and nature tended to denigrate both when juxtaposed against men and culture. This was the theme of her 1978 book *Woman and Nature*, a poetic dramatization of women's oppression and one of the founding texts of ecofeminism. A third skeptic, Catherine Roach, looking at a then popular poster of Earth photographed from space and accompanied by the slogan "Love Your Mother," deplored the assumptions embedded in it. It encouraged the idea that mothers and nature are nurturing in the same way. They are not. "We expect our mothers to love us in a way we can never expect the environment to love us. There is no 'Mother Nature' wanting to nurture and care for us, nor 'Mother Earth' who loves us." Much better, said Roach, to get rid of these irksome dualisms (woman/man, nature/culture), because they "encourage the belief that 'culture' and humanity are quite apart from 'nature,' and that we humans may thus use and abuse the environment at will."[10]

Deep ecology and ecofeminism thrived in the academy in the 1980s and 1990s among scholars in women's studies, religion, philosophy, and literary criticism. On the face of it, neither was likely to have much of a political impact in a pragmatic, materialist society like the United States, especially when they repudiated industrialization and called for a wholesale transformation of human relations. Still, as Bill Devall noted, the legislation of the early 1970s, above all the Endangered Species Act, did appear to offer recognition in law, even by hardheaded members of Congress, that species other than humans have an intrinsic worth quite apart from their usefulness to humanity.[11]

BIOREGIONALISM

One possible application of deep ecology was bioregionalism, the idea that small communities should replace giant nation-states and that people should seek to consume only what they or their neighbors could produce. A bioregion is an area large enough to sustain diverse plant and animal communities, but small enough to permit human-scale interactions without cars, telephones, or computers. Its boundaries are natural (watersheds, rivers, and shorelines) rather than political lines drawn on maps. Bioregionalists objected to foods traversing the earth in jet aircraft and container ships when they could be grown in one's own garden or nearby. As one sympathetic writer expressed it, to be a bioregionalist meant "becoming part of a community already present— the natural community of beasts and birds and fish and plants and rivers and mountains and plains and sea. It means becoming part of the . . . environment of a particular natural region instead of imposing a human-centered technological order on the area."[12]

Bioregionalism also meant getting to know the ecology and biology of one's immediate surroundings. Can you map the flow of streams and rivers in your neighborhood? Do you know which plants and trees in your neighborhood are indigenous and which exotic, the mating behavior of local bird populations, or the way of life of the indigenous peoples who lived here before you? What local species are threatened with extinction, and how many days are there until the next full moon?

Like deep ecology, bioregionalism was supposed to be a praxis, not just an academic interest. Bioregionalists should be busy tending gardens, clearing streams and restoring waterways, pressuring local government to adopt sustainable practices, protesting corporate globalism, and learning the principles of ecology.[13]

Peter Berg (1937–2011) founded the Planet Drum Foundation in 1973 to popularize this idea. He and the ecologist Raymond Dasmann (1919–2002) published *Reinhabitation* in 1978, a guide to bioregionalism. Reinhabitation, they wrote, "involves learning to live-in-place in an area that has been disrupted and injured through past exploitation. It involves becoming native to a place through becoming aware of the particular ecological relationships that operate within and around it." David Haenke, a homesteader in the Ozarks, organized the first bioregional conference in 1984, and this "Continental Congress," as the conference called itself, reconvened every two years after that.[14]

Kirkpatrick Sale (born 1937), a radical journalist and former anti–Vietnam War activist, wrote about the possibilities of bioregionalism in *Human Scale* (1980) and *Dwellers in the Land* (1985). Convinced that industrial gigantism was depleting resources, poisoning the world, and creating "a vast psychic distance between humans and nature," he sought a radically decentralized alternative. In small cities of 250,000 or fewer, he wrote, surrounded by bioregions that could provide for their needs, dwellers' lives would be more communal, less stressful, and less beset by crime, loneliness, addiction, and other pathologies. He argued that such centers would be more democratic, more congenial to spiritual life, and that work would be less alienating because its results could be directly observed in the community.[15]

Sale was offering a profoundly unhistorical vision. History suggests that when autonomous, localized societies had the opportunity to link up with neighboring areas or to participate in widening markets, they almost invariably said yes. A more materialistic life was never forced on citizens—they eagerly embraced it. Increases in economic and political scale, moreover, made decentralized groups much less likely to fight each other. It was not easy to find historical evidence for the idea that small, decentralized communities would live in peace and harmony. Neither did Sale offer any mechanism for the transition from urban industrial civilization to bioregionalism.

A very different application of the bioregionalism idea came from two Rutgers University professors of geography, Frank and Deborah Popper. They proposed in 1987 that a vast area of the High Plains, 136,000 square miles spanning ten states, should be set aside to become a national "buffalo commons." This was the area that homestead farmers had settled in the 1870s and 1880s only to discover, in most cases, that it was too dry to be dependable as farmland. Its population had been shrinking ever since, including a sharp decline during the Dust Bowl era of the 1930s. Even the irrigation-intensive farming taking place there could not last, they believed, because of the depletion of the underground Ogallala Aquifer. What better way to acknowledge natural realities than to let the land revert to the condition it had experienced for centuries before the arrival of white settlers? Immense herds of buffalo had wandered there once and might do so once more.[16]

The Poppers, however, discovered that the remaining local population, though small in number, was tenacious in its affection for the High Plains. Journalist Anne Matthews spent a year traveling with them and wrote an entertaining and informative book about the experience, *Where the Buffalo Roam* (1992). She describes the Poppers' talks about the buffalo commons in small towns across the plains and the angry rebuttals and scornful newspaper editorials they provoked. The Poppers summarized Hardin's "tragedy of the commons" to explain the failed human attempt to exploit the area. The 1990 census also confirmed that the area was still losing population such that, as they put it, the old frontier now seemed primed to return. Rebuffed at first, the Poppers eventually recognized the need to include Native Americans, small towns, local property owners, profit-oriented buffalo ranchers, universities, and NGOs in their planning. They managed to usher in a piecemeal revival of buffalo habitat in dozens of smaller areas across the Great Plains.[17]

Not all environmentalists were convinced by the arguments for deep ecology, even if they were sympathetic to the impulse. Deep ecology assumed, incoherently, that humans could create a system of ethics that was not meant to relate principally to themselves. Too often, their critics noted, deep ecologists asserted that the earth *wanted* or *needed* something. What they really meant, of course, was that *they* wanted other people to act in certain ways because of their expectation of environmentally benign outcomes. But "nature" doesn't *want* anything, and neither does the earth.[18]

Economists tended to be even less sympathetic. Deepak Lal, an Indian economist working in the United States, pointed out that deep ecology, with its calls to abandon industrialization, would be treated throughout much of the developing world not as a harbinger of benign change but as a strange new form of Western imperialism. It would deny poor countries the opportunity to industrialize or to create longed-for higher standards of living comparable to those of the West. Samuel Huntington had suggested in an influential article just after the Cold War that the secular West was now involved in a "clash of civilizations" against various forms of fundamentalism in the rest of the world. Inverting that claim, Lal argued that radical ecology was itself a form of religious fundamentalism whose devotees were immune to rational refutation, with dangerous consequences for international development and political stability.[19]

MONKEYWRENCHING

The early civil rights movement under Martin Luther King, Jr., was studiously nonviolent and prayerful. By the mid-1960s parts of the Student Nonviolent Coordinating Committee (SNCC) and new groups like the Black Panthers were becoming dissatisfied with remaining passive in the face of segregationist violence. In the same way, some militant young environmentalists began in the 1970s to propose dramatic and forceful actions when the political and procedural approach to reform seemed to be moving too slowly.[20]

Their guru was Edward Abbey, the author of *Desert Solitaire*. His novel *The Monkey Wrench Gang* (1975) was the tale of four Westerners—

a doctor, a river guide, a Vietnam veteran, and a hippie feminist—dedicated to preventing the degradation of the desert landscape. In daredevil style, they cut down power pylons with chain saws, set fire to roadside billboards, sabotage strip-mining equipment, pour Karo syrup and sand into the gas tanks of bulldozers, and dream of blowing up the Glen Canyon Dam. They are contemptuous of mainstream environmentalists and don't even observe the conventional niceties—they drive pickup trucks and fling beer cans from the open windows. The three male characters bear many similarities to Abbey's own character and the whole novel is unmistakably a wish-fulfillment fantasy.[21]

Scattered acts of environmentally motivated mischief were already taking place in the late 1960s and early 1970s. A mysterious activist nicknamed "the Fox," for example, found a way to block the drains pouring poisonous effluent from a soap factory into the Fox River in Illinois. Later he dumped fifty pounds of raw sewage in the executive offices of the U.S. Steel Corporation and left reeking skunks on the doorsteps of executives from polluting corporations. Becoming a folk hero and successfully preserving his anonymity, the Fox enjoyed positive press from Chicago columnist Mike Royko and even drew a tribute from the commissioner of the federal government's Water Quality Administration. Only much later was his real identity disclosed—he was a middle school biology teacher named James Phillips (1931–2001).[22]

Greenpeace also favored illegal direct action, first coming to public attention in 1970 when its founders, a group of

Edward Abbey, author of *Desert Solitaire* and *The Monkey Wrench Gang*.

Canadian antinuclear activists, tried to prevent an American nuclear weapons test off Alaska by sailing into the test zone. Later they and an offshoot organization, the Sea Shepherd Conservation Society, harassed whaling fleets, attacked trawlers, interrupted seal hunts, and vandalized whaling stations. Incensed that the French government was still testing nuclear weapons in the early 1980s, Greenpeace conducted a tense sequence of confrontations with French naval vessels in the South Pacific Ocean. This face-off culminated in the sinking of the Greenpeace ship *Rainbow Warrior* by French commandos in the harbor of Auckland, New Zealand, which killed one of the men on board. The scandal that ensued (locally nicknamed "Underwatergate") was a public relations disaster for the French government. Two of the commandos were imprisoned, and France was forced to pay reparations of $8 million to Greenpeace.[23]

Radical environmental activism picked up speed and energy in 1979 with the creation of Earth First!, whose slogan was "No compromise in defense of Mother Earth." Its founder, Dave Foreman, was a former Goldwater conservative and Young American for Freedom who had dropped out of the Marine Corps and then out of biology graduate school. After a decade working as a lobbyist for the Wilderness Society, Foreman became dissatisfied with the compromises that defined environmental politics in Washington. Environmentalism by the late 1970s, he believed, had become so routine and so humorless that it had ceased to be interesting. "The environmental groups were becoming indistinguishable from the corporations they were supposedly fighting," he told one interviewer. Hiking in the New Mexico desert with his friends, Foreman conceived a new approach to revitalize the movement. His group hammered out a series of goals, honoring the deep ecology principles that all living things had an equal right to existence, that the earth was dramatically overpopulated by humans, and that the true moral criterion of every act was whether it benefited earth.[24]

When the Reagan administration took office in early 1981, with its antienvironmentalist appointments at Interior (James Watt) and the EPA (Anne Gorsuch), it provoked a rage among environmentalists that made many among them (at least briefly) receptive to the idea of direct action. Earth First! created a media sensation that spring by releasing a massive roll of black plastic down the front of the Glen Canyon Dam in Arizona. When photographed from a distance, it appeared to be a great crack in the dam itself. Foreman's friend Edward Abbey was on hand, and in a speech for the occasion ("Free the Colorado!") he praised this symbolic destruction of what was, to him, one of the most hated symbols of Western development.[25]

Although Earth First! had a group of recognized founders, at first it had no offices, no address, and no publications. An infrastructure of newsletters and related foundations subsequently developed. Foreman himself published *Ecodefense: A Field Guide to Monkeywrenching* (1985), which included details on how to destroy bulldozers and spike trees. Spiking consisted of driving big nails into the trunks of old and valued trees, then marking them with a spray-painted "S" so that loggers would leave them alone—otherwise the spikes would damage chain saws and destroy circular saw blades in the sawmills. The driving of the spikes itself did not kill the trees. One incident of a shattering saw blade against a spiked log in 1987 badly wounded a sawmill worker in Cloverdale, California. Earth First! denied responsibility, noting that the tree in question was not an old-growth specimen and was not marked. Their aim in spiking trees in the first place was to *say* that they had done so and identify the spikes, in order to prevent the trees from being felled.[26]

Foreman, who was frequently arrested, justified extralegal actions as morally necessary because of the acute threat to the environment.

> We're in a war . . . the war of industrial civilization against the natural world. If you look at what the leading scientists are telling us, we could lose one-third of all species in the next 40 years. We're being told that by the end of the century the only large mammals left will be those we choose to allow to continue to exist. We're in one of the great extinction episodes in three and a half billion years of evolution.

Foreman also told a reporter that the earth was dangerously overpopulated and that AIDS in Africa could be an example of nature healing itself. Rather than send aid to AIDS and famine victims, he argued, "the best thing would be to let nature seek its own balance, to let the people there just starve."[27]

Over the next few years, people from dozens of decentralized groups claiming an Earth First! affiliation chained themselves to trees and bulldozers, sabotaged road-building machines, and pulled out survey- ors' stakes along proposed new roads in remote areas. They were some- times able to delay projects for long enough that more mainstream environmental organizations could arrange court injunctions. Activists also realized that the damage they caused increased the developers' insurance costs and might eventually tempt them to yield. Foreman remarked that bulldozers, made from iron ore, were "the Earth, trans- mogrified into a monster destroying itself. By monkeywrenching it, you liberate a bulldozer's dharma nature, and return it to the Earth."[28]

Earth First! continued to hold an annual meeting called the Round River Rendezvous, usually in a woodland camp where members ex- changed ideas, plans, speeches, and music. The religious and mystical overtones of the group, and its wild high spirits, can be glimpsed in this fragment of a speech by Foreman:

> Look at me! Sired by a hurricane, dam'd by an earthquake, half brother to the cholera, nearly related to the smallpox on my mother's side! Why, I could eat nineteen oil execu- tives and a barrel of whiskey for breakfast when I'm in ro- bust health, and a dead bulldozer and a bushel of dirt-bikers when I'm ailin' . . . I crack Glen Canyon Dam with a glance. The blood of timber executives is my natural drink, and the wail of dying forest supervisors is music to my ears.

When asked whether Earth First! was part of the political left, he re- sponded, "At its best, Earth First! offers a way forward that the left would be wise to learn from. We aren't rebelling against the system because we are sour on life. We're fighting for beauty, for life, for joy. We kick up our heels in delight at a wilderness day." Cofounder Howie Wolke, arrested by an ax-wielding Chevron employee at the scene of a

spontaneous Earth First! action in 1986 (he had been pulling up surveyors' stakes), was sent to prison in Wyoming. While serving his sentence he wrote *Wilderness on the Rocks*, whose mood and zany rhetoric
are also highly characteristic of the Earth First! mentality and idiom.[29]

Earth First! activist and journal editor Christopher Manes defended
their method of direct action in *Green Rage* (1990). The imminence of
mass extinctions, he wrote, meant that no more time could be lost. We
now lived in a "culture of extinction" in which the rapid shrinkage of
habitat and its division into "islands" by urbanism and road building
appeared to be annihilating thousands of species per year, many of
which had not even been studied and named. The creatures most likely
to survive this holocaust were "mobile, adaptable, and opportunistic . . .
rats, roaches, sparrows, gulls, and weeds." The mainstream environmentalists were so feeble in the face of this destruction, he added, that
direct action was vital. He believed that the heads of the Audubon Society and the Sierra Club had more in common with President Reagan
and James Watt than with Earth First! But suppose everyone did become involved, bringing the traditional economy to a grinding halt?
"Many of us in the Earth First! movement would like to see human beings live much more like the way they did fifteen thousand years ago . . .
with hunter-gatherer, shifting-agriculture economies of tribal people."[30]

In 1989 the FBI—suspicious ever since learning about Foreman's
how-to guide to ecosabotage—infiltrated an Arizona branch of Earth
First! that called itself EMETIC. The infiltrator's signal led FBI agents
to the scene of an action—the group was trying to topple an electrical
transmission tower, part of the Central Arizona Project. The authorities
had hoped to find Foreman among the activists, but he was elsewhere.
Even so, he was arrested at dawn the next morning in his Tucson home
and charged with conspiracy. Evidence at the trials strongly pointed to
the infiltrators as provocateurs, urging the actual Earth First! members
on to more violent acts. Foreman was able to plea-bargain on a lesser
charge and was given five years' probation while the EMETIC activists
were sent to prison.[31]

Two other prominent figures among radical environmentalists, Judi

Bari and Darryl Cherney, were injured—Bari very badly—when an exploding pipe bomb destroyed their car in 1990. The FBI and the Oakland police, which already had them under surveillance, took them to the hospital but also arrested them, claiming that they had made the bomb and were planning to use it as part of an Earth First! action. Bari and Cherney strenuously denied the charge. They countered that the agencies had tried to kill them as part of an escalating series of harassments. The charges were dropped and the bombing remained unsolved, but the Earth First!–ers eventually won a $4 million civil suit against the police and the FBI.[32]

At the time of the explosion, Bari and Cherney had been arranging "Redwood Summer," an action to save old-growth redwoods in the Pacific Northwest. Bari came from an East Coast old-left family and was interested in the logging workers' situation even while prioritizing the preservation of old-growth trees. "Sitting-in" had first become famous in racially segregated Southern diners during the late 1950s. Environmental sit-in activists would climb high into the old-growth trees' canopy and dare loggers to cut them down, anticipating that the possibility of injury or death would deter them. Earth First! recognized that their actions were valuable only to the extent they could draw media attention, which in turn might persuade the political authorities to halt the logging. Ad hoc at first, tree sitting became more systematic in the 1990s as other environmental groups worked out how to keep shifts of protesters in the trees all the time, as well as how to feed them, maintain communications, and publicize their work in the media. Sitters gave themselves new names (Lorax, Spring, Sprite) and named the trees, too (Grandma, Yggdrasil) to further their sense of community. It was a dangerous game; in 1998 a Humboldt County, California, tree sitter named David "Gypsy" Chain was killed by a falling tree. Julia "Butterfly" Hill, on the other hand, sat in an endangered California redwood, "Luna," for 738 days, wrote a New Age spiritual memoir about the experience, and was ultimately able to save it.[33]

By then, Earth First! had split into two factions. Foreman's swagger and antipopulation rhetoric had led to accusations from social justice activists in the group that he was an "ecofascist." His friend and co-founder Howie Wolke, disliking the influence of the group's feminist contingent, said Earth First! had lost its original character and had become a group of "militant vegan feminist witches for wilderness."[34]

The social ecologists looked for ways to blend environmental protection with concern for working and poor people. Murray Bookchin, an anarchist and influential speaker and writer on the American left since the era of World War II, was a representative figure on this side of the deep ecology movement. Insisting that environmental concern must never overshadow the quest for social justice, he had been dismayed by Foreman's statements about AIDS and his apparent willingness to accept large-scale human die-offs. At a 1987 conference in Amherst, Massachusetts, Bookchin described Earth First!–ers as "barely disguised racists, survivalists, Daniel Boones and outright social reactionaries." He went on to claim that they "feed on human disasters, suffering and misery, preferably [in] third world countries" and that their ideas were "an ideological toxic dump." In the same vein, the ecofeminist Ynestra King denounced Foreman and his friends as "a bunch of guys who have set themselves up as the self-appointed protectors of another virgin—the virgin wilderness" and noted that "they represent nothing more than the Daniel Boone mentality in ecological drag."[35]

As Bookchin saw it, Earth First!'s failure to distinguish among different types of people was a fatal deficiency, because it implied that all humans were equally to blame for the plundering of the environment. "Let's face it, when you say a black kid in Harlem is as much to blame for the ecological crisis as the president of Exxon, you are letting one off the hook and slandering the other. Such talk by environmentalists makes grassroots coalition building next to impossible . . . All this loose talk of 'we' masks the reality of social power and social institutions."[36]

Invited to debate Foreman in 1989 in New York, Bookchin became more conciliatory. Both of them, he said, were equally revolted at the capitalist plundering of the environment and equally convinced of the need to resist it by all means legal and extralegal. "Dave and I are complementary. Dave and Earth First! work on preserving the wilderness; I and others are trying to create a new grassroots municipal politics, a new cooperative economics, a new pattern of science and technology to go along with their direct action."[37]

CRITICS OF DEEP ECOLOGY

Mainstream environmentalists were often horrified by acts of ecological sabotage, or "ecotage," which became more destructive in the late 1990s and early 2000s with the rise of the Earth Liberation Front (ELF). They feared that the work they had undertaken so painstakingly over the last few decades would now be discredited. They now had to worry about what looked like a crazy, radical fringe that was likely to do more harm than good. Doug Scott, director of the Sierra Club, told a *New York Times* reporter in 1990, "I have no use for tree spiking and other tactics which in their ideal form might look like a moral statement but which threaten to harm people . . . Individuals ought to take responsibility for the consequences of their political actions, but action in the night is on a slippery slope down toward terrorism."[38]

On the other hand, the radicals' actions made the mainstream look more moderate and reasonable than would otherwise have been possible. They could also sometimes draw attention to an issue, such as the cutting of old-growth redwoods or the decline of spotted owl habitat, which would then win the more systematic attention of the established environmental groups. Besides, mainstream environmentalists sometimes cast a rueful glance in the direction of their more radical colleagues. "I honor Earth First! for having the guts to do the things they do," said Brock Evans, vice president of the Audubon Society in 1990. "It's not for me, but I understand why they do what they do. And, ultimately, we all help each other."[39]

Foreman himself understood that the emergence of Earth First! had created opportunities for mainstream environmental groups. "As a result of our staking out a position of unapologetic, uncompromising wilderness lovers with a bent for monkey-wrenching and direct action, I think we have allowed the Sierra Club and other groups to actually take stronger positions than they would have before, and yet appear to be more moderate than ever." Some mainstream environmentalists echoed his point. A Sierra Club administrator commented: "When Earth First! is out there demanding a hundred million acres of wilderness and we know we can only get ten million I can turn to a congressman and say, Look, we're the voice of reason." Christopher Manes described the relationship between moderates and radicals as a "surly symbiosis."[40]

But academic environmental writers were unconvinced and tended to see the radicals as delusional. Martin Lewis, for example, a professor of historical geography at George Washington University, wrote a denunciation of the radicals as dangerous romantics. Their extremism, he wrote, enabled antienvironmentalists to discredit responsible moderates by deliberately associating the two. Besides, "radical environmentalism's ecology is outdated and distorted, its anthropology stems from naïve enthusiasms of the late 1960s and early 1970s, and its geography reflects ideas that were discredited sixty years ago." Most ecoradicals, he added, "show an unfortunate ignorance of history and a willful dismissal of economics." If everyone really did live bioregionally and depended on simple organic farming, they would tend to revert to the long tradition among farmers of having large families, thus worsening the population problem. Their "scale-appropriate" technologies would probably be *less* efficient than those being developed by industry; by turning away from the world of science and research they would be denying themselves the facilities and resources to develop better ones. Worst of all, the mass depopulation of the great cities would put far more pressure on endangered species and their habitat than they already faced.[41]

Like it or not, said Lewis, who certainly considered himself an environmentalist, capitalism offers us the best opportunity to resolve our environmental problems because of its powers of innovation and its ingenuity in creating more efficient and less wasteful technologies. No amount of wishful thinking can take us into an arcadian utopia, so we must make the best of what we already have. Luckily, he believed, there was reason to hope: "Recent economic progress has come to demand a certain dematerialization of value, based on miniaturization and

the development of lightweight, energy efficient, composite materials."
Fiber-optic cables and silicon chip miniaturization in the computer industry were examples. Lewis also pointed out that economic growth
did not necessarily mean more smoke-belching factories; it could and
should mean ever greater miniaturization, efficiency, and sustainability. Although he was eager to distance himself from Julian Simon, Lewis
agreed with the cornucopian economist that capitalist firms developing, for example, solar energy, "should be hailed and supported as environmental heroes, not denounced as technocratic and capitalistic
eco-villains."[42]

RADICAL ENVIRONMENTALISTS REMAINED a small minority
through the 1990s and into the new millennium. Often alienated from
the conventions of contemporary society, they sought a dramatic transformation of everyday life and a completely new approach to interactions between humans and the natural world. They were not able to
provoke a large-scale revolt against industrialism and the consumer
society, however, such that voluntary abandonment of electricity, motor
vehicles, and imports remained very unusual. Radical environmentalism thrived on college campuses, in departments of environmental
studies, women's studies, and literary criticism, where it coexisted with
the familiar academic traditions of tenure and peer-reviewed publication. Economics departments, by contrast, were much less likely to host
environmental radicals.

But despite their limited reach, the radicals were a valuable part of
the era's environmental debates. Just as libertarians were willing, on
one side, to think about the consequences of dismantling government
programs to improve the environment, so the radicals were willing to
contemplate a drastic reordering of human life. Thought experiments
of this kind sometimes spin off useful insights, even if the framework in
which they develop is bizarre. At the edges, radicals of left and right
contributed a fund of ideas and insights that might otherwise have
been overlooked.

Even so, on the great policy questions of the era the deep ecologists were almost totally irrelevant. The scale of the American economy is immense, such that any effort to deindustrialize the nation and turn to bioregionalism would create dislocation and suffering on a Wagnerian scale. It would require a horrifying degree of coercion and would generate fanatical opposition. The industrial and consumer way of life, for all its imperfections, enjoys mass support.

Environmental radicalism persists today, among people who believe that the world's situation has never been worse. The editors of *Earth First! Journal*, for example, claim that we are witnessing "the last dying gasp of a crumbling empire, desperately digging for the last drops of fossil fuel that it can dredge up and burn, leaving a wake of destruction in its path unrivaled in the history of the world." It urges its readers to fight back, using "the weapons of biocentrism, anti-oppression, deep ecology and solidarity."[43]

Advocates for the radical agenda in the years since 2000, in such publications as *Earth First! Journal, Treehugger, Green Anarchy,* and *Earth Island News* continued to assert the unity of theory and practice, disdaining a merely analytical response to the situation. Some added that earth activism was not only imperative but also therapeutic. One wrote that until she took action, "oppression felt like an insurmountable monster that I had no hope of conquering," but that the mere act of protesting against the cutting of old-growth forests provoked in her "a dramatic sense of power."[44]

This determined posture cannot disguise the reality that the radical movement has suffered in the wake of 9/11. Actions that would once have been prosecuted merely as mischievous or, at worst, as vandalism are now condemned as acts of terrorism, which makes the perpetrators vulnerable to extraordinary reprisals. Congress held hearings on "eco-terrorism" in 2002 while the FBI declared it their most serious domestic threat. These disproportionate claims prompted radicals to retort that the Red Scare of the 1950s had morphed into a "Green Scare" of the 2000s. In each case, they claimed, powerful government agencies were overreacting to a minor threat as a way of justifying repression and intolerance. Even the leading scientific journal *Nature* protested against the misnomer.[45]

Activists arrested for environmental "actions" faced the prospect of long, even lifelong, prison terms. The FBI's Operation Backfire was a 2005 sweep of suspected arsonists, men and women who had burned down a ski lodge in Vail, Colorado, a wildlife research center, and the headquarters of a lumber company in Oregon, and had toppled a power pylon near Bend, also in Oregon, without harming or killing anyone. They belonged to the Earth Liberation Front and the Animal Liberation Front. One among them, William Rodgers ("Avalon"), committed suicide in his prison cell. Another, Daniel McGowan, pleaded guilty to terrorism from fear that he might otherwise face a life sentence. His plight, the moral ambiguity of his actions, and the seven-year sentence he ultimately drew from the courts are the subject of Marshall Curry's fine documentary film *If a Tree Falls*. Similarly, Caltech physics graduate student William Cottrell faced an eight-year sentence for setting fire to a Hummer dealership in Southern California.[46]

Another radical, this one nonviolent, Tim DeChristopher, was imprisoned for making high bids at a Utah auction in December 2008, in the hope of preventing oil companies from getting cheap drilling leases near Arches and Canyonlands National Parks. Unable to pay (never intending to do so), he was sentenced to two years in prison and fined ten thousand dollars. He believed the oil companies were recklessly contributing to climate change and told the court at his sentencing that "my intent at the time of the auction and now was to expose, embarrass, and hold accountable the oil and gas industry, to a point that it cut into their $100 billion profits." Outside the Salt Lake City courtroom, sympathetic demonstrators blocked traffic and chanted songs—twenty-six more were arrested. He too became a cause célèbre, subject of Beth and George Gage's documentary film *Bidder 70*.[47]

The risks of breaking the law on behalf of environmental beliefs are higher than ever, and a twenty-first-century protestor, even one who is studiously nonviolent, has to anticipate harsher punishment than his or her predecessors in the 1970s and 1980s. The fact that in 2013, during the Keystone XL pipeline protests, even the Sierra Club authorized civil disobedience for the first time in its long history demonstrates the continuing lure of such dramatic symbolic acts. The club's executive director, Michael Brune, was among those arrested, explaining his action as part of a continuing protest against policies that contribute to global warming. No wonder: from the time it first made headlines in 1988, no environmental question has had a greater capacity to raise controversy, anger, and a sense of emergency than global warming.[48]

CHAPTER 9

GLOBAL WARMING

THROUGHOUT THIS BOOK I have tried to emphasize that the best way to understand environmental problems is to study them historically. That is as true with global warming as with everything else. Two things become clear straightaway. The first is that the earth has a long history of climate fluctuation and change, nearly all of which was not caused by human activity. Preindustrial societies were powerless to influence the climate, but they nevertheless adapted to both rises and declines in average temperature. We should find this history reassuring. It should make us *expect* climate change rather than regard it as alarming, and it should make us at least guardedly confident that, with all the resources of modern life, we will be able once again to adapt.

The second point is that humanity has a long history of making predictions about the future, nearly all of which have turned out to be wrong. The staggering complexity of the world makes it impossible for even the most ingenious methods of prediction to incorporate all the relevant factors. Predictions have always said far more about the world in which they were made than about actual future realities. When we read predictions made in the year 1900 about the world of the year 2000, for example, we learn plenty about the preoccupations of the late 1890s but nothing at all about the actual millennium. By analogy, it is reasonable to expect that climate predictions made today will tell us much more about the people who are making them than about the future they purport to describe.

Think about the idea of global warming in the light of these two insights. Claims that the world was heating up because of human action made headlines for the first time in the late 1980s. Computer climate model projections showed that a planetary disaster lay ahead unless the nations of the world acted collectively to reduce emissions of carbon dioxide and other greenhouse gases. Advocates of these claims argued that worldwide warming would cause the polar ice caps to melt, sea levels to rise, coasts to flood, tropical diseases to migrate northward, and millions of people to suffer dislocation, famine, flood, and premature death. Humanity, they feared, could not survive except by undertaking massive shifts in its way of life.

The story broke at the same time a series of earlier apocalyptic possibilities fell out of favor. It coincided, for example, with the end of the Cold War, when it suddenly seemed far less likely that the world would end in a massive exchange of nuclear missiles. It coincided also with a period in which oil prices were falling after OPEC's failure to restrict output. Oil and most other raw materials were cheaper and more abundant in 1990 than they had been in 1980, making it much more difficult to sustain claims like those in *The Limits to Growth* and the *Global 2000* report, with their predictions of "inevitable" privation and austerity in the very near future. Environmental catastrophism, in other words, did not disappear at the end of the Cold War. Instead, it transferred its energy to another fraught future scenario.

The global warming crisis, like earlier environmental scares, included a plea to affluent Westerners to abandon their self-indulgent way of life. Like the earlier crises, it implied that human abuse of the planet had reached an intolerable pitch, that disaster lay just around the corner, and that it was a disaster we had brought on ourselves through greed and stupidity. Like the earlier crises, it carried familiar echoes of the long American tradition of jeremiad: the self-flagellation of a prosperous and successful people afraid that they had turned away from righteousness and must now face condign punishment.

It was true that carbon dioxide levels in the atmosphere were rising, and it was true that average temperatures were rising. Whether there was a simple cause-and-effect connection between these two trends was less certain, and whether the continued rise of carbon dioxide would also lead to a corresponding continued rise in temperature far into the future was unknowable. The phenomenal complexity of climate, many aspects of which were not yet well understood, made such a simple correlation dubitable. Strangely, this intangible and speculative issue, unlikely to cause actual harm for decades to come, led to a mass mobilization of political energy throughout the developed world.

It was certainly a good idea—now as always—not to be wasteful or profligate with resources. It was a good idea to continue seeking alternative energy sources and to make existing energy sources more efficient. On the other hand, it was not a good idea to devote massive resources to cutting carbon dioxide emissions if, in doing so, other worthwhile ends could no longer be pursued. The great paradox of the 1990s and 2000s was that poor people in developing countries continued to suffer from malnutrition, smoke inhalation, and remediable diseases and to die from drinking contaminated water, while developed nations discussed astronomically expensive carbon dioxide abatement schemes whose benefits were highly conjectural and could only be realized—if at all—in the distant future.

Today there is an immense literature on global warming. Ecologists, physicists, political scientists, economists, climatologists, meteorologists, biologists, astronomers, and authors from many other disciplines have written on the topic, demonstrating the immense variety of types of expertise necessary to grasp it fully. But few historians have written about the issue, and so far as I know none has devoted much thought to comparing the proposed popular response to global warming with earlier events. For example, few have paused to ask: How would we benefit now if our grandparents and great-grandparents had exercised more self-restraint and self-denial? Would we live better if they had exercised greater prudence and self-control?

In most instances the answer is surely no. If the Victorians had denied themselves the economic growth of which they were capable, they would have bequeathed to us a poorer world, not a richer one. If we were to discover that they had voluntarily held back from the enjoyment of new resources out of concern for their distant descendants, we would be more likely to think them quaint than noble, since it was impossible for them to know, in 1860, what sorts of activities would be pursued and valued in 2014 and what sort of commodities we would need. In the same way, most sacrificial actions undertaken now for the sake of our own distant descendants might well appear to *them* as comically irrelevant.

However, there are a few cases where the answer is yes. We *do* benefit from the fact that the Victorians finally realized they were driving many species to extinction. Their belated decision to restrain themselves came too late for the passenger pigeon, but it did bequeath to us the wolves, buffalo, mountain lions, and many bird species that have since recovered. Extinction is a once-and-for-all proposition and we surely owe our ancestors a debt of gratitude for trying to prevent it. That is worth remembering as we speculate about our obligations to our successors on the earth.

Global warming, like most other environmental issues, can best be understood in historical context. As with pollution, population, and urban sprawl, we should treat it as a real problem, but a manageable one. It is one of the problems of success. The rising human carbon footprint may be troublesome, but it is a side effect of the creation of immense benefits. The search for remedies is worthwhile so long as it does not do more harm to society than the ostensible benefits it seeks to achieve.

THE "WARMERS"

The problem of climate change first came to public notice, paradoxically, because of concerns about global *cooling*. In 1971 Stephen Schneider, a NASA scientist, estimated that increasing levels of atmospheric dust caused by rapid industrialization would lead to significant worldwide cooling in the coming decades, and that the mean surface temperature of the earth could fall by as much as 3.5 degrees Celsius. Temperature records between 1940 and 1970 showed a downward trend and seemed to support Schneider's forecast. Other scientists, such as Reid Bryson, professor of meteorology at the University of Wisconsin, had noticed that large areas of the earth were affected by dust from farming and forestry, haze from industry, and clouds created by aircraft contrails. He agreed with Schneider that they would reduce the amount of sunlight reaching the earth's surface and would therefore have a cooling effect. *Science News* reported that "a temperature decrease of this magnitude, if sustained over a period of several years, might be sufficient to trigger an ice age."[1]

The possibility of a global cooling trend made headlines in the 1970s. Stephen Schneider, later a global warming advocate, advanced the idea.

In 1975 a report from the U.S. National Academy of Sciences confirmed this possibility. According to one observer, this report, written in a tone of "repressed alarm," represented "a warning by some of the world's most conservative, prestigious, cautious scientists that an Ice Age beginning in the near future . . . was not impossible." Schneider himself was aware that rising carbon dioxide levels in the atmosphere might offset some of the cooling, but he believed the "greenhouse effect" was limited and that, after the first one or two degrees, more carbon dioxide did not imply more warming. The front cover of *Science News* on March 1, 1975, showed an immense glacier crushing New York's skyscrapers next to the headline "The Ice Age Cometh?" In 1976

Bryson wrote that a majority of climate scientists now believed the earth's temperature was changing and "of that majority, a majority believe that the longer trend will be downward."[2]

Well-funded scientific studies of temperature decline, by the National Academy of Sciences and others, ended with speculation about how society might compensate for shorter growing seasons, severer winters, and advancing ice sheets. Lowell Ponte's 1976 book *The Cooling* painted a grim picture of the effects of a process that he insisted had already begun. Fog was chilling Southern California, frost and snow were damaging Brazilian coffee harvests, an entire fleet carrying supplies to Alaska pipeline workers had been frozen into the heaviest pack ice in decades, and glaciers were advancing so rapidly in Alaska, China, Iceland, Canada, and Russia that they threatened human settlements.

> If the cooling continues . . . we could possibly witness the beginning of the next Great Ice Age. Conceivably, some of us might live to see huge snowfields remaining year-round in northern regions of the United States and Europe. Probably we would see mass global famine in our lifetimes, perhaps even within a decade. Since 1970, half a million human beings in northern Africa and Asia have starved because of floods and droughts caused by the cooling climate.

Similarly, a British TV documentary of 1974 warned of a possible coming "snow-blitz," adding that a new ice age might be triggered at any moment.[3]

In fall 1983 a group of scientists led by Cornell and NASA astronomer Carl Sagan (1934–1996) announced in a press conference that severe human-induced cooling would be one of the effects of a nuclear war. Those not killed in the blast and radiation, Sagan warned, would die in the ensuing freeze, the "nuclear winter," as smoke from burning cities along with dust and debris rising into the atmosphere occluded the sun. At its worst, the chill would prevent photosynthesis, cause a mass crop failure, and condemn to starvation even people who had been remote from the actual nuclear explosions. These claims amplified the fears explored in the previous year by the journalist Jonathan Schell, whose book *The Fate of the Earth* had won a Pulitzer Prize.[4]

Within five years, however, concern about global cooling had all but disappeared, replaced by a more impassioned claim that the real hazard was global *warming*. The scientist who first made headline news with the idea was James Hansen of NASA's Goddard Institute for Space Studies. An expert on the atmosphere of Venus, Hansen had become interested during the 1980s in long-term trends in the earth's atmosphere. He showed in 1988 that there had been a perceptible warming effect since the 1880s (when significant data collection began) of between 0.5 and

NASA scientist James Hansen, whose testimony before Congress in 1988 helped turn the idea of global warming into a political issue.

0.7 degrees Celsius. He also showed that the four warmest years on record had all been in the 1980s. In dramatic testimony before the Senate Energy and Natural Resources Committee in June 1988, on a very hot day in Washington, Hansen said the earth was already feeling the effects of global warming and that it was "time to stop waffling so much and say that the evidence is pretty strong that the greenhouse effect is here." He added that the Midwest and Southeast now faced the prospect of regular blazing summers and droughts.[5]

In a speech that December, Hansen also predicted that hurricanes would become more powerful than ever, with winds up to 225 miles per hour. He even offered a bet to all comers that one of the next three years would be the hottest ever recorded, and in 1990 he won, against climatologist Hugh Ellsaesser, who doubted that Hansen's data were conclusive. Hansen was convinced that small changes in temperature could have dramatic consequences and that it would be unwise to assume slow, linear change as temperatures rose gradually: "That makes it prudent to be very careful about how hard we're pushing the climate system, because we just don't know when it might respond in a very non-linear way."[6]

In 1988, the same year as Hansen's congressional testimony, the World Meteorological Organization and the United Nations jointly created the Intergovernmental Panel on Climate Change (IPCC), a hybrid organization made up of scientists and politicians. The IPCC was charged with sponsoring research, monitoring results, and reporting regularly on the state of the field and its implications. It issued its first report in 1990, confirming the warming trend but admitting to a wide range of uncertainties about its cause and its future development.[7]

Stephen Schneider, who had warned of global cooling in the 1970s, reappeared in the late 1980s as a leading advocate of human-induced global *warming*. His 1989 book *Global Warming: Are We Entering the Greenhouse Century?* blended scientific studies with policy recommendations. He now described the greenhouse effect as a much more serious threat than he had previously recognized, and anticipated the possibility of a five-degree rise in global temperature, perhaps as soon as 2050. Schneider urged the industrial nations to take drastic steps to prevent continued warming.[8]

Science historian Spencer Weart notes that the late 1980s and early 1990s was the moment when the environmental movement really began to take notice of the issue of potential climate change.

> Groups that had other reasons for preserving tropical forests, promoting energy conservation, slowing population growth, or reducing air pollution could make common cause as they offered their various ways to reduce emissions of CO_2. Adding their voices to the chorus were people who looked for arguments to weaken the prestige of

large corporations. For better or worse, global warming became firmly identified as a "green" issue.

The new evidence appeared to be stronger than the earlier evidence about cooling. Even so, as Weart remarks, "it was an extraordinary novelty that such a thing became a political question at all. Global warming was invisible, no more than a possibility, and not even a current possibility." He sees the surge of popular interest as testimony to the rising capacity of a well-educated general public to grasp abstractions and consider distant contingencies, particularly those related to the environment.[9]

Central to the explanation of why global temperatures might be rising was the increase of greenhouse gases, in particular carbon dioxide (CO_2), water vapor, methane, nitrous oxides, and chlorofluorocarbons. Industrial processes and the burning of biomass generate CO_2 as a waste gas. An atmosphere rich in greenhouse gases holds more heat from the sun rather than dissipating it into space. The intensive industrialization and deforestation of the world after 1945, and more recently of China and India, had increased the quantity of CO_2 in the atmosphere. The respected atmospheric scientist C. D. Keeling had been taking annual readings from a mountaintop site at Mauna Loa in Hawaii since 1957, which showed an unwavering upward trend through the later years of the twentieth century. Readings of about 315 parts per million in 1957 had reached about 350 parts per million by 1990 and have since moved into the 390s.[10]

It was possible to trace not only recent and current levels of atmospheric CO_2, but also CO_2 levels in earlier centuries, by sampling arctic ice cores. The technique was invented by a Danish scientist, Willi Dansgaard, in the 1950s and 1960s, and perfected around 1980. By drilling into the deep ice of Greenland and Antarctica, which had been accumulating for centuries, scientists were able to analyze the composition of the tiny air bubbles trapped in the ice. The deeper the stratum of the ice core, the earlier the year it represented. These ice core experiments established that CO_2 levels had always been higher during interglacial periods and lower during recurrent ice ages, suggesting a close correlation between a CO_2-rich atmosphere and global warmth. Readings from the most recent levels, after the industrial revolution, were the highest.[11]

The revolution in computer technology of the 1960s and 1970s enabled climate scientists to undertake ever more complicated forecasting experiments. Their aim was to simulate atmospheric conditions all over the world and predict how increases in greenhouse gases would affect them over the coming decades and centuries. An effective general circulation model (GCM) would have to account for such factors as the difference between land and sea areas, prevailing winds, cloud patterns, differences in temperature at various altitudes, changes in vegetation, shifts in ocean currents, and even, ideally, such extraterrestrial factors as changes in solar radiation and sunspot activity. The model would need good data from tens of thousands of points all over the earth's surface, all of which could then be transfigured into computer language. It depended on a high degree of abstraction from empirical data. This kind of climate modeling, with ostensibly long-term predictive value, was alien to meteorologists, who were constantly updating their own models in light of daily or hourly shifts in the weather. To feel confident that their *future* projections were accurate, moreover, the climate modelers would also need to be able to read *backward* accurately. In other words, could they show, given data from the present, what had happened over the preceding centuries? If they could, their projections would be far more deserving of confidence than if they could not, and this problem hamstrung the early GCM modelers of the 1980s and 1990s.[12]

The modelers soon learned that tiny variations in the information they fed into the computers could lead to large variations in outcome. That might prove, as critics of the methodology suggested, that there was simply too much randomness in climate across the whole world and too many variables to make computer modeling meaningful. On the other hand, it might suggest that small changes in initial conditions could have vast consequences later—an insight with ominous implications when considered in light of climate change. The complexity of the computer models continued to increase and the quality of observational data from all over the world improved with each passing year.[13]

Anxious commentators, extrapolating from the computer studies, speculated that continued warming could have grave consequences. First, it might thaw the polar ice caps and glaciers, potentially raising sea levels and threatening coastal areas with inundation. The breakup of the immense Antarctic Larsen Ice Shelf in 1995 offered vivid evidence to support this possibility.[14] Second, it might accelerate desertification, making tropical areas uninhabitable and generating large numbers of "environmental refugees." Third, global warming might trigger changes in the familiar ocean currents and prevailing winds, with immense consequences for the most heavily settled parts of the world. For example, if the warm Gulf Stream no longer flowed northeast from the Caribbean to the Irish Sea, it might make Northern Europe much colder than before. A related possibility was that changing ocean conditions might create more, and fiercer, hurricanes. Fourth, it would destabilize the habitat of endangered species and contribute to a wave of extinctions. Fifth, it could also increase the likelihood of severe infectious disease outbreaks as tropical and subtropical diseases migrated to formerly temperate zones.[15]

Paleoclimatologists, interested in the question of why ice ages begin and end, also began to theorize that these changes might be sudden rather than gradual. Excavations and ice core work in the early 1990s suggested that just a few decades had sometimes been enough to witness a radical change in climate conditions, suggesting that small temperature changes had initiated very powerful positive feedback effects. We could not depend on everything happening gradually, but might suddenly reach a tipping point at which catastrophic changes happened all at once.[16] In 1998 an article on "The Great Climate Flip-Flop" in the *Atlantic Monthly* popularized this idea. The author, William Calvin (a popular science writer and professor of medicine at the University of Washington), declared that the changes "would occur too quickly for us to make readjustments in agricultural productivity and supply; it would be a potentially civilization-shattering affair, likely to cause an unprecedented population crash." The hypothesis provided the scientific scenario for a 2004 Hollywood movie, *The Day After Tomorrow*, in which the cities of the American Northeast suddenly become arctic wastelands, forcing a mass migration of the U.S. population into Central America.[17]

Nearly everyone involved admitted that the subject of global warming was fraught with uncertainties, especially in the 1980s and early 1990s. They acknowledged that it was difficult to distinguish between "climate" and "weather." Many writers on the topic were drawn to anecdotes that seemed to suggest that anomalous weather events were increasing, and were signs of imminent disaster. A further complication arose in 1991 when Mount Pinatubo, a volcano in the Philippines, erupted, spewing millions of tons of sulfur dioxide and other debris into the atmosphere and creating a measurable plume around the world. It was probably the biggest volcanic eruption of the twentieth century, and for a while global temperatures dropped. The eruption therefore inhibited studies that sought to measure atmospheric warming.[18]

Numerous writers in the late 1980s and early 1990s were struck by the degree to which scientists like Hansen were entering the policy realm, where their political naivete was sometimes painfully obvious. One political scientist familiar with Machiavellian realities wrote:

> Some science- and engineering-trained architects of greenhouse response strategies appear to suffer from the expectation, unfounded in the political arena, that policy arguments win on their merits. Others seem to assume that science education is all that is needed to galvanize public support for climate stabilization. In short, the facile treatment of greenhouse politics by some atmospheric scientists suggests that policymakers may have as much to *teach* scientists about the political process as they have to *learn* from them about changes in our atmosphere.[19]

Stephen Schneider agreed with Hansen that climate modelers needed to speak out in public if they were convinced that there was no other way to express the urgency of the situation. In a 1989 interview with the journalist Jonathan Schell, Schneider meditated on the ethics of scientists raising the alarm:

> As scientists we are ethically bound to the scientific method, in effect promising to tell the truth, the whole truth, and nothing but—which means that we must include all the doubts, the caveats, the ifs, ands, and buts. On the other hand, we are not just scientists but human beings as well. And like most people we'd like to see the world a better place, which in this context translates into our working to reduce the risk of potentially disastrous climatic change. To do that we need to get some broad-based support, to capture the public's imagination. That, of course, entails getting loads of media coverage. So we have to offer up scary scenarios, make simplified, dramatic statements, and make little mention of any doubts we might have. This "double ethical bind" we frequently find ourselves in cannot be solved by any formula. Each of us has to decide what the right balance is between being effective and being honest. I hope that means being both.

Schneider himself led one of the IPCC working groups, founded the journal *Climatic Change*, won a MacArthur Fellowship, and spoke regularly on popular television news and chat shows to publicize the idea of a global warming menace.[20]

Remarks like this candid admission from Schneider raised the question of whether it was possible to make an absolute separation between science and policy. David Demeritt, a theoretical geographer, speculated that the convergence of science and policy was putting a subtle pressure on the scientists themselves, even those who avoided joining the political argument:

> How to conduct this experiment or measurement? Whether to trust that datum or result? Whose interpretation to believe? Such questions are the stuff of everyday scientific

practice, and they depend on trust and professional judgment. Try as we might to be scrupulously impartial and open-minded, these decisions remain socially saturated . . . Unfortunately, public representations of science seldom acknowledge the irreducibly social dimension of scientific knowledge or practice.

He watched a group of climate modelers at work and noted that its members felt an implicit obligation to conform to a set of policy expectations.[21]

While Hansen, Schneider, and many others provided the scientific data, no one did more to popularize the idea of global warming as a potentially immense problem than Al Gore. A Democratic senator from Tennessee, Gore staked out a position on environmental issues during the 1980s. In a *New York Times* op-ed in 1989, for example, he compared the situation of global warming to the year 1938: we had, he declared, reached a new "ecological Kristallnacht." Just as the world then had faced the Nazi menace, so now it faced an "environmental holocaust." Global warming was undeniable, he declared, and like resource depletion, deforestation, ozone depletion, and species extinctions, it was getting worse. "Just as a drug addict needs increasing doses to produce the same effect, our global appetite for the earth's abundance grows each year." He flayed the George H. W. Bush White House for its inaction. His book *Earth in the Balance* (1992) described global warming as "the most serious threat that we have *ever* faced" and urged the nation and the world to act "boldly, decisively, comprehensively, and quickly." Then he became vice president in 1992, raising hopes of a new approach from the White House.[22]

Reality did not match Gore's hopes. As always, different government agencies pulled in different directions, and President Clinton was eager not to give the impression that he favored abatement of global warming over economic growth. Gore himself was politically hardheaded enough to know that he couldn't expect the electorate to welcome economic hardships. He therefore asserted that it would be possible to cut

CO_2 emissions without restricting growth—it would simply have to be cleaner and more intelligent growth than ever before. He admitted to the environmental writer Bill McKibben that practical politicians like himself, who understood the magnitude of the global warming problem, were in a difficult bind: "The maximum that is politically feasible, even the maximum that is politically imaginable right now, still falls short of the minimum that is scientifically and ecologically necessary." The election of a sharply counterenvironmental and conservative Congress in the midterm elections of 1994 made things from his point of view even worse than before.[23]

Gore was convinced that an international agreement on CO_2 abatement was vital, and he believed that the United States, as the leading industrial power, should take the initiative. Making and enforcing an international treaty would be difficult, however, because developing nations like China and India, among the worst emitters of greenhouse gases, did not want to restrict their industrial growth. They had a weaker scientific infrastructure and resented being asked to make sacrifices on behalf of a hypothetical future benefit, especially when the developed world already enjoyed the material advantages that they were trying to achieve for themselves.[24]

Gore gave a dramatic speech at the international conference that considered global warming at Kyoto in 1997. He urged the governments of the assembled delegates to sign a protocol agreeing to cut emissions of greenhouse gases back to 1990 levels by the year 2012. Poorer countries, including China and India, would be exempted from the requirement. Because they were exempt, however, the U.S. Senate— heavily lobbied by a skeptics' organization, the Global Climate Coalition—voted ninety-five to zero against the protocol. It was a jarring disappointment for Gore, further exacerbated by his narrow loss to George W. Bush in the presidential election of 2000 and Bush's decision not to follow the protocol.[25]

Once out of office, Gore devoted more of his time than ever before to the global warming issue and developed a multimedia slideshow designed to present the evidence in the most compelling form. After delivering the talk hundreds of times in American cities and around the world, he collaborated with filmmaker Davis Guggenheim to make *An Inconvenient Truth* (2006). The film shows Gore giving his presentation in a folksy style to an audience of concerned citizens. Guggenheim also intersperses episodes from Gore's political and personal life, culminating with the controversial events of the 2000 election. He also includes film clips of Antarctic ice shelves collapsing into the sea, of areas once covered in glaciers now laid bare, and of hapless hurricane victims in New Orleans just after Hurricane Katrina in August 2005. It ends with a somber Gore declaring that global warming is not just a scientific issue, but a moral one. America must once again summon the political will to overcome it, just as it did to win the Revolutionary War, end slavery, give women the vote, and end segregation. The film was well received, won two Oscars, and boosted public awareness of the issue.[26]

THE GLOBAL WARMING SKEPTICS

Gore was a highly controversial figure and plenty of influential intellectuals and politicians disagreed entirely with his view. On global warming, as on many other environmental issues, skeptics cast doubt on whether they were looking at an accurate picture of the earth's probable future or just a computer-projected illusion. They pointed out that it is extremely difficult to disentangle "climate" from "weather" and to detect real trends in the midst of the confusing "noise" generated by thousands of readings from countless different stations. They also wondered whether warming, even if real, was as apocalyptic as Hansen, Schneider, Gore, and others implied. Might it not be another real but manageable problem?

Besides, was it not possible that the atmosphere responded to warming with negative feedback effects, preserving a rough equilibrium rather than triggering sudden shifts? Some observers believed it did. In 1988, A. James Wagner at the National Weather Service explained to

New York Times journalist Malcolm Browne: "A global increase in temperature would increase evaporation from the oceans, thereby producing more clouds and rainfall. Rain falling on land might cool the land and subsequently cool the air over the land. The increased cloud cover, moreover, would reflect more sunlight away from the earth than normal as a result of this compensation." Variations on this theme—that the problem was self-correcting rather than self-reinforcing—proved very persistent as the debates continued.[27]

Skeptics tried other explanations, too. Some, agreeing that global temperatures had risen during the last century, argued that it was not possible to be certain that human activity was the cause. Why was it, they asked, that the warming between 1900 and 1940 was greater than the warming *since* 1940? If industry was the principal cause, the increased industrialization of the post–World War II era should have made the curve steeper in those decades rather than shallower. Yet between 1940 and 1975 there had been a long pause before the upward trend resumed—long enough, at least, to give rise to the global cooling scare.[28]

We now know enough about the history of the earth, said other skeptics, not to expect long-term climate equilibrium. The planet has always experienced variations, the most dramatic of which were the ice ages. Clearly the earlier shifts were not caused by human activity. In recorded history we know that the period around the year AD 1000 was relatively warm, enough that Viking settlers could live and farm in Greenland, which would be impossible today. We also know that in Shakespeare's time (the late 1500s and early 1600s) the River Thames in London froze hard every year and was the site of a fair, ice-skaters, and a market, whereas today it never freezes.[29]

Since climate change clearly predated the industrial revolution, something other than human action must have caused it. The ultimate source of the earth's climate is the sun, whose own workings were being studied throughout the twentieth century. As early as 1800 British astronomers and economists noted a correlation between sunspot activity and food prices, suggesting that more sunspots created warmer weather and better harvests. In the 1990s a group of Danish scientists showed a strong relationship between sunspot activity and the global warming of their own era. Their idea was confirmed by the Columbia University geologist Gerard Bond, who concluded in 2001 that "the Earth's climate system is highly sensitive to extremely weak perturbations in the Sun's energy output" and that "solar variability will continue to influence climate in the future." Another Danish scientist, Henrik Svensmark, showed a relationship between the intensity of cosmic rays from solar wind and the creation of atmospheric clouds. These discoveries offered a theoretical challenge to the claim that anthropogenic CO_2 was the decisive factor.[30]

Skeptics also criticized the influential "hockey stick" graph published in the journal *Nature* in 1998 by computer modelers Michael Mann, Raymond Bradley, and Malcolm Hughes (MBH98). The graph showed that after centuries of more or less constant temperatures, there had been a sudden and completely unprecedented temperature rise in the late twentieth century, taking the world into an era of superheating that it had never experienced before. The curve looked like a hockey stick laid on its side, with a long, flat handle and a sudden upward-curving end to represent the recent warming. The graph reappeared in the IPCC's 2001 report.[31]

A Canadian businessman, Stephen McIntyre, recognized the hockey stick curve as similar to those illustrating stock market promotions that promised sudden and unprecedented profits. The recent high-tech stock market bust prompted him to check the data and the authors' statistical methods from scratch. Finding numerous errors, omissions, and guesses in the authors' work, and confronting their steady refusal to cooperate, he redrew the graph. It showed "that early fifteenth-century values exceeded twentieth-century values, contradicting the MBH98 conclusion of twentieth-century uniqueness." The hockey stick, and its assertion of unparalleled warming, disappeared. He was amazed that no one at *Nature* or IPCC had checked the basic research and mathematics. As McIntyre and his collaborator Ross McKitrick wrote, the experience raised serious questions about the adequacy of peer review: "In the private sector, no one would build an oil refinery based on an academic article. There is a process of engineering due diligence . . . Yet governments will make far larger, costlier decisions based on the chimerical standard of academic peer review." Other scholars' studies gradually led to the discrediting of the hockey stick curve.[32]

If James Hansen and Stephen Schneider were the most prominent scientific exponents of global warming as a real problem, Richard Lindzen and Fred Singer were the most prominent scientific skeptics. Lindzen, a professor of meteorology at MIT and a member of the National Academy of Sciences, had already made major contributions to the understanding of how the atmosphere works. Almost as soon as global warming began to make headlines in 1988 he began publicly to challenge the pessimistic scenarios, arguing that the atmosphere takes care of itself with powerful negative feedback effects and that the detected temperature rise was within the range of experimental error. Lindzen added in later articles that even a doubling of atmospheric CO_2 would probably result in a permanent temperature rise of less than one degree Celsius, "which is well within the range of natural variability," and that the computer models remained far too primitive and too remote from reality to deserve observers' full confidence.[33]

He also seized on anomalies in the data, such as the fact that measurements from 1999 showed significant warming at ground level but not in the upper atmosphere. Since greenhouse warming meant by definition that the atmosphere warmed the earth's surface, this was a surprising finding. "If you don't have warming in the atmosphere and you do have it at the surface, the surface [warming] is not a greenhouse response," he argued. But despite his doubts, Lindzen played a prominent role in researching and writing the IPCC Assessment Reports of 1995 and 2001. He defended the scientific work his panels presented, but protested that the Summary for Policymakers in 2001 represented a political distortion of the findings. He also told Congress that members of the panel were pressured to declare a greater confidence in the computer models than they sometimes felt: "Throughout the drafting sessions, IPCC 'coordinators' would go around insisting that criticism of models be toned down, and that 'motherhood' statements be inserted to the effect that models might still be correct despite the cited faults. Refusals were occasionally met with ad hominem attacks. I personally witnessed coauthors forced to assert their 'green' credentials in defense of their statements."[34]

Singer, like Lindzen, had a distinguished career in government and academia, which included supervising the building and launching of a system of meteorological satellites, a stint as policy adviser to the Environmental Protection Agency, and a distinguished professorship in environmental sciences at the University of Virginia. He too knew how to use the publicity offered by congressional testimony, press, and broadcast media. In 1990, just after the creation of the IPCC, Singer founded the Science and Environmental Policy Project, which became a center for scientific work on the uncertainties and ambiguities of climate change. In a barrage of letters to *Science,* the *Washington Post,* and the *New York Times* and frequent appearances on radio and television shows, he emphasized the unreliability of computer modeling as a predictor of future climate. He also argued the need for skepticism about the accuracy of temperature-measuring stations throughout the world, con-

Bjorn Lomborg, Denmark's "skeptical environmentalist."

cluding that we probably could not even know *whether* the temperature was rising or falling. Singer, like Lindzen, noted that satellites did not confirm the rising temperature patterns being derived from ground temperature readings.[35]

Singer believed the Kyoto Protocol was based on inadequate science and that it falsely implied the existence of a scientific consensus. It was also worthless in practice: "Enforcing its targets would reduce global temperature in 2050 by only 0.05 degrees C, a virtually undetectable amount." Singer raised the possibility, also favored by some economists, that on balance warming would be beneficial, not harmful: "GNP would increase, with agriculture and forestry benefiting the most." Singer's 1999 book *Hot Talk, Cold Science* expanded these ideas. Singer became a polarizing figure, widely admired by other global warming skeptics but bitterly hated by advocates. His willingness to work with oil and coal corporations and with conservative think tanks was explored at length in popular and scholarly rebuttals to his claims.[36]

The most energetic skeptic of all was Bjorn Lomborg (born 1965), a Danish statistician and political scientist. Lomborg's thick tome *The Skeptical Environmentalist*, first published in his home country in 1998, then in England and the United States in 2001, subjected every controversial environmental issue to statistical analysis. In most cases, he concluded, the standard orthodoxy, or what he called "The Litany," is wrong, and we have a seriously skewed idea of which environmental problems are the most serious and which we can most effectively remedy. The best way to safeguard the earth, he argued, was to enable humans to become wealthier, because wealthy societies are more resilient and better able to protect themselves in the face of new threats. He deplored the one-sided media coverage of global warming, noting that "the typical reporting on global warming tells us all the bad things that could happen from CO_2 emissions but few or none of the bad things that could come from overly zealous regulation of such emissions." In his view, global warming was real but could not be unambiguously attributed to human action. It had several benign consequences, he believed, and was not a harbinger of catastrophe.[37]

The Skeptical Environmentalist provoked a firestorm of controversy, even prompting the Danish Committee on Scientific Dishonesty to investigate Lomborg. It found him guilty of bias, selective citation, misleading use of statistics, and failure to uphold adequate scientific standards. On appeal, however, the judgment was overturned by the Danish Ministry of Science, Technology, and Innovation, which pointed out that the committee had not identified any specific examples of deception. He emerged from the dispute as controversial as ever, now with a new job as head of his country's Environmental Evaluation Institute.[38]

Lomborg followed up with a new book, *Cool It: The Skeptical Environmentalist's Guide to Global Warming*, in 2007. Reaffirming that global warming was taking place and conceding that its origins were at least in part anthropogenic, he emphasized cost-effective responses to the problem. In his view, it was a grave mistake for governments to commit themselves to expensive CO_2-reduction programs in line with Kyoto because their future beneficiaries were impossible to identify and because such programs would only delay the effects of the warming by a few years. "Such a course is especially debatable in a world where billions of people live in poverty, where millions die of curable diseases, and where these lives could be saved, societies strengthened, and environments improved at a fraction of the cost."[39]

Cool It was packed with challenges to prevailing wisdom. Lomborg demonstrated that polar bear populations in the Arctic were increasing, despite widespread reporting by Al Gore and others that the melting of the ice was causing their numbers to dwindle. He reminded readers that far more people die of cold than of heat every year and that global warming affected the most northerly and southerly latitudes more than the temperate and torrid zones, so that Europe and the United States would feel relatively slight effects. Among the many positive effects of moderate warming would be a reduction in the number of deaths from cardiovascular and respiratory disease. One of the organizations he supervised, the Copenhagen Consensus, was a group of economists who studied the cost-effectiveness of different methods of helping humanity. They had discovered, wrote Lomborg, that in terms of cost per life saved, it was much wiser to work on HIV/AIDS prevention, malaria abatement, and third world nutrition than on Kyoto-style CO_2 reductions.[40]

Lomborg's core argument was that each generation should do what it could with its limited resources to help people who were suffering in that moment, rather than trying to aid future generations. The best way to do this was to enable nations to become wealthier, because wealth gave them so much more resilience and flexibility. The control of malaria—once very common in America—illustrated this point. He showed that when the Centers for Disease Control set out to eradicate malaria after World War II, they found a close correlation between vulnerability and income. It might be true that global warming would make more people in temperate zones theoretically susceptible to malaria, he admitted, but it was worth remembering that the United States had eradicated it during a period of warming because it had become wealthier. "Studies show that when countries get to an annual income of about $3,100 per person, they can eradicate malaria, because their personal wealth will allow them to buy more protection and treatment, while their societies will be sufficiently able to provide general health care and environmental management, such as house spraying and mosquito eradication." Global warming, he added, was not going to reintroduce malaria to the United States and Northern Europe, because these were wealthy societies equipped with the full repertoire of remedies.[41]

Although Lindzen, Singer, Lomborg, and most of the other outspoken warming skeptics were connected to the political right, the global warming theory also took a few knocks from the political left. Some radical social scientists described attempts to impose restrictions on the industries of the developing world as a form of "environmental colonialism" or "environmental orientalism." They pointed out that Western scientists' and policy makers' claim that global warming affected people everywhere was only half true. In countries where hunger, contaminated water supplies, smoke inhalation, endemic disease, high child mortality, and war were the daily realities of life, it was hardly more than a cruel joke to tell people that they faced the threat of a possible five degrees of warming over the next century and that preventing it should be their chief priority. Besides, observers in developing countries suspected that the governments of the industrial "North" were using global warming to gain tactical *economic* advantage over one another and over the poor "South." Two Indian economists wrote: "Pious rhetoric of global stewardship of the planet notwithstanding, the real battles over climate change are being fought over issues of trade and national competitiveness in the context of greenhouse policies." The concerns of the South had been almost entirely neglected, they wrote, even though the South would be asked to shoulder much of the burden.[42]

THE GLOBAL WARMING DEBATE reprised many characteristics of earlier environmental controversies. Each side believed that its opponents were acting in bad faith, accused them of ulterior motives, and declared that the other's proposed action (or inaction) was the gateway to disaster. Each side also had a distinctive rhetoric. Advocates of anthropogenic global warming routinely declared, from about 1990 onward, that they represented an overwhelming majority of all responsible scientists. They attributed their opponents' dissent to the fact that they were funded by oil, coal, and manufacturing interests, which stood to lose millions of dollars if fossil fuel use was restricted. Ross Gelbspan, author of *The Heat Is On* (1997), was typical in this respect: "A major battle is under way. In order to survive economically, the biggest enterprise in human history—the worldwide coal and oil industry—is at war with the ability of the planet to sustain civilization. The trillion-dollar-a-year coal and oil industry is pitted against the oceans, forests, ice caps, and mountains of the earth as we know them today."[43]

Global warming skeptics, conversely, rarely failed to mention that prowarming advocates were merely the latest manifestation of a sectarian radicalism. These radicals, they wrote, had failed to convince the world with their earlier false alarms about population, food, and natural resources, and now they were trying again with an even graver, but equally overblown, scenario of apocalypse. "Now global warming is the *cause du jour.*" Not only were they wrong on the facts, said the skeptics, but they had devised a political solution to offer that would infringe on the free market and citizens' liberties, increase the danger of coercive or totalitarian government, and unnecessarily lower standards of living for nearly everyone. Having failed in the 1970s to provoke a large-scale switch to alternative energy sources in response to the crises of 1973 and 1979, they had now seized on a new pretext to push the same old agenda.[44]

Skeptics also argued that their opponents had a financial as well as an intellectual stake in the outcome. Adherence to the anthropogenic warming orthodoxy had become essential to anyone who hoped to secure funding from the big foundations and government agencies. Peer reviewers would reject research projects that challenged it. "Green" technology had meanwhile become a big business and its developers had a stake in the validity of theory. One skeptic wrote that "without a deal as made at Kyoto . . . large investments would be lost. Technology seeking new markets and money seeking investment opportunities in sequestering carbon would find it more difficult to obtain subsidies or helpful regulations." In her view, nations signed the treaty not from altruistic concern for the future welfare of the earth, but in the expectation of a direct economic benefit. She also noted that, despite efforts at presenting a united front, the IPCC was inwardly plagued by disagreements that were at least as much political as scientific.[45]

The earth itself, of course, did not offer decisive answers to the big climate questions, though there was little evidence to suggest that the situation was deteriorating dramatically. Some climatologists predicted that global warming would cause ever intensifying hurricanes, but the years after Katrina's assault on New Orleans in 2005 saw a mysterious lull in hurricane activity. Anomalous weather events continued, but did not provide unambiguous evidence in support of anthropogenic warming. A slight cooling trend even set in after 2002. Meanwhile, signatories to the Kyoto Protocol set to work to reduce carbon emissions. They tried to increase the use of alternative energy from renewable sources (wind, solar, and wave action) and to sequester greenhouse gases at source, and they drafted agreements to reduce deforestation. The European Union, where such efforts were particularly intense, discovered in the late twentieth and early twenty-first centuries that it was extraordinarily difficult to generate enough electricity from alternative sources, because they did not lend themselves to dependable bulk production. With each passing year the Kyoto targets seemed more daunting, and the probability that they would not be met loomed ever larger.

CHAPTER 10

ENVIRONMENTAL ISSUES
OF THE 1990S

AMERICA'S GLOBAL WARMING ANTAGONISTS had the precious advantage of a free press in which they could exchange views, reproaches, and even insults in public view. From the 1940s through the new millennium, the fact that all interested parties were able to publish their environmental views made effective outcomes much more likely: problems could be identified, evidence weighed, and appropriate remedies sought. The ending of the Cold War in 1989–1990, bringing decades of Soviet secrecy to a close, showed by contrast the appalling environmental dangers of autocracy and repression. The Soviet Union, lacking a free press, committed to high levels of industrialization without safeguards, and extraordinarily repressive against its own peoples, had created an environmental nightmare. No one in the United States had suffered even a fraction of the environmental degradation endured by the Soviet republics and Eastern Europe.

As the arduous project of cleaning up the post-Soviet world began, however, scientific and industrial advances in the West continued to raise new environmental questions. One concerned the rights and wrongs of genetically modified crops. James Watson and Francis Crick had explained the structure of DNA in 1953, opening up vast new areas of genetic research. By the 1980s their successors were experimenting with artificially modifying plants, with an eye to creating crops that could resist insects, fungi, drought, and cold. The argument in favor of such crops was that they held out the promise of greater and more dependable harvests to feed the world's growing population. The argument against them, widely held in Europe and America, was that such plants could never have evolved without human intervention and might mutate or crossbreed with other species in dangerous ways. They also appeared to put unprecedented economic power in the hands of the companies that patented the new crop strains.

A second and related question was the capacity of endangered species, plant and animal, to endure. In a world ever more dominated by human projects, and constantly exposed to new chemicals, new machines, new pharmaceuticals, and the spread of urban civilization, could unspectacular creatures—often confined to local and specialized habitats—survive? Similarly, what was the long-term genetic effect on humans of prolonged exposure to new chemicals? Gross forms of toxic pollution undoubtedly declined in the last thirty years of the twentieth century, but subtler threats remained, and the 1990s bore witness to new fears about nonlethal threats to human endocrines.

The Soviet environmental mess was glaring, blatant, and measurable in the most basic ways; Soviet contamination had poisoned generations, shortening life expectancy, creating chronic public health problems, and often failing to achieve expected productivity. The American issues, by comparison, were ambiguous. Genetically modified crops *might* have harmful effects in the long run, but were highly beneficial in the short. The question of species loss also proved unexpectedly elusive in the 1990s. Some endangered species had already been brought back from the brink of extinction, but these tended to be the "charismatic megafauna," such as eagles, wolves, and mountain lions, that had made the issue popular in the first place. Surprisingly, it remained difficult to say with confidence even *whether* the extinction of insects, corals, mosses, and other noncharismatic life forms was accelerating or whether human measures to protect them were succeeding.

THE SOVIET LEGACY

The end of the Soviet Union and its empire in Eastern Europe trans-formed the world's geopolitical situation. Western observers, given easy access for the first time in generations, were horrified by the environ-mental degradation this vast area had suffered under Soviet programs of forced industrialization. The Chernobyl disaster of 1986 had been so severe that even the secrecy-obsessed Soviet government had been un-able to hide it. Visitors now realized that Chernobyl was merely the visible tip of an immense iceberg of environmental spoliation. Environ-mental concerns may actually have contributed to the fall of the Soviet system. According to the *Economist* in 1989, "[T]he preservation of na-ture has become a national obsession . . . Green feelings now run as deep, and are as politically challenging, as anywhere in the world . . . The most influential informal organizations in the Soviet Union are the so-called popular fronts . . . pressing for greater political, cultural and economic autonomy. Most began as green lobbies."[1]

Soviet cities suffered from extraordinarily high levels of smoke and smog pollution. Moreover, as an immediately post-1989 report showed, "Almost three fourths of the nation's surface water is polluted; one fourth is completely untreated. By themselves, the two giant ministries of energy and metallurgy account for half the air pollution. Untreated, wa-terborne agricultural, industrial and human wastes together threaten to kill the Sea of Azov, the Black Sea, and the Caspian, and have turned giant rivers, including the Volga, the Dneipr, and the Don, into open sewers." Public health levels were so low, diets so poor, and medical care so inadequate that more than half of young Soviet men were found to be unfit for military service.[2]

The destruction of the Aral Sea in Central Asia (now part of Uzbeki-stan and Kazakhstan) was among the most catastrophic of Soviet blun-ders, dwarfing anything that had happened in the United States. A body of water covering 26,300 square miles, the Aral had for centuries hosted a thriving fishing industry and had yielded fifty thousand tons of fish per year as recently as the 1950s. The reedy wetlands at its edge had been habitat for thousands of other species. The Soviet government, eager to achieve self-sufficiency in cotton production, created large-scale irrigation projects, diverting water from the Aral Sea's tributary rivers, the Syr and Amu. These projects essentially drained the sea, whose level began to sink and whose shores shrank away starting in the early 1960s. By the end of the Cold War in 1989, fishing fleets had become rusted hulks, lying on sands miles from the sea itself, while the fragmentary remains of the lake were no more than a handful of salty pools. The surrounding wetlands had been destroyed.[3]

The disappearance of the sea affected the local climate, making average summer temperatures higher than before and winter temperatures lower. The whole region became much drier, and salt-laden windstorms began to create a dust hazard that damaged much of the irrigated farmland the project had created. The seabed, which some Soviet officials had anticipated turning into pastureland, became instead an alkaline wasteland. Even the canals that carried away the river water had been so poorly made that an estimated 70 percent of their water was lost to leakage. Leaking water flooded and undermined adjacent houses and damaged fields and orchards. Chemical-intensive farming polluted local wells, causing a sharp rise in cases of intestinal disease and infections of the liver, pancreas, and gallbladder. As a Western observer concluded, a project begun under the slogan "Millions of Tons of Cotton—at Any Cost" had ended in a situation of "catastrophic costs and no production whatsoever." Western health organizations like Doctors Without Borders struggled in the ensuing years to handle the public health fallout of the scheme.[4]

The years after the breakup of the Soviet Union continued to bring harrowing environmental news. The post-Soviet republic of Ukraine, now left with the legacy of the Chernobyl disaster, was probably the worst affected. Its minister of the environment said that two-thirds of his country's fifty-two million people had been exposed to elevated levels of radiation, with an anticipated future impact of between twenty thousand and forty thousand cancer deaths. An extraordinary cynicism on the part of the Soviet government had led to the unnecessary sacrifice of many Ukrainians' lives in the weeks immediately after the disaster, when evacuations were delayed and when emergency workers were given no protective clothing and no warning of the hazards they faced.[5]

Much of Eastern Europe, which had been politically dominated for forty-five years by the Soviet Union, was also afflicted. An area of southern Poland, the northern Czech Republic, and southeastern Germany, lying on a heavily exploited coalfield, became known as the "Black Triangle" because of elevated levels of pollution. Coal mining, power stations, and the use of coal for domestic heating generated high levels of sulfur dioxide and dust emissions, and smog-based fogs so thick they could bring cities to a standstill. Poor epidemiological studies, lack of environmental laws, and an odious tradition of government secrecy worsened an already difficult situation. Reports from the area immediately after the Cold War ended demonstrated high levels of lung cancer, emphysema, chronic bronchitis, and other respiratory diseases among its population. A *New York Times* article from the Romanian metallurgical towns of Baia Mare and Copsa Mica also reported high levels of contamination, where "even new shoots of grass are covered with a greasy black film" and where life expectancy, at fifty, was twenty years shorter than for the country as a whole. Studies of children showed elevated levels of lead in bones and teeth and widespread bronchial illnesses. Yet the local townspeople dreaded the closing of their factories, which would take away their livelihood.[6]

American environmental organizations had often criticized American companies for causing pollution and for their eagerness to shirk or minimize regulation. They nevertheless recognized that the situation on the other side of the Iron Curtain, where citizens were unable to protest and where regulation was slack, had been incomparably worse. In 1990, for example, Lester Brown's Worldwatch Institute, an environmental watchdog, condemned the intemperate use of high-sulfur brown coal throughout Eastern Europe and the area's neglect of environmental controls. Brown had often been a scourge to capitalist industrialists, but now even he declared that "the lack of market forces kept these countries from realizing the impressive gains in energy efficiency registered in the West after the oil shocks of the Seventies . . . Their weak economies still preclude major investments in pollution control." One of the principal achievements of the post–Cold War decades was the rapid improvement of environmental standards in parts of the former Soviet Bloc as the old Warsaw Pact nations of Eastern Europe were incorporated into the European Union.[7]

GENETICALLY MODIFIED FOODS

The 1990s bore witness to the first commercial launch of genetically modified crops. A generation of molecular biologists had followed Watson and Crick's insights on DNA by working on the genetic modification of plants and animals. Rapid progress in the 1970s and 1980s led to a Supreme Court decision (*Diamond v. Chakrabarty*, 1980) upholding manufacturers' right to patent engineered species. In 1994 a company called Calgene marketed a type of genetically modified tomato that ripened without softening. In subsequent years, genetically modified (GM) variants of soybeans, corn, and sugar beet followed. "BT corn," one of the most successful of these variants, even contained its own pesticide, *Bacillus thuringiensis*. A GM soybean was resistant to powerful herbicides like Roundup. As a result, that herbicide could be applied just once during the growing season and would suppress all the weeds growing around the corn until harvest.[8]

The advantages of genetically modified crops for farmers were significant. They could be engineered to suit consumer preferences and to better fit the conditions in which they were grown. Drought-resistant genes could improve crops' durability in dry areas. Fish genes for endurance of cold weather could give strawberries and potatoes a resistance to otherwise lethal late frosts. Pest-resistant crops like BT corn yielded more at harvest time, diminished the need for pesticide spraying, and alleviated the problem of contaminated runoff from heavily treated fields. Herbicide resistance engineered into the crops also decreased the amount of tillage needed to suppress weeds during the growing season, which in turn discouraged soil erosion, another great scourge of intensive agriculture. "Gold" varieties of rice were created in 1999 by Ingo Potrykus and Xudong Ye, modified to include more vitamin A, addressing the chronic nutrition problems—and frequent blindness—suffered by people living in areas where rice was the staple food.[9]

Advocates of GM foods pointed out that the creation of desired traits was now quick and reliable, whereas selective crossbreeding, the traditional means of developing traits, was time-consuming and not always reliable. Here was a way to ensure a continuing food supply for the earth's growing population. It was true that food supplies had more than kept pace with worldwide population growth. Still, the world's population was expected to reach six billion by the year 2000 and was going to continue increasing for at least another half century after that, even though rates of growth had slowed. GM crops might be the surest way of feeding this vast new population and carrying on the humane work that the green revolution had begun.[10]

Before they could be marketed in the United States, GM crops had to be approved by the Department of Agriculture, the EPA, and the Food and Drug Administration (FDA), each of which imposed safety criteria. Former president Jimmy Carter, himself a farmer, was an enthusiast for GM crops. Since leaving the White House he had been involved in low-tech health and nutrition programs in the third world and had become an authority on the subject. "By increasing crop yields," he wrote in the *New York Times* in 1998, "GM organisms reduce the constant need to clear more land for growing food. Seeds designed to resist drought and pests are especially useful in tropical countries, where crop losses are often severe." He also enumerated their potential medical and nutritional benefit, and urged skeptics not to stand in the way of their widespread export. Norman Borlaug, who had won a Nobel Prize in 1970 for his work on hybrid crop plants, was also an enthusiastic supporter of GM.[11]

GM foods were, nevertheless, acutely controversial. Among their most vocal and outspoken opponents was Jeremy Rifkin, an environmental activist and author of *The Biotech Century* (1998). Rifkin compared genetic engineering to the delusion of the old alchemists, who had tried to turn base metals into gold. Genetic engineering struck Rifkin as another false quest for perfection, motivated not by altruism but by greed. Worse, it pointed to a revival of eugenics, the science of artificially perfecting humanity, which had been disgraced and discredited by Adolf Hitler. Similarly, Prince Charles, heir to the British throne, denounced GM foods in a *Daily Telegraph* editorial in 1998 as a form of playing God and as an excessively risky step that, once taken, could not be undone. The prince wrote, "Once genetic material has been released into the environment it cannot be recalled . . . If something does go badly wrong we will be faced with the problem of clearing up a kind of pollution which is self-perpetuating."[12]

Many other less prominent figures also raised various alarms. First, how would GM crops fit into preestablished environments? Was it possible that "rogue" GM plants would have unforeseen consequences in the wild, crossbreeding with unmodified varieties or displacing them completely? Although BT corn was effective at killing crop pests, it also killed other insects indiscriminately, many of which were harmless. Critics pointed out that the pesticide effect of the crops was likely to weaken over time as resistant varieties of insects evolved and reproduced. Suppose cross-fertilization of the Roundup-resistant crops with common plants led to the development of "superweeds." Already by 1997 a wide array of organizations, including the Sierra Club, Greenpeace, and an alliance of organic farmers, was petitioning the EPA to suspend its approval of BT corn.[13]

Second, GM crops could be patented and licensed. For millennia farmers had saved a part of one year's crop to plant as seeds in the following year. No longer. Now the farmer had to buy his seed each year from the manufacturer. This relationship gave the manufacturers immense power and was already, by the late 1990s, making GM crops one of the most lucrative commodities in the world. Would third world buyers, whose needs were the greatest, be able to afford GM crops, or would they be the preserve only of the rich nations, further widening the gap between the rich "North" and the poor "South"? Even if the food were given away, would the recipients accept it? In 2002 six African nations declined food aid from the United States because it was genetically engineered. Five eventually relented, but Zambia continued to refuse.[14]

GM foods also raised health concerns for some critics. A controversial paper in *Lancet* in 1999 by Arpad Pusztai and Stanley Ewen described damage to the digestive tract of rats that had been fed on genetically modified potatoes. Critics also pointed out that as more people became susceptible to dangerous allergies, modifying crops with genes from other species might provoke worse allergy problems.[15]

Critics of GM farming argued that the green revolution of the 1940s to the 1970s had itself raised crop yields sufficient to feed the world and that the reason some people were still hungry related to political instability and repression, not a lack of available food overall. Dave Toke, a British analyst of the GM controversy, noted that "world hunger" was often cited as a motive for producing the crops but that the actual producers and marketers of GM foods showed little interest in famine relief. He wrote: "[P]erhaps the 'GM crops will alleviate world hunger' storyline serves as a general rhetorical rejoinder to green claims that GM crops are the product of corporate villains who care only for profits." Certainly the GM food producers never suggested that they would emulate the NGOs and foreign aid programs that had freely distributed green revolution crops throughout the world in the previous generation.[16]

The most intense criticism came from Europe, where skepticism about American corporations and a lack of trust in government regulators created a hostile environment from the outset. In a broadside against all forms of genetic engineering, the British science journalist Andy Rees wrote: "We live at a time when the all-pervading Big Business lobby, and its huge influence on the media, has shifted received wisdom far away from commonsense and brainwashed us with half-truths, bad science, and outright lies. Nowhere have they done this more effectively than the GM debate, where the biotech lobby has poured colossal resources into its aggressive and proactive PR machine."[17]

Despite these concerns, GM food crops caught on very quickly in the United States during the 1990s, and no popular movement opposed their spread. By 2000 it was difficult for consumers to avoid buying GM food, because conventional and GM varieties were not marketed separately. In the European Union, by contrast, popular resistance to GM foods was much stronger and manufacturers were required to specify on their labels whether food products included GM ingredients.[18]

In 2000 the international Cartagena Protocol on Biosafety was signed at a convention in Montreal, designed to take effect when endorsed by fifty nations. Export shipments now had to specify whether they included GM crops, and importing nations could decide to reject GM imports even without scientific proof that they were harmful. This was an expression of the "precautionary principle" for which Greenpeace and other environmental groups had long argued. Discussions in the previous two years in Seattle and Cartagena, Colombia, had been inconclusive, but this time the representatives were able to reach acceptable terms, consonant with the Biological Diversity Convention of Rio de Janeiro of 1992. The United States, as principal producer of GM foods, bargained hard to limit the provisions of the treaty, but recognized that it must be conciliatory to preserve valuable export markets.[19]

By the early years of the twenty-first century, accordingly, GM food appeared to be in a similar situation to that of nuclear power. Whatever its merits, GM's unpopularity among many potential consumers inclined many farmers to leave it alone. In 2004 Monsanto announced that it would not put a new form of GM wheat on the market due to fears that it would limit American farmers' ability to sell the crop on the world market. Disagreements over GM foods embodied the clash of philosophies that we have seen repeatedly throughout this book. To people who accepted the legitimacy of manipulating nature in our own interest, it seemed logical to modify crops if doing so made them pest- and herbicide-resistant, increased their yields, and made them hardier in marginal settings. Those who objected to the idea of "playing God" with the natural world, conversely, were dismayed at the hubris of such experiments and feared that GM tampering was both immoral and dangerous. It is noteworthy, however, that there was very little protest against *medical* uses of genetic engineering, such as the production of insulin (after 1982) and other drugs, even among groups that opposed GM foods.[20]

ENDANGERED SPECIES II

A similar clash of worldviews was apparent in the continuing dispute over the future of endangered species. Since the passage of the Endangered Species Act in 1973, the U.S. Fish and Wildlife Service (FWS) and the National Oceanic and Atmospheric Administration (NOAA) had been required to decide which species of plants and animals to designate as endangered. They were heavily lobbied by environmental organizations that recognized the benefits of getting rare plants and animals onto the list. Sometimes a species truly was in danger of becoming extinct, as in the case of the California condor and the bald eagle. At other times, listing was more of a stratagem in political battles with ulterior objectives. As we saw earlier, the snail darter had no friends before objectors to the Tellico Dam recognized that it might well become a trump card in bringing the TVA dam project to a halt.

The FWS and NOAA were also required, when a species was listed, to make arrangements with the states to ensure the preservation and protection of its habitat, since habitat loss and degradation were the chief causes of endangerment and extinction. Economic considerations were not allowed to influence decisions about which species to protect—only the best available scientific evidence was counted as relevant, according to a 1982 amendment to the law (which closed a loophole that had been opened during the Tellico Dam controversy). FWS and NOAA would next have to submit recovery plans explaining how they intended to facilitate the revival of endangered species. A committee of seven experts considered all petitions for exemption from the act in cases where vital interests clashed.[21]

By the 1990s, many of the species listed were corals, marine plants, and insects, most of which were unknown to ordinary Americans. Acute controversy swirled around two more familiar species, however: wolves and spotted owls. Throughout most of American history, wolves had been hunted because they were a threat to domestic livestock. Colonies and then states had often paid bounties to wolf hunters, who used guns, steel traps, and poisoned carcasses to take their targets.

Belated recognition that wolves might become extinct led to a radical change of direction; they were listed under the Endangered Species Act in 1974 and their populations began slowly to revive. Wildlife biologists recognized, however, that in order to thrive, the wolves needed sufficiently large populations so they would not suffer from the genetic deterioration that comes with inbreeding. Because they were predators at the top of the food chain, moreover, they needed a wide territory to support relatively small numbers, and very large areas had to be available as wolf range, mostly outside federally controlled land.[22]

Among the controversial environmental questions of the late 1980s and the 1990s was whether to reintroduce wolves to Yellowstone National Park in northwestern Wyoming or simply to wait and hope, in the expectation that eventually they would return on their own by ranging down from the Canadian Rockies, where populations still flourished. Officially, wolves had been absent from Yellowstone since 1926, though occasional sightings were still reported. The Endangered Species Act prohibited the introduction of new animals to a site if an original population still lived there, which made the legality of reintroduction doubtful. Visitors to the park strongly supported the idea of bringing back the wolves. Wyoming and Montana ranchers living around the park, on the other hand, regarded revival or reintroduction as equally unwelcome because the wolves would prey on their cattle and sheep.[23]

Wildlife enthusiasts were pleasantly surprised to find in the late 1980s that President Reagan's head of the National Park Service, William Mott, favored the idea of bringing back the wolves. He also suggested that an environmental organization, Defenders of Wildlife, should offer to pay compensation to ranchers whose animals were killed by the wolves. Defenders agreed and established a fund, which quickly gathered a hundred thousand dollars in voluntary contributions.[24] The outcome of a long debate was the reintroduction of fifteen wolves, captured in Alberta and released in Yellowstone in January 1995, to immense media fanfare. Almost at once they formed packs, reproduced, and began to change the ecology of the park itself. As top predators they displaced the coyotes, a change that affected other parts of the food chain. As one enthusiast observed:

> In some areas 50 percent or more of the coyotes have been killed or displaced by wolves, as the latter reclaim their position of dominance in Yellowstone. Because coyotes are voracious consumers of voles, ground squirrels, and pocket gophers, biologists are predicting that a diminished coyote population will translate into more food for the park's owls, hawks, badgers, foxes, and pine martens; anecdotal observations suggest these other predators are, in fact, on the increase.

The wolves also became effective elk hunters, which gratified park rangers who were concerned that the elk were overgrazing the park's aspen and willow stands. Elk carcasses also provided a new food supply to scavenging animals like eagles, ravens, and foxes.[25]

Centuries of human aversion, and even the villainous role of wolves in tales like "Little Red Riding Hood," still made it difficult for some people to consider them sympathetically. During the Yellowstone debate, a representative in the Montana state assembly offered vivid congressional testimony about the "throaty death-moans of lambs" and showed photographs of still living cattle horribly mauled in wolf attacks. Wyoming's Common Man Institute issued pamphlets about wolves' attacks on people, describing them as "the most cruel and destructive animals on the North American continent," the moral equivalent of mass murderers. Among the more outspoken critics of protecting the wolves was Helen Chenoweth, a Republican congresswoman from Idaho and Wise Use advocate.[26]

Chenoweth was one of the many Republican freshmen who took their seats after the dramatic midterm election of 1994 and signed Newt Gingrich's "Contract with America." When the Endangered Species Act came up for renewal in 1996, the Wise Use movement sought to curtail it severely, especially as it applied to habitat protection on privately owned land. Their stance won them the nickname of "the extinction lobby" from indignant environmentalists. Other groups supported them, including the Endangered Species Coordinating Council and the National Endangered Species Act Reform Coalition, misleadingly titled organizations sponsored by corporations that sought a relaxation of the act's rigor. The American Farm Bureau Federation, which also favored reducing the reach of the act, said that farmers were being victimized by "toads, owls, chubs, suckers, rats and bats, bugs and weeds."[27]

Northern spotted owls, like the Yellowstone wolves, became a symbol of wider human anxieties. In the Pacific Northwest, the habitat of this owl subspecies had shrunk steadily in the face of aggressive logging of old-growth forests. An Audubon Society audit suggested in 1986 that there were only fifteen hundred breeding pairs left in the nation and urged the Fish and Wildlife Service to add it to the list of threatened species. In the Reagan era, the FWS was dragging its feet on this and other listings because it foresaw that the new listings would displease powerful lumbering interests. By then a backlog of several hundred plants and animals awaited inclusion on the list, each of which had to be systematically studied and evaluated in a slow and costly process. Finally, a lawsuit forced the issue and the U.S. District Court in *Northern Spotted Owl v. Hodel* (1988) agreed with the plaintiffs that Secretary of the Interior Donald Hodel had stalled the case of the spotted owl for political reasons.[28]

Hodel and his successor, Manuel Lujan, were so annoyed by the decision that they speculated in public on the need to weaken the provisions of the Endangered Species Act when it came up for renewal. President George H. W. Bush, who'd described the northern spotted owl as "that little furry feathery guy," also said he would not sign the act in its current form. By then the terms of the act were threatening the completion of large-scale engineering projects: the mottled-bellied spotted frog, for example, had prevented completion of a major irrigation project in central Utah.[29]

In 1990, nevertheless, the spotted owl was added to the endangered species list as "threatened." An unusually well-written statement, "Conservation Strategy for the Northern Spotted Owl," drafted by Forest Service scientist Jack Ward Thomas, affirmed that the owls would face extinction if logging were not restricted. It agreed with environmental activists' claims that the northern spotted owl was an "indicator species," whose welfare mirrored the welfare of countless other species in the same area. A federal judge ordered most logging to stop in 1991 in order that a sustainable three thousand pairs of owls might thrive. It was important, conservationists believed, that the breeding pairs not be isolated in little "islands" of old-growth trees separated by large clear-cut zones. Instead, old-growth forest must be continuous in order to create a large and uninterrupted habitat area.[30]

At a 1993 "Owl Summit Meeting" in Portland, incoming president Bill Clinton heard evidence from both sides and claimed that the problem could be resolved in a way that preserved both owls and jobs. He brokered a plan that lifted court-imposed injunctions and got at least some loggers back to work. By then, further studies were casting doubt on whether the claims of endangerment had been entirely justified. Northern spotted owls were discovered living in large numbers in California and in second-growth as well as old-growth forest. They turned out to be a more adaptable species than original studies had implied. Severe limitations were still placed on logging corporations in the name of preserving the owls. Throughout the controversy, the Wise Use activists and "Class of '94" Republicans claimed that thousands of jobs in the logging and sawmill industries were at stake, along with the economic well-being of the entire Pacific Northwest.[31]

Conservative Republicans received an unexpected check in 1996 when the Evangelical Environmental Network (EEN) came out in favor of upholding the Endangered Species Act in its full rigor. To dilute the act in the name of economic growth or "Wise Use" would, they said, be to violate God's will, according to which mankind must act as steward for all other species. This unforeseen development from inside the GOP's electoral alliance frightened many Republicans away from their anti-ESA rhetoric. Newt Gingrich himself, then speaker of the House of Representatives, said that although Republicans wanted less federal meddling in citizens' lives, they also wanted "to ensure the maximum bio-diversity. Frankly, every species we lose is a level of knowledge about life which is irreplaceable."[32]

Alongside the political wrangling over wolves and spotted owls, wildlife biologists were conducting a difficult theoretical debate about endangerment and extinction. Ever since the near extinction of the buffalo around 1900 and the death of the last passenger pigeon in 1914, they had understood that to hunt an animal relentlessly and destroy its habitat was bound to diminish its numbers, perhaps to the point of annihilation. Not until after World War II, however, had a mathematical ecologist, Frank Preston, created an equation relating habitat area to species abundance. His "species-area curve," introduced in the journal *Ecology* in 1962, purported to demonstrate a definite relationship that could be graphed exactly. The smaller an area was, the smaller the number of species that could inhabit it. The equation's curve showed that as a habitat area shrank, the number of species would decline gradually but then, as it shrank further, would decline far more sharply.[33]

Preston's theory was elaborated in the 1960s by the ecologists E. O. Wilson and Robert MacArthur and summarized in their 1967 book *The Theory of Island Biogeography*. An "island" was either a literal island in water or an area whose ecology was distinct from that of the surrounding area, such as a park in an urban area. Wilson's graduate student Daniel Simberloff put the theory to the test by killing all the life (mainly insects) on a few tiny Florida islets after doing a complete species census. He then monitored the recovery of life in the ensuing months, to see whether the number of species was eventually replicated. It was, with islands closest to the mainland recovering more quickly than those further out to sea. Islands reduced in size by cutting away part of their area mechanically regained a smaller number of species, apparently vindicating Preston's theory.[34]

In the early 1970s Jared Diamond, a UCLA ecologist, added an important new dimension to the theory: animals adapted only to a very particular habitat faced global rather than just local extinction if their habitat was destroyed or diminished. This insight led some ecologists to claim that the clearance of large areas in the Amazon rain forest was causing the extinction of thousands of species every year. The problem with verifying this claim was that many of the species (mainly insects) living in the rain forest had never been identified or named in the first place—their presence was hypothesized rather than established as fact. After reading a wide array of articles estimating the rate of annual extinctions, two ecologists, Edward Connor and Earl McCoy, published a long cautionary article in the *American Naturalist* in 1979. They concluded that it was impossible to correlate rain forest destruction with reliable numbers about extinction and endangerment.[35]

Preston's theory was limited by the fact that it could not specify the *rate* at which extinctions would take place. Many observers knew that populations might decline but still hang on for a century or more when their habitat was disturbed before going extinct. Another pair of ecologists, William Boecklen and Nicholas Gotelli (both graduate students of Simberloff's), demonstrated a huge variation in forecasts about the prospect of extinctions in a Kenyan game park, ranging from 0.5 percent of all species at the low end to 95.5 percent at the high end. In other words, they wrote, predictions according to the current state of knowledge were almost worthless. Simberloff, once confident about the species-area curve and its predictive power, responded to his students' discovery by admitting to a new humility.[36]

In sum, no one knew for sure how many species were going extinct, or at what rate, even though nearly all shared the fear that extinctions were happening at much more than the "natural" rate. This was one of the many areas of environmental controversy in which different authors offered persuasive yet mutually contradictory accounts of the situation. Paul and Anne Ehrlich argued in *Extinction* (1981) that nothing was more important than preserving species from extinction.[37] Charles Mann and Mark Plummer, by contrast, argued in *Noah's Choice* (1995) that Congress had unwittingly given the nation an impossible task when it expressed the intention of saving *all* endangered species. They showed in detail the difficulty of preserving enough habitats for each of America's hundreds of endangered species. Beetles, birds, butterflies, fish, and mammals made very different demands, required different types of land, and often an immense amount of it. Their needs stood squarely athwart other valuable uses for land. They showed that the owners of private land where endangered species might be found had a perverse incentive to *destroy* any individuals they discovered, lest the operations of the act prevent them from developing their land if word leaked out. Without minimizing the severity of the issue, Mann and Plummer argued that there were circumstances in which permitting the extinction of a particular beetle species, for example, might be justifiable for economic or humanitarian reasons. To pretend otherwise was to live in a fool's paradise.[38]

By the turn of the new millennium, the question of when and why species should be *removed* from the endangered species list had also become controversial. The question was inevitably political and the George W. Bush administration was eager to compress the list. Wildlife advocacy groups nearly always opposed removal, arguing that populations could shrink again if no longer protected and that endangered animals were being taken off the list prematurely for political rather than genuinely ecological reasons. There was nevertheless scope for some optimism by 2000. The outgoing Clinton administration had removed twenty-nine species from endangered status, including the gray wolf and the symbol of the republic itself, the bald eagle. These top predators at least had responded well to protection and their populations were rebounding.[39]

Even so, when habitats shrank, environmentalists occasionally found themselves in the awkward position of struggling to defend one rare species against the predation of another one. By the 1990s, for example, Sierra bighorn sheep living at the highest altitudes of the Sierra Nevadas were jeopardized by mountain lions. The lions, earlier hunted almost to extinction but now protected by a California state referendum, had staged a comeback in the late twentieth century and seemed likely to annihilate the remaining bighorns. Should they be culled? "For many conservationists," wrote Paul Rauber in *Sierra*, "it is a bitter draught to contemplate the killing of a noble creature they once fought to protect. Yet once we start playing God . . . by granting special protection to mountain lions . . . we seem obliged to continue." To simply let nature take its course would be "to erase the Sierra Nevada bighorn from the book of life." Biologists were able in this instance to work out which individual lions were killing sheep; the federal government then authorized their killing, as a way to preserve the mountain sheep, with the result that the bighorn herd survived at least into the twenty-first century.[40]

Mountain lions were troublesome in other ways. The city of Boulder, Colorado, prided itself on creating a hospitable environment for once endangered species with the result that, in the 1980s, deer, elk, and coyotes were commonly sighted in the city, at times becoming nuisances. In January 1991, however, a mountain lion killed jogger Scott Lancaster inside city limits and partially ate his body. The local authorities expected an anti-lion backlash, but did not get it. One of Lancaster's friends commented at the memorial service that to be eaten by a lion was "kind of fitting for him . . . He was a real outdoorsy guy." Another added: "It felt like it was part of nature, and it was part of the earth, and it was part of the way that things work and the way that the cycle happens." Lancaster's former high school English teacher even claimed that "Scott would have been angry that the lion was shot. He would have been angry that his body was not left there for the lion to finish."[41]

Another aspect of "playing God" was the recognition that some species were so close to extinction that the only way to save them was by breeding them in captivity in the hope of reintroducing them, when partly grown, into the wild. The red wolf, the Florida panther, and the California condor were all rescued in this way. Reintroduction worked only if the animals could fend for themselves, and only if there was sufficient habitat in which they might thrive. On first being released, some of them showed a tendency to favor human company and not to be scared of motor vehicles and other hazards to their lives. Loggers, farmers, and hunters opposed reintroduction, especially if the new species was a predator that might kill farm or game animals, or if they feared that the presence of the animals would impose restrictions on their ability to develop or modify their property. Most states devoted far more funds to promoting hunting than to protecting predators, so the politics and economics of reintroduction tended to be lopsided. It would work only if the conditions that had led to imminent extinction in the first place were somehow changed. Luckily, an increased understanding of predators' necessary role, and a growing sympathy for endangered species, helped several of these programs succeed in the 1990s and the new millennium.[42]

ECOTOURISM

Experience in Africa and Asia suggested that bans on the hunting of endangered species and on cutting timber in game reserves and national parks were ineffective, especially when hunting and firewood gathering were parts of the tradition of indigenous peoples. Organizations dedicated to wildlife protection gradually realized that they needed to give local peoples an incentive to preserve the animals and the trees rather than merely prohibiting their destruction. Ecotourism appeared to be the answer. Projects around the world offered some encouraging signs, preserving elephants in Africa and Thailand, harp seals in Labrador, and distinctive rain forest habitat in Zaire and Costa Rica. To make these projects work well, local people had to be employed as guides, rangers, and hotel workers at game reserves. They would then have a direct economic incentive to care for the animals and prevent poaching.[43]

Ecotourism was also an effective way to bring together constituencies that were otherwise likely to disagree. The long confrontation in the Pacific Northwest between wilderness advocates on one side and loggers fearing unemployment on the other might be resolved if tourism to the *uncut* redwood trees could become profitable. Similarly, creating an ecotourism constituency among Alaskans, giving them an incentive to protect and preserve the environment, might counterbalance prodevelopment forces there.

By the 1990s steady increases in American families' incomes and steadily rising awareness of environmental issues had created a large potential constituency for environmentally themed vacations. A generation of ecoentrepreneurs stood ready to serve them. One of the most inventive was Stanley Selengut, creator of Maho Bay Camps in the American Virgin Islands. Selengut had begun the project in 1977, trying to build the resort in such a way as to minimize its environmental impact. The resort's "eco-tents" were built without the use of heavy equipment and were constructed from ChoiceDek, which was made from recycled milk jugs and sawdust. The tents and chalets were equipped with solar-generated electricity and rainwater showers that were fed from black sun-warmed rooftop barrels. Visitors had to monitor their own water use and hand-pump only as much as they needed. "People actively involved in supervising their resources become conservation-minded," said Selengut. His intention was to raise their environmental awareness as well as offer them enjoyable vacations.[44]

Selengut was eager to employ local people from the islands in craft projects. In the 1990s he created a second resort, the Refuge at Ocklawaha, north of Orlando, Florida. It was funded by local government, a grant from the Pew Charitable Trusts, whose managers were impressed by Selengut's educational aims, and by the Audubon Society, which recognized the benefits of building the resort adjacent to a large wetland restoration project. Selengut was cautiously optimistic that the model he had created might catch on more widely, though he recognized that large-scale developers would probably be less concerned than he with sustainability and with adaptation to local conditions.[45]

A less ambitious form of ecotourism became standard practice in the national parks, as visitors took hikes, canoe rides, and tours with rangers and biologists designed to educate them about the local flora and fauna and to teach them about the pressures facing the parks themselves. Wilderness backpackers learned to "leave no trace," packing out everything they had taken into the area. Outdoor equipment companies like REI, Slumberjack, and L.L.Bean began to sew instructions onto their sleeping bags explaining these Leave No Trace principles.[46]

There was a paradox inherent in ecotourism, however. Citizens were more likely to take an interest in the natural world and in conservation if they experienced it regularly. Yet the sheer fact that they began coming in such large numbers was itself a potential hazard. Edward Abbey had sensed this problem in the 1960s, a time of rapidly rising numbers in the national parks and monuments. In the introduction to *Desert Solitaire* he had written, "Do not jump into your automobile next June and rush out to the Canyon country hoping to see some of that which I have attempted to evoke in these pages." Later he feared that he had indeed contributed to the deterioration of Arches National Monument by attracting ever larger crowds each year. When the United Nations organized a conference in Quebec in 2002 to celebrate the "International Year of Ecotourism," its spokesman estimated that ecotourism was growing at two or three times the rate of all other forms of tourism. He admitted that aggressive developers were disrupting many sites and that too many visitors were damaging fragile sites in Thailand and Nepal. The slopes of Mount Everest had become a junkyard of former expeditions' abandoned gear. A group of antiglobalism activists set up their own campaign, the "International Year of Stopping Ecotourism."[47]

Wildlife and conservation biologists also began to fear that human disturbance, even when well intentioned, was damaging the habitat of endangered species and degrading fragile landscapes. Government agencies that promoted ecotourism were vulnerable to bureaucratic forces that could be harmful to the land in question. Changes in regime, especially in politically volatile areas of the world, could lead to abrupt changes in the protection of ecotourism areas. Meanwhile, entrepreneurs, even high-minded ones, were trying to make ecotourism pay, and often favored projects that significantly changed the landscape, such as the building of paved roads, lodges, campgrounds, and improved sewage facilities. They had to balance the austerity that sustainable living implies with the desire for luxury and convenience that goes with high-priced vacations.[48]

Some critics objected to ecotourism simply because it was a form of leisure. In an influential 1995 article, historian Richard White pointed out that the environmental movement, especially the part of it devoted to wilderness preservation, had somehow detached itself and its interests from *work*. No wonder, he wrote, that angry loggers sported bumper stickers that read, "Are you an environmentalist or do you work for a living?" How, he wondered, could work and environmental awareness be reconciled?[49]

ENDOCRINE DISRUPTORS

One of the bestselling and most widely discussed popular science books of the 1990s was *Our Stolen Future* (1996) by a zoologist, Theo Colborn, a journalist, Dianne Dumanoski, and a foundation head, John Myers. Vice President Al Gore wrote the preface, in which he compared the book to Rachel Carson's *Silent Spring*. Colborn had earned her PhD later in life, at the age of fifty-eight, after years of ranching in Colorado, then joined a Conservation Foundation study of Great Lakes wildlife in the late 1980s. There she documented bizarre behaviors and discovered reproductive abnormalities in otters, snapping turtles, and other species, especially those that fed on lake fish. Theorizing that synthetic chemicals were affecting the animals' hormone functions, she organized a meeting in 1991 of specialists from a wide variety of relevant disciplines at the Wingspread conference center in Racine, Wisconsin. Participants debated her hypothesis that low-level exposure to synthetic chemicals was affecting animals' endocrine systems and damaging the sexual development of their progeny.[50]

One of the participants, Frederick vom Saal, a physiologist from the University of Missouri, had earlier shown that tiny variations in animals' prenatal exposure to hormones could have severe consequences for their development and behavior. He recognized the importance of the conference in formulating a new general theory: "Wingspread was like a religious experience," he wrote. "The evidence presented was incredible . . . The magnitude and seriousness of the problem became very clear." The group's 1991 "Wingspread Statement" summarized evidence in support of the hypothesis that synthetic chemicals were "endocrine disruptors," whose effects showed up not in the adult animals subjected to the chemicals, but in their offspring. *Our Stolen Future* carried the idea, five years later, to a much wider audience.[51]

Summarizing a wide variety of scientific studies but presenting their findings in an excitable popular style, the authors of *Our Stolen Future* argued that long-lasting chemicals (persistent organic pollutants, or POPs) could have harmful consequences for humans too. These chemicals were insidious, the authors argued, because they worked inconspicuously, sometimes in microscopic trace amounts, and disrupted natural hormone or endocrine patterns with effects that sometimes took decades to become apparent. "What we fear most immediately is not extinction but the insidious erosion of the human species. We worry about the power of hormone-disrupting chemicals to undermine and alter the characteristics that make us uniquely human." They cited examples from "sentinel species" in nature: of eagles neglecting to nurture their hatchlings, female herring gulls forming same-sex pairs, diminished penis size in alligators, and sharp population declines among bears, mink, and otters. The clearest human consequences appeared to be a rising incidence of sexual underdevelopment and a long-term decline in men's sperm counts. Other possible effects included rising rates of attention deficit disorder and hyperactivity.[52]

Synthetic chemicals, wrote the authors, sometimes mimic estrogen and other hormones and block them from acting effectively. DDT, one of the chemicals at the center of *Silent Spring*, was among these mimics. Others included dioxin, DES (diethylstilbestrol), and PCBs (polychlorinated biphenyls). They broke down very slowly, so that a lifetime of exposure would lead to significant accumulation in a mother's body by the time she was mature and pregnant, even if her exposure had generally been low. Collectively these chemicals were undermining reproductive health, yet they remained widespread, and were joined every year by hundreds of threatening new substances.[53]

Colborn and her coauthors admitted, however, that it was difficult to specify exactly which chemicals caused which afflictions, because so many synthetics were now in wide circulation. The burden of proof was, at present, laid at the door of people who believed they had suffered harm from chemical contaminants. Responsibility ought to be shifted to manufacturers, they argued, forcing them to demonstrate that their chemicals were *not* endocrine disruptors before being permitted to market them. The authors came close to arguing that the manufacturing of chemicals should stop almost completely. They also urged the scientific and policy communities to move beyond the "cancer paradigm" in their approach to toxic chemicals. Until then, the great issue for toxicologists at sites like Love Canal had been high doses of toxic substances and their carcinogenic potential. Endocrine disruption was different—harder to detect and sparked by much smaller doses—but perhaps equally significant in the long run.[54]

Our Stolen Future rapidly attracted detractors as well as champions. Bruce Ames, a microbiologist at Berkeley already famous as an environmental cancer skeptic, described it as "lousy science." Stephen Safe, a toxicologist at Texas A&M, argued that the trace amounts of the chemicals in question were too small to have an effect on humans and were dwarfed in volume by natural hormones. Elizabeth Whelan of the American Council on Science and Health called the book "an alarmist tract with a polemical style, clearly crafted for its political, not scientific, impact." In a slashing attack in the *Washington Post*, Ronald Bailey, author of *Eco-Scam* (1993) and *The True State of the Planet* (1995), noted that the book was being promoted by "Fenton Communications, the same PR firm that brought us Meryl Streep and the Alar Scare," and that it was an ideologically motivated attack on the chemical industry rather than genuine science. "People eat 40 million times more natural plant estrogens than they do synthetic estrogens each day. Synthetic estrogens are thousands to millions of times weaker than the estrogen produced by the body." Bailey added that ever since the ban on DDT in the early 1970s, background levels in the United States had been *dropping* steadily, not rising, as Colborn implied. The Chemical Manufacturers' Association, meanwhile, dedicated funds to refuting the book and prepared written comments to help chemical companies' spokespeople respond to it.[55]

Even so, enough concerned citizens and politicians were alarmed that Congress decided to take action. In 1996 it passed the Food Quality Protection Act and the Safe Drinking Water Estrogenic Substances Screening Program Act. It ordered the EPA to develop a testing program on all commercial chemicals to determine their endocrine-disrupting characteristics and to regulate those that appeared to carry an imminent risk. The researchers reviewed more than three hundred scientific articles already published on the issue, agreeing that evidence of harm to certain animals was clear, but that there was not yet any conclusive evidence of harm to humans. An interim report from the National Research Council admitted in 1999 that most aspects of the subject remained controversial and opaque, because the chain of causation between the initial pollution and the eventual harm could extend over decades. Its committee members' difficulties stemmed not just from the science, but also from uncertainty about how to think about the issue:

> Much of the division among committee members appears to stem from different views of how we come to know what we know. How we understand the natural world and how we decide among conflicting hypotheses about the natural world is the province of epistemology. Committee members seemed to differ on some basic epistemological issues, which led to different interpretations and conclusions on the issues of hormonally active agents in the environment.

A similar 2003 report by the EPA admitted to a high level of continuing uncertainty, adding that studies on eighty-seven thousand chemicals already in production were needed, in substances used in such diverse products as foods, pesticides, insecticides, lawn care agents, cosmetics, and plastics. Meanwhile, a second Wingspread Statement (1998) urged the adoption of a precautionary principle: that advocates for the use of synthetic chemicals should shoulder the burden of proof even if harm to human health was not scientifically proven.[56]

Sheldon Krimsky, a professor of urban environmentalism and public health at Tufts University, followed this controversy closely and published *Hormonal Chaos* in 2000, a history of the endocrine disruption controversy. Bringing a new level of sophistication to the debate, Krimsky showed how Colborn had in effect created a new scientific paradigm with her challenge to carcinogenesis as the main issue in environmental toxicology. He also showed how interested constituencies (of scientists, and of policy makers) had influenced the presentation of the issue, and how media decisions impacted the development of hormone disruption as a major *political* phenomenon. The publicity surrounding *Our Stolen Future* had, for example, opened up new sources of funding: "Scientists in a variety of subfields of molecular and cellular biology, toxicology, and environmental sciences, taking notice of the new funding opportunities, began to reorient their model systems to compete for a share of the newly available grant money." In other words, the hypothesis created a constituency that then had a vested interest in its validity. Despite a sympathetic treatment of Colborn herself, and an interesting comparison of the media's treatment of her with its treatment of Rachel Carson thirty-five years earlier (both women, both in some ways outsiders to the scientific mainstream), Krimsky left the reader in no doubt that her hypothesis was very far from proven. Summarizing the "precautionary principle," he remarked that "it may be considered rational to act as if the hypothesis were true while retaining one's scientific skepticism."[57]

Colborn herself created TEDX (The Endocrine Disruption Exchange), a clearinghouse for information and concerns about the hormone receptor problem. By the early twenty-first century she was urging consumers not to use plastic water or food containers because phthalates, a chemical in the plastic, was one of the most suspicious and potentially damaging endocrine disruptors. The *New York Times* columnist Nicholas Kristof raised what was becoming the standard response to this and several other ambiguous environmental issues: "One of the conundrums for scientists and journalists alike is how to call prudent attention to murky and uncertain risks, without sensationalizing dangers that may not exist."[58]

Various research projects also linked endocrine disruption to rising rates of breast cancer, asthma, obesity, and the early onset of puberty in girls. Nancy Langston, a professor of history and environmental studies at the University of Wisconsin, Madison, wrote a history of endocrine-disrupting chemicals, focusing on diethylstilbestrol (DES), which had been prescribed to millions of pregnant women to prevent miscarriage while also being fed to poultry and cattle as a growth agent in the 1940s, 1950s, and 1960s. Langston remarked that as an academic her "typical bias is to be skeptical," but that her research findings prompted her to speculate about her own family members: "Of the five women in my immediate family, all have had a string of reproductive issues: miscarriages, infertility, endless fibroids, diseased fallopian tubes, ectopic pregnancies, cervical dysplasia, hysterectomies, excised ovaries, suspicious mammograms and breast biopsies . . . Each of these is linked, in laboratory studies on animals and in epidemiological studies on women, to endocrine disruptors." But as she also admitted, "not a single one of us can point to a specific reproductive problem and pinpoint a specific exposure as the cause."[59]

Another book, published in the same year as *Our Stolen Future*, bore witness to the decade's intense and continuing preoccupation with the links between chemical pollution and threats to health. Jonathan Harr's *A Civil Action* told the true story of a class-action lawsuit, *Anderson v. Cryovac*, against two Massachusetts corporations, Beatrice Foods and W. R. Grace, whose pollution of groundwater wells with trichloroethylene (TCE) had allegedly caused a cluster of leukemia cases among local children. Winner of the National Book Critics Circle Award, Harr's book made clear how difficult it was for citizens to win a tort case of this kind. They had to prove that the particular defendants in question had contaminated the groundwater and that the contaminants did in fact cause leukemia, both of which claims could be (and were) disputed by defendants, whose legal strategy was to bankrupt the plaintiffs' attorney through delays and costly scientific testing. Written as a human interest drama and focusing on the plaintiffs' attorney, Jan Schlichtmann, *A Civil Action* taught a wide American audience (most of whom would never have waded through the technical literature on these issues) just how complicated the epidemiology, technology, law, and politics of pollution could be. The site itself, in Woburn, Massachusetts, eventually became a Superfund site, and Grace and Beatrice were obliged to pay for the cleanup.[60]

Hollywood also recognized the box office potential of this topic and dedicated several major productions to health and environment stories. Characteristically, these films simplified immensely complex topics into examples of plucky little David facing up to and slaying mighty Goliath. For example, John Travolta starred in a successful movie version of *A Civil Action* (1998). Two years later Julia Roberts starred in *Erin Brockovich* (2000), which was based on a similar story. Its heroine was a researcher for a Southern California lawyer named Ed Masry, who had been her attorney in a traffic accident case. She uncovered evidence that Pacific Gas and Electric (PG&E) had for many years been leaking toxic chromium compounds into the water supply of Hinkley, California. She connected the leaks to an array of severe illnesses afflicting the townspeople, including cancers, reproductive failure, miscarriage, Hodgkin's lymphoma, and many others. In the ensuing lawsuit, the utility company was forced to pay damages of $333 million to 648 citizens of Hinkley, which at the time was the highest tort settlement in American history.[61]

Brockovich herself then became a consumer advocate, declaring on her Web site that "this gutsy broad doesn't apologize for who she is" and that she was dedicated to "being the voice for those who don't know how to yell." Here too, however, the link between the chemical and the illnesses remained uncertain. Writing on chromium hazards in the journal *Environmental Health Perspectives,* two science writers noted that to drink water contaminated with chromium 6 was much less dangerous than to inhale the chemical "because ingested Cr(VI) is converted to inactive trivalent chromium in the stomach. Many experts also claim that the exposures were too low to cause health effects and that there are few data linking Cr(VI) exposures to the Hinkley residents' symptoms." In other words, the simple cause-and-effect relationship on which the film's moral energy depended might not have been quite so clear in fact.[62]

THE CONTRAST BETWEEN American and ex-Soviet environmental issues by the 1990s was glaring. No constituency defended the dirty and degraded situation of the Soviet Union and its Eastern European satellites after the fall of communism. Environmental degradation there, especially at Chernobyl, had caused or accelerated the deaths of thousands. All the interested parties in the post-Soviet world, internal and external, joined hands to seek ways of improving a shattered environment. Filthy residual effects and hazardous work conditions kept life expectancy in the former Soviet zone distinctly shorter than in the environmentally protected West.[63]

How different was the situation in the United States, where environmental controversies continued to churn but where right and wrong were far more difficult to determine, and where intelligent people could make objectively powerful arguments on both sides of most issues. By the 1990s most American environmental hazards were nonlethal and more often involved aesthetic and economic questions than matters of life and death. A popular 1998 book, ominously entitled *Ecology of Fear*, considered the environmental problems confronting Los Angeles. It contained a possibly inadvertent reassurance to its readers in that the death rate from nearly all of the environmental threats it considered had, over the last few decades, been close to zero.[64]

As Americans celebrated the millennium they lived in a much cleaner and safer environment than they had in 1970. Their lives were more seriously threatened by overeating, smoking, and lack of exercise than by external environmental hazards—all issues, in other words, subject to their own control. A wide array of government programs and departments kept close watch over their work conditions, air quality, water quality, new pharmaceuticals, food purity, and public health. Even AIDS, one of the great health scourges of the 1980s and 1990s, was becoming amenable to medication, greatly increasing its victims' capacity to survive.

Has the passage of time clarified any of the confusions of the 1990s? Concern about endocrine disruption persists, with widespread research backed by federal funding. Some experiments now suggest that phthalates (a common additive in plastics and cosmetics) are linked to the onset of type 2 diabetes and cancer. Pediatric studies have also linked pesticides and the widely used chemical BPA (bisphenol A) to autism and hyperactivity in children.[65]

Bruce Blumberg, a biologist at the University of California, Irvine, recently invented the word "obesogen" to describe endocrine-disrupting chemicals that prompt weight gain. His work with mice shows that exposure to trace amounts of an obesogen in utero or at birth can create a lifetime disposition to obesity and can be passed down to the creatures' offspring. The implication is that exposure of pregnant women to comparable chemicals might create vulnerability in their children. Further experiments are testing exposure to industrial and pharmaceutical chemicals as the trigger for metabolic changes. These findings have coincided with widespread public concern over obesity among children, expressed by First Lady Michelle Obama and many others. A White House Taskforce on Childhood Obesity in 2010 was receptive to endocrine studies implicating environmental chemicals.[66]

The widespread industrial use of suspected endocrine disruptors (even in such mundane products as ATM receipts, wallpaper, and vinyl blinds) makes it difficult or impossible to avoid their presence, but pregnant women and new mothers feel an understandable urge to do just that. One journalist notes that "the household chemical purge may be developing into a ritual of new parenthood, a counterpoint to the traditional baby shower." Whether the risk is really significant remains in doubt, however. He adds, "Depending on whom you ask, it's a media-induced mass hysteria, an eco-marketing trend, a public health campaign or a stealth environmental movement—possibly all of the above."[67]

Canada, Denmark, and France decided to ban BPA in 2010 (Japan and China followed the next year), whereas the European Union as a whole has declined to do so, stating that "data currently available do not provide convincing evidence of neurobehavioral toxicity of BPA." Spokespeople for the American chemical manufacturers also deny the charge of endocrine disruption, asserting that when used properly their products are entirely benign and have been through exhaustive safety testing before going on the market. The EPA, meanwhile, has delayed making a decision, commissioned new studies, and left consumers to decide for themselves whether they face a risk, and if so how severe.[68]

The state of endangered species is as tantalizing and as contradictory as the news on endocrine disruptors. On the one hand, the success of wolf recovery programs has been so effective that Congress took the wolf off the endangered species list in 2011. Several of the plains and mountain states at once authorized wolf hunts, prompting the animals' champions to fear that they now face a second plunge toward extinction. Animal behaviorists were particularly frustrated that seven wolves wearing high-tech collars with GPS technology, which facilitated the study of packs' ranging behavior, were among those shot in the 2012 hunts.[69]

News is sometimes simultaneously good and bad. The grizzly bear is recovering so well, and its numbers increasing so healthily, that it too was removed from the endangered species list in 2007. Less reassuring is the fact that grizzlies killed three people in separate incidents during the summer of 2011, two in Yellowstone and one on the Montana-Idaho border. Lethal grizzly attacks are the subject of Werner Herzog's superb film *Grizzly Man*, about an eccentric environmentalist, Timothy Treadwell, who spent thirteen summers living among and filming the bears in Alaska, but was ultimately mauled to death and partially eaten by them.[70]

The first new American bird species to be discovered in a century, the Gunnison sage grouse, was identified (in Utah and Colorado) as recently as the year 2000 by scientists who were delighted, but who also warned that it was so localized, and its habitat so threatened, that it was in immediate danger of extinction. For unloved species, especially bugs and amphibians, or creatures unknown except to specialists, the news is nearly always bad, as competition from invasive species, habitat loss, climate change, and pollution threatens their capacity to survive.[71]

Even with good intentions, the agencies responsible for listing species face a difficult situation. Under pressure to preserve and improve habitat for species already on the list, they are also lobbied hard by advocates for new species. In 2011 a pair of organizations, the Center for Biological Diversity and WildEarth Guardians, sued the Fish and Wildlife Service to force it to speed up its decisions on more than eight hundred candidate species. The court ordered the service to resolve all its pending applications by 2018. Since the listing of a species also requires the preservation of critical habitat, everyone involved in using (or hoping to use) the land in question becomes an interested party. Each new listing generates more friction, especially when the creature is not widely known or admired and has no symbolic value. The FWS expects further lawsuits from aggrieved farmers, developers, hunters, and off-road recreationists. No outcome can possibly satisfy all parties because the values brought to the debate differ so widely and so fundamentally.[72]

CHAPTER 11

THE NEW MILLENNIUM

EVERY ENVIRONMENTAL CONTROVERSY of the post–World War II era involved disagreements about danger and health. They also involved aesthetic questions—what should the world look like? By the turn of the millennium the health questions were becoming, if anything, even more prominent, despite continuing rises in life expectancy. The tobacco industry, after fighting a decades-long rearguard, began to lose costly lawsuits to lung cancer patients. Government campaigns against smoking had contributed to the shift in public and legal opinion, and the federal government had underwritten much of the research that proved tobacco's dangers. Should government now play a comparable role in campaigning against unhealthy foods, or did they constitute a different kind of risk? How often should it intervene to help citizens take care of themselves?

Another persistent question was whether resources were becoming scarcer or more plentiful. As we have seen, there was some evidence that they were becoming more plentiful. The Carter administration in the late 1970s, however, had taken the "scarcer" view and created subsidies for the manufacture of biofuels. There was perhaps no more perfect example of good intentions leading to bad results, environmental and economic, than the story of biofuels. The subsidies had created a new industry that campaigned hard to keep the money flowing, despite accumulating evidence that, all factors considered, biofuels were *less* "green" than the fossil fuel alternative. Worse, the industry was diverting crop supplies into fuel manufacture sometimes raising food prices worldwide.

The quest for sustainable supplies of electricity was comparable. Wind and solar power, said their advocates, were infinite, abundant, clean, and renewable. This might be true in theory, but not given the actual technologies of the early 2000s. Wind turbines depended on inconsistent winds, were costly, difficult, and dirty to build, were ugly, required immense land areas but returned only a miserly supply of power, demanded an immense infrastructure of wires and pylons, and might even be health hazards. Solar power was, at least for the moment, even less viable as a large-scale energy source and provided less than 1 percent of America's electricity. The wind and solar industries, however, like the biofuel makers, created a constituency and garnered political subsidies.

Meanwhile the global warming debate rolled on. Advocates of the theory that anthropogenic warming was going to cause traumatic consequences in the future continued to interpret unusual weather events as evidence, though the term "warming" had now given way to the more ambiguous term "climate change." Even with more sophisticated computer models, advocates of a general crisis were dependent on highly theoretical projections and could not say with confidence what exactly would result, where, or when. Some speculated that "geoengineering" the planet would prove necessary—finding technological ways to compensate for persistent warming. Scientists who had been skeptical were in general agreement by the early 2000s that there *was* a slight global temperature rise, but they tended to attribute it to natural variation or to solar activity as much as to human production of greenhouse gases. The 2012 deadline for the first Kyoto emission reductions came and went, demonstrating a massive failure on the part of the industrial nations to actually cut back their CO_2 emissions. In the skeptics' view, it did not really matter.

THE ANTITOBACCO CAMPAIGN

Citizens unaware of most environmental controversies were likely to have strong feelings about tobacco, which can fill a small environment (a room!) with extraordinarily high levels of smoke pollution. It was not often regarded as an environmental issue at the time, but we should look at it as one in retrospect, since a key objective of environmentalism was to protect citizens from unhealthy atmospheric contaminants. The fact that millions of people subjected themselves to the smoke voluntarily does not change the reality that it was more lethal in the late twentieth century than any other form of pollution.

On no other issue relating to health and the environment had such a scientific consensus developed by the year 2000. Whereas nearly every aspect of the endocrine disruptor controversy remained ambiguous, no respectable constituency doubted any longer that smoking leads to lung cancer, emphysema, and other life-threatening diseases. After the first surgeon general's warning in 1964, Congress had imposed a ban on tobacco advertisements on television and radio in 1971. In the ensuing years smoking was gradually banned in restaurants and workplaces. The pace of these changes was remarkable. Anyone born in 1925, for example, would have grown up in an era in which the popular idols of Hollywood and professional sports enhanced their appeal by smoking. By their sixtieth birthdays, on the other hand, smoking was an increasingly stigmatized activity, subject to immense negative propaganda.[1]

Subsequent research had established, by the 1980s, the hazards of secondary smoke. Nonsmokers in the presence of smokers faced elevated health hazards. A National Academy of Sciences report in 1986 demonstrated "that children of smokers were twice as likely to suffer from respiratory infections, bronchitis, and pneumonia than children whose parents did not smoke." Surgeon General C. Everett Koop followed this report by confirming that "the right of the smoker to smoke stops at the point where his or her smoking increases the disease risk in those occupying the same environment." He added that an estimated three thousand deaths each year were caused by secondary smoke.[2]

Litigation against the tobacco companies intensified. Lung cancer victims sued, arguing that the manufacturers had deliberately withheld knowledge of the harmful effects of smoking. The companies could no longer claim that the scientific evidence was ambiguous. Instead, they defended themselves with the claim that the adverse health effects were well known and that smokers had made an individual "lifestyle" choice to accept these risks. They were asserting their rights as Americans! But as the historian Allan Brandt remarks: "Generating enthusiasm for smokers' rights proved difficult when the vast majority of smokers were already deeply ambivalent about their own habit. Most polls indicated that most smokers *wanted* to quit."[3]

The antismoking offensive gathered momentum. Congress banned smoking on all internal aircraft flights in 1990. A court decision in 1994 in favor of the state of Mississippi enabled it to recover from tobacco companies the Medicaid costs it had incurred while treating smokers' lung diseases. That landmark decision led nearly all the other states to try the same approach. Rather than submit one by one to fifty such cases, the tobacco companies came to a general settlement with the states' attorneys general in 1998. The Master Settlement Agreement (MSA) required the tobacco industry to pay the states $246 *billion* in health care reparations over the next twenty-five years.[4]

Many public health advocates were nevertheless disappointed: they had hoped to bring the tobacco companies to their knees or drive them out of business completely. Part of the MSA agreement was that the tobacco manufacturers would now be exempt from class-action lawsuits. The states that accepted the payout from the corporations were not even obliged to spend the money on antismoking campaigns.[5] Among those disappointed by the MSA was David Kessler, administrator of the Food and Drug Administration. Appointed by George H. W. Bush in 1990, he had stayed on under President Clinton and led an effort to prove that the tobacco companies had deliberately cultivated addiction by raising the nicotine level in cigarettes. In other words, he showed that cigarettes were drugs and that they therefore fell under the jurisdiction of his agency. The FDA issued restrictive regulations, but the Supreme Court overturned them in 2000, on the grounds that the agency had exceeded its mandate, and that only Congress had the power to declare tobacco a drug.[6]

The first massive decisions against the tobacco companies in *individual* lawsuits, however, also came in 1999. Plaintiffs could now argue that tobacco was not only harmful but addictive and that, accordingly, addicted smokers had not made an entirely free choice. Two California juries were persuaded. One awarded damages of $51 million to Patricia Henley (later reduced to $26 million) and a second awarded $21.5 million to Leslie Whiteley. Whiteley's case was significant in that the plaintiff, a forty-year-old lung cancer victim at the time of the suit, had begun smoking in 1972, seven years *after* government health warnings had begun to appear on cigarette packs.[7]

The tobacco companies remained liable to individual litigation in the ensuing years but showed no signs of falling into bankruptcy or going out of business. On the contrary, they reacted to an increasingly hostile legislative and judicial situation in the United States by ramping up the export of tobacco to developing nations. Cultivating strong links with foreign governments that had little history of consumer regulation, they were able to market aggressively in countries where cigarettes were among the first minor luxury items consumers could afford. Smoking became almost universal among men, then among women in China even as it declined in the United States. As a result, wrote Brandt in 2007, "the cigarette will cause far more deaths in this new century than it did in the last, irrespective of innovative and effective clinical and public health interventions in the future. At no moment in human history has tobacco presented such a dire and imminent risk to human health as it does today."[8]

The smoking controversy raised ethical and environmental questions that also applied to other issues. If government had a stake in restraining tobacco corporations on the grounds that their product was harmful to health, should it also intervene to restrict citizens' access to fatty foods? Nutrition, like smoking, has not usually been a central concern of environmentalists, but perhaps it should be. If tiny traces of synthetic chemicals in the atmosphere were affecting citizens' health and welfare, as many believed, surely there should be a correspondingly greater interest in the much larger quantity of synthetics they were consuming along with their daily three square meals.

The cover of one issue of *Fortune* magazine in 2003 pictured a French fry in an ashtray, and asked: "Is Fat the Next Tobacco?" In other words, would "Big Food" face the same kind of attack in the 2000s as had Big Tobacco in the 1990s? Obesity was widespread. Large food corporations like Archer Daniels Midland, Monsanto, and Cargill certainly had an incentive to sell more food than American consumers actually needed, which put them in a situation in some ways analogous to that of the tobacco companies.[9]

The new decade witnessed a spate of popular books about Americans' dietary habits, showing that they were harmful both to citizens' own health and to the environment. The most effective was Eric Schlosser's *Fast Food Nation* (2001). Schlosser, an energetic investigative journalist, examined the agricultural and industrial activities that preceded any customer's request for a hamburger and French fries in a fast-food restaurant. He described the insanitary and cruel conditions of animal feedlots where beef cattle were force-fed to gain weight, the meat-processing plants where overworked and underpaid laborers (often illegal immigrants) violated health and safety standards, sometimes taking "crank" and other illegal drugs to keep themselves going, the secret laboratories where flavor enhancement chemicals were brewed, and the sterile, chemical-drenched fields where potatoes for French fries grew.[10]

Schlosser remarked about fast food what Kessler and many other antitobacco campaigners had said about cigarettes: "Fast food is heavily marketed to children and prepared by people who are barely older than children. This is an industry that both feeds and feeds *off* the young." It contributed to an epidemic of obesity among children. It also accelerated trends in farming toward monoculture and intensive chemical treatments of crops, and against the survival of family farming. Summarizing the unsustainable characteristics of this type of industrialized farming, he wrote:

> By embracing [the] industrial model of agriculture—one
> that focuses narrowly on the level of inputs and outputs,

that encourages specialization in just one crop, that relies heavily on chemical fertilizers, pesticides, fungicides, herbicides, advanced harvesting and irrigation equipment— American farmers have become the most productive farmers on earth. Every increase in productivity, however, has driven more American farmers off the land. And it has left those who remain beholden to the companies that supply the inputs and the processors that buy the outputs.

Giant food-processing corporations were the clear winners in this situation, said Schlosser. At one end of the food chain they underpaid farmers for their crops, and at the other end they overcharged, undernourished, and overfattened the hapless consumers.[11]

Michael Pollan, a nature journalist, looked at other aspects of the situation. In *The Botany of Desire* (2001), he too visited the potato farms where McDonald's French fries began their lives. "The typical potato grower," wrote Pollan, "stands in the middle of a bright green circle of plants that have been doused with so much pesticide that their leaves wear a dull white chemical bloom and the soil they're rooted in is a lifeless gray powder. Farmers call this a 'clean field,' since, ideally, it has been cleansed of all weeds and insects and disease—of all life, that is, with the sole exception of the potato plant. A clean field represents a triumph of human control, but it is a triumph that even many farmers have come to doubt." No wonder they found genetically modified potatoes an attractive new alternative—they needed far fewer poisonous additives. On the other hand, Pollan was convinced that the GM farmers were living on borrowed time and that sooner or later insect resistance would develop, nullifying the advantage offered by GM potatoes. Better than either, he concluded, was the organic farm he also visited whose owner practiced polyculture, planting many different crops, or many different types of potato, in the same field, edging them with flowers that encouraged a variety of insects to compete, and growing potatoes that were safe to eat straight from the ground.[12]

Just as the tobacco industry eventually provoked a legislative and judicial reaction, so did the manufacturers of the unhealthiest foods.

First Lady Michelle Obama launched an initiative against childhood obesity in 2010, urging children to exercise more and eat less junk food. School districts began to ban carbonated soft drinks and snack food vending machines; some states specified that packaged foods should be labeled with the number of calories they contained. The food industry's trade associations argued that individuals should be free to choose their own lifestyle rather than have to submit to the dictates of the "food police" or "food fascists," that of course fatty foods should be eaten in moderation, and that exercise was as important as diet. They also promised to regulate themselves and to offer healthier alternative foods on their menus, while diminishing the hard sell to children. Academic studies of these initiatives were skeptical. One summarized that "industry self-regulation does not adequately protect children from inappropriate marketing of unhealthful foods."[13]

Meanwhile, an organic food movement continued to thrive for at least a part of American society. Characteristically, the same upper-middle-class people who were likely to become active in environmental organizations were also likely to be most conscientious about what they ate and drank. The rise of the "slow food" movement, as its name suggests, made a point of opposing all the characteristics of its "fast" rival. A New York Times journalist defined slow food in 2001 as "a gastronomic version of Greenpeace: a defiant determination to preserve unprocessed, time-intensive food from being wiped off the map." As part of the rising protest against globalism, its activists in Europe and North America were eager to preserve distinctive local tastes rather than submit to the homogenization of the big corporations. Perhaps inevitably, big corporations hastened to pander to this fashion, quickly becoming the principal purveyors of putatively local delicacies.[14]

BIOFUELS

The American agricultural situation at the start of the new millennium was paradoxical in many ways. The story of ethanol fuel offers a glimpse of the ways in which environmental concerns, energy policy, foreign policy, and farm subsidies came together to create a complex and morally ambiguous situation. Back in the 1970s, anxiety about depending on oil supplies from the politically unstable Middle East had led to the search for domestic alternatives. The Alaska pipeline was one result. Another was the first subsidies for ethanol, approved by Congress in 1978 in the National Energy Act. Ethanol, an alcohol made from corn, soybeans, sugarcane, or other plants, could be added to gasoline to make an effective fuel, and producers were offered a forty-cent-per-gallon federal subsidy (later fifty-one cents) to make it. It seemed to be "greener" than fossil fuel because it was renewable, generated less carbon dioxide while burning, and was a less harmful gasoline additive than either lead or methyl tertiary butyl ether.[15]

Improvements in ethanol-making technology and a sharp rise in oil prices after 2000 made it increasingly attractive. Many American farmers switched to growing corn because they could sell it to fuel manufacturers for a subsidized high price. They were also protected by an excise tax on imported ethanol, which forestalled Brazilian competition. However, corn grown for ethanol production could no longer be used as food, with the result that the available corn supply for food diminished, driving up its price worldwide. This problem was made more acute since corn was also being diverted to feed animals that were destined to be consumed as meat. A United Nations agriculture spokesperson declared in 2007 that it was a "crime against humanity" to manufacture food-based biofuels when people were going hungry. Other branches of the UN demurred, citing the anti–global warming benefits. Environmental organizations also divided on the issue, with some advocating biofuels as a great future hope and others deploring them.[16]

United States automakers began manufacturing "flex-fuel" cars that could run on a blend of 85 percent ethanol and 15 percent gasoline (E85) instead of conventional gasoline. Flex-fuel cars were given distinctive yellow gas tank caps. Very few gas stations outside the farm belt of the Midwest actually offered E85, however, so most flex fuel cars continued to run on gasoline alone, or a lower blend known as

E10. Customers complained that their cars' gas mileage deteriorated when they used these blends, and that marine engines using ethanol ran poorly.[17]

Skeptics, including several prominent environmentalists, became increasingly indignant about the pursuit of a national subsidized ethanol policy. The production of corn took a lot of energy (often from tractors and crop-spraying planes using nonrenewable fossil fuels) and had profound environmental effects. It required intensive nitrogen and phosphorus compounds for fertilizer and pesticide, which leached into groundwater and became "a major source of . . . nitrate, nitrite, and pesticide residues in well water." Depending on which factors were included, ethanol could be shown to take more energy to produce than it ultimately provided. David Pimentel, a Cornell professor of entomology who had long been active on environmental issues, concluded in 2005 that converting corn to ethanol actually consumed 29 percent more energy than the fuel produced. He added that extending corn cultivation for more ethanol production would contribute to the already serious problem of soil erosion. "I'm sympathetic, and I wish that ethanol production was a net positive," he told an interviewer. "But I'm a scientist first and an agriculturalist second. I don't think the U.S. will meet its goals with biofuels." Timothy Searchinger, a scholar of environmental economics at Princeton, and Joseph Fargione at the Nature Conservancy drew similar conclusions in papers from 2008, adding that the greenhouse gases contributed by ethanol, when all stages of its production were factored in, were *worse* than those from conventional fossil fuels.[18]

"Biodiesel" from soybeans was another workable fuel, but economic studies showed that neither it nor corn ethanol could come close to supplying a significant percentage of American energy needs in the near future. Even diversion of the whole U.S. corn and soybean crop to ethanol production would not provide enough to supply all of America's vehicles—one estimate reckoned it would provide less than 10 percent. An alternative possibility, much touted after 2005, was that production of ethanol from cellulose or other nonfood plants might become economically viable. It would be particularly attractive if the source plant could be grown on wasteland or if the ethanol could be derived from what were otherwise waste products, such as cornstalks and wood chips. These alternatives were collectively known as "cellulosic ethanol." Besides not taking corn out of the food supply, they were global warming "friendly," absorbing more CO_2 while growing than they produced when burning. Under the terms of the 2005 Energy Policy Act, the federal government provided $385 million to support the development of cellulosic ethanol. It also established a target of 136 billion gallons of ethanol to be produced each year by 2022, more than seven times the production total of 2005.[19]

Subsidies on such large scales ensured a continuing growth in ethanol production, whether gasoline prices rose or fell. Environmental groups became increasingly concerned that land currently protected from farming monoculture, under the federal Conservation Reserve Program and similar schemes, would be brought back into production rather than being devoted to the preservation of plant biodiversity and wetlands. That in turn would adversely affect the preservation of habitat for diverse animal and bird species.[20]

The structure of American politics played a vital role in the ethanol debate. The fact that the Iowa caucus was the first hurdle for any aspiring presidential candidate, along with the fact that Iowa was a major corn-growing state, encouraged candidates from all parties to talk about ethanol in glowing terms. The farm states of the Midwest and the Great Plains are mostly low in population, but are well represented in the U.S. Senate (since two U.S. senators come to Washington from each state, no matter the size of its population). Corn-growing subsidies were very popular in those areas, and the farm bloc in the Senate was able to preserve them even in the face of recurrent protests about bloated federal budgets. Archer Daniels Midland (ADM), one of the agribusiness giants and the single biggest manufacturer of corn ethanol, lobbied Democrats and Republicans to preserve the status quo. Its CEO, Dwayne Andreas, campaigned hard for ethanol, describing it in patriotic and populist terms as "the Midwest versus the Middle East" and as "corn farmers versus the oil companies." One skeptical writer, James Bovard, noted the consequences:

> Nothing symbolizes ADM's political exploitation of Americans better than ethanol. Ethanol has become a magic obeisance button for politicians. Simply mention the word and politicians grovel like trained dogs, competing to heap the most praise on ethanol and its well-connected producers. Regardless of how uncompetitive the product may be, politicians have for years talked about ethanol as if it were the agricultural equivalent of holy water. Ethanol producers have received a de facto subsidy of nearly $10 billion since 1980—yet they continue demanding more, more, more.

A lobbying group supported by ADM, the Renewable Fuels Association, became a powerful shaper of the debate in Washington.[21]

In 2010 the benefits and drawbacks of ethanol remained acutely controversial. On the one hand, the EPA continued to insist, despite some evidence to the contrary, that corn-based ethanol reduced greenhouse emissions. On the other hand, the National Association of Clean Air Agencies deplored the EPA's decision to increase the safe level of ethanol from 10 to 15 percent, arguing that it produced more nitrogen oxides and other smog-related pollutants than fossil fuel. The issue of diverting food from a hungry world also persisted. "Thanks to Washington," wrote one columnist, "four of every ten ears of corn grown in America—the source of 40 percent of the world's production—are shunted into ethanol," with the result that food supplies in the rest of the world fell and prices increased. He echoed David Pimentel's earlier complaint that more energy was used in making ethanol than it could possibly return. Other critics continued to insist that ethanol could never be more than a small contributor to America's overall fuel needs and that it made far more sense to work on improving vehicles' gas mileage than it did to boost alternative fuels.[22]

ELECTRIC SHOCKS

The search for cheap, abundant, and clean electricity was as complex as the search for cheap, abundant, and renewable vehicle fuels. The environmental movement had begun in part as a reaction against the pollution to which coal mining and coal-fired power stations were major contributors. The acid rain crisis of the 1980s had also placed dirty power stations in the spotlight, as had growing concern about power stations' emission of greenhouse gases. Natural gas was not so dirty as coal, and was a popular choice for new power stations after 1980, but it too was a nonrenewable fossil fuel. For a while nuclear power had seemed a potentially viable alternative, but, as we've seen, it failed to live up to its early promise, proving too costly and creating severe difficulties with the safe disposal of used fuel rods. Accidents at Three Mile Island and Chernobyl further chilled its prospects, as did concern that terrorists might steal uranium.

The third principal source of electricity, along with coal and nuclear, was hydropower. It too, unfortunately, had severe adverse environmental effects, because it could be made only by flooding valleys, which transformed the landscape, destroyed farmland, wrecked migratory fish runs, and modified rivers' ecosystems beyond recognition. Throughout much of the West hydroelectric projects like the Glen Canyon Dam were bitterly hated symbols to environmentalists of American industrial rapacity at its worst. Earth First!'s theatrical "cracking" of the dam and Marc Reisner's 1986 book *Cadillac Desert* were classic embodiments of this antidam sentiment.[23]

Viable alternative sources of electricity included solar, wind, geothermal (using geological heat sources), and tidal power. All could be made to work on a small scale, and all were steadily improved after 1970, but none could generate enough electricity to displace traditional methods. Neither could they be competitive in terms of cost, so research and development depended heavily on government subsidies. When *Sierra* magazine surveyed the situation at the start of the new millennium, it noted that "renewable" energy sources were stuck at just under 2 percent of American consumption, largely because it could not be made in sufficient quantities and was not competitive in price. "Efforts to entice environmentally conscious consumers to pay extra for 'green power,'" it added ruefully, "have attracted only a small number of energy altruists." *Sierra* romanticized families that had found ways to live "off the grid" with photovoltaic solar cells and individual-scale wind generators, but admitted that these cases were exceptional.[24]

About half of America's renewable electricity in the new decade was provided by wind power, but that was barely 1 percent of the nation's overall output. The Clinton administration announced in 1999 a goal of generating 20 percent of the nation's electricity with renewable technologies by the year 2020. It noted that Sweden, Denmark, Spain, and Germany already derived a much greater percentage—up to 10 percent—of their electricity from the wind. These European nations had discovered several advantages with the method, however. Once established, giant wind turbines were economical to run and could be sited in shallow seas as well as on land. They were sources of national pride, even tourist attractions, and seemed to bear witness to the European Union's commitment to reducing its carbon footprint. A Danish company, Vestas, dominated the world market for high-tech wind turbines and made rapid strides between 1990 and 2005 in increasing their size and making them quieter.[25]

The drawbacks of wind energy were also significant, however, and some environmental activists turned against it. First, the turbines were expensive and difficult to build, often requiring very high conventional energy outputs. Second, they took up a great deal of real estate. Third, they were noisy and distracting, creating an irritating high-pitched whine and a flickering effect for local residents as their great rotating blades momentarily shadowed the sun. Fourth, they were unsightly, and usually depressed property values. They also created a wildlife hazard, killing large numbers of birds and bats that flew into them. The Audubon Society sued the owners of the Altamont Pass Wind Farm in California when it killed more than a thousand birds in one year, including twenty-four endangered golden eagles. The place best suited to wind turbines in the United States, the Great Plains, was remote from the cities where additional power was most needed, so transmission would require a heavy additional infrastructure of wires and pylons.[26]

Most important, wind turbines could not run all the time because the wind does not blow all the time. From a practical standpoint this was their greatest weakness. The wind does not blow at the same rate even in habitually windy places, so turbines could only ever be *part* of a power production system, usually requiring backup from conventional fossil fuel sources. Despite improvements, the turbines had severe operational limitations. They were vulnerable not only to periods of calm but also to excessively high winds. They could not start spinning until the wind blew at about ten or fifteen miles per hour, but they also had to be stopped and taken off-line when the wind reached forty or fifty miles per hour. Otherwise, they were liable to malfunction or to break completely. "It is always possible," admitted one advocate of wind power, "that the machines will 'run away,' meaning that the winds will become so powerful so quickly that the braking mechanisms don't have time to work. When that happens, the turbines spin faster and faster, destroying the braking mechanisms and eventually blowing themselves and the entire structure apart and scattering their huge blades over the countryside."[27]

Doubts about wind power accumulated on both sides of the Atlantic. John Etherington's 2009 book *The Wind Farm Scam* was particularly scathing. The author, a retired professor of ecology from the University of Wales, demonstrated how uneconomical wind power was and how only a pattern of tax incentives and hidden subsidies kept it going—all at the expense of hapless consumers. He showed how rarely wind generators could actually operate at full capacity, how they had to be supported by coal- and natural gas–powered stations, and concluded that, while costing a fortune, their contribution to the UK's power needs was so minuscule that they could contribute virtually nothing to reducing greenhouse gases.[28]

Meanwhile, an American doctor, Nina Pierpont, reported her discovery of what she called "wind turbine syndrome," an affliction suffered by people who lived two miles or less from giant wind farms and were affected by very low frequency sound waves, or "infrasound." This was much more than mere annoyance at the humming or beating sound of the turbines themselves, she said, and included such symptoms as sleep disorders, headaches, dizziness, nausea, panic attacks, and vertigo. She speculated, in a self-published book, that the low-frequency noise characteristic of the turbines had a physiological effect on people continuously subjected to it. Wind industry advocates countered her claims by noting that she had merely selected a few case studies from people who lived near wind farms and had health issues, rather than running a systematic epidemiological study with a control group. Pierpont nevertheless became a popular figure among citizen groups trying to prevent the construction of wind farms in their neighborhoods.[29]

A network of Internet sites sprang up bringing together these various objections and linking NIMBY communities that were trying to prevent wind farms from being built in their neighborhoods. They noted that wind power, like ethanol production, benefited from heavy government subsidies and that it was boosted for political reasons. Nevertheless, political support for wind energy persisted. President Obama toured a turbine factory in Iowa on Earth Day 2009 and told its workforce, "The choice we face is between prosperity and decline. We can remain the world's leading importer of oil, or we can become the world's leading exporter of clean energy." The American Wind Energy Association developed as an important lobby in Washington, countering the antiwind arguments at every point and emphasizing that theirs was a "green," safe, renewable, and benevolent industry. It claimed that "development of just ten percent of the wind potential in the ten windiest states would reduce total United States emissions of CO_2 by almost a third." Moreover, it was continuing to improve the technology, raising efficiency and reducing price year after year.[30]

The Solar Electric Power Association made comparable claims about harnessing the power of the sun. It lobbied successfully for tax credits as a stimulus to the solar industry but was much less advanced than wind power by 2014. Potentially, solar could provide more energy than all other sources combined (all of which are, ultimately, sun related). For the moment, however, the high cost of large-scale solar power production kept it at the experimental stage. It was already effective for local, decentralized uses such as powering road signs, flashlights, calculators, wristwatches, and domestic water supplies in warm areas.

Ecologist Daniel Botkin was optimistic that solar power would become the decisive technology, because solar collectors were less intrusive than giant turbines, could be sited on rooftops, and were rapidly improving in efficiency and declining in cost. He calculated that "the total energy demand in the United States . . . could be met if photovoltaics occupied 1.7% of the land." Sooner or later, he believed, solar power would play a central role in solving the world's energy needs. In the short run, however, solar power remained unviable because the panels could not be made at a competitive price or with sufficient productivity. Solyndra, a solar power company founded with "green" fanfares in 2005 and benefiting from hefty federal subsidies, was forced to declare bankruptcy in 2011.[31]

Renewable electricity sources developed through the first decade of the new millennium, with costs coming down gradually toward a point where at least some might be able to compete with traditional sources, especially if the prices of oil, natural gas, and coal continued to rise or show extreme volatility. In her 2009 book *Global Warming Is Good for Business*, business journalist Kimberly Keilbach points out that the United States has a highly entrepreneurial tradition, and that where advocates of the old ways see only crises, innovators recognize moments of opportunity. "There are many individuals and organizations operating in the United States today who have embraced the changes that global warming and energy security have brought about and who are discovering ways to impact our world in a positive manner. They are working toward a greener future, where human beings can build environmentally sustainable lives *and* make a buck."[32]

Even more enthusiastic is Amory Lovins, whose Rocky Mountain Institute compiled a distinguished record on energy questions between the 1980s and the 2010s. Lovins is eloquent on the topic of how many savings can be made by improving efficiency, and as a consultant to the Department of Defense, Walmart, and other corporations he has shown them ways of making huge savings with the technology they already possess. His 2011 book *Reinventing Fire* anticipates that by 2050 the economy will have grown by 150 percent, that it will have freed itself almost entirely from fossil fuels and nuclear power, that vehicles will be electrically powered, strong, and safe, drawing on electricity supplies that are decentralized, renewable, and clean. Profits will be up, greenhouse gases down, and ingenious entrepreneurs will have found countless ways to make their fortunes, leaving behind older technologies as completely as computers annihilated typewriters. It is a bracing and gratifying prospect that some of his critics have found almost too good to be true.[33]

Innovation was certainly better than carrying on in the old way with electricity-generating projects that scanted environmental concerns. The authoritarian regime in China, while receptive to some forms of entrepreneurship by the early twenty-first century, continued to ignore more than half a century of American environmental experience. The Three Gorges Dam, planned in the 1980s, begun in 1993, and finished in 2006, was comparable to projects undertaken in the United States seventy years earlier, when the Hoover and the Grand Coulee Dams were built across the Colorado and Columbia Rivers. Six hundred feet high, a mile across, and creating a 410-mile-long reservoir, the Three Gorges Dam became the biggest power station in the world, generating 22,500 megawatts of power. It was also designed to prevent chronic flooding of the Yangtze and its tributaries. But like the blundering Soviet project that had drained and wrecked the Aral Sea region, it brought as much catastrophe and tragedy as it did progress.[34]

First, the flooding of fertile farmland displaced a population of over one million people, destroyed the means of their livelihood, and submerged areas of ancient historical and archaeological interest. Second, the dam was sited too far upstream to prevent severe flooding, much of which was caused year after year by heavy rainfall farther downstream or in the tributaries of rivers that flowed into the Yangtze below the dam.[35] Third, the river flowing into the reservoir carried hundreds of thousands of tons of silt. This annual load was now destined to settle behind the dam and gradually make the reservoir shallower, reducing its overall capacity and its ability to forestall flooding. Silt would also clog the generator turbines. By no longer flowing into the lower valley, finally, the nutrients the river had historically carried to farms in the Chinese lowlands would be lost.[36]

The Chinese government did not permit the kind of outspoken debate over this project that was routine in the United States, where for half a century environmentalists had condemned such dam-building entities as the Bureau of Reclamation and the Army Corps of Engineers. When Dai Qing, a journalist, published her book *Yangtze! Yangtze!* summarizing many of the hazards, she was sent to a high-security jail for ten months. Undeterred, she told Western journalists that the only positive outcome of the project was to create a new environmental awareness among the Chinese people and to prompt the formation of "green" interest groups.[37]

The Chinese government set to work on other valleys farther upstream to create a linked series of dams, each of which would have the same effects as Three Gorges but would, in theory, forestall the premature silting of the main dam. These dams caused further alarm to observers worldwide, who noted that one, on the Jinsha River, was to be sited on an active earthquake fault and that others would accelerate the extinction of rare plant and animal species.[38]

Belatedly, in 2007, the Chinese government began to concede in official announcements that it was encountering severe environmental consequences that it had not adequately anticipated: "[D]enial suddenly gave way to reluctant acceptance that the naysayers were right." It admitted that landslides and an increase in seismic activity raised the possibility of a major earthquake, that the area had suffered an increase in waterborne diseases like schistosomiasis, that rare plant and animal habitats were being damaged or destroyed, and that the area's climate was beginning to change. In dry years, dramatically reduced flow below the dam stranded ships and created a freshwater crisis in Shanghai, while salt water moved farther upstream than hitherto. Even so, the Chinese government declared its continued commitment to hydroelectricity.[39]

INVASIVE SPECIES

Ever since Columbus, plants and animals from the New World had traveled to Europe, while plants and animals from Europe and Africa had come to the Americas. From the early nineteenth century exotic species were brought from Asia, too, further transforming the American landscape. Wheat, vines, horses, pigs, honeybees, and cattle, none native to the Americas, played a vital role in the history of the continent, but so did unwelcome pests and weeds. Species could run wild in America when they found no local competition, or could be so well suited to particular ecological niches that they replaced the indigenous plants and creatures previously thriving there.[40]

In the twentieth and twenty-first centuries, the pace of invasive species takeovers appeared to be increasing. Several newcomers caused widespread destruction. Consider just two: kudzu and zebra mussels. Kudzu was imported from Japan to the American South between 1876 and the 1930s as a fast-growing plant that appeared suitable to prevent soil erosion. It could also be used as a nitrogen fixer in poor soil, as an animal feed, and as a decorative domestic plant. Rapidly exceeding its importers' hopes, it ran wild across the South, smothering trees, electric utility poles and lines, unoccupied houses, and fallow fields. Tenacious, hard to remove, capable of growing a foot per day, and growing from a hard-to-kill taproot weighing up to four hundred pounds, kudzu continued to spread. By 2000 it was found in half of the states, and as far from its original Southern range as Oregon. In 1970 the one-time "miracle vine" had been redesignated a weed by the Department of Agriculture. *Time* magazine in 1999 named its introduction among the one hundred worst ideas in American history.[41]

Zebra mussels were troublesome in the same way. Native to the Caspian and Black Seas in southern Russia, they had spread across Europe in the nineteenth century and then appeared in the Great Lakes in 1986, probably brought in the ballast water of Eastern European freighters. Capable of rapid reproduction, they could also cling to hard surfaces. They soon coated rocks and the hulls of ships and dockyard pilings, clogged the intakes of power plants and dams, and consumed the phytoplankton on which many other species depended for food. Fish stocks in the Great Lakes declined sharply. The zebra mussels spread rapidly by latching on to pleasure boats and Mississippi barges, soon infesting rivers and lakes throughout the union. Municipal water supply operators and factory owners found them difficult and costly to remove. They also imparted a nasty odor to drinking water, "like dirty socks at the bottom of a college freshman's laundry bag," according to one report. The closely related quagga mussel, another invasive, compounded these problems and proved able to live at greater depths than the zebra mussel.[42]

New invasive species alarms made headlines every few years, sometimes accompanied by wry admissions that the creatures had been brought in on purpose, only to then spread out of control. For example, Asian carp, originally introduced to Southern lakes and ponds in the 1970s as algae eaters, began making their way north toward the Great Lakes in the ensuing decades. They could grow as big as one hundred pounds, ate half their own body weight every day, and displaced all the other fish in areas they came to dominate. The state of Illinois spent twenty million dollars building electric barriers in the Chicago Sanitary and Ship Canal to try to forestall their arrival in the lakes, and even speculated about closing the canal altogether. In addition to the economic implications, they provoked an acute ecological concern. Invasives like kudzu, zebra mussels, and Asian carp could push jeopardized native species over the brink to extinction. How often that had happened in the past, and whether the arrival of invasives might sometimes create opportunities for new speciation, was itself a source of scientific controversy.[43]

How to control invasive species taxed the ingenuity of farmers, cities, and watershed managers. Legislation forced oceangoing ships to flush their ballast tanks in deep waters before entering the Saint Lawrence Seaway and the Great Lakes. In an era of recurrent food fads, including the "Paleolithic diet" (eat only what the cavemen ate) and the "locavore diet" (eat only what grows locally), one suggestion was to make invasive species part of the food supply, sometimes renaming them to make them appear more attractive. Recipes for kudzu began appearing in American cookbooks in the late twentieth century. Though it was hard to imagine ways to eat zebra mussels, associated as they were with salmonella and a form of botulism, fishery biologists suggested renaming the Asian carp "Kentucky tuna" to make it sound more palatable. A San Francisco parks department worker named Rachel Kesel suggested the "invasive species diet." Taras Grescoe, a Canadian travel writer, dealt with the issue in his award-winning book *Bottomfeeder: How to Eat Ethically in a World of Vanishing Seafood* (2008).[44]

GLOBAL WARMING, CONTINUED

Controversy over global warming further intensified in the early twenty-first century. A broad consensus had developed among scientists studying the climate that the warming of the post-1970 decades was real. The degree to which it was human induced and the degree to which it was linked to anthropogenic production of carbon dioxide remained unclear. Even more convoluted were the questions of whether warming was the most serious problem confronting humanity and what responses might be most appropriate. Even the strongest advocates of the anthropogenic warming theory admitted that its future consequences remained uncertain, depending on which inputs to the computer models were used, how accurate they were, whether negative feedback effects might mitigate the warming, and whether changes would be linear.[45]

Many of the world's governments had pledged themselves, as part of the Kyoto Protocol of 1997, to restrict greenhouse gas emissions, but hardly any succeeded in doing so. Some of the "dirtiest" developing nations had been exempted from the treaty and even signatories who made a good-faith effort found compliance difficult or impossible. Others, notably the United States, had declined even to participate.

Meanwhile, global CO_2 emissions increased about 2 to 3 percent each year and atmospheric carbon concentrations grew by one or two parts per million, reaching about 380 parts per million in 2010.[46]

Most of the scientists and policy makers associated with the Intergovernmental Panel on Climate Change were intellectually and professionally committed to the idea that it *was* the most serious of all environmental problems. They were pleased to see the award of a Nobel Peace Prize jointly to the IPCC and to Al Gore in 2007. Figures who had risen to prominence on the issue remained active advocates of drastic action, none more than Stephen Schneider and James Hansen. Schneider's 2009 book *Science as a Contact Sport* was a scientific autobiography, describing the central role he had played in the changing climate disputes of the last forty years. It explained in detail the tortuous work involved in formulating IPCC statements that both the scientists and the politicians were willing to accept, and his own attempt to give an exact quantifiable value to words and phrases like "probable," "discernable," and "high confidence."[47]

Schneider reiterated a point he had made from the outset: that scientists must get involved in policy making rather than simply leave it to the politicians. Even when the exact consequences of warming remained uncertain, the general danger was unmistakable, he believed, making preventive action essential. He tried to discourage journalists from reporting climate issues by getting representative quotations from both sides. To do so was to play into the hands of the "deniers" by implying that there was no scientific consensus, as tobacco lobbyists had done successfully for years. In his view there *was* a strong consensus among the climate scientists, with skeptics coming only from other disciplines, making their opinions less relevant.[48]

Hansen, whose congressional testimony in 1988 had first made the issue of global warming front-page news, also wrote an autobiography around the issue. *Storms of My Grandchildren* (2009) describes how, as a federal employee (director of NASA's Goddard Space Center), he had struggled to impress on members of the George W. Bush administration the seriousness of the climate change situation, only to be met with increasing levels of denial. Administrators had even tried to prevent him from talking to the press without prior government approval. Buoyed by the election of President Obama, Hansen was soon disappointed at the new president's eagerness for compromise and his reluctance to take drastic measures on environmental causes. In Hansen's view the cap-and-trade approach to reducing CO_2 emissions, or the Kyoto approach, was inadequate as it was easy to circumvent and brought down emissions too slowly. A straight tax on emissions would be much better, he believed, if high enough to force businesses to change their ways.[49]

Hansen also believed that nuclear power, for all its hazards, was the best short-term solution to producing electricity without greenhouse gases. Longer-term policy depended on a switch to clean renewables. Meanwhile, he was infuriated by fossil fuel companies' lobbying against tight fuel-efficiency standards, which he regarded not merely as evidence of a scientific difference of opinion or even as normal political hardball, but as criminal activity. In a speech to the National Press Club in 2008, which also invoked the tobacco precedent, he declared:

> Special interests have blocked transition to our renewable energy future. Instead of moving heavily into renewable energies, fossil companies choose to spread doubt about global warming, as tobacco companies discredited the smoking-cancer link. Methods are sophisticated, including funding to help shape school textbook discussions of global warming. CEOs of fossil energy companies know what they are doing and are aware of long-term consequences of business as usual. In my opinion these CEOs should be tried for high crimes against humanity and nature.

Hansen was now convinced that the IPCC estimates of rising sea levels were, if anything, too cautious, and that the rate of melting of the polar ice sheets was even faster than he had believed in the 1990s.[50]

Hansen, Schneider, and many others were joined by scientists with second thoughts. James Lovelock, for example, the originator of the

Gaia hypothesis, had at first taken the view that the earth was a self-regulating mechanism and that it would provide negative feedback effects to counteract anthropogenic warming. In 2004, however, after studying *positive* feedback systems in the Arctic, in tropical forests, and in the oceans, Lovelock became convinced that "the resiliency of the system was gone" and that "the whole system is in failure mode." He now foresaw the crossing of a tipping point, after which the earth would recalibrate itself in a much hotter equilibrium state.[51]

As the world's industrial leaders proved unable, in the years after Kyoto, to scale back their CO_2 emissions, scholars, governments, and entrepreneurs began to look for ways to adapt to climate change. Schneider himself cowrote *Preparing for Climate Change* in 2010, in which he advocated a dual approach to the problem. Mitigation remained his primary concern, but he also began to consider faster ways of adapting to it. The boldest adaptation schemes required "geoengineering," or interventions on a global scale to counteract the effects of warming. These included pumping sulfate particles into the stratosphere to reflect more sunlight back into space, an idea studied in detail by Edward Teller and Lowell Wood. Other possibilities included building giant scrubbers to take CO_2 out of the air and convert it into harmless compounds, capturing CO_2 and sequestering it in underground geological formations, or simply (at the low-tech end) painting roads and roofs white to increase heat reflection. The two great problems with such schemes, as the science journalist Jeff Goodell pointed out, were that they could have unforeseen side effects and that they could distract governments from the more important job of reducing emissions at source. Any scheme that left the CO_2 in the atmosphere would have to be done repeatedly and would not remedy CO_2's other harmful effects, such as acidification of the ocean and damage to marine corals.[52]

Among the most troublesome problems confronting anthropogenic warming theorists and politicians was the knowledge that even their most sophisticated GCM computer models lacked specific information about how conditions would change in *particular places*, and how those particular places should adapt. All agreed that overall warming did not mean that all places in the world would get hotter at the same rate. Some might face localized cooling, others might confront increased rainfall, and others again more drought. The best the models could do was to offer limited guidance with "horizontal resolutions" of between one hundred and five hundred kilometers. Unfortunately, "there is a gap between the scale on which models produce consistent information and the scale on which humans act." Neither could the models predict with confidence whether dramatic "tipping point" events might occur, nullifying projections that assumed linearity. Even with the assumption of linearity, projections for each decade further into the future became less certain.[53]

Other scholars remained skeptical not just about these particular problems but about the whole theory, and doubted whether evidence accumulated over the previous twenty years all pointed in the same direction. Even those who agreed that anthropogenic warming was real differed greatly in their judgment as to how much it would change the world in the coming decades and whether it was a major or minor problem. Just as Hansen and Schneider remained prominent alarmists, so Richard Lindzen and Fred Singer remained active on the side of the skeptics. Lindzen participated in the IPCC reports of 1995 and 2001 and was a member of the National Academy of Sciences panel that prepared the report "Climate Change Science: An Analysis of Some Key Questions" (2001). He agreed that there was a connection between rising CO_2 levels and rising temperatures but believed that it had been greatly overstated. Other relevant factors included solar variations, ocean cycles, and the still not well understood working of clouds. He also noted in 2009 that the warming appeared to have stopped over the foregoing decade. There had been "no surface-measured warming since 1997 and no statistically significant warming since 1995."[54]

Lindzen bitterly resented the attempt to discredit his own work, and that of other skeptics, by the alarmists. Just as they accused him of being a flack for the oil and coal corporations, so he accused them of conspiring to promote the idea of an emergency for the sake of more federal funding:

Ambiguous scientific statements about climate are hyped by those with a vested interest in alarm, thus raising the political stakes for policy makers who provide funds for more science research to feed more alarm to increase the political stakes . . . [T]here is a sinister side to this feeding frenzy. Scientists who dissent from the alarmism have seen their grant funds disappear, their work derided, and themselves libeled as industry stooges, scientific hacks or worse. Consequently, lies about climate change gain credence even when they fly in the face of the science that supposedly is their basis.

Lindzen was nevertheless able to continue publishing in peer-reviewed journals. His prestige gave other scientific and political skeptics a lodestar.[55]

Singer wrote two new books on the issue, *Unstoppable Global Warming: Every 1,500 Years* (2006) and *Climate Change Reconsidered* (2009). Both argued against the anthropogenic warming theory. He also appeared in a 2007 British television documentary, *The Great Global Warming Swindle*. Singer agreed that CO_2 was a greenhouse gas and that the volume of CO_2 in the atmosphere was rising because of human actions, but argued that so many other factors were involved in global climate changes that human action could not be isolated as the sole determinative factor. He was also convinced that alarmists were dedicated not merely to cutting emissions but to restraining economic growth—that there was an ideological dimension to their concern. He repeated the familiar argument that economic growth makes societies stronger, more resilient, and better able to face whatever challenges lie ahead.[56]

An important new voice on the skeptics' side was the physicist Freeman Dyson, a distinguished fellow of the Princeton Institute for Advanced Study who could not easily be linked to energy company payrolls or right-wing media. On the contrary, he was a regular contributor to the left-liberal *New York Review of Books*. Long famous for his faith in technology, he argued in 2008 that genetic engineering would enable humanity to develop a strain of "carbon-eating trees" that would take care of the rising atmospheric CO_2. He later added that carbon-eating phytoplankton in the sea might have the same effect, while an array of giant kites in Antarctica could provoke heavier snowfall there and prevent sea levels from rising.[57]

In a meditation on the intensity of the debate, Dyson concluded that "there is a worldwide secular religion . . . [of] environmentalism" and that it had replaced the earlier secular religion of socialism. That was on the whole a good thing, he believed, because "environmentalism, as a religion of hope and respect for nature . . . is one that we can all share." Unfortunately, he continued, some devotees of this new secular religion had "adopted as an article of faith the belief that global warming is the greatest threat to the ecology of our planet" and had come to depict global warming skeptics not simply as people who had drawn different conclusions on the basis of the evidence, but as *enemies*. The reality was different. "Many of the skeptics are passionate environmentalists. They are horrified to see the obsession with global warming distracting public attention from what they see as more serious and more immediate dangers to the planet, including problems of nuclear weaponry, environmental degradation, and social injustice."[58]

As the scientific and political communities became increasingly polarized, however, it became more difficult for anyone to keep in touch with both sides, each of which tended to think the very worst of the other. The ecologist Daniel Botkin, who had been involved in climate research since the 1960s, wrote that he was "deeply saddened by the intense politicization of global climate change." He had friends on both sides of the global warming debate, "yet each side is convinced that the other is initiating a new McCarthyism against them as people," so that the debate "appears to have devolved into double paranoia and worse."[59]

A major conference on climate change was scheduled for December 2009 in Copenhagen. Just before it opened, the publication of a trove of e-mails from climatologists at the University of East Anglia's Climatic Research Unit (CRU) by a hacker named "FOI" appeared to show that the institute had suppressed data that contradicted the anthropogenic warming hypothesis. Rather than release the data in response to a freedom of information request, which they were required to do by British law, the unit's employees had destroyed it. The e-mails also showed a pattern of secrecy and impatience with contradictory findings. In one, CRU director Phil Jones noted that the editor of the journal *Climate Research* had recently accepted for publication an article that cast doubt on the orthodox view. "I will be e-mailing the journal *Climate Research* to tell them I'm having nothing to do with it until they rid themselves of this troublesome editor," he declared. His American correspondent, Michael Mann, of Penn State University, answered:

> This was the danger of always criticizing the skeptics for not publishing in the "peer reviewed" literature. Obviously they found a solution to that—take over a journal! So what do we do about this? I think we have to stop considering *Climate Research* as a legitimate peer-reviewed journal. Perhaps we should encourage our colleagues in the climate research community to no longer submit to, or cite papers in, this journal.

In another e-mail, Jones said he was determined to exclude two peer-reviewed papers from an IPCC report "even if we have to redefine what peer-review literature is." Inevitably the media began referring to these disclosures as "Climategate."[60]

These embarrassing revelations encouraged skeptics' belief that an unethical attempt was being made to enforce conformity on behalf of a consensus. Pat Michaels, another skeptic, confirmed that "over the years it has become increasingly difficult for anyone who does not view global warming as an end-of-the-world issue to publish papers." Fred Singer added that the leak "has shown that the surface temperature data that the IPCC relies on is based on distorted raw data and algorithms that they will not share with the science community." Moreover, he wrote, CRU scientists "have taken control of the IPCC process and they have smeared opponents personally, rather than critiquing the research."[61]

. . .

GLOBAL WARMING REMAINS the strangest crisis in American history. As a phenomenon whose current manifestations are almost imperceptible, it has none of the characteristics of an ordinary political issue and cannot mobilize a significant electoral constituency. So many short-term problems confront the nation, especially after the financial crisis of 2008, that global warming has become relatively less newsworthy. It nevertheless continues to elicit a wide range of political responses. By now environmental responsibility has become a touchstone for almost everyone in political life, as universal and as vague as "progressivism" a hundred years ago or "anticommunism" fifty years ago. Sharp disagreements persist on the degree to which government programs should regulate industry, but there is a broad consensus on the need for clean air, clean water, food safety, and workplace safety. These objectives have all been achieved by federal and state regulation, systematic application of rules, and a generation of environmental education at all levels that has helped citizens internalize the relevant principles.

If American industry once dragged its feet and complied only reluctantly, a large part of it is by now invested in green projects. They benefit from the existence of strict rules, sometimes lobby to maintain them, and profit from the sale of green technologies. Oil and chemical companies have become adept at "greenwashing," advertising themselves as zealous advocates for environmental protection. If environmentalists think such claims hypocritical, they can nevertheless be consoled by the thought that hypocrisy is the tribute that vice pays to virtue.

CONCLUSION

THE UNITED STATES IS CLEANER, safer, healthier, and better provided with national parks today than it was in 1945. Its people live longer, smoke less, are better educated, are less vulnerable to occupational illnesses, accidents, and fatalities, enjoy a higher standard of living, and share their country with an array of species that have been brought back from the brink of extinction. For anyone interested in the environment, there is much to be proud of.

The clean air acts of the 1960s and 1970s greatly improved air quality throughout the United States. According to the EPA, between 1980 and 2009 (the latest year for which figures are available) emissions of carbon monoxide declined 61 percent and emissions of sulfur dioxide declined by 65 percent. These achievements are particularly gratifying since they took place at the same time as a 122 percent increase in the gross national product, a 95 percent increase in the number of vehicle-miles traveled, and a 35 percent rise in population.[1]

Among the most successful government interventions was the phasing out of lead in gasoline, which had been linked to brain damage in children and retardation of their cognitive and behavioral development. Legislation specified that cars manufactured and sold after 1976 would have to run on unleaded gasoline. When President Reagan's EPA administrator Anne Gorsuch declined to enforce this law, the public outcry prompted the Reagan administration to *accelerate* the phaseout of leaded gasoline. Atmospheric lead declined 97 percent between

1980 and 2009. This achievement, along with the almost complete curtailment of smoking in public places, means that most Americans are much less vulnerable to environmental hazards in their everyday lives than they were in 1945. Serious attempts to regulate hazardous chemicals in the environment and to clean up toxic waste dumps also bear witness to the development of the political will to improve public health and safety.[2]

Clean water acts greatly reduced the pollution of American lakes and rivers. The Cuyahoga River, for example, notorious for catching fire in 1969, was subjected in the ensuing decades to a rigorous recovery program, removing pollutants, restricting industrial uses, and creating shoreline parkland. A report on progress early in the new millennium noted that "breeding populations of Great Blue heron and Bald Eagle, sentinel species, have returned," that wild turkey and Canada geese had been successfully reintroduced, and that "deer and beaver populations have naturally increased." The river is now popular with fishers, and the fish themselves are edible.[3]

Rural as well as urban environmental policy has succeeded in many ways since 1945. The Endangered Species Act, enacted in 1973 and extended since, has facilitated successful intervention to prevent the extinction of gray and red wolves, mountain lions, bald eagles, California condors, and alligators. The controversies over the snail darter and the spotted owl have also shown a genuine willingness, at the highest levels of government, to consider the survival needs of unspectacular creatures as well as the economic needs of citizens. The extension of the national park system and the designation of more areas as wilderness has ensured their survival for the enjoyment of subsequent generations. More than thirty new national parks have been created, generating a park system of 84 million acres in all (131,000 square miles), and including new parks in Alaska, Arizona, California, Colorado, the Dakotas, Minnesota, Nevada, Texas, Utah, and Washington. The national forests now cover a further 192 million acres of public land.[4]

Despite frequent lamentation about the destruction of forests, meanwhile, the entire United States, especially east of the Mississippi River, has experienced a profound and continuous process of *reforestation.*

"Whatever measure is taken," writes forest historian Michael Williams, "the conclusion seems unavoidable that the forest is building up today rather than declining." He adds that "the evidence of one's eyes is better than statistics. Regrowth can be seen everywhere, and one is struck by the robustness of the forest." Reversion of abandoned farmland to forest, fire control, the decline of the use of firewood and lumber as a building material, and improved management have all contributed to this resurgence. Damage to red spruce trees from acid rain was limited to high ground and then mitigated by the 1990 Clean Air Act. Other tree species, better protected than ever before, flourish in such areas as the Carolina Appalachians, which were clear-cut in the late nineteenth and early twentieth centuries.[5]

Today all young Americans receive a rudimentary education in environmental awareness, learning in school that they ought not to drop litter, and that they ought to recycle reusable containers, avoid wasting water, and (especially in the West) take precautions against forest fires. Schools encourage students not to waste paper, linking conservation to the protection of forests. Such activities might be, and sometimes are, dismissed as merely "light green," but their cumulative effect is significant. No politician can ignore the generalized pattern of respect for "the environment" in his or her policy proposals.

This generally positive situation does not mean, obviously, that no environmental concerns remain. The environmental movement has often devoted itself to redressing problems that are the side effects of economic success, a phenomenon that persists up to the present. The immense housing boom of the late twentieth and early twenty-first centuries has led to the widening sprawl of metropolitan areas like Atlanta, Houston, Dallas, Phoenix, and Los Angeles. Houses are bigger than ever, use more resources, generate more wastes, and feature ever larger vehicles in their driveways. While Europe taught itself to drive efficient, economical cars, some Americans appeared to take a perverse pleasure in doing just the opposite, buying massive and inefficient sport-utility vehicles. The biggest and most vulgar of these vehicles was the Hummer, introduced by General Motors in 1998 based on the military Humvee and defiantly oblivious of environmental concerns.

An "ecoterrorist" attack on a California Hummer dealership in 2003 demonstrated their significance as a flashpoint for environmentalist anger.[6]

The nation's energy future remains in serious question. The rate of increase in energy use over the last six decades means that the United States is still dependent on foreign oil supplies, many of them from politically volatile nations. Possible substitutes have been disappointing. Ethanol, wind power, solar power, and geothermal all work in particular places, but usually on a small scale, or else become economically viable only with subsidies. None of them is yet poised to become a major substitute for petroleum. The development of hydraulic fracturing ("fracking") in the 1990s has been a mixed blessing. On the one hand it produces vast new supplies of oil and gas from American sources, reducing the nation's dependence on foreign suppliers and creating work and investment within the United States. On the other hand it generates dirty flowback water, increases the risk of blowouts at wellheads, and releases such potent greenhouse gases as methane.

Nuclear power remains controversial too. Avoided by American energy companies for two decades after Three Mile Island, it started to regain respectability in the early twenty-first century. The 2011 earthquake and tidal wave at Fukushima that swamped a nuclear power station raised new doubts about its safety. Meanwhile, the designated nuclear waste disposal site at Yucca Mountain has never come online. Years of tenacious politicking by Nevada's representatives and senators stalled the project and in 2011 President Obama abandoned it altogether. If nuclear power is to revive as a major source of electricity generation, the waste disposal problem will have to be solved. The threat it presents to American principles of democracy, public accountability, and transparency makes nuclear power, in any case, a very dubious and troublesome panacea.

Energy questions also loom in the future of American agriculture. In some ways American farming is an incredible success story. Less than 2 percent of the population is now capable of feeding the other 98 percent, with large surpluses left over. On the other hand, this level of productivity uses a great deal of energy and other resources, raising the question of whether it is sustainable. "Superbugs" and "superweeds" are developing resistance to genetically modified crops. The depletion of aquifers remains a nagging problem. From year to year, well pumps bring water from greater depths to irrigate farms in the Midwest and on the Great Plains. Their exhaustion or salination, predicted regularly after 1980, might eventually challenge the domestic food supply.

Side by side with domestic conditions, it is important to judge the international environmental situation. The Montreal Protocol of 1987 set the gold standard for international cooperation. After widespread agreement among atmospheric scientists that the thinning of the stratospheric ozone layer was related to chlorofluorocarbons, the treaty's signatories agreed to phase out their production and to use less harmful substitutes. In other respects, international action has been less effective. The signatories to the Kyoto Protocol of 1997 made promises to cut carbon dioxide emissions that they found they could not, or would not, keep. Some nations, notably the United States and Australia, refused even to sign, and an influential segment of scientists and politicians continued to doubt that reducing emissions of greenhouse gases was in practice the best way to confront global warming.

Phenomenal rises in world food production, thanks first to the green revolution and then to genetically modified crops, forestalled the catastrophic worldwide famines that were forecast in the 1950s and 1960s, even though the population has swelled since then from about two billion to over seven billion. However, glaring inequalities in nutrition and food distribution persist. In 2014 tens of millions of people around the world still suffer from malnutrition and undernourishment; extraordinarily difficult questions about how (and whether) to respond remain controversial. Surpluses from the United States and Europe, when sent to poor countries in Africa and Asia, undercut the price of locally grown food, prompting some farmers to abandon the land and swell urban populations. Their underemployment and political volatility, in turn, prompt governments to subsidize food imports, keeping prices low as a way of muting political dissent. Some advocates of third world development have argued in recent years that Western aid programs, though well intentioned, nearly always do more harm than good and should be stopped. Meanwhile, the leading environmental causes of preventable death throughout the world in the early twenty-first century remain very low tech: smoke inhalation from wood and dung fires, and the ingestion of contaminated drinking water.

More than half a century of experience has shown by now that environmental issues are a central concern of the American people. The controversies surrounding them, however, have also shown that none are simple. Only in the early stages, when the solution seemed a matter of cleaning up severely polluted landscapes and providing clean air and water, did something like a consensus develop. But as the problems grew ever more complex, opinions polarized and animosities deepened. Philosophical issues, questions about the purpose of life, economic disagreements about how to deploy limited resources, and political disagreements about what practical steps were feasible, beset every proposal. Democrats remained generally proenvironmentalist; Republicans became enviroskeptics. Although the relevant sciences have gained in sophistication and accuracy, and although human understanding of natural processes has improved immensely, science alone is never going to provide answers to the all-important ethical questions. As the nation emerges from the Great Recession, we find a wide range of environmental questions still before us, still unresolved.

MY INTENTION IN UNDERTAKING this book has been to explain the history of American environmental controversies since World War II and to encourage an optimistic attitude toward the environmental future. First, I hope to have shown that America's environmental problems have been *manageable* problems. Scientists, media, and activists often claimed that the nation, or even the whole of humanity, faced catastrophe. Such claims were false, with the single exception of general nuclear war, which really could have annihilated humanity. All the other problems, though often complicated and serious, were susceptible to intelligent human intervention and mitigation. When the nation mobilized the political will, it was effective in providing remedies. Legislation and regulation, though sometimes imperfect and clumsy, have transformed the environment for the better.

Environmental problems should be studied historically. History teaches us that industrialization has done far more good than harm in the world, and will probably continue to do so into the future. Without it, nearly everyone in the world would be wretchedly poor (as indeed nearly everyone in the world was before the industrial revolution). Life expectancy would be low, infant mortality high, education scanty, nutrition poor, and everyday life cramped, narrow, and monotonous. In the United States industrialization, over the long run, has led to a richer way of life for nearly everyone, opened up areas of choice, increased individual freedom, increased health and life expectancy, improved nutrition, increased access to education, improved communications, and strengthened democracy. It has also generated sufficient surplus wealth to enable the nation to take its environmental problems seriously.

I believe that what worked for the United States will work for the rest of the world. Wealth is better than poverty, and the people who suffer the most are the world's poorest people. So long as they live in underdeveloped countries they will remain vulnerable; hope lies in the prospect of industrialization. It is of course easy to dislike industrialization, which in the short run is dirty and messy and usually accentuates social inequalities. In the long run, however, it is the necessary prelude to the collective improvement of human welfare. It is much better to live in a dirty industrialized country, such as India or China today, than a clean rural one, like Haiti or Sudan, and better still to live in a clean industrialized society like the United States.

As nations become richer they become more resilient and better able to devote resources to safeguarding their people. The very poorest Americans today are in some respects richer than the very richest people in colonial America. In the famous opening sentence of *The Affluent Society* John Kenneth Galbraith wrote: "Wealth is not without its advantages and the case to the contrary, though it has often been made, has never proved widely persuasive." True. Suffering people throughout the world want to be wealthier because more wealth increases their chances of staying alive and enabling their children to live. Environmentalism is always going to be most persuasive and successful when linked to increasing industrial wealth. It is going to be least convincing when coupled with calls for self-denial, a steady-state economy, or an end to growth.

Thinking sensibly about the environment means learning to accept several paradoxes. First is the paradox that industrial capitalism, the system that has *caused* the problem of pollution, is better equipped to *solve* it than any alternative, especially when coupled with political democracy. We know this because industrialization behind the Iron Curtain, during the long years of the Cold War, was much dirtier than in the capitalist West. In the Eastern Bloc, the state owned and ran all the industries, market incentives to clean up pollution were absent, and a repressive, secretive political system prevented citizens from complaining or taking action. The lack of a free press and freedom of expression, along with the lack of alternative sources of initiative apart from the state, made the whole of Eastern Europe and the Soviet Union vulnerable to environmental disasters like Chernobyl and the destruction of the Aral Sea. Western experience, by contrast, shows that open democratic societies, once aroused to the dangers of pollution, have the institutional means to remedy it. Citizens took action on their own initiative, used the free press and the judiciary, and lobbied their governments successfully to enhance environmental protection. Government programs, though often imperfect, were then able to reduce pollution even as the number of people, vehicles, factories, and power stations continued to increase.

Second is the paradox that the anticipation of catastrophe can often contribute to preventing it. The intense and widely shared fear of nuclear weapons after World War II, with which this book began, prompted nearly everyone involved to look for ways to contain and limit the damage they might cause. On the face of it, no other weapon in the history of the world has been so little used. A second glance shows, however, that nuclear weapons *were* being used when they sat in their silos. Using nuclear weapons actually meant, above all, deterring potential adversaries by *threatening* to fire them. Mutual deterrence worked brilliantly throughout the Cold War, limiting America's capacity to intervene in the Soviet Bloc but also safeguarding the West against Soviet aggression. The two sides even had a high incentive to cooperate in restricting tests—the Atmospheric Test Ban Treaty of 1963 benefited everyone by reducing the level of radioactive fallout in the atmosphere. Even with this most dangerous threat, in other words, the political system found a way to combine an effective strategic policy with minimal environmental harm.

Closely related is the paradox that "inevitable" events don't always happen. From the vantage point of today, the belief among intelligent people in the 1950s and 1960s that rising populations were *bound* to lead to famines seems reasonable enough. How could world population double in just twenty-five years after World War II without exceeding the world's ability to feed them? The fact that the green revolution and then the development and spread of genetically modified crops more than kept pace is astonishing testimony to the fertility of human imagination as well as to the fertility of the earth and its people. The positive outcome of what looked like an apocalyptic situation inspires faith in human creativity and gives us reason to hope for the successful resolution of other "inevitable" crises.

What looks like altruism toward our successors—especially our distant successors—is paradoxically unlikely to win their gratitude. The meaning of events changes with the passage of time, such that one era's apparent crisis can seem irrelevant, even quaint, to later generations. Of course we should always be aware of the future and concerned about safeguarding future generations, but we should be thinking far more seriously about safeguarding the welfare of our own generation. Limited resources should be devoted to saving and improving jeopardized lives today rather than hypothetical lives in the future. If, for example, an anti–global warming policy retards economic growth in the present, it is likely to cause more harm than good. The study of history shows us how bad we are at predicting the future (predictions tell us far more about the time in which they were made than about the times they ostensibly predicted). It also shows that unforeseen events and developments soon render irrelevant our expectations for more than the immediate future.

The fifth of these paradoxes is that we can sometimes tempt ourselves into believing that a situation is worsening largely because it has, in fact, improved. The increase in cancer cases in the post–World War II era, for example, made it reasonable to believe at first glance that environmental carcinogens were exposing people to greater health hazards than ever before. But these were the years in which the *detection* of cancer became far better than ever before, so that fewer cases went undiagnosed. They were also the years in which life expectancy was increasing steadily, enabling more people—who in earlier generations had died young from other causes—to live long enough to contract cancer. It was, in other words, one of the problems that come with success.

Readers of these pages might conclude that I am overoptimistic or that, like Voltaire's Dr. Pangloss, I think that ours is the best of all possible worlds. Let me state unequivocally that I am no Pangloss, and that I am acutely aware of the seriousness of our environmental situation. We do continue to confront many grave questions: securing safe, clean energy supplies for the long-term future, preserving endangered species, coping with the coevolution of bacteria, insects, and other pests in response to our medicines and pesticides, continuing to restrict the proliferation of nuclear weapons, ensuring the preservation of biotic diversity, preparing to cope with the effects of global warming, and looking for effective ways to carry the benefits of basic health care, nutrition, and safety to the developing world. None of them is easy, all of them carry costs, and all provoke intense disagreements about how they should be carried out.

On the other hand, I have faith in the institutions of democracy and capitalism. Democracy can often seem deadlocked (so it seems as I write, in 2014). It often moves slowly, sometimes more in response to special interests' preferences than in response to the general population's actual needs. But when the population becomes sufficiently aroused, as it did in the late 1960s and early 1970s, it can convey its concerns effectively to its political representatives, who will act upon them. The legislative transformation with regard to the environment accomplished in those years is reassuring. So is the discovery that, as environmental concern became widespread throughout American society in the 1970s and 1980s, dozens of entrepreneurs recognized opportunities to profit while improving the environment. The last forty years have witnessed hundreds of inventions related to recycling, improving energy efficiency, miniaturization, and substitution of dangerous chemicals with more benign alternatives, enabling us to have a far more productive economy with far less pollution and waste. This is the terrain on which we stand, and which gives us every reason to be hopeful as we face the future.

NOTES

INTRODUCTION

1. A. Costandina Titus, *Bombs in the Backyard: Atomic Testing and American Politics* (Las Vegas: University of Nevada Press, 1986), 36–38.
2. Titus, *Bombs in the Backyard*, 38–42, quotes from 41, 42.
3. Barton C. Hacker, *Elements of Controversy: The Atomic Energy Commission and Radiation Safety in Nuclear Weapons Testing, 1947–1974* (Berkeley: University of California Press, 1994), 139–52, quote from 148. Ralph Lapp, *The Voyage of the Lucky Dragon* (New York: Harper, 1958).
4. Carolyn Kopp, "The Origins of the American Scientific Debate over Fallout Hazards," *Social Studies of Science* 9 (November 1979), 403–22. Ralph Lutts, "Chemical Fallout, Rachel Carson's *Silent Spring*, and the Environmental Movement," *Environmental Review* 9 (Autumn 1985), 210–25.
5. Howard Ball, *Justice Downwind: America's Atomic Testing Program in the 1950s* (New York: Oxford University Press, 1986). Christopher Emery, "Fifty Years After Bikini Atoll," *Frontiers in Ecology and the Environment* 2 (April 2004), 119.

CHAPTER 1

1. On the religious response to Hiroshima, see: Patrick Allitt, *Religion in America Since 1945: A History* (New York: Columbia University Press, 2004), 1–2, 12. John Hersey, *Hiroshima* (New York: Knopf, 1946). David Bradley, *No Place to Hide* (1946. Hanover: University of New Hampshire Press, 1984), quoted in Allan Winkler, *Life Under a Cloud: American Anxiety About the Atom* (New York: Oxford University Press, 1993), 91.
2. Philip L. Fradkin, *Fallout: An American Nuclear Tragedy* (Tucson: University of Arizona Press, 1989). On the films about nuclear apocalypse, see Paul Boyer, *By the Bomb's Early Light: American Thought and Culture at the Dawn of the Nuclear Age* (New York: Pantheon, 1985), 352–55.
3. Eugene Rabinowitch, "Living with H-Bombs," *Bulletin of the Atomic Scientists* 11 (January 1, 1955), 5–8. See also H. J. Muller, "How Radiation Changes the Genetic Constitution," *Bulletin of the Atomic Scientists* 11 (November 1955), 329–52.
4. Eugene Rabinowitch, "Pugwash—History and Outlook," *Bulletin of the Atomic Scientists* 13 (September 1957), 243–48; Committee II, "Social Responsibility of Scientists," ibid., 252. See below, chapter 9, on the issue of scientists' responsibility to participate in the political aspect of the global warming controversy.
5. Ted Goertzel et al., *Linus Pauling: A Life in Science and Politics* (New York: Basic, 1995), 143–48. Lawrence S. Wittner, *Confronting the Bomb: A Short History of the World Nuclear Disarmament Movement* (Stanford, CA: Stanford University Press, 2009), 55–74. Louise Zibold Reiss, "Strontium 90 Absorption by Deciduous Teeth," *Science* 134 (November 24, 1961), 1669–73.

6. Peter Goodchild, *Edward Teller: The Real Dr. Strangelove* (London: Weidenfeld and Nicolson, 2004), 274–79. On the threshold question, see: Jack Schubert, "Fetal Irradiation and Fallout," *Bulletin of the Atomic Scientists* 15 (June 1959), 253–56; "Safe So Far," *Bulletin of the Atomic Scientists* 15 (October 1959), 352.

7. Winkler, *Life Under a Cloud*, 101–7. Marie Smith, "500 Women Picket for Peace: Letters to First Ladies," *Washington Post*, November 2, 1961, D1.

8. Richard Andrews, *Managing the Environment, Managing Ourselves: A History of American Environmental Policy*, second edition (New Haven, CT: Yale University Press, 2006), 212–13. Benjamin Greene, *Eisenhower, Science Advice, and the Nuclear Test-Ban Debate, 1945–1963* (Stanford, CA: Stanford University Press, 2006).

9. L. T. Evans, *Feeding the Ten Billion: Plants and Population Growth* (Cambridge, UK: Cambridge University Press, 1998).

10. Warren Thompson, "Population," *American Journal of Sociology* 34 (May 1929), 959–75. A mature statement of demographic transition theory is F. W. Notestein, "Economic Problems of Population Change," *Proceedings of the 8th International Conference of Agricultural Economists* (New York: Oxford University Press, 1953), 13–31.

11. For a summary of debates over causation of demographic transition, see Jean-Claude Chesnais, *The Demographic Transition: Stages, Patterns, and Implications*, translated from French by E. and P. Kreager (Oxford, UK: Clarendon, 1992).

12. Fairfield Osborn, *Our Plundered Planet* (Boston: Little, Brown, 1948). William Vogt, *Road to Survival* (New York: W. Sloane, 1948), quote from 28.

13. Thomas Malthus, *An Essay on the Principle of Population* (1798. New York: Norton, 2004).

14. On neo-Malthusianism, see: Madeline Gray, *Margaret Sanger: A Biography of the Champion of Birth Control* (New York: R. Marek, 1979). Karl Sax, *Standing Room Only: The Challenge of Overpopulation* (Boston: Beacon Press, 1955). Aldous Huxley, *Brave New World Revisited* (New York: Perennial, 1958).

15. For the history of the Rockefeller and PPF programs, see Matthew Connelly, *Fatal Misconception: The Struggle to Control World Population* (Cambridge, MA: Belknap Press of Harvard University Press, 2008). For the Draper report, see "The Numbers Game," *Time* 75 (January 11, 1960).

16. Glen L. Johnson and C. Leroy Quance, eds., *The Overproduction Trap in U.S. Agriculture* (Baltimore: Resources for the Future/Johns Hopkins University Press, 1972).

17. Ester Boserup, *The Conditions of Agricultural Growth: The Economics of Agrarian Change Under Population Pressure* (London: Allen and Unwin, 1965).

18. Earl Parker Hanson, *New Worlds Emerging* (New York: Duell, Sloan and Pearce, 1949).

19. Alden Hatch, *Buckminster Fuller: At Home in the Universe* (New York: Crown, 1974); for "ephemeralization," see 143.

20. David Kinkela, *DDT and the American Century: Global Health, Environmental Politics, and the Pesticide that Changed the World* (Chapel Hill: University of North Carolina Press, 2011).

21. John H. Douglas, "The New Green Revolution," *Science News* 106 (October 5, 1974), 218–19. Lennard Bickel, *Facing Starvation: Norman Borlaug and the Fight Against Hunger* (New York: Reader's Digest Press, 1974). Evans, *Feeding the Ten Billion*, 114–48.

22. Bess Furman, "Catholics Oppose Use of Aid Funds in Birth Control," *New York*

Times, November 26, 1959, A1. E. W. Kenworthy, "State Department Says Food Output Exceeds Population Growth," *New York Times,* December 3, 1959, A1.

23. Aldo Leopold, *A Sand County Almanac and Sketches Here and There* (1949. New York: Oxford University Press, 1987), 41. On Leopold's life, see Julianne Lutz Newton, *Aldo Leopold's Odyssey* (Washington, D.C.: Island Press/Shearwater, 2006).

24. Leopold, *Sand County Almanac,* 201–26, quote from 224–25.

25. Marjory Stoneman Douglas, *Everglades: Sea of Grass,* sixtieth anniversary edition, ed. Robert Fink (1947. Sarasota, FL: Pineapple Press, 2007), 5, 349.

26. Rachel Carson, *Under the Sea Wind: A Naturalist's Picture of Ocean Life* (New York: Simon and Schuster, 1941); *The Sea Around Us* (New York: Oxford University Press, 1951); *The Edge of the Sea* (Boston: Houghton Mifflin, 1955). On Carson's life, see Linda Lear, *Rachel Carson: Witness for Nature* (New York: Henry Holt, 1997).

27. Carson quoted in Paul Brooks, *The House of Life: Rachel Carson at Work* (Boston: Houghton Mifflin, 1972), 147.

28. Sigurd Olson, *The Singing Wilderness* (New York: Knopf, 1956); *Listening Point* (New York: Knopf, 1958), 4, 7. On Olson's life, see David Backes, *A Wilderness Within: The Life of Sigurd F. Olson* (Minneapolis: University of Minnesota Press, 1997).

29. Olson, *Listening Point,* 151. On the therapeutic aspect of wilderness advocacy, see Roderick Nash, *Wilderness and the American Mind* (New Haven, CT: Yale University Press, 1967), 245.

30. Michael P. Cohen, *History of the Sierra Club, 1892–1970,* 2 vols. (San Francisco: Sierra Club Books, 1988). David Brower, *For the Earth's Sake: The Life and Times of David Brower* (Salt Lake City: Peregrine Smith, 1990). Nash, *Wilderness and the American Mind,* 211–21.

31. Marc Reisner, *Cadillac Desert: The American West and Its Disappearing Water* (New York: Viking, 1986), 222–63. John McPhee, *Encounters with the Archdruid* (New York: Farrar, Straus and Giroux, 1971), 153–58. For Brower's mea culpa over Glen Canyon, see his "The Place No One Knew" (1963) in Steven Stoll, *U.S. Environmentalism Since 1945: A Brief History with Documents* (New York: Palgrave Macmillan, 2007), 46–49.

32. McPhee, *Encounters,* 21. Charles Park, *Affluence in Jeopardy: Minerals and the Political Economy* (San Francisco: Freeman Cooper, 1968). Robert Wernick, "Let's Spoil the Wilderness," *Saturday Evening Post* 238 (November 6, 1965), 12, 16.

33. Nash, *Wilderness and the American Mind,* 221–27. David Reisman, *The Lonely Crowd: A Study of the Changing American Character* (New Haven, CT: Yale University Press, 1950). William Whyte, *The Organization Man* (Garden City, NY: Doubleday, 1956). Sloan Wilson, *The Man in the Gray Flannel Suit* (New York: Simon and Schuster, 1955).

34. Kenneth Jackson, *The Crabgrass Frontier: The Suburbanization of the United States* (New York: Oxford University Press, 1985).

35. Richard Pells, *The Liberal Mind in a Conservative Age* (New York: Harper and Row, 1985), 196–99. Morton White, *The Intellectual Versus the City: From Thomas Jefferson to Frank Lloyd Wright* (New York: Oxford University Press, 1977). John Keats, *The Crack in the Picture Window* (Boston: Houghton Mifflin, 1956).

36. Adam Rome, *The Bulldozer in the Countryside* (New York: Cambridge University Press, 2001), 87–118 (sanitation); 153–88 (erosion); 45–86 (energy).

37. Rome, *Bulldozer in the Countryside,* 8. See also Christopher C. Sellers, *Crabgrass Crucible: Suburban Nature and the Rise of Environmentalism in Twentieth-Century America* (Chapel Hill: University of North Carolina Press, 2012). Sellers emphasizes that for suburbanites themselves, the presence of more "nature" than they could enjoy in central city districts was one of the principal attractions of their districts.

38. Kevin Kruse, *White Flight: Atlanta and the Making of Modern Conservatism* (Princeton, NJ: Princeton University Press, 2007). Robert Caro, *The Power Broker: Robert Moses and the Fall of New York* (New York: Knopf, 1974).

39. Jane Jacobs, *The Death and Life of Great American Cities* (New York: Random House, 1961). On her life and career, see also Alice Sparberg Alexiou, *Jane Jacobs: Urban Visionary* (New Brunswick, NJ: Rutgers University Press, 2006), and Anthony Flint, *Wrestling with Moses: How Jane Jacobs Took On New York's Master Builder and Transformed the American City* (New York: Random House, 2009).

40. For positive reviews of Jacobs, see Paul Kutsche, untitled review, *American Anthropologist* 64 (August 1962), 907–14. For negative reviews, see Arthur T. Row, untitled review, *Yale Law Journal* 71 (July 1962), 1597–602; Paul Pretzschner, untitled review, *Antioch Review* 22 (Spring 1962), 130–36.

41. Galbraith quoted in Andrew Rome, "Give Earth a Chance: The Environmental Movement and the Sixties," *Journal of American History* 90 (September 2003), 529.

42. William L. Thomas, ed., *Man's Role in Changing the Face of the Earth* (Chicago: University of Chicago/Wenner-Gren Foundation, 1956). Preston E. James, "Man's Role in Changing the Face of the Earth: A Review," *Economic Geography* 33 (July 1957), 267–74, quotes from 270.

43. Evans, *Feeding the Ten Billion,* 223.

CHAPTER 2

1. Lynn Page Snyder, "The Death Dealing Smog over Donora, Pennsylvania: Industrial Air Pollution, Public Health Policy, and the Politics of Expertise," *Environmental History Review* 18 (Spring 1994), 117–39. See also: "Federal Experts Will Study Smog," *New York Times,* November 19, 1948, 55; Bess Furman, "Government Spurs Poisoned Air Study," *New York Times,* October 14, 1949, 29.

2. "Western Wind When Wilt Thou Blow," *Time* 88 (August 20, 1965), 45. "Menace in the Skies," *Time* 89 (January 1, 1966), 60–69. "Cleaning the Air," *Time* 89 (May 20, 1966), 94. Chip Jacobs and William Kelly, *Smogtown: The Lung-Burning History of Pollution in Los Angeles* (Woodstock, NY: Overlook Press, 2008), 9. "Monoxide Rides the Freeways," *Time* 87 (February 19, 1965), 74.

3. Jerry Hubschman, "Lake Erie: Pollution Abatement, Then What?," *Science* 171 (February 12, 1971), 536–40. "Time for Transfusion," *Time* 88 (August 20, 1965), 74. In the ensuing decades, the problem was largely rectified by regulation and reduction of phosphorus discharges. See William McGucken, *Lake Erie Rehabilitated: Controlling Cultural Eutrophication* (Akron, OH: University of Akron Press, 2000).

4. James Ridgeway, "Gunboats on the Raritan," *New Republic* 148 (June 1, 1963), 17–19; "Down by the Styx," *New Republic* 149 (August 31, 1963), 8; "Speaking of Reorganization," *New Republic* 151 (November 21, 1964), 16.

5. "When Noise Annoys," *Time* 88 (August 19, 1966), 26.

6. Gladwin Hill, "Lake's Pollution Vexes Governors," *New York Times*, May 11, 1965, 33. "Who Is to Police Pollution?," *Time* 89 (February 10, 1967), 22. Gladwin Hill, "The Politics of Pollution," *Nation* 201 (October 11, 1965), 220–23. "Air Pollution," *National Review* 19 (March 7, 1967), 234.

7. "Environment: Tragedy in Oil," *Time* 93 (February 14, 1969), 29–31. Harvey Molotch and Marilyn Lester, "Accidental News: The Great Oil Spill as Local Occurrence and National Event," *American Journal of Sociology* 81 (September 1975), 235–60.

8. Carol E. Steinhart and John S. Steinhart, *Blowout: A Case Study of the Santa Barbara Oil Spill* (North Scituate, MA: Duxbury Press, 1972), 2–15.

9. David and Richard Stradling, "Perceptions of the Burning River: Deindustrialization and Cleveland's Cuyahoga River," *Environmental History* 13 (July 2008), 515–35, quote from 517. The authors emphasize that the river was less polluted by 1969 than it had been in the 1950s.

10. Kenneth Slocum, "The Dying Lake," *Wall Street Journal*, February 10, 1969, 1. "The Cities: The Price of Optimism," *Time* 94 (August 1, 1969), 51–52. "The Age of Effluence," *Time* 91 (May 10, 1968), 58–62. See also Gaylord Nelson, "The National Pollution Scandal," and Frank Graham, Jr., "The Mississippi Fish Kill," in Glen Love and Rhoda Love, eds., *Ecological Crisis: Readings for Survival* (New York: Harcourt, Brace, Jovanovich, 1970), 141–51, 153–71.

11. Allan M. Brandt, *The Cigarette Century: The Rise, Fall, and Deadly Persistence of the Product That Defined America* (New York: Basic, 2007), 1–158.

12. Robert N. Proctor, *Cancer Wars: How Politics Shapes What We Know and Don't Know About Cancer* (New York: Basic, 1995), 101–10. Naomi Oreskes and Erik Conway, *Merchants of Doubt: How a Handful of Scientists Obscured the Truth on Issues from Tobacco to Global Warming* (New York: Bloomsbury, 2010), 14–23.

13. Brandt, *Cigarette Century*, 237.

14. Rachel Carson, *Silent Spring* (1962. Boston: Houghton Mifflin, 1987).

15. Ibid., 1–3 (vision), 19–20 (diagrams), 23 (babies).

16. Ibid., 89–91 (Detroit), 267–70 (resistant mosquitoes).

17. Ibid., 8.

18. Ibid., 297.

19. Linda Lear, *Rachel Carson: Witness for Nature* (New York: Henry Holt, 1997), 457–80.

20. Ibid., 412–27, 461–63. I. L. Baldwin, "Chemicals and Pests," *Science* 137 (September 28, 1962), 1042–43. Lamont Cole, "Rachel Carson's Indictment of the Wide Use of Pesticides," *Scientific American* 207 (December 1962), 173–80.

21. Barry Commoner, *Science and Survival* (New York: Viking, 1967).

22. Ibid., 55.

23. Robert Gottlieb, *Forcing the Spring: The Transformation of the American Environmental Movement* (Washington, D.C.: Island Press, 1993), 256.

24. Paul Ehrlich, *The Population Bomb* (New York: Sierra Club/Ballantine, 1968). "That Population Explosion," *Time*, January 11, 1960, cover. Paul Paddock and William Paddock, *Famine 1975! America's Decision: Who Will Survive?* (Boston: Little, Brown, 1967).

25. Ehrlich, *Population Bomb*, cover.

26. Ibid., 15 (Delhi), 36 ("battle is lost"), 44 (famine).

27. Ibid., 88 (abortion), 139 (sterilization), 144 (Catholic teaching).

28. Ibid., 138 ("whatever steps"), 46–67 ("dying planet"). For biographical details

on Ehrlich, see Rachel Scheuering, *Shapers of the Great Debate on Conservation* (Westport, CT: Greenwood, 2004), 129–41.

29. Ben Wattenberg, "The Nonsense Explosion," in Daniel Callahan, ed., *The American Population Debate* (Garden City, NY: Doubleday, 1971), 96–109.

30. See, for example, in ibid.: Donald Bogue, "The End of the Population Explosion," 44–54, and Frank Pollara, "Trends in U.S. Population," 55–67.

31. Garret Hardin, "The Tragedy of the Commons," *Science* 162 (December 13, 1968), 1243–48.

32. Ibid., 1247.

33. Ibid., 1244.

34. Ibid., 1245.

35. Lynn White, "The Historical Roots of Our Ecological Crisis," *Science* 155 (March 10, 1967), 1203–7, quote from 1204.

36. Ibid., 1205.

37. Ibid., 1206–7.

38. "Fighting to Save the Earth from Man," *Time* 95 (February 2, 1970), 60–70; "The Paul Revere of Ecology," ibid., 62–64.

39. Barry Commoner, *The Closing Circle: Nature, Man, and Technology* (New York: Knopf, 1971). On Commoner's life, see Michael Egan, *Barry Commoner and the Science of Survival: The Remaking of American Environmentalism* (Cambridge, MA: MIT Press, 2007).

40. Commoner, *Closing Circle*, 296.

41. Ibid., 38, 41, 45, 46.

42. See, for example, these generally positive reviews: "*The Closing Circle* by Barry Commoner," *New Republic* 165 (November 6, 1971), 28–29; "Environment, the Price of Progress," *Time* 98 (November 1, 1971), 64. For more critical reviews, see: James Walls, "Ecodoom," *Family Planning Perspectives* 5 (Winter 1973), 64; Laura Fermi, untitled review of Commoner and others, *American Scientist* 60 (May/June 1972), 386.

43. Constance Holden, "Ehrlich Versus Commoner: An Environmental Fallout," *Science* 177 (July 21, 1972), 245–47. Kendrick Frazier, "Beyond the Ehrlich-Commoner Dispute," *Science News* 102 (August 12, 1972), 99. See also: Robert J. Trotter, "Super Scientists of the Media," *Science News* 107 (June 7, 1975), 370–72, 375; Egan, *Barry Commoner*, 131–35.

44. Todd Gitlin, *The Sixties: Years of Hope, Days of Rage* (New York: Bantam, 1987), 206–21.

45. On Abbey's life, see James Cahalan, *Edward Abbey: A Life* (Tucson: University of Arizona Press, 2003).

46. Edward Abbey, *Desert Solitaire: A Season in the Wilderness* (1968. New York: Ballantine, 1971), 6, 34.

47. Ibid., 117.

48. Ibid., 45–68 ("industrial tourism"), 55 ("make the bums range"). On Earth First!, see chapter 7 below.

49. Don Hopey and David Templeton, "In 1948, Smog Left Deadly Legacy in Donora," *Pittsburgh Post-Gazette*, December 12, 2010, A9.

50. Richard Mertens, "Clean Water Act at 40: Is It Failing to Meet New Pollution Challenges?," *Christian Science Monitor*, October 18, 2012. James Salzman, "Why Rivers No Longer Burn," *St. Paul Pioneer Press*, December 16, 2012.

CHAPTER 3

1. Adam Rome, "Give Earth a Chance," *Journal of American History* 90 (September 2003), 534, 537.
2. Richard Nixon, "Annual Message to the Congress on the State of the Union," January 22, 1970, American Presidency Project, www.presidency.ucsb.edu /ws/?pid=2921.
3. Adam Rome, "The Genius of Earth Day," *Environmental History* 15 (April 2010), 194–205. Bill Christofferson, *The Man from Clear Lake* (Madison: University of Wisconsin Press, 2004), 3, 4, 305, 311.
4. "Post-Moratorium," *New Republic* 162 (May 2, 1970), 9.
5. Raymond Coffey, "Teach-In on the Environment," *Nation* 210 (April 6, 1970), 390.
6. Rome, "Give Earth a Chance," 546.
7. "Who Pays for Anti-Pollution," *National Review* 22 (February 10, 1970), 124–25. "Conservation: High Priority," *National Review* 22 (January 27, 1970), 70, 72.
8. Biographical details from "William D. Ruckelshaus: First Term," at www.epa .gov. Quote is from Andrews, *Managing the Environment*, 230. Edmund Russell III, "Lost Among the Parts Per Billion: Ecological Protection at the United States Environmental Protection Agency, 1970–1993," *Environmental History* 2 (January 1997), 29–51.
9. A complete list of these laws can be found in Andrews, *Managing the Environment*, 425–28.
10. "The Sierra Club as Lobbyist: An Interview with Brock Evans," *Journal of Forest History* 30 (October 1986), 182–91, quote from 183. Susan Schrepfer, "The Nuclear Crucible: Diablo Canyon and the Transformation of the Sierra Club, 1965–1985," *California History* 71 (Summer 1992), 212–37, quote from 214.
11. Russell Train, *Politics, Pollution, and Pandas: An Environmental Memoir* (Washington, D.C.: Island Press, 2003).
12. John Quarles, *Cleaning Up America: An Insider's View of the Environmental Protection Agency* (Boston: Houghton Mifflin, 1976), 58.
13. Rome, *Bulldozer in the Countryside*, 10. Andrews, *Managing the Environment*, 218–21.
14. Andrews, *Managing the Environment*, 209. Terence Kehoe, "Merchants of Pollution? The Soap and Detergent Industry and the Fight to Restore Great Lakes Water Quality," *Environmental History Review* 16 (Autumn 1992), 21–46.
15. Ralph Nader, *Unsafe at Any Speed* (New York: Grossman, 1965). On Nader's life and career, see Justin Martin, *Nader: Crusader, Spoiler, Icon* (Cambridge, MA: Perseus, 2002).
16. Elinor Langer, "Auto-Safety: Nader vs. General Motors," *Science* 152 (April 1, 1966), 47–50. Marti Mueller, "Nader: From Auto Safety to a Permanent Crusade," *Science* 166 (November 21, 1969), 979–83.
17. L. J. C., "Environmental Defense Fund: Yannacone Out as Ringmaster," *Science* 166 (December 26, 1969), 1603. Christopher Stone, *Should Trees Have Standing: Toward Legal Rights for Natural Objects* (1972. Palo Alto, CA: Tioga Publishing, 1988).
18. Luther J. Carter, "DDT: The Critics Attempt to Ban Its Use in Wisconsin," *Science* 163 (February 7, 1969), 548–51, quote from 548. Thomas R. Dunlap, "DDT on Trial: The Wisconsin Hearing, 1968–1969," *Wisconsin Magazine of History* 62 (Autumn 1978), 2–24.

19. Andrew Spielman and Michael D'Antonio, *Mosquito: A Natural History of Our Most Persistent and Deadly Foe* (New York: Hyperion, 2001), 143–67, quote from 165.

20. Kenneth Boulding, "The Economics of the Coming Spaceship Earth," in H. H. Jarrett, ed., *Environmental Quality in a Growing Economy* (Baltimore: Resources for the Future/Johns Hopkins University Press, 1966), 3–14.

21. Donella Meadows et al., *The Limits to Growth: A Report for the Club of Rome's Project on the Predicament of Mankind* (New York: Universe Books, 1972), 23–24. Comment from Robert Gillette, "The Limits to Growth: Hard Sell for a Computer View of Doomsday," *Science* 175 (March 10, 1972), 1088–92.

22. Meadows et al., *Limits to Growth*, 29, 51.

23. Ibid., 194.

24. Herman Daly, "Toward a Steady State Economy," in John Harte and Robert Socolow, eds., *Patient Earth* (New York: Holt, Rinehart and Winston, 1971). Herman Daly, "In Defense of a Steady-State Economy," *Journal of Agricultural Economics* 54 (December 1972), 945–54, quote from 946. For commentary, see also Hazel Henderson, "The Limits of Traditional Economics: New Models for Managing a 'Steady State Economy,'" *Financial Analysts Journal* 3 (May/June 1973), 28–87.

25. E. F. Schumacher, *Small Is Beautiful: Economics as if People Mattered* (New York: Harper Colophon, 1973). On Schumacher's life, see Barbara Wood, *Alias Papa: A Life of Fritz Schumacher* (London: Jonathan Cape, 1984).

26. Schumacher, *Small Is Beautiful*, 54–55. Wood, *Alias Papa*, 361–62.

27. Ernest Callenbach, *Ecotopia* (1975. Berkeley, CA: Heyday Books, 2004).

28. Callenbach, *Ecotopia*, afterword, 170–71. Andrew G. Kirk, *Counterculture Green: The Whole Earth Catalog and American Environmentalism* (Lawrence: University Press of Kansas, 2007).

29. Petr Beckmann, *Eco-Hysterics and the Technophobes* (Boulder, CO: Golem Press, 1973), quote from 167. John Maddox, *The Doomsday Syndrome* (New York: McGraw Hill, 1972).

30. Kuznets cited in James A. Weber, *Grow or Die!* (New Rochelle, NY: Arlington House, 1977), 20.

31. Wilfred Beckerman, *Two Cheers for the Affluent Society: A Spirited Defense of Economic Growth* (New York: Saint Martin's, 1974), x.

32. Wilfred Beckerman, "Economists, Scientists, and Environmental Catastrophe," *Oxford Economic Papers* 24 (November 1972), 327–44.

33. Beckerman, *Two Cheers*, 28, 35.

34. Ben Wattenberg, *In Search of the Real America: A Challenge to the Chaos of Failure and Guilt* (1974. New York: Capricorn, 1978), 7.

35. Ibid., 153–57, 175.

36. Ibid., 176.

37. Ibid., 182 ("pollution abatement laws"), 237–38 ("Americans understand"), 235 (well-to-do elite).

38. Lester Thurow, *The Zero-Sum Society: Distribution and the Possibilities for Economic Change* (1980. New York: Penguin, 1981), 104–5.

39. Ibid., 120.

40. Kenneth Bridbord and David Hanson, "A Personal Perspective on the Initial Federal Health-Based Regulation to Remove Lead from Gasoline," *Environmental Health Perspectives* 117 (August 2009), 1195–1201. George Gonzalez, "Urban

Growth and the Politics of Air Pollution: The Establishment of California's Automobile Emission Standards," *Polity* 35 (Winter 2002), 213–36. Robert J. Naiman et al., "Freshwater Ecosystems and Their Management: A National Initiative," *Science* 270 (October 27, 1995), 584–85.

41. Gerald Barney, *Global 2000: The Report to the President* (1980. Arlington, VA: Seven Locks Press, 1988), 1.

42. T. Selden, A. Forrest, and J. Lockhart, "Analyzing the Reductions in US Air Pollution Emissions, 1970–1990," *Land Economics* 75 (February 1999), 1–21. The authors suggest that advanced economies are all likely to experience an "inverted-U"-shaped curve, according to which pollution increases in the early stages of industrialization but then diminishes as the economy matures, diversifies into services as well as manufacturing, and improves its efficiency. For the libertarian view, see Indur Goklany, *Clearing the Air: The Real Story of the War on Air Pollution* (Washington, D.C.: Cato Institute, 1999).

43. Andrews, *Managing the Environment*, 228.

44. Ibid., 223, 250–51, 270.

45. Richard Kosobud, ed., *Emissions Trading: Environmental Policy's New Approach* (New York: John Wiley, 2000). A. Danny Ellerman et al., eds., *Markets for Clean Air: The U.S. Acid Rain Program* (New York: Cambridge University Press, 2000).

46. Andrews, *Managing the Environment*, 234.

47. See, for example, "Clearing the Air for Clean Air," *New York Times,* March 4, 1981, A26; Philip Shabecoff, "Emission Curbs Termed Feasible," *New York Times,* June 24, 1981, A19.

48. Bruce Yandle, Maya Vijayaraghavan, and Madhusudan Bhattarai, "Income and the Race to the Top," in Terry Anderson, ed., *You Have to Admit It's Getting Better: From Economic Prosperity to Environmental Quality* (Stanford, CA: Hoover Institution, 2004), 83–108.

49. Chip Jacobs and William J. Kelly, *Smogtown: The Lung-Burning History of Pollution in Los Angeles* (Woodstock, NY: Overlook Press, 2008), 352.

50. See, for example, Bob Beauprez, "How the EPA Connives with Greens on Policy," *Washington Times,* June 10, 2013, B1.

51. "Manchin Was Essential to Chemical Proposal," *Charleston Daily Mail,* May 28, 2013, 4A. "Biotechnology Industry Organization: TSCA Reform Will Encourage Innovation and Pollution Prevention, BIO Says," Biotechnology Industry Organization press release, May 30, 2013. "An Opening to Strengthen Chemical Regulations," *New York Times,* May 30, 2013, A22.

CHAPTER 4

1. On the background to the crisis, see Martin V. Melosi, "Energy and Environment in the United States: The Era of Fossil Fuels," *Environmental Review* 11 (Autumn 1987), 167–88.

2. Daniel Yergin, *The Prize: The Epic Quest for Oil, Money, and Power* (New York: Simon and Schuster, 1991), 572–73. Joshua Ashenmiller, "The Alaska Pipeline as an Internal Improvement, 1963–1973," *Pacific Historical Review* 75 (August 2006), 461–90.

3. Dan O'Neill, "H-Bombs and Eskimos: The Story of Project Chariot," *Pacific Northwest Quarterly* 85 (January 1994), 25–34. Reisner, *Cadillac Desert*, 217–20. Michael C. Robinson, "The Relationship Between the Army Corps of Engi-

neers and the Environmental Community, 1920–1969," *Environmental Review* 13 (Spring 1989), 1–41.

4. Peter Coates, *The Trans-Alaska Pipeline Controversy* (Bethlehem, PA: Lehigh University Press, 1991).

5. Ibid., 200–201 (block quote), 191 ("Cumberland Gap").

6. James P. Roscow, *800 Miles to Valdez: The Building of the Alaska Pipeline* (Englewood Cliffs, NJ: Prentice Hall, 1977).

7. Ira Chernus, *Eisenhower's Atoms for Peace* (College Station: Texas A&M University Press, 2002).

8. Robert J. Duffy, *Nuclear Politics in America: A History and Theory of Government Regulation* (Lawrence: University Press of Kansas, 1997). Steven Del Sesto, *Science, Politics and Controversy: Civilian Nuclear Power in the United States, 1946–1974* (Boulder, CO: Westview Press, 1979).

9. James M. Jasper, *Nuclear Politics: Energy and the State in the United States, Sweden, and France* (Princeton, NJ: Princeton University Press, 1990), 109. On the California controversy, see also Thomas Wellock, *Critical Masses: Opposition to Nuclear Power in California, 1958–1978* (Madison: University of Wisconsin Press, 1998).

10. Andrews, *Managing the Environment, Managing Ourselves: A History of American Environmental Policy,* second edition (New Haven, CT: Yale University Press, 2006), 183–85.

11. Petr Beckmann, *The Health Hazards of NOT Going Nuclear* (Boulder, CO: Golem Press, 1976), 12.

12. Nader quoted in Sheldon Novick, *The Electric War: The Fight over Nuclear Power* (San Francisco: Sierra Club Books, 1976), 313. John Shattuck, "Nuclear Power and the Constitution," *Nation* 229 (November 3, 1979), 430–33.

13. Beckmann, *Health Hazards,* 99.

14. Glenn Seaborg, *The Atomic Energy Commission Under Nixon* (New York: St. Martin's, 1993), 115.

15. Bernard Cohen, "Exaggerating the Risks," in Michio Kaku and Jennifer Trainer, eds., *Nuclear Power: Both Sides: The Best Arguments For and Against the Most Controversial Technology* (New York: Norton, 1983), 78.

16. Martin, *Nader,* 173.

17. Ibid., 174.

18. Richard Rashke, *The Killing of Karen Silkwood: The Story Behind the Kerr-McGee Plutonium Case* (Boston: Houghton Mifflin, 1981). Martin, *Nader,* 175.

19. Rasmussen, however, estimated the probability of such an uncontrollable reactor meltdown as once in a billion reactor-years. For a critical history of the Rasmussen Report's genesis and method, however, see Daniel Ford, *Meltdown* (New York: Simon and Schuster, 1986), 136–66.

20. Seaborg, *Atomic Energy Commission,* 115. Harvey Wasserman, "High Tension in the Energy Debate: The Clamshell Reaction," *Nation* (June 18, 1977), 744–49. On the role of the anti–nuclear *weapons* movement in the anti–nuclear power debate, see Lawrence S. Wittner, *Confronting the Bomb: A Short History of the World Nuclear Disarmament Movement* (Stanford, CA: Stanford University Press, 2009), 120–24.

21. Richard Munson, "The Price Is Too High," *Nation* 228 (May 12, 1979), 521, 536–39.

22. Samuel Walker, *Three Mile Island: A Nuclear Crisis in Historical Perspective* (Berkeley: University of California Press, 2004).

23. *Kemeny Commission Findings: Oversight: Hearing Before the Subcommittee on Energy Research and Production* (Washington, D.C.: U.S. Government Printing Office, 1980). Joan Aron, *Licensed to Kill? The Nuclear Regulatory Commission and the Shoreham Power Plant* (Pittsburgh: University of Pittsburgh Press, 1998).

24. Stephen Croall, *The Anti-Nuclear Handbook* (New York: Pantheon, 1978), 4.

25. Alvin Weinberg, *The Second Nuclear Era: A New Start for Nuclear Power* (New York: Praeger, 1985). Glenn Seaborg, *Modern Alchemy* (River Edge, NJ: World Scientific, 1994). Edward Teller, ed., *Fusion* (New York: Academic Press, 1981). David Lilienthal, *Atomic Energy: A New Start* (New York: Harper and Row, 1980).

26. Mark Hertsgaard, *Nuclear Inc.: The Men and Money Behind Nuclear Energy* (New York: Pantheon, 1983), 179.

27. Cohen, "Exaggerating the Risks," 72. Hertsgaard, *Nuclear Inc.*, 191. Hertsgaard adds that "the credibility of Teller's statement was shaken . . . when NRC Commissioner Peter Bradford wrote the *Journal* a letter refuting many of Teller's claims and pointing out a piercing irony: Dresser Industries, which paid for the Teller ad, was the company that manufactured the faulty valve whose failure led to the accident at Three Mile Island."

28. John Gofman, "George Orwell Understated the Case," in Kaku and Trainer, *Nuclear Power*, 66. Cohen, "Exaggerating the Risks," 71–72.

29. Scott Fenn, *The Nuclear Power Debate: Issues and Choices* (New York: Praeger, 1981), 16–19.

30. Gordon Sims, *The Anti-Nuclear Game* (Ottawa: University of Ottawa Press, 1990), 20 (on relative risk). Richard Rhodes, *Nuclear Renewal: Common Sense About Energy* (New York: Viking, 1993). Bernard Cohen, *Before It's Too Late: A Scientist's Case for Nuclear Energy* (New York: Plenum, 1983).

31. Cohen, "Exaggerating the Risks," 75.

32. Seaborg, *Atomic Energy Commission*, 185–86. Rhodes, *Nuclear Renewal*, 103–12.

33. Rhodes, *Nuclear Renewal*, 54–79. William Lanouette, "Atomic Energy, 1945–1985," *Wilson Quarterly* 9 (Winter 1985), 90–131 (see box "Toute Nucléaire!," 102).

34. Bernard Cohen, *The Nuclear Energy Option: An Alternative for the 90s* (New York: Plenum, 1990), 257–71.

35. See, for example, Alvin Weinberg, *Continuing the Nuclear Dialogue* (La Grange Park, IL: American Nuclear Society, 1985), especially Part III, "Faust Redeemed, Post Three Mile Island," 101–51.

36. On the history of the Yucca Mountain fiasco, see Robert W. Collin, *The Environmental Protection Agency: Cleaning Up America's Act* (Westport, CT: Greenwood, 2006), 97–102.

37. Biographical details based on James Udall, "Amory Lovins: Walking the Soft Path," *Sierra* 75 (January 1990), 128–33.

38. Amory Lovins, *World Energy Strategies: Facts, Issues, and Options* (1973. San Francisco: Friends of the Earth International, 1975), quote from 125.

39. Amory Lovins and John H. Price, *Soft Energy Paths: Toward a Durable Peace* (San Francisco: Friends of the Earth International, 1977), 38, 39.

40. Amory Lovins and L. Hunter Lovins, *Energy/War: Breaking the Nuclear Link* (San Francisco: Friends of the Earth, 1980).

41. Udall, "Amory Lovins." David Riggle, "Amory Lovins: From Megawatts to Hypercars," *In Business* 17 (March/April 1995), 18–22. On continuing to improve efficiency, see Amory Lovins, "Energy, People, and Industrialization," *Population and Development Review* 16 supplement (1990), 95–124.

42. John M. Broder, "Canadian Visits U.S. to Promote Oil Pipeline," *New York Times,* April 10, 2013, A16. Carol Freedenthal, "Protesters Give Many Reasons to Stop Keystone XL Coming South," *Pipeline and Gas Journal* 240 (March 2013), 20. Marty Durbin, "Keystone XL Will Pipe Energy and Economic Security to the U.S.," *Pipeline and Gas Journal* 238 (August 2011), 86.

43. Dan Frosch, "Keystone Pipeline Foes Vent in Nebraska," *New York Times,* April 19, 2013, A12.

44. Judith Mernit, "Taking It to the Streets," *High Country News* 45 (February 18, 2013), 3, 5. John M. Broder, "Keystone XL Protesters Seized at White House," *New York Times Blogs,* February 13, 2013, www.green.blogs.nytimes.com/2013/02/13

45. Jason Mark, "The Fission Division," *Earth Island. Journal* 22 (Autumn 2007), 37–43. Matilda Lee, "The Big Divide: Is Ideology Holding Back Greens from Embracing Nuclear Power?," *Ecologist* 40 (August 2011), 17–19. George Monbiot, "Evidence Meltdown," April 4, 2011, at www.monbiot.com. Stewart Brand, "Nuclear Power Is Safe, Sound . . . and Green," *Earth Island Journal* 25 (Winter 2011), 48–50.

46. Mark, "Fission Division," 41.

47. "Japan's Nuclear Future: Don't Look Now," *Economist,* April 20, 2013, at www.economist.com. Svenne Juris, "The Case for a Return to Nuclear Power," *Environmentalist* 32 (September 2012), 346–52.

48. "Fracked Off," *Economist,* June 1, 2013, online at www.economist.com.

CHAPTER 5

1. William U. Chandler, *The Myth of the TVA: Conservation and Development in the Tennessee Valley, 1933–1983* (Cambridge, MA: Ballinger, 1984), 161–66.

2. David Etnier, *The Fishes of Tennessee* (Knoxville: University of Tennessee Press, 1993). William Wheeler and Michael McDonald, *TVA and the Tellico Dam, 1936–1979: A Bureaucratic Crisis in Post-Industrial America* (Knoxville: University of Tennessee Press, 1986).

3. "Fish in a Porkbarrel," *New Republic* 178 (April 8, 1978), 15–16. Wheeler and McDonald, *TVA and Tellico,* 211. Zygmunt J. B. Plater, "Tiny Fish, Big Battle," *Tennessee Bar Journal* 44 (April 2008). Kenneth Murchison, *The Snail Darter Case: The TVA Versus the Endangered Species Act* (Lawrence: University Press of Kansas, 2007).

4. Baker quoted in Phillip F. Kramer, *Deep Environmental Politics: The Role of Radical Environmentalism in Crafting American Environmental Policy* (Westwood, CT: Greenwood, 1998), 160–61.

5. Wheeler and McDonald, *TVA and Tellico,* 212, 216–17. Joanne Omang, "Wee Snail Darter Alive and Well Far from Home," *Washington Post,* November 8, 1980, A1.

6. Paul Ehrlich and Anne Ehrlich, *Extinction: The Causes and Consequences of the Disappearance of Species* (New York: Ballantine, 1981).

7. Martin F. J. Taylor et al., "The Effectiveness of the Endangered Species Act: A Quantitative Analysis," *BioScience* 55 (April 2005), 360–67, quote from 361. For a list of recovered species and the years in which they were added to and then removed from endangered status, see the Web site of the U.S. Fish and Wildlife Service, http://ecos.fws.gov.

8. Norman Myers, *The Sinking Ark: A New Look at the Problem of Disappearing Species* (New York: Pergamon Press, 1979).

9. Norman Myers and Dorothy Myers, "From Duck Pond to the Global Commons: Increasing Awareness of the Supranational Nature of Emerging Environmental Issues," *Ambio* 11 (1982), 195–201, quote from 198.

10. Peter Singer, *Animal Liberation: A New Ethics for Our Treatment of Animals* (New York: New York Review Press, 1975), quote from 270. See also Holmes Rolston III, "Duties to Endangered Species," *BioScience* 35 (December 1985), 718–26.

11. Singer, *Animal Liberation*, 185. See, for example, these reviews: David Hull, "The Rights of Animals," *Science* 192 (May 14, 1976), 679–80; Bill Puka, untitled review, *Philosophical Review* 86 (October 1977), 557–60.

12. This passage is based on Lois Gibbs, *Love Canal: My Story* (Albany: State University of New York Press, 1982); Allan Mazur, *A Hazardous Enquiry: The Rashomon Effect at Love Canal* (Cambridge, MA: Harvard University Press, 1998).

13. Gina B. Kolata, "Love Canal: False Alarm Caused by Botched Study," *Science* 208 (June 13, 1980), 1239–42.

14. Adeline Levine, *Love Canal: Science, Politics, and People* (Lexington, MA: Lexington Books, 1982). David Dickson, "Love Canal Continues to Fester as Scientists Bicker over the Evidence," *Ambio* 9 (1980), 257–59.

15. Beverly Paigen, "Controversy at Love Canal," *Hastings Center Report* 12 (June 1983), 29–37. Phil Brown and Richard Clapp, "Looking Back on Love Canal," *Public Health Reports* 117 (March/April 2002), 95–98.

16. Robert Emmet Hernan, *This Borrowed Earth: Lessons from the Fifteen Worst Environmental Disasters Around the World* (New York: Palgrave, 2010), 91–100.

17. John Hird, "Environmental Policy and Equity: The Case of Superfund," *Journal of Policy Analysis and Management* 12 (Spring 1993), 323–43. Harold C. Barnett, "Crimes Against the Environment: Superfund Enforcement at Last," *Annals of the American Academy of Political and Social Science* 525 (January 1993), 119–33. Mark Haggerty and Stephanie Welcomer, "Superfund: The Ascendance of Enabling Myths," *Journal of Economic Issues* 37 (June 2003), 451–59.

18. Barnaby Feder, "In the Clutches of the Superfund Mess," *New York Times,* June 16, 1991, F1.

19. Story of John Tsigounis recounted in Bruce G. Siminoff, *Victim: Caught in the Environmental Web* (Lakewood, CO: Glenbridge, 1993), 13–14. I regret that I have been unable to discover how the case was eventually resolved.

20. Lois Gibbs, *Dying from Dioxin: A Citizen's Guide to Reclaiming Our Health and Rebuilding Democracy* (Boston: South End Press, 1995).

21. Andrews, *Managing the Environment*, 248–49, 265.

22. Charles Lee, "Toxic Waste and Race in the United States," in Bunyan Bryant and Paul Mohai, *Race and the Incidence of Environmental Hazards: A Time for Discourse* (Boulder, CO: Westview Press, 1992), 10–27.

23. Commission for Racial Justice, *Toxic Wastes and Race in the United States* (New York: United Church of Christ, 1987). Lena Williams, "Race Bias Found in Location of Toxic Dumps," *New York Times,* April 16, 1987, A20:1.

24. Robert Bullard, *Dumping in Dixie: Race, Class, and Environmental Quality,* third edition (Boulder, CO: Westview Press, 2000).

25. Bryant and Mohai, *Race and the Incidence*, introduction, 2.

26. Gary Boulard, "Combating Environmental Racism," *Christian Science Monitor,* March 17, 1993, 8. On "Cancer Alley," see also Barbara Koeppel, "Cancer Alley, Louisiana," *Nation* 269 (November 8, 1999), 16–24.

27. Marianne Lavelle and Marcia Coyle, "Unequal Protection: The Racial Divide

in Environmental Law," *National Law Journal* 15 (September 21, 1992). Gregg Easterbrook, *A Moment on the Earth: The Coming Age of Environmental Optimism* (New York: Viking, 1995), 467. For details of the Reilly and Clinton rulings, see Tom FitzGerald and Liz Edmondson, "Environmental Justice 101," Kentucky Resources Council, www.kyrc.org/webnewspro/125303806957977.shtml.

28. "Fighting 'Environmental Racism,'" *New York Post*, May 18, 1998, 36. See also Matthew Rees, "Black and Green," *New Republic* (March 2, 1992), 15–16. Rees argued that the siting of dumps correlated far more closely with social class than with race, chiefly because "poorer areas are likely to have less expensive land."

29. Johnine Brown, "Chasing the Tail of Environmental Racism: Is There a Pit Bull Attached?," *Illinois Legal Times*, June 1994, 5. Jim Ritter, "Waste Study Finds No Racism in Siting," *Chicago Sun-Times*, October 25, 1994, 3.

30. Gerald Markowitz and David Rosner, *Deceit and Denial: The Deadly Politics of Industrial Pollution* (Berkeley: University of California Press/Millbank Memorial Fund, 2002), 267–86. Paul Hoversten, "EPA Puts Plant on Hold in Racism Case," *USA Today*, September 11, 1997, 3A. Robyn Blumner, "EPA Aims at Racism, Hits Minorities," *Journal of Commerce*, October 8, 1998, 7A. "Dubious Claim," *Paducah Sun*, December 16, 2005.

31. Dorceta Taylor, "Can the Environmental Movement Attract and Maintain the Support of Minorities?," in Bryant and Mohai, *Race and the Incidence*, 28–54, quote from 39.

32. Andrews, *Managing the Environment*, 325–27.

33. R. E. Benedict, *Ozone Diplomacy* (Cambridge, MA: Harvard University Press, 1991). Oreskes and Conway, *Merchants of Doubt*, 107–35.

34. Gene E. Likens, Richard F. Wright, James N. Galloway, and Thomas J. Butler, "Acid Rain," *Scientific American* 241 (October 1979), 43–51. Oreskes and Conway, *Merchants of Doubt*, 66–106. Philip Shabecoff, "Acid Rain Report Confirms Concern," *New York Times*, September 6, 1990, A24:1.

35. Robert Lovely, "Wisconsin's Acid Rain Battle: Science, Communication, and Public Policy, 1979–1989," *Environmental History Review* 14 (Autumn 1990), 20–48, quote from 33.

36. Oreskes and Conway, *Merchants of Doubt*, 267–74.

37. J. Raloff, "Is Ozone Giving Acid Rain a Bad Name?," *Science News* 128 (November 2, 1985), 279. Philip Shabecoff, "Acid Rain Report Unleashes a Torrent of Criticism," *New York Times*, March 20, 1990, C4:1. Easterbrook, *Moment on the Earth*, 167. On the decline of the red spruce in the Vermont mountains, see Charles E. Little, *The Dying of the Trees* (New York: Penguin, 1995), 17–35.

38. Maureen Dowd, "Bush, in Ottawa, Now Vows to Pursue Acid Rain Pact," *New York Times*, February 11, 1989, A1:3. Jared Raloff, "Acid Assessment: The State of the Science," *Science News* 137 (February 24, 1990), 119–24.

39. Trip Gabriel, "Greening the White House," *New York Times*, August 13, 1989, 6, 25:1.

40. Easterbrook, *Moment on the Earth*, 176.

41. Ted Steinberg, *Down to Earth: Nature's Role in American History*, second edition (New York: Oxford University Press, 2009), 255. Margaret Taylor, Edward Rubin, and David Hounshell, "Regulation as the Mother of Invention: The Case of SO_2 Control," *Law and Policy* 27 (April 2005), 348–78.

42. Edward Krug and Charles Frink, "Acid Rain on Acid Soil: A New Perspec-

tive," *Science* 221 (1983), 520–25. Jerome Dobson, Richard Ruh, and Robert Peplies, "Forest Blowdown and Lake Acidification," *Annals of the Association of American Geographers* 80 (September 1990), 343–61. Easterbrook, *Moment on the Earth*, 168.

43. Howard Kurtz, "Is Acid Rain a Tempest in a News Media Teapot?," *Washington Post*, January 14, 1991, A3. Edward Krug, "Environmental Zealots Squelch Critics," *St. Louis Post-Dispatch*, June 20, 1991, C3. Warren Brookes, "Scientific McCarthyism at the EPA?," *Washington Times*, May 1, 1991, G3.

44. Aaron Wildavsky and Robert Owen Rye, "The Effects of Acid Rain on the United States (with an Excursion to Europe)," in Aaron Wildavsky, *But Is It True? A Citizen's Guide to Environmental Health and Safety Issues* (Cambridge, MA: Harvard University Press, 1995), 274–303, quote from 277.

45. R. Monastersky, "Acid Precipitation Drops in United States," *Science News* 144 (July 10, 1993), 22.

46. Samuel Epstein, *The Politics of Cancer* (San Francisco: Sierra Club Books, 1978), 19, 1. Proctor, *Cancer Wars*, 57–64.

47. See, for example, Paul Stolley, review of Epstein, *Politics of Cancer*, in *Journal of Public Health Policy* 1 (March 1980), 97–99; Douglas Hands, review of ibid., *Journal of Economic Literature* 18 (June 1980), 654–56.

48. Proctor, *Cancer Wars*, 61–62.

49. Edith Efron, *The Apocalyptics: Cancer and the Big Lie* (New York: Simon and Schuster, 1984).

50. Ibid., 345–49, 364–68.

51. Proctor, *Cancer Wars*, 88.

52. Kerry Rodgers, "Multiple Meanings of Alar After the Scare: Implications for Closure," *Science, Technology and Human Values* 21 (Spring 1996), 177–97.

53. Rodgers, "Multiple Meanings," 180.

54. Daniel Koshland, "Scare of the Week," *Science* 244 (April 7, 1989), 9.

55. Philip Shabecoff, "Apple Scare of '89 Didn't Kill Market," *New York Times*, November 13, 1990, A28:1.

56. Paul Shrivastava, *Bhopal: Anatomy of a Crisis* (Cambridge, MA: Ballinger, 1987). Clayton Trotter et al., "Bhopal, India, and Union Carbide: The Second Tragedy," *Journal of Business Ethics* 8 (June 1989), 439–54. Pushpa Bhargava, "The Bhopal Tragedy: A Middle Word," *Economic and Political Weekly* 20 (June 1, 1985), 962–65. David Davidar, "Beyond Bhopal: The Toxic Waste Hazard in India," *Ambio* 14 (Spring 1985), 112–16.

57. Yuri Shcherbak, "Ten Years of the Chernobyl Era," *Scientific American* 274 (April 1996), 44–49.

58. John F. Ahearne, "Nuclear Power After Chernobyl," *Science* 236 (May 8, 1987), 673–79.

59. John Keeble, *Out of the Channel: The Exxon Valdez Oil Spill in Prince William Sound* (New York: HarperCollins, 1991). Art Davidson, *In the Wake of the Exxon Valdez: The Impact of the Alaskan Oil Spill* (San Francisco: Sierra Club Books, 1990). Michael Bowen and F. Clark Power, "The Moral Manager: Communicative Ethics and the 'Exxon Valdez' Disaster," *Business Ethics Quarterly* 3 (April 1993), 97–115.

60. Bowen and Power, "Moral Manager," 101.

61. Keeble, *Out of the Channel*, 87–91.

62. Charles H. Peterson et al., "Long-Term Ecosystem Response to the Exxon Val-

dez Oil Spill," *Science* 302 (December 19, 2003), 2082–86. Jeff Wheelwright, *Degrees of Disaster: Prince William Sound: How Nature Reels and Rebounds* (New Haven, CT: Yale University Press, 1996). Marguerite Holloway, "Soiled Shores," *Scientific American* 265 (October 1991), 91–102.

63. Viktoria Harzl and Matthias Pickl, "The Future of Offshore Oil Drilling: An Evaluation of the Economic, Environmental, and Political Consequences of the Deepwater Horizon Incident," *Energy and Environment* 23 (July 1, 2012), 757–70.

64. "Spills and Bills," *Economist,* February 9, 2013, online.

65. Arne Jernelov, "The Threats from Oil Spills: Now, Then, and in the Future," *Ambio* 39 (July/September 2010), 353–66.

66. "Report Regarding the Causes of the April 20, 2010 Macondo Well Blowout," Bureau of Ocean Energy Management, Regulation and Enforcement, September 14, 2011, online at http://docs.lib.noaa.gov/noaa_documents/DWH_IR/reports/dwhfinal.pdf. Charles H. Peterson et al., "A Tale of Two Spills: Novel Science and Policy Implications of an Emerging New Oil Spill Model," *BioScience* 62 (May 1, 2012), 461–70.

67. See, for example: Lisa Margonelli, "A Spill of Our Own," *New York Times,* May 2, 2010, A12; Richard Steinberg, "How Did BP's Risk Management Lead to Failure?," *Compliance Week,* July 20, 2010, online.

CHAPTER 6

1. On the rise of the New Right, see Patrick Allitt, *The Conservatives: Ideas and Personalities Throughout American History* (New Haven, CT: Yale University Press, 2009), 224–54.

2. The first comprehensively antienvironmentalist book I have been able to find is Melvin Grayson and Thomas Shepard, Jr., *The Disaster Lobby: Prophets of Ecological Doom and Other Absurdities* (Chicago: Follett, 1973).

3. Barry Goldwater, *With No Apologies: The Personal and Political Memoirs of U.S. Senator Barry Goldwater* (New York: William Morrow, 1979), 296–97.

4. On the history of this relationship and the relative weakness of the BLM prior to 1976, see Maitland Sharpe, "The Sagebrush Rebellion: A Conservationist's Perspective," *Rangelands* 2 (December 1980), 232–34.

5. Trudie Olson, "The Sagebrush Rebellion," *Rangelands* 2 (October 1980), 195–99, quote from 195.

6. R. McGregor Cawley, *Federal Land, Western Anger: The Sagebrush Rebellion and Environmental Politics* (Lawrence: University Press of Kansas, 1993). Jonathan Lash, Katherine Gillman, and David Sheridan, *A Season of Spoils: The Reagan Administration's Attack on the Environment* (New York: Pantheon, 1984), 237–39, 260–67.

7. On the Reagan era and the environment, see Samuel P. Hays, *Beauty, Health, and Permanence: Environmental Politics in the United States, 1955–1985* (New York: Cambridge University Press, 1987), 491–526. Quote from Barbara Mikkelson, "Ronald Reagan: 'If You've Seen One Tree . . . ,'" www.snopes.com/quotes/reagan/redwoods.asp.

8. Biographical information on Watt is based on Scheuering, *Shapers of the Great*

Debate, 171–84. Lash, Gillman, and Sheridan, *Season of Spoils*, 7–10, 82–100, 231–32.

9. Peter Staler and Gary Lee, "The Trouble with Watt," *Time* 117 (May 11, 1981), 52. "The Legacy of James Watt," *Time* 122 (October 24, 1983), 31. Walter Isaacson, "A Watt that Produces Steam," *Time* 118 (August 3, 1981), 17–18.

10. Scheuering, *Shapers of the Great Debate*, 179. Isaacson, "Watt that Produces Steam."

11. George Will, *The Morning After: American Successes and Excesses* (New York: Basic, 1986), 147–48.

12. Keller quoted in "Legacy of James Watt."

13. William Henry III, "This Ice Queen Does Not Melt," *Time* 119 (January 18, 1982).

14. Maureen Dowd, "Superfund, Supermess," *Time* 121 (February 21, 1983).

15. Wilbur Edel, *The Reagan Presidency* (New York: Hippocrene, 1992), 30–33.

16. Steven Weisman, "President Names Ruckelshaus Head of Troubled EPA," *New York Times*, March 22, 1983, A1:6. Some environmentalists still had doubts because Ruckelshaus had been working at Weyerhaeuser, a large lumber company in the Pacific Northwest. See Robert Lindsey, "Ruckelshaus's Ties Split Environmental Leaders," *New York Times*, March 26, 1983, A1:8. George Church, "Reagan Makes His Moves," *Time* 122 (October 24, 1983), 20–24.

17. Bernard Friedan, *The Environmental Protection Hustle* (Cambridge, MA: MIT Press, 1979). William Tucker, *Progress and Privilege* (New York: Anchor, 1982). Herbert Meyer, *The War Against Progress* (Friday Harbor, WA: Storm King Press, 1979). Quote is from M. Stanton Evans, "Dark Horses," *National Review* (August 22, 1980), 1037.

18. Allan May, *A Voice in the Wilderness* (Chicago: Nelson-Hall, 1978), 22.

19. Jeffrey Nelligan, "Out of Control," *National Review* 34 (April 16, 1982), 422–23. Lynn Dwyer et al., "Property Rights Case Law and the Challenge to the Endangered Species Act," *Conservation Biology* 9 (August 1995), 725–41.

20. Richard Epstein, *Takings: Private Property and the Power of Eminent Domain* (Cambridge, MA: Harvard University Press, 1985). David Helvarg, *The War Against the Greens* (San Francisco: Sierra Club Books, 1994), 307–15. David Dunlap, "Resolving Property 'Takings,'" *New York Times*, August 23, 1992, 10:1.

21. Julian Simon, *The Ultimate Resource* (Princeton, NJ: Princeton University Press, 1981), 9–10.

22. Ibid., 4–5.

23. Ibid., 5.

24. Ibid., 18–19, 349–51.

25. Ibid., 15–29.

26. Ibid., 32–50.

27. Ibid., 27. John Tierney, "Betting on the Planet," *New York Times*, December 2, 1990, 6:52.

28. Tierney, "Betting on the Planet." Ehrlich's summary of the bet and its outcome can be found in Paul Ehrlich and Anne Ehrlich, *Betrayal of Science and Reason: How Anti-Environmental Rhetoric Threatens Our Future* (Washington, D.C.: Island Press, 1996), 100–101. The Ehrlichs claim that the prices of only three of the metals went down in the 1980s, which contradicts the *New York Times* account (itself based on graphs from *Metal Week*). They write: "Paul and his colleagues

ended up paying a small sum on the bet"—a rather disingenuous way of describing 57 percent of the initial amount.

29. Virginia Abernethy, "How Julian Simon Could Win the Bet and Still Be Wrong," *Population and Environment* 13 (Fall 1991), 3–7. Ed Regis, "The Doomslayer," *Wired* 5 (February 1997), www.wired.com/wired/archive/5.02/ffsimon_pr.html.

30. Julian Simon, *A Life Against the Grain: The Autobiography of an Unconventional Economist* (New Brunswick, NJ: Transaction, 2002), 297–313. Dennis Ahlburg, "Julian Simon and the Population Growth Debate," *Population and Development Review* 24 (June 1998), 317–27, quote from 320.

31. Herman Kahn, *On Thermonuclear War* (Princeton, NJ: Princeton University Press, 1960).

32. Julian Simon and Herman Kahn, eds., *The Resourceful Earth: A Response to Global 2000* (New York: Basil Blackwell, 1984), 2. D. Gale Johnson, "World Food and Agriculture," ibid., 67–112.

33. Amartya Sen, "Population: Delusion and Reality," *New York Review of Books* 41 (September 22, 1994), online at www.nybooks.com/articles/archives/1994/sep/22/population-delusion-and-reality/.

34. Ben Wattenberg, *The Good News Is the Bad News Is Wrong* (New York: Simon and Schuster, 1984), 20.

35. Ibid., 370–78.

36. Ibid., 65–6. Ben Wattenberg, *The Birth Dearth* (New York: Pharos Books, 1987).

37. Mary Douglas and Aaron Wildavsky, *Risk and Culture* (Berkeley: University of California Press, 1982), 9.

38. Ibid., 10.

39. Wildavsky, *But Is It True?*.

40. Ibid., 78–9, 120.

41. Ibid., 446–47.

42. Stephen Breyer, *Breaking the Vicious Circle: Toward Effective Risk Regulation* (Cambridge, MA: Harvard University Press, 1993), quote from 16.

43. Ronald Bailey, *Eco-Scam: The False Prophets of Ecological Apocalypse* (New York: St. Martin's, 1993). Charles Murray, *Losing Ground: American Social Policy, 1950–1980* (New York: Basic, 1984).

44. Easterbrook, *Moment on the Earth*.

45. Wallace Kaufman, *No Turning Back: Dismantling the Fantasies of Environmental Thinking* (New York: Basic, 1994), 7.

46. Ibid., 39–46.

47. Biographical information on Ray is based on Scheuering, *Shapers of the Great Debate*, 89–100, and on Kurt Kim Schaefer, "Right in the Eye: The Political Style of Dixy Lee Ray," *Pacific Northwest Quarterly* 93 (Spring 2002), 81–93. See also Gary Taubes, "The Ozone Backlash," *Science* 260 (June 11, 1993), 1580–83.

48. Dixy Lee Ray with Lou Guzzo, *Trashing the Planet: How Science Can Help Us Deal with Acid Rain, Depletion of the Ozone, and Nuclear Waste (Among Other Things)* (Washington, D.C.: Regnery Gateway, 1990). Dixy Lee Ray and Lou Guzzo, *Environmental Overkill: Whatever Happened to Common Sense?* (New York: Harper-Collins, 1993), ix, 6–7, 77–79.

49. Louis S. Richman, "Bringing Reason to Regulation," *Fortune* 126 (October 19, 1992). For greater elaboration of business reactions to environmental legislation, see also: Sheldon Kamieniecki, *Corporate America and Environmental*

Policy: How Often Does Business Get Its Way? (Stanford, CA: Stanford University Press, 2006). Hays, *Beauty, Health, and Permanence*, 287–328.

50. Terry Anderson and Donald R. Leal, *Free Market Environmentalism* (San Francisco: Pacific Research Institute for Public Policy/Westview Press, 1991).

51. Ibid., 21 (quote), 158–59 (permit trading).

52. Paul Raubner, "Wise Guise," *Sierra* 76 (May 1991), 70.

53. David Helvarg, "The Institute for Innovative Plunder," *Sierra* 80 (March 1995), 34. Sierra Club fund-raising letter quoted in Benjamin Kline, *First Along the River: A Brief History of the U.S. Environmental Movement*, fourth edition (Lanham, MD: Rowman and Littlefield, 2011), 133.

54. William Poole, "Neither Wise Nor Well," *Sierra* 77 (November 1992), 58. Keith Schneider, "Environment Laws Are Eased by Bush as Election Nears," *New York Times*, May 20, 1992, 1:4.

55. Timothy Egan, "Look Who's Hugging Trees Now," *New York Times*, July 7, 1996, 6:28. Biographical information on Chenoweth-Hage is based on Scheuering, *Shapers of the Great Debate*, 157–69.

56. Richard White, "The Current Weirdness in the West," *Western Historical Quarterly* 28 (Spring 1997), 4–16, quote from 9.

57. Allitt, *The Conservatives*, 236–45, 267–70.

58. David Orr and David Ehrenfeld, "None So Blind: The Problem of Ecological Denial," *Conservation Education* 9 (October 1995), 985–87.

59. Paul Ehrlich and Anne Ehrlich, *The Population Explosion* (New York: Simon and Schuster, 1990).

60. Ehrlich and Ehrlich, *Betrayal of Science and Reason*, 203–12. Daniel Sarewitz, "Science and Sensibility," *Science* 274 (October 11, 1996), 198.

61. See, for example, "Apocalypse Perhaps a Little Later," *Economist*, March 30, 2013, online.

62. "Thousands Gather for Stop the Frack Attack Rally," Sierra Club *Compass*, July 30, 2012, http://sierraclub.typepad.com/compass/2012/07/thousands-gather-for-stop-the-frack-attack-rally.html.

63. Robert H. Nelson, "The Fractured Left," *Weekly Standard* 18 (April 29, 2013), 26–29. Kevin Williamson, "The Truth About Fracking," *National Review*, February 20, 2012, 31. See also William Tucker, "America's Oil Revival," *American Spectator*, February 8, 2013, http://spectator.org/archives/2013/02/08/americas-oil-revival.

64. See, for example, Fareed Zakaria, "An Alternative to Oil," *Washington Post*, March 30, 2012, A17.

CHAPTER 7

1. Donald Worster, *Nature's Economy: A History of Ecological Ideas*, second edition (New York: Cambridge University Press, 1994), 209–20.

2. Ibid., 294–310. On Lindeman, see also Paul Colinvaux, *Why Big Fierce Animals Are Rare: An Ecologist's Perspective* (Princeton, NJ: Princeton University Press, 1978), 24–27.

3. Worster, *Nature's Economy*, 362–68.

4. James Lovelock, *Gaia: A New Look at Life on Earth* (New York: Oxford University Press, 1979), 3. Worster, *Nature's Economy*, 379–87.

5. Worster, *Nature's Economy*, 391, 408–10. Joseph H. Connell and Ralph O. Slay-

ter, "Mechanisms of Succession in Natural Communities and Their Role in Community Stability and Organization," *American Naturalist* 111 (November/December 1977), 1119–44.

6. Colinvaux, *Why Big Fierce Animals*, 208.

7. S. T. A. Pickett and P. S. White, *The Ecology of Natural Disturbance and Patch Dynamics* (Orlando, FL: Academic Press, 1985), xiii, 374.

8. Daniel Simberloff, "A Succession of Paradigms in Ecology: Essentialism to Materialism and Probabilism," *Synthese* 43 (1980), 3–39.

9. Ibid., 25.

10. Daniel Botkin, *Discordant Harmonies: A New Ecology for the Twenty-First Century* (New York: Oxford University Press, 1990), 130.

11. Ibid., 77–80.

12. Ibid., 189.

13. William C. Summers, "Hans Zinsser: A Tale of Two Cultures," *Yale Journal of Biology and Medicine* 72 (1999), 341–47.

14. Hans Zinsser, *Rats, Lice and History: The Biography of a Bacillus* (Boston: Little, Brown, 1934), vii, 168, 300.

15. Paul Sears, *Deserts on the March* (1935. Washington, D.C.: Island Press, 1988), 4.

16. "Interview: Roderick Nash," *Environmental History* 12 (April 2007).

17. Roderick Nash, *Wilderness and the American Mind* (1967. New Haven, CT: Yale University Press, 1982), 13–17.

18. Ibid., 84–95 (Thoreau), 122–40 (Muir).

19. Ibid., 1, 379–88.

20. Alfred Crosby, biographical summary at his Web site, www.awcrosby.com/.

21. Alfred Crosby, *The Columbian Exchange: Biological and Cultural Consequences of 1492* (Westport, CT: Greenwood, 1972), 64–121.

22. Ibid., 31, 219.

23. William H. McNeill, *Plagues and Peoples* (Garden City, NY: Doubleday, 1976), 4.

24. Ibid., 6.

25. Donald Worster, *Dust Bowl: The Southern Plains in the 1930s* (New York: Oxford University Press, 1979).

26. Ibid., 80–94.

27. Ibid., 4–8.

28. Ibid., 239. Donald Worster, *Rivers of Empire: Water, Aridity, and the Growth of the American West* (New York: Pantheon, 1985).

29. William Cronon, *Changes in the Land: Indians, Colonists, and the Ecology of New England* (New York: Hill and Wang, 1983), 12–13.

30. Ibid., 9, 11.

31. Martin Melosi, "Urban Pollution: Historical Perspective Needed," *Environmental Review* 3 (Spring 1979), 37–45. Martin Melosi, *Garbage in the Cities: Refuse, Reform, and the Environment, 1880–1980* (Chicago: Dorsey Press, 1981); on horses, see 24–25. See also, for example: Craig Colten, "Industrial Wastes in Southeast Chicago: Production and Disposal," *Environmental Review* 10 (Summer 1986), 93–105; Daniel Zarin, "Searching for Pennies in Piles of Trash: Municipal Refuse Utilization in the United States," *Environmental Review* 11 (Autumn 1987), 207–22; Kehoe, "Merchants of Pollution?," 21–46; Raymond Smilor, "Personal Boundaries in the Urban Environment: The Legal Attack on Noise, 1865–1930," *Environmental Review* 3 (Spring 1979), 24–36.

32. Frederick Jackson Turner, "The Significance of the Frontier in American His-

tory," *Annual Report of the American Historical Association for the Year 1893* (Washington, D.C.: Government Printing Office, 1894), 199–227. On the range and durability of this approach, see Richard White and Patricia Nelson Limerick, *The Frontier in American Culture*, ed. James R. Grossman (Berkeley: University of California Press, 1994).

33. Patricia Nelson Limerick, *The Legacy of Conquest: The Unbroken Past of the American West* (New York: Norton, 1987), 9.

34. Ibid., 124–25.

35. Stephen Pyne, *Fire in America: A Cultural History of Wildland and Rural Fire* (1982. Seattle: University of Washington Press, 1997), 3–4.

36. Stephen Pyne, "Firestick History," *Journal of American History* 92 (March 1990), 1132–41.

37. See, for example: Stephen Innes, untitled review, *Journal of Interdisciplinary History* 15 (Summer 1984), 154–57; Donald Worster, untitled review, *Agricultural History* 58 (July 1984), 508–9; Calvin Martin, untitled review, *Pacific Historical Review* 53 (November 4, 1984), 506–8. For a Cronon-esque study of another region, see Timothy Silver, *A New Face on the Countryside: Indians, Colonists, and Slaves in South Atlantic Forests, 1500–1800* (New York: Cambridge University Press, 1990). Janny Scott, "An Environmentalist on a Different Path," *New York Times*, April 3, 1999, online at nytimes.com.

38. William Cronon, *Nature's Metropolis: Chicago and the Great West* (New York: Norton, 1991), quote from 7.

39. Ibid., 145.

40. Richard White, untitled review, *Environmental History Review* 16 (Summer 1992), 85–91.

41. William Cronon, "A Place for Stories: Nature, History, and Narrative," *Journal of American History* 78 (March 1992), 1347–76.

42. Ibid., 1349, 1352.

43. William Cronon, "The Trouble with Wilderness," reprinted in his *Uncommon Ground: Rethinking the Human Place in Nature* (New York: Norton, 1996), 69–90, quotes from 79, 85.

44. Samuel Hays, "The Trouble with Bill Cronon's Wilderness," *Environmental History* 1 (January 1996), 29–32. Michael P. Cohen, ibid., 33–42. Snyder quoted in Scott, "Environmentalist on a Different Path."

CHAPTER 8

1. Arne Naess, "The Shallow and the Deep, Long-Range Ecology Movement: A Summary," *Inquiry* 16 (Spring 1973), 95–100, quotes from 95 and 96.

2. Bill Devall, "John Muir as Deep Ecologist," *Environmental Review* 6 (Spring 1982), 63–86, quote from 65.

3. Bill Devall and George Sessions, *Deep Ecology: Living as if Nature Mattered* (Salt Lake City: Peregrine Smith Books, 1985), 7, 70.

4. Dolores LaChapelle quoted in "Talking on Water," *Sierra* 79 (May 1994), 72. Holmes Rolston III, *Philosophy Gone Wild: Essays in Environmental Ethics* (Buffalo, NY: Prometheus, 1986), 120.

5. Roderick Nash, *The Rights of Nature: A History of Environmental Ethics* (Madison: University of Wisconsin Press, 1989), 150.

6. Arne Naess and David Rothenberg, *Ecology, Community and Lifestyle: Outline of*

an Ecosophy (New York: Cambridge University Press, 1989), 156. See also Phillip Cramer, *Deep Environmental Politics: The Role of Radical Environmentalism in Crafting American Environmental Policy* (Westport, CT: Praeger, 1998).

7. Ynestra King quoted in Nash, *Rights of Nature*, 144. For an introduction to the very extensive literature of ecofeminism, see: Mary Mellor, *Feminism and Ecology* (New York: New York University Press, 1997); Heather Eaton, *Introducing Ecofeminist Theologies* (New York: Continuum, 2005); Ynestra King, "What Is Eco-Feminism?," *Nation*, December 12, 1987, 702.

8. Marija Gimbutas, *Goddesses and Gods of Old Europe, 6500–3500 BC: Myths and Cult Images* (Berkeley: University of California Press, 1982). Marija Gimbutas, *The Language of the Goddess: Unearthing the Hidden Symbols of Western Civilization* (San Francisco: Harper and Row, 1989). Riane Eisler, *The Chalice and the Blade: Our History, Our Future* (San Francisco: Harper and Row, 1987). See also Kirkpatrick Sale, "Ecofeminism—A New Perspective," *Nation*, September 26, 1987, 302–5. On the religious aspect of ecofeminism, see Patrick Allitt, *Religion in America Since 1945: A History* (New York: Columbia University Press, 2003), 127–32.

9. Janet Biehl, *Finding Our Way: Rethinking Ecofeminist Politics* (New York: Black Rose, 1993), quote from 5.

10. Susan Griffin, *Woman and Nature: The Roaring Inside Her* (New York: Harper and Row, 1978). Catherine Roach, "Loving Your Mother: On the Woman-Nature Relation," *Hypatia* 6 (Spring 1991), 46–59, quotes from 49, 54.

11. Bill Devall, "The Deep, Long-Range Ecology Movement, 1960–2000: A Review," *Ethics and the Environment* 6 (2001), 18–41.

12. Dave Foreman, *Confessions of an Eco-Warrior* (New York: Crown, 1993), 44.

13. Mike Carr, *Bioregionalism and Civil Society: Democratic Challenges to Corporate Globalism* (Vancouver: University of British Columbia Press, 2004). Carolyn Merchant, *Radical Ecology: The Search for a Livable World* (New York: Routledge, 1992), 217–22.

14. Berg quoted in Carr, *Bioregionalism*, 74.

15. Kirkpatrick Sale, *Human Scale* (New York: Coward, McCann and Geoghegan, 1980). Kirkpatrick Sale, *Dwellers in the Land: The Bioregional Vision* (San Francisco: Sierra Club Books, 1985), quote from 22.

16. Deborah Popper and Frank Popper, "Great Plains: From Dust to Dust," *Planning*, December 1987, 12–19.

17. Anne Matthews, *Where the Buffalo Roam* (New York: Grove, 1992). See also Sara Dant Ewart, "Bioregional Politics: The Case for Place," *Oregon Historical Quarterly* 103 (Winter 2002), 439–51.

18. The principal arguments are well summarized in Martin W. Lewis, *Green Delusions: An Environmentalist Critique of Radical Environmentalism* (Durham, NC: Duke University Press, 1992).

19. Deepak Lal, "Eco-Fundamentalism," *International Affairs* 71 (July 1995), 515–28.

20. The following section is based on Donald R. Liddick, *Eco-Terrorism: Radical Environmental and Animal Liberation Movements* (Westport, CT: Praeger, 2006).

21. Edward Abbey, *The Monkey Wrench Gang* (1975. New York: Avon, 1976).

22. Douglas Martin, "James Phillips, 70, Environmentalist Who Was Called the Fox," *New York Times*, October 22, 2001.

23. John Dyson, *Sink the Rainbow! An Enquiry into the Greenpeace Affair* (London:

Gollancz, 1986). Ramesh Thakur, "A Dispute of Many Colours: France, New Zealand, and the 'Rainbow Warrior' Affair," *World Today* 42 (December 1986), 209–14.

24. Foreman quoted in Steve Chase, ed., *Defending the Earth: A Dialogue Between Murray Bookchin and Dave Foreman* (Boston: South End Press, 1991), 38. See also: Martha Lee, *Earth First! Environmental Apocalypse* (Syracuse, NY: Syracuse University Press, 1995); Liddick, *Eco-Terrorism*, 56.

25. B. J. Bergman, "Wild at Heart," *Sierra* 83 (January/February 1998), 24–29.

26. Dave Foreman, *Eco-Defense: A Field Guide to Monkeywrenching* (Tucson, AZ: Ned Ludd Books, 1985). Christopher Manes, *Green Rage: Radical Environmentalism and the Unmaking of Civilization* (Boston: Little, Brown, 1990), 11.

27. Trip Gabriel, "If a Tree Falls in the Forest, They Hear It," *New York Times Magazine*, November 4, 1990, 34.

28. Chase, *Defending the Earth*, 46.

29. Liddick, *Eco-Terrorism*, 58. Manes, *Green Rage*, 10. Chase, *Defending the Earth*, 54. Howie Wolke, *Wilderness on the Rocks* (Tucson, AZ: Ned Ludd Books, 1991).

30. Manes, *Green Rage*, 26.

31. Susan Zakin, *Coyotes and Town Dogs: Earth First! and the Environmental Movement* (New York: Viking, 1993). Peter C. List, *Radical Environmentalism: Philosophy and Tactics* (Belmont, CA: Wadsworth, 1993). C. Keyser, "Compromise in Defense of Earth First!," *Sierra* 76 (November/December 1991), 45–47.

32. Gabriel, "If a Tree Falls," 37. On Cherney, see also Bob Doran, "Infamous Troubadour: The Life, Times and Future of Darryl Cherney," *North Coast Journal Weekly*, February 17, 2005, www.northcoastjournal.com/021705/cover0217.html.

33. Heather Millar and Jennifer Hattam, "Generation Green," *Sierra* 85 (November/December 2000), 36ff. Julia Hill, *The Legacy of Luna* (New York: HarperOne, 2001).

34. Joe Kane, "One Man's Wilderness," *Sierra* 85 (March/April 2000), 46ff.

35. Bookchin quoted in Kirkpatrick Sale, "Deep Ecology and Its Critics," *Nation* 246 (May 14, 1988), 671. King, "What Is Eco-Feminism?," 731.

36. Bookchin quoted in Chase, *Defending the Earth*, 31.

37. Ibid., 36.

38. Gabriel, "If a Tree Falls."

39. Brock Evans quoted in Cramer, *Deep Environmental Politics*, 15.

40. Chase, *Defending the Earth*, 39. Manes, *Green Rage*, 18.

41. Lewis, *Green Delusions*, 11.

42. Ibid., 10, 16–17.

43. "Eco-Liberation: The Renewal of Radical Environmentalism," editorial, *Earth First! Journal* 33, no. 1, online at http://earthfirstjournal.org/.

44. Rachel Lee, "In the Wild, We Are Free from Abuse," *Earth First! Journal* 33, no. 1.

45. For protests against the concept of "ecoterrorism," see, for example, Ed Quillen, "The Latest Trend in Name-Calling," *High Country News* 40 (June 9, 2008), 7. See also "Unwise Branding," *Nature* 447 (May 24, 2007), 353.

46. Michael Janofsky, "11 Indicted in 17 Cases of Sabotage in West," *New York Times*, January 21, 2006, A9. On Cottrell, see Judith Lewis, "A Terrible Thing to Waste," *LA Weekly*, February 28, 2007.

47. Kirk Johnson, "Utah Man Convicted in Fraud at 2008 Energy Auction," *New York Times*, March 4, 2011, A14. Derek P. Jensen, "DeChristopher Sentence Riles Protestors, Spurs Arrests," *Salt Lake Tribune*, July 26, 2011. Jennifer Dobner, "Green Hero Goes to Jail," *Australian Financial Review*, July 28, 2011, 14.

48. John M. Broder, "Police Arrest Keystone XL Protesters," *New York Times*, February 13, 2013.

CHAPTER 9

1. "Question for the (Ice) Age," *Science News* 100 (July 17, 1971), 39. For an intellectual biography of Schneider, see Regina Nuzzo, "Profile of Stephen H. Schneider," *Proceedings of the National Academy of Sciences* 102 (November 1, 2005), 15725–27.

2. Lowell Ponte, *The Cooling* (Englewood Cliffs, NJ: Prentice Hall, 1976), 4, 29. Reid Bryson, preface to Ponte, xi. *Science News* 104 (March 1, 1975), cover.

3. Ponte, *The Cooling*, xiv. Spencer Weart, *The Discovery of Global Warming*, revised and expanded edition (Cambridge, MA: Harvard University Press, 2008), 88.

4. Carl Sagan, "Nuclear War and Climatic Catastrophe," *Foreign Affairs* 62 (Winter 1983), 257–92. Jonathan Schell, *The Fate of the Earth* (New York: Avon, 1982), 75–90.

5. Philip Shabecoff, "Global Warming Has Begun, Expert Tells Senate," *New York Times*, June 24, 1988, A1.

6. Philip Shabecoff, "Ferocious Storms and Drought Seen," *New York Times*, December 7, 1988, A25. Richard Kerr, "Global Temperature Hits Record Again," *Science* 251 (January 18, 1991), 274. R. Monastersky, "Buying Time in the War on Global Warming," *Science News* 139 (March 23, 1991), 183.

7. Weart, *Discovery of Global Warming*, 152–57.

8. Sid Perkins, "Cooling Climate 'Consensus' of 1970s Never Was," *Science News* 174 (October 9, 2008), 5–6. Stephen H. Schneider, *Global Warming: Are We Entering the Greenhouse Century?* (San Francisco: Sierra Club Books, 1989).

9. Weart, *Discovery of Global Warming*, 151.

10. Ibid., 34–37. For the Keeling curve itself, see keelingcurve.ucsd.edu.

11. Weart, *Discovery of Global Warming*, 70, 126.

12. David Demeritt, "The Construction of Global Warming and the Politics of Science," *Annals of the Association of American Geographers* 91 (June 2001), 307–37.

13. Weart, *Discovery of Global Warming*, 55–61.

14. Ross Gelbspan, *The Heat Is On: The High Stakes Battle over Earth's Threatened Climate* (Reading, MA: Addison Wesley, 1997), 2.

15. Ibid., 22–23, 138, 145, 160–62.

16. Ibid., 30–31.

17. William Calvin, "The Great Climate Flip-Flop," *Atlantic Monthly* 281 (January 1998), 47–64, quote from 47.

18. P. Minnis et al., "Radiative Climate Forcing by the Mount Pinatubo Eruption," *Science* 259 (March 5, 1993), 1411–15. Brian Soden et al., "Global Cooling After the Eruption of Mount Pinatubo: A Test of Climate Feedback by Water Vapor," *Science* 296 (April 26, 2002), 727–30.

19. Lamont C. Hempel, "Greenhouse Warming: The Changing Climate in Science and Politics," *Political Research Quarterly* 46 (March 1993), 213–39.

20. Stephen Schneider, "Don't Bet All Environmental Changes Will Be Benefi-

cial," *American Physical Society News* 5 (August/September 1996). In this article Schneider defends himself against critics who had misquoted the remark, first made to the journalist Jonathan Schell in an interview with *Discover* magazine in 1989.

21. Demeritt, "Construction of Global Warming and the Politics of Science," 309.
22. Al Gore, "An Ecological Kristallnacht," *New York Times*, March 19, 1989, 4:27. Al Gore, "To Skeptics on Global Warming," *New York Times*, April 22, 1990, 4:27. Al Gore, *Earth in the Balance: Ecology and the Human Spirit* (Boston: Houghton Mifflin, 1992).
23. Keith Schneider, "Gore Meets Resistance in Effort for Steps on Global Warming," *New York Times*, April 19, 1993, A:17. "Mr. Clinton, Meet Mr. Gore," editorial, *New York Times*, April 20, 1993, A:28. Bill McKibben, "Not So Fast," *New York Times*, July 23, 1995, 6:24.
24. Weart, *Discovery of Global Warming*, 166–67.
25. Richard N. Cooper, "Toward a Real Global Warming Treaty," *Foreign Affairs* 77 (March/April 1998), 66–79.
26. A. O. Scott, "Warning of Calamities with a Scholarly Tone," *New York Times*, May 24, 2006, E1.
27. Malcolm Browne, "Was That a Greenhouse Effect? It Depends on Your Theory," *New York Times*, September 4, 1988, 4:1.
28. Lawrence Solomon, *The Deniers* (Minneapolis: Richard Vigilante Books, 2008), 57–74.
29. Weart, *Discovery of Global Warming*, 105–20, 158–61.
30. Henrik Svensmark and Nigel Calder, *The Chilling Stars: A New Theory of Climate Change* (London: Icon, 2007). G. Bond, B. Kromer et al., "Persistent Solar Influence on North Atlantic Climate During the Holocene," *Science* 294 (December 7, 2001), 1257–66, quotes from 1266. See also David Schneider, "Living in Sunny Times," *American Scientist* 93 (January/February 2005), 22, 24.
31. M. E. Mann, R. S. Bradley, and M. K. Hughes, "Global-Scale Temperature Patterns and Climate Forcings over the Past Six Centuries," *Nature* 392 (1998), 779–87.
32. Ross McKitrick, "The Mann et al. Northern Hemisphere 'Hockey Stick' Climate Index: A Tale of Due Diligence," in Patrick Michaels, ed., *Shattered Consensus: The True State of Global Warming* (Lanham, MD: Rowman and Littlefield, 2005), 20–50. Quotes from 27, 48. Solomon, *The Deniers*, 9–22.
33. Richard Kerr, "Greenhouse Skeptic Out in the Cold," *Science* 246 (December 1, 1989), 1118–19. Richard Lindzen, "Can Increasing Carbon Dioxide Cause Climate Change?," *Proceedings of the National Academy of Sciences* 94 (August 5, 1997), 8335–42, quote from 8342.
34. Richard Monastersky, "As Globe Warms, Atmosphere Keeps Its Cool," *Science News* 157 (January 22, 2000), 53. "Testimony of Richard Lindzen Before the Senate Commerce Committee," May 1, 2000, accessed online at www.lavo isier.com.au/articles/climate-policy/science-and-policy/Lindzen_McCain.pdf.
35. Biographical information on Singer is based on Scheuering, *Shapers of the Great Debate*, 115–27. Fred Singer, "Climate Claims Wither Under the Luminous Lights of Science," *Washington Times*, November 29, 1994, 16. Fred Singer, "Climate Change and Consensus," letter, *Science* 271 (February 2, 1996), 581–82.
36. Fred Singer, "Is Kyoto Dead?," *Washington Times*, May 6, 2001, B4. Fred Singer, *Hot Talk, Cold Science: Global Warming's Unfinished Debate* (Oakland, CA:

Independent Institute, 1999). For the critique of Singer, see Aaron McCright and Riley E. Dunlap, "Defeating Kyoto: The Conservative Movement's Impact on U.S. Climate Change Policy," *Social Problems* 50 (August 2003), 348–73.

37. Bjorn Lomborg, *The Skeptical Environmentalist: Measuring the Real State of the World* (New York: Cambridge University Press, 2001), 318–19.

38. Lone Frank, "Greens See Red over Revisionist's New Job," *Science* 295 (March 8, 2002), 1817. Richard Norgaard, "Optimists, Pessimists, and Science," *BioScience* 52 (March 2002), 287–92.

39. Bjorn Lomborg, *Cool It: The Skeptical Environmentalist's Guide to Global Warming* (New York: Vintage, 2007), ix.

40. Ibid., 5, 15, 39, 44.

41. Ibid., 101.

42. Arun Agrawal and S. Narain, *Global Warming in an Unequal World* (New Delhi: Centre for Science and Environment, 1991). Suzanna Sawyer and Arun Agrawal, "Environmental Orientalisms," *Cultural Critique* 45 (Spring 2000), 71–108. Ambuj Sagar and Milind Kandlikar, "Knowledge, Rhetoric and Power: International Politics of Climate Change," *Economic and Political Weekly* 32 (December 6–12, 1997), 3139–48, quote from 3147.

43. Gelbspan, *Heat Is On*, 8.

44. Roy Spencer, *Climate Confusion* (New York: Encounter, 2008), 5.

45. Sonja Boehmer-Christiansen, "Science, Equity, and the War Against Carbon," *Science, Technology and Human Values* 28 (Winter 2003), 69–92, quote from 74.

CHAPTER 10

1. "Russia's Greens: The Poisoned Giant Wakes Up," *Economist* 312 (November 4, 1989), 23–26.

2. Murray Feshbach and Alfred Friendly, Jr., *Ecocide in the USSR: Health and Nature Under Siege* (New York: Basic, 1992), 3.

3. Norman Precoda, "Requiem for the Aral Sea," *Ambio* 20 (May 1991), 109–14.

4. Ibid., 114. Ian Small et al., "Acting on an Environmental Health Disaster: The Case of the Aral Sea," *Environmental Health Perspectives* 109 (June 2001), 547–49.

5. Murray Feshbach, *Ecological Disaster: Cleaning Up the Hidden Legacy of the Soviet Regime* (New York: Twentieth Century Fund Press, 1995), 31. Zhores Medvedev, *The Legacy of Chernobyl* (New York: Norton, 1992).

6. Wieslaw Jedroychowski, "Review of Recent Studies from Central and Eastern Europe Associating Respiratory Health with High Levels of Exposure to Traditional Air Pollutants," *Environmental Health Perspectives* 103 (March 1995), 15–21. "Romania Town's Prosperity Means Pollution," *New York Times*, August 16, 1992, 1:8.

7. "Report Warns of Pollution in Eastern Europe," *New York Times*, January 21, 1990, 1:17.

8. Daniel Kevles, "Ananda Chakrabarty Wins a Patent: Biotechnology, Law, and Society, 1972–1980," *Historical Studies in the Physical and Biological Sciences* 25 (Spring 1994), 111–35. Terrance Hurley et al., "Risk and the Value of BT Corn," *American Journal of Agricultural Economics* 86 (May 2004), 345–58. Alan J. Gray, "Ecology and Government Policies: The GM Crop Debate," *Journal of Applied Ecology* 41 (February 2004), 1–10.

9. Lisa Weasel, *Food Fray: Inside the Controversy over Genetically Modified Food* (New York: Amacom, 2009), 68–81.

10. Paul Lurquin, *High Tech Harvest: Understanding Genetically Modified Food Plants* (Boulder, CO: Westview Press, 2002).

11. Ingrid Wickelgren, "Please Pass the Genes," *Science News* 136 (August 19, 1989), 136. Jimmy Carter, "Who's Afraid of Genetic Engineering?," *New York Times*, August 26, 1998, A21. Klaus Leisinger, "Yes, Stop Blocking Progress," *Foreign Policy* 119 (Summer 2000), 113–22. Weasel, *Food Fray*, 59–65.

12. Jeremy Rifkin, *The Biotech Century* (New York: Jeremy Tarcher/Putnam, 1998). Charles Arthur, "Biotech Firms Hit Back at Charles," *Independent* (London), June 9, 1998, 9.

13. S. Perkins, "Transgenic Plants Provoke Petition," *Science News* 152 (September 27, 1997), 199.

14. Dietmar Harhoff et al., "Some Simple Economics of GM Food," *Economic Policy* 16 (October 2001), 265–99. Weasel, *Food Fray*, 1–2, 88–94.

15. Andy Rees, *Genetically Modified Foods: A Short Guide for the Confused* (London: Pluto Press, 2006), 15–16, 140–44.

16. Dave Toke, *The Politics of GM Food: A Comparative Study of the UK, USA, and EU* (London: Routledge, 2004), 7.

17. Rees, *Genetically Modified Foods*, 1.

18. David Barboza, "Foods Put Companies in a Quandary," *New York Times*, June 4, 2000, 1:1. Marian Burros, "US Plans Long-Term Studies on Safety of Genetically Altered Foods," *New York Times*, July 14, 1999, A18.

19. Andrew Pollack, "130 Nations Agree on Safety Rules for Biotech Food," *New York Times*, January 30, 2000, 1:1.

20. "Whither GM Corn?," *Environment* 41 (December 1999), 9. Andrew Pollack, "Monsanto Shelves Plan for Modified Wheat," *New York Times*, May 11, 2004, C5:1.

21. Shannon Petersen, *Acting for Endangered Species: The Statutory Ark* (Lawrence: University Press of Kansas, 2002). Brian Czech and Paul Krausman, *The Endangered Species Act: History, Conservation Biology, and Public Policy* (Baltimore: Johns Hopkins University Press, 2001). Kathryn Kohm, ed., *Balancing on the Brink of Extinction: The Endangered Species Act and Lessons for the Future* (Washington, D.C.: Island Press, 1991).

22. Bruce Hampton, *The Great American Wolf* (New York: Henry Holt, 1997). Rick McIntyre, *A Society of Wolves: National Parks and the Battle over the Wolf* (Stillwater, MN: Voyageur Press, 1993). Richard P. Thiel, *The Timber Wolf in Wisconsin: The Death and Life of a Majestic Predator* (Madison: University of Wisconsin Press, 1993).

23. Christopher K. Williams et al., "A Quantitative Summary of Attitudes Toward Wolves and Their Reintroduction, 1972–2000," *Wildlife Society Bulletin* 30 (Summer 2002), 575–84.

24. Hampton, *Great American Wolf*, 195–225.

25. David Wildove, *The Condor's Shadow: The Loss and Recovery of Wildlife in America* (New York: Anchor, 1999), 60–61.

26. Hampton, *Great American Wolf*, 216. Philip Brick and R. McGreggor Cawley, *A Wolf in the Garden: The Land Rights Movement and the New Environmental Debate* (Lanham, MD: Rowman and Littlefield, 1996).

27. Paul Rauber, "An End to Evolution," *Sierra* 81 (January 1996), 28–34.

28. Timothy Egan, "Ruling on Owl Stirs New Hope for Trees," *New York Times,* November 18, 1988, A:16.

29. Petersen, *Acting for Endangered Species,* 108, 87.

30. Joan Hamilton, "The Owl and the Scientist," *Sierra* 76 (July 1991), 20–22. Tim Hilchey, "Study Raises Concern over Plan to Protect Northern Spotted Owl," *New York Times,* December 14, 1993, C4.

31. Gregg Easterbrook, "The Birds," *New Republic* 210 (March 28, 1994), 22–28.

32. Petersen, *Acting for Endangered Species,* 118.

33. F. W. Preston, "The Canonical Distribution of Commonness and Rarity, Part I," *Ecology* 43 (Spring 1962), 185–215.

34. Robert H. MacArthur and E. O. Wilson, *The Theory of Island Biogeography* (Princeton, NJ: Princeton University Press, 1967). Charles C. Mann and Mark L. Plummer, *Noah's Choice: The Future of Endangered Species* (New York: Knopf, 1995), 60–61.

35. Edward Connor and Earl McCoy, "The Statistics and Biology of the Species-Area Relationship," *American Naturalist* 113 (June 1979), 791–883. Mann and Plummer, *Noah's Choice,* 63.

36. Mann and Plummer, *Noah's Choice,* 68–69.

37. Ehrlich and Ehrlich, *Extinction.*

38. Mann and Plummer, *Noah's Choice,* 212–38. See also the sharply critical review by David Blockstein, "False Choices," *BioScience* 46 (June 1996), 458–59.

39. Petersen, *Acting for Endangered Species,* 125.

40. Paul Rauber, "The Lion and the Lamb," *Sierra* 86 (March/April 2001), 32–42.

41. David Baron, *The Beast in the Garden: A Modern Parable of Man and Nature* (New York: Norton, 2004), 226.

42. Jan DeBlieu, *Meant to Be Wild: The Struggle to Save Endangered Species Through Captive Breeding* (Golden, CO: Fulcrum, 1991).

43. Marnie Bookbinder et al., "Ecotourism's Support of Biodiversity Conservation," *Conservation Biology* 12 (December 1998), 1399–404.

44. Karen Madsen, "A Green Getaway," *E—The Environmental Magazine* 14 (January/February 2003), 46–47.

45. Jerome Goldstein, "The Logical Path of an Ecotourism Pioneer," *In Business* 21 (July/August 1999), 18–19.

46. Michael Tennesen, "The Road Less Traveled," *National Parks* 72 (May/June 1998).

47. Abbey, *Desert Solitaire,* xii. Adam Piore, "Trouble in Paradise," *Newsweek,* July 22, 2002, 42.

48. Jack Coburn Isaacs, "The Limited Potential of Ecotourism to Contribute to Wildlife Conservation," *Wildlife Society Bulletin* 28 (Spring 2000), 61–69.

49. Richard White, "'Are You an Environmentalist or Do You Work for a Living?': Work and Nature," in William Cronon, ed., *Uncommon Ground: Rethinking the Human Place in Nature* (New York: Norton, 1995), 171–85.

50. Mark Hertsgaard, "A World Awash in Chemicals," *New York Times,* April 7, 1996, 7:25.

51. Vom Saal quoted in Sheldon Krimsky, *Hormonal Chaos: The Scientific and Social Origins of the Environmental Endocrine Hypothesis* (Baltimore: Johns Hopkins University Press, 2000), 25.

52. Theo Colborn, Dianne Dumanoski, and John Peterson Myers, *Our Stolen Future: Are We Threatening Our Fertility, Intelligence, and Survival? A Scientific Detective*

Story (New York: Dutton, 1996), 234. For a more detached corroboration of these findings, see also Dore Hollander, "Environmental Effects on Reproductive Health: The Endocrine Disruption Hypothesis," *Family Planning Perspectives* 29 (March/April 1997), 82–86, 89.

53. Colborn, Dumankski, and Myers, *Our Stolen Future*, 68–76.

54. Ibid, 239–49.

55. Whelan, quoted in Krimsky, *Hormonal Chaos*, 97. Gina Kolata, "Chemicals That Mimic Hormones Spark Alarm and Debate," *New York Times*, March 19, 1996, C1. Ronald Bailey, "Hormones and Humbug: A New Expose Is One Part Pseudo-Science, Two Parts Hype, Three Parts Hysteria," *Washington Post*, March 31, 1996, C3. Maurice Zeeman, "Our Fate Is Connected With the Animals," *BioScience* 46 (July/August 1996), 542–45.

56. Nancy Langston, *Toxic Bodies* (New Haven, CT: Yale University Press, 2010), 15. Gina Kolata, "Experts Unsure of Effects of a Type of Contaminant," *New York Times*, August 4, 1999, A16. Jason Vogel, "Tunnel Vision: The Regulation of Endocrine Disruptors," *Policy Sciences* 37 (December 2004), 277–303.

57. Krimsky, *Hormonal Chaos*, 57.

58. Nicholas Kristof, "Chemicals and Our Health," *New York Times,* July 16, 2009, A27. See also Nicholas Kristof, "Cancer from the Kitchen," *New York Times,* December 6, 2009, WK:11.

59. Langston, *Toxic Bodies*, xii.

60. Jonathan Harr, *A Civil Action* (New York: Vintage, 1996). See also Leonard Glantz, "A Most Uncivil Action," *Public Health Reports* 113 (January/February 1998), 87–89.

61. Carl Cranor, *Toxic Torts* (New York: Cambridge University Press, 2006).

62. Erin Brockovich, "My Story," on Brockovich's Web site, www.brockovich.com/my-story/. Cheryl Pellerin and Susan M. Booker, "Reflections on Hexavalent Chromium: Health Hazards of an Industrial Heavyweight," *Environmental Health Perspectives* 108 (September 2000), A402–7.

63. Laura Henry, *Red to Green: Environmental Activism in Post-Soviet Russia* (Ithaca, NY: Cornell University Press, 2010).

64. Mike Davis, *Ecology of Fear: Los Angeles and the Imagination of Disaster* (New York: Vintage, 1999).

65. Rachel Pomerance, "How Safe Are Your Cosmetics?," *USNews.com*, July 31, 2012. Nicholas Kristof, "Big Chem, Big Harm?," *New York Times*, August 26, 2012, SR11.

66. Wendee Holtcamp, "Obesogens: An Environmental Link to Obesity," *Environmental Health Perspectives* 120 (February 2012), A62–68. Nicholas Kristof, "Warnings from a Flabby Mouse," *New York Times,* January 20, 2013, SR11. Linda Birnbaum, "Is Supersize More Than Just Too Much Food?," *Environmental Health Perspectives* 120 (June 2012), A223–24.

67. Michael Tortorello, "Is It Safe to Play Yet?," *New York Times*, March 15, 2012, D1.

68. Ian Austen, "Canada Declares BPA, a Chemical in Plastics, to Be Toxic," *New York Times*, October 14, 2010, A14. Kara Sissell, "Industry Disputes Findings of Cleaning Products Study," *Chemical Week*, March 12–19, 2012, 33.

69. Jim Dutcher et al., "Don't Forsake the Gray Wolf," *New York Times*, June 8, 2013, A19. Nate Schweber, "Research Animals Lost in Wolf Hunts Near Yellowstone," www.green.blogs.nytimes.com, November 28, 2012.

70. Jim Robbins, "A Summer of Humans v. Grizzlies," www.green.blogs.nytimes

.com, September 19, 2011. On Treadwell, see also Mike Lapinski, *Death in the Grizzly Maze: The Timothy Treadwell Story* (New York: Falcon, 2005).

71. John W. Fitzpatrick, "Newly Discovered, Nearly Extinct," *New York Times,* March 7, 2013, A27. Brian Gratwicke, Thomas Lovejoy, and David Wildt, "Will Amphibians Croak Under the Endangered Species Act?," *BioScience* 62 (February 2, 2012), 197–202.

72. Michael Wines, "Endangered or Not, But at Least No Longer Waiting," *New York Times,* March 7, 2013, A12.

CHAPTER 11

1. On the rise of the industry, its advertising, its cultivation of celebrities, its innovations, and its gradual loss of credibility in the face of public health inquiries, see Richard Kluger, *Ashes to Ashes: America's Hundred-Year Cigarette War, the Public Health, and the Unabashed Triumph of Philip Morris* (New York: Knopf, 1996).

2. Brandt, *Cigarette Century,* 292–93.

3. Ibid., 300.

4. Barry Meier, "Tobacco Windfall Begins Tug of War Among Lawmakers," *New York Times,* January 10, 1999, 1:1. Brandt, *Cigarette Century,* 305 (aircraft ban), 432 (Master Settlement Agreement).

5. Brandt, *Cigarette Century,* 432–35.

6. David Kessler, *A Question of Intent: A Great American Battle with a Deadly Industry* (New York: PublicAffairs, 2001).

7. Harriet Chiang, "$20 Million Jury Award to Smoker," *San Francisco Chronicle,* March 28, 2000, A1.

8. Brandt, *Cigarette Century,* 450.

9. *Fortune* article and cover summarized in Kelly Brownell and Kenneth Warner, "The Perils of Ignoring History: Big Tobacco Played Dirty and Millions Died. How Similar Is Big Food?," *Milbank Quarterly* 87 (March 2009), 259–94.

10. Eric Schlosser, *Fast Food Nation: The Dark Side of the All-American Meal* (New York: Harper, 2005).

11. Ibid., 9, 119.

12. Michael Pollan, *The Botany of Desire* (2001. New York: Random House, 2002), 199–225, quote from 217.

13. Brownell and Warner, "Perils of Ignoring History," 265. Alexandra Lewin, Lauren Lindstrom, and Marion Nestle, "Food Industry Promises to Address Childhood Obesity: Preliminary Evaluation," *Journal of Public Health Policy* 27, no. 4 (2006), 327–48, quote from 341.

14. Lawrence Osborne, "Slow Food," *New York Times,* December 9, 2001, 6:1. Anne Menley, "Extra Virgin Olive Oil and Slow Food," *Anthropologica* 46, no. 2 (2004), 165–76.

15. Wallace E. Tyner, "The US Ethanol and Biofuels Boom: Its Origins, Current Status, and Future Prospects," *BioScience* 58 (July/August 2008), 646–53.

16. Grant Ferrett, "Biofuels 'Crime Against Humanity,'" BBC News, October 27, 2007, online at http://news.bbc.co.uk/2/hi/7065061.stm.

17. Kate Galbraith, "Ethanol Stirs Up a Mutiny," *New York Times,* July 26, 2008, C1.

18. Jim Motavalli, "Solution or Distraction? An Ethanol Reality Check," *New York Times,* May 14, 2006, 12:1. Elisabeth Rosenthal, "Studies Call Biofuels a Greenhouse Threat," *New York Times,* February 8, 2008, A9.

19. Robert Bryce, "Five Myths About Breaking Our Foreign Oil Habit," *Washington Post,* January 13, 2008, B3. Jason Hill, Erik Nelson, Stephen Polasky, and Douglas Tiffany, "Environmental, Economic, and Energetic Costs and Benefits of Biodiesel and Ethanol Biofuels," *Proceedings of the National Academy of Sciences* 103 (July 25, 2006), 11206–211. Alexei Barrionuevo, "Six Get Grants from U.S. to Support Bio-Refineries," *New York Times,* March 1, 2007, C3.

20. Joseph E. Fargione et al., "Bioenergy and Wildlife: Threats and Opportunities for Grassland Conservation," *BioScience* 59 (October 2009), 767–77.

21. Alexei Barrionuevo et al., "For Good or Ill, Boom in Ethanol Reshapes Economy of Heartland," *New York Times,* June 25, 2006, 1:1. James Bovard, "Archer Daniels Midland: A Case Study in Corporate Welfare," CATO Institute Policy Analysis #241, online at www.cato.org/pubs/pas/pa-241.html.

22. Matthew L. Wald, "EPA Approves Use of More Ethanol in Gasoline," *New York Times,* January 22, 2011, B7. Steven Mufson, "A Boost for Corn-Based Ethanol?," *Washington Post,* February 4, 2010, A15. Steven Rattner, "The Great Corn Con," *New York Times,* June 25, 2011, A19.

23. Reisner, *Cadillac Desert.* See also Richard White, *The Organic Machine: The Remaking of the Columbia River* (New York: Hill and Wang, 1995). White describes the complete transformation of the Columbia River over the course of the twentieth century by hydroelectric power projects.

24. Paul Rauber, "Looking to a Future Where Every Fifth Watt Is Green," *Sierra* 87 (March/April 2002), 16. "Unplugged," *Sierra* 78 (September 1993), 23.

25. Bret Schulte, "Energy Efficiency from the Wind," *U.S. News and World Report,* March 26, 2007, online at www.usnews.com.

26. Mark Landler, "Wind Power and Resistance," *New York Times,* November 23, 2007, C1. Clifford Krauss, "Move Over, Oil: There's Money in Texas Wind," *New York Times,* February 23, 2008, A1. Daniel Botkin, *Powering the Future* (Upper Saddle River, NJ: Pearson/FT Press, 2010), 138 (eagles at Altamont).

27. Russell Ray, "Wind Power: Hot Air or Valid Energy Source?," *Tulsa World,* March 13, 2005. Quote is from Botkin, *Powering the Future,* 129.

28. John Etherington, *The Wind Farm Scam* (London: Stacey International, 2009).

29. Nina Pierpont, *Wind Turbine Syndrome* (Lowell, MA: King Printing, 2009). See also Patrick Cassidy, "Wind Turbine Safety Questioned," *Cape Cod Times* (Hyannis, MA), June 15, 2011.

30. Marty Durlin, "Wind Farms—Not in My Back Yard," *Ruidoso News* (New Mexico), March 19, 2009. Sheryl Stolberg, "Obama Hails Wind Energy on Earth Day Visit to Iowa," *New York Times,* April 23, 2009, A17. See the "Siting" section of the American Wind Energy Association Web site, www.awea.org/index.aspx.

31. Botkin, *Powering the Future,* 151. Todd Woody, "Solyndra: Pay Some Investors Before Taxpayers in Solar Flame Out," *Forbes* (September 6, 2011), online at www.forbes.com/sites/toddwoody/2011/09/06/solyndra-pay-some-investors-before-taxpayers-in-solar-flame-out/.

32. Kimberly Keilbach, *Global Warming Is Good for Business* (Fresno, CA: Quill Driver Books, 2009), xiii.

33. Amory Lovins, *Reinventing Fire* (New York: Chelsea Green, 2011). Author's interview with Mr. Lovins, Atlanta, July 29, 2013. For a skeptical rejoinder to Lovins, see the review by Ted Trainer in *Energy Bulletin* (September 15, 2012) reprinted online at www.resilience.org/stories/2012-09-15/review-reinventing-fire-amory-lovins. Trainer says in part, "Lovins always has an enthusiasti-

cally optimistic view of probable future trends in costs. However discussion of
all issues to do with energy, resources, technology, environment and consumption should be based on the assumption that in the near future there are very
likely to be large and irreversible rises in the prices of energy, resources, materials, construction, plant and technology."

34. Steven Mufson, "Floods Leave Beijing Eager for New Dam: Critics Say
Huge Project Will Not Tame Deadly Flow," *Washington Post,* August 6, 1996, A11.
Mara Hvistendahl, "China's Three Gorges Dam: An Environmental Catastrophe?," *Scientific American,* March 25, 2008, online at www.scientificamerican
.com/article.cfm?id=chinas-three-gorges-dam-disaster.

35. Jane McCartney, "Greed for Energy Threatens to Dam Legendary Gorge,"
Times (London), May 9, 2006, 40.

36. Shi Jiangto, "Mega Dams Meant to Control Siltation Will Add to Ecological Woe, Experts Warn," *South China Morning Post,* February 27, 2008.

37. Mary Anne Toy, "What Cost as China Tames Mother River?," *The Age* (Mel-
bourne), May 20, 2006, 20.

38. John Gittings, "Seismic Risk Behind Three Gorges Dam," *Guardian Weekly,*
July 11, 2003, 3.

39. Hvistendahl, "China's Three Gorges Dam."

40. Crosby, *Columbian Exchange,* 64–121.

41. Derek H. Alderman, "Channing Cope and the Making of a Miracle Vine," *Geo-
graphical Review* 94 (April 2004), 157–77.

42. Raad Cawthon, "Chicago Fights Mussels with All Its Might," *Philadelphia
Inquirer,* January 5, 1999, A3. John Collins Rudolf, "Tiny, Clingy, and Destructive, Mussel Makes Its Way West," *New York Times,* June 17, 2008, F3.

43. Monica Davey, "Be Careful What You Fish For," *New York Times,* December 13,
2009, WK3. On the biologists' debate, see Carl Zimmer, "Friendly Invaders,"
New York Times, September 9, 2008, F1.

44. James Gorman, "A Diet for an Invaded Planet," *New York Times,* January 2,
2011, WK3. Taras Grescoe, "How to Handle an Invasive Species? Eat It," *New
York Times,* February 20, 2008, A21.

45. Weart, *Discovery of Global Warming,* 177–204.

46. Dale Jamieson, "Talking About the Weather," *BioScience* 60 (September
2010), 639–42.

47. Stephen Schneider, *Science as a Contact Sport* (Washington, D.C.: National Geographic, 2009), 148–54.

48. Ibid., 259.

49. James Hansen, "Only a Carbon Tax and Nuclear Power Can Save Us," *Austra-
lian,* March 11, 2010, 12. On Hansen's struggles with the bureaucracy, see Mark
Bowen, *Censoring Science: Inside the Political Attack on Dr. James Hansen and the
Truth of Global Warming* (New York: Dutton, 2008).

50. James Hansen, *Storms of My Grandchildren: The Truth About the Coming Climate
Catastrophe and Our Last Chance to Save Humanity* (New York: Bloomsbury, 2009).
Hansen quote is in Schneider, *Science as a Contact Sport,* 121–22. On sea levels,
see Jeff Goodell, *How to Cool the Planet: Geoengineering and the Audacious Quest to
Fix the Earth's Climate* (Boston: Houghton Mifflin Harcourt, 2010), 103.

51. Goodell, *How to Cool the Planet,* 101–2.

52. Michael Mastrandrea and Stephen Schneider, *Preparing for Climate Change* (Cambridge, MA: MIT Press, 2011). Goodell, *How to Cool the Planet,* 17–19, 109–34 (Wood and Teller).

53. Naomi Oreskes, David Stainforth, and Leonard Smith, "Adaptation to Global Warming: Do Climate Models Tell Us What We Need to Know?," *Philosophy of Science* 77 (December 2010), 1012–28.

54. For a history of the debate from a skeptic's or doubter's point of view, see Christopher Booker, *The Real Global Warming Disaster: Is the Obsession with "Climate Change" Turning Out to Be the Most Costly Scientific Blunder in History?* (New York: Continuum, 2009). Committee on the Science of Climate Change, *Climate Change Science: An Analysis of Some Key Questions* (Washington, D.C.: National Academy Press, 2001). Lindzen quoted in Michael Fumento, "Where Did All the Warming Go?," *Washington Times,* December 7, 2009, A19.

55. Richard Lindzen, "Climate of Fear," *Wall Street Journal,* April 12, 2006. Online at http://heartland.org/sites/all/modules/custom/heartland_migration/files /pdfs/20143.pdf.

56. S. Fred Singer and Dennis T. Avery, *Unstoppable Global Warming: Every 1500 Years* (Lanham, MD: Rowman and Littlefield, 2007). Craig Idso and Fred Singer, *Climate Change Reconsidered: The Report of the Nongovernmental International Panel on Climate Change* (Chicago: Heartland Institute, 2009).

57. Freeman Dyson, "The Question of Global Warming," *New York Review of Books,* June 12, 2008, www.nybooks.com/articles/archives/2008/jun/12/the-question-of-global-warming/. William Nordhaus, Dimitri Zenghelis, Leigh Sullivan, and Freeman Dyson, "'The Question of Global Warming': An Exchange," *New York Review of Books,* September 25, 2008, www.nybooks.com/articles/archives/2008/ sep/25/the-question-of-global-warming-an-exchange/.

58. Dyson, "Question of Global Warming."

59. Daniel Botkin, "Overheated," *BioScience* 60 (July/August 2010), 552–53.

60. Mann cited by L. Gordon Crovitz, "Enemies of Science," *National Post,* December 1, 2009, A17. Deborah Saunders, "The Inquisition of Global Warming," *San Francisco Chronicle,* December 1, 2009, A16.

61. "Time to Investigate Global Warming Collusion Claims," editorial, *Orange County Register,* November 24, 2009. Fred Singer, "Climate Skeptic: We Are Winning the Science Battle," *Reuters,* December 14, 2009.

CONCLUSION

1. www.epa.gov/airtrends/aqtrends.html.

2. www.edf.org/documents/2695_cleanairact.htm.

3. www.epa.gov/greatlakes/aoc/cuyahoga/CR-RAP-01-02.pdf.

4. www.cr.nps.gov/history/park_histories/index.htm. See, for example, this account of New York State reforestation: www.dec.ny.gov/lands/4982.html.

5. Michael Williams, *Americans and Their Forests: A Historical Geography* (New York: Cambridge University Press, 1989), 467–70.

6. See, for example, the 2007 news story "Eco-Vandals Attack Hummer in D.C.," CBS News, www.cbsnews.com/stories/2007/07/18/national/main3070288 .shtml.

IMAGE CREDITS

INDEX